PROOF THEORY

Proof Theory

A selection of papers
from the Leeds Proof Theory Programme 1990

edited by

Peter Aczel
University of Manchester

Harold Simmons
University of Manchester

and

Stanley S. Wainer
University of Leeds

CAMBRIDGE
UNIVERSITY PRESS

Published by the Press Syndicate of the University of Cambridge
The Pitt Building, Trumpington Street, Cambridge CB2 1RP
40 West 20th Street, New York, NY 10011-4211, USA
10 Stamford Road, Oakleigh, Victoria 3166, Australia

First published 1992

British Library cataloguing in publication data available

Library of Congress cataloguing in publication data available

ISBN 0 521 41413 X hardcover

Transferred to digital printing 2004

CONTENTS

PREFACE

This is a collection of ten refereed papers presented at an international Summer School and Conference on Proof Theory held at Bodington Hall, Leeds University between 24th July and 2nd August 1990. The meeting was held under the auspices of the "Logic for Information Technology" (Logfit) initiative of the UK Science and Engineering Research Council, in collaboration with the Leeds Centre for Theoretical Computer Science (CTCS). The principal funding came from SERC Logfit under contract SO/72/90 with additional contributions gratefully received from the British Logic Colloquium and the London Mathematical Society. There were 100 participants representing at least twelve different countries: Belgium, Canada, Estonia, France, Germany, Italy, Japan, Norway, Sweden, Switzerland, USA and UK.

The first three papers printed here represent short lecture courses given in the summer school and are intended to be of a more instructional nature, leading from basic to more advanced levels of 'pure' proof theory. The others are conference research papers reflecting a somewhat wider range of topics, and we see no better way of ordering them than alphabetically by author.

The programme of lectures given at the meeting is set out overleaf. Though not all of the invited speakers were able to contribute to this volume we believe that what remains provides rich flavours of a tasty subject.

Our thanks are due to the referees, to the staff at Bodington Hall for their hospitality, to Frances Johnson of 'Concilia' for helpful and efficient conference management, to Pat Boyes of the Leeds School of Mathematics for general secretarial help and large amounts of duplicating, and to Matt Fairtlough and Caroline Wainer for their back-up and assistance.

Peter Aczel (Manchester), Harold Simmons (Manchester), Stan Wainer (Leeds)

August 1992.

LOGIC FOR IT

The University of Leeds
CTCS
Centre for Theoretical Computer Science

LEEDS PROOF THEORY 1990 PROGRAMME

Summer School Lectures 25 July - 30 July 1990

S. WAINER (Leeds) 3hrs.	*Basic Proof Theory*
L. WALLEN (Oxford) 4hrs.	*Elementary Proof Theory and Search*
T. COQUAND (Gothenburg) 4hrs.	*Generalized Type Systems*
W. POHLERS (Münster) 4hrs.	*Proof Theory and Ordinal Analysis*
H. SCHWICHTENBERG (Munich) 4hrs.	*Proofs as Programs*
L. PAULSON (Cambridge) 2hrs.	*Applications of Proof Theory to ISABELLE*

Conference Lectures 30 July - 2 August 1990

W. BUCHHOLZ (Munich)
Simplified Ordinal Analysis of Impredicative Theories.

S. BUSS (San Diego)
The Undecidability of K-Provability in Sequent Calculus.

A. CICHON (London)
Proof Theory and Rewrite Systems.

G. DOWEK (Rocquencourt)
Some Problems on the Design of a Mathematical Vernacular.

S. FEFERMAN (Stanford) 3hrs.
Logics and Type Systems for Functional Programming Languages.

F. HONSELL (Udine)
Reasoning about Lambda Terms in Domain Models.

D. HOWE (Cornell)
Applied Proof Theory in NuPRL.

N. MENDLER (Manchester)
Inductive Types via Initial Algebras in Martin-Löf Type Theory.

G. MINTS (Tallinn) 2hrs.
Resolution Calculi for Predicate Modal Logic.
Interplay between Proof Theory and Constructive Ideology in USSR 1950-70.

R. POLLACK (Edinburgh)
Implicit Syntax.

M. RATHJEN (Münster)
Predicative Fragments of Kripke-Platek Set Theory.

W. SIEG (Carnegie-Mellon)
Finite Type Extensions of Fragments of Arithmetic.

J. ZUCKER (McMaster)
Provably Computable Functions on Abstract Data Types.

Basic proof theory

S. WAINER & L. WALLEN

Basic Proof Theory

S.S. WAINER,
Dept. of Pure Mathematics, University of Leeds, U.K.
L.A. WALLEN,
Computing Laboratory, University of Oxford, U.K.

§ 1 Introduction

This paper is an amalgam of two introductory lecture courses given at the Summer School. As the title suggests, the aim is to present fundamental notions of Proof Theory in their simplest settings, thus: Completeness and Cut-Elimination in Pure Predicate Logic; the Curry-Howard Correspondence and Normalization in the core part of Natural Deduction; connections to Sequent Calculus and Linear Logic; and applications to the Σ_1-Inductive fragment of arithmetic and the synthesis of primitive recursive bounding functions. The authors have tried to preserve a (readable) balance between rigour and informal lecture-note style.

§ 2 Pure Predicate Logic—Completeness

Classical first order predicate calculus (PC) is formulated here essentially in "Schütte-Ackermann-Tait" style, but with *multisets* instead of *sets* of formulas for sequents. It is kept "pure" (*i.e.*, no function symbols) merely for the sake of technical simplicity. The refinement to multiset sequents illuminates the rôle of the so-called *structural inferences* of *contraction* and *weakening* in proof-theoretic arguments.

The language of PC. The language consists of

- Individual variables: $x_0, x_1, x_2, \ldots$;
- Predicate symbols: $P_0, \bar{P}_0, P_1, \bar{P}_1, \ldots$ occurring in complementary pairs;
- Logical symbols: $\vee$ (or), $\wedge$ (and), $\exists$ (some), $\forall$ (all);
- Brackets for unique readability.

Formulas $A, B, \ldots$ are built up from atoms: $P(x_{i_1}, \ldots, x_{i_k})$, $\bar{P}(x_{i_1}, \ldots, x_{i_k})$, by applying $\vee$, $\wedge$, $\exists x$ and $\forall x$. Note that negation $\neg$ and implication $\rightarrow$ are not included as basic logical symbols. Negation is *defined* by De Morgan's Laws: $\neg P \equiv \bar{P}$; $\neg\bar{P} \equiv P$; $\neg(A \vee B) \equiv \neg A \wedge \neg B$; $\neg(A \wedge B) \equiv \neg A \vee \neg B$; $\neg\exists x A \equiv \forall x \neg A$; $\neg\forall x A \equiv \exists x \neg A$. Implication $A \to B$ is *defined* to be $\neg A \vee B$. The reason for presenting logic in this way is that we want to exploit the duality between $\vee$ and $\wedge$, and $\exists$ and $\forall$. The price paid is that we cannot present intuitionistic logic in this way, since De Morgan's Laws are not intuitionistically valid.

Derivability in PC. Rather than deriving single formulas we shall derive finite multisets of them $\Gamma = \{A_1, A_2, ..., A_n\}$ meaning "A_1 or A_2 or ... or A_n". Γ, A means $\Gamma \cup \{A\}$ where the union sign ($\cup$) here is union of multisets.

The Proof-Rules of PC are (with any Γ and Δ):

$$\text{(Axioms)} \quad P(x_{i_1}, \ldots, x_{i_k}), \bar{P}(x_{i_1}, \ldots, x_{i_k})$$

$$(\vee)\ \frac{\Gamma, A_0, A_1}{\Gamma, (A_0 \vee A_1)} \qquad (\wedge)\ \frac{\Gamma, A_0 \quad \Delta, A_1}{\Gamma, \Delta, (A_0 \wedge A_1)}$$

$$(\exists)\ \frac{\Gamma, A(x')}{\Gamma, \exists x A(x)} \qquad (\forall)\ \frac{\Gamma, A(x')}{\Gamma, \forall x A(x)} \quad x' \text{ not free in } \Gamma$$

$$(\mathrm{C})\ \frac{\Gamma, A, A}{\Gamma, A} \qquad (\mathrm{W})\ \frac{\Gamma}{\Gamma, A}$$

$$(\mathrm{Cut})\ \frac{\Gamma, C \quad \Delta, \neg C}{\Gamma, \Delta} \quad C \text{ is the "cut formula."}$$

We shall use $\vdash_{PC} \Gamma$ to mean that there is a PC-derivation of Γ from axioms.

EXERCISES. Show that for all Γ and all A,

(1) $\vdash_{PC} \Gamma, \neg A, A$. (Hint: prove $\vdash \neg A, A$ by induction on the "build-up" of A, then use weakening. Call this (Axiom$'$).

(2) If $\vdash_{PC} \Gamma, (A_0 \wedge A_1)$ then $\vdash_{PC} \Gamma, A_0$ and $\vdash_{PC} \Gamma, A_1$.

(3) If $\vdash_{PC} \Gamma, \forall x A(x)$ then $\vdash_{PC} \Gamma, A(t)$, for any term (*i.e.*, variable) t.

Alternative formulations. The ($\vee$) rule is often formulated as:

$$(\vee')\ \frac{\Gamma, A_i}{\Gamma, (A_0 \vee A_1)} \quad i = 0 \text{ or } 1,$$

which is easily seen to be equivalent to ($\vee$) in the presence of contraction and weakening. Moreover, the rules are usually understood as working over sets instead of multisets. In the set approach the rules with two premises ($\wedge$) and (Cut) can be given the same contexts Γ, *i.e.*,

$$(\wedge') \quad \frac{\Gamma, A_0 \quad \Gamma, A_1}{\Gamma, (A_0 \wedge A_1)} \qquad\qquad (\mathrm{Cut}') \quad \frac{\Gamma, C \quad \Gamma, \neg C}{\Gamma}.$$

If the axioms are taken as in the above exercise, both contraction and weakening can be dropped with no change in the set of provable sequents. The system comprising (Axiom$'$), ($\vee'$), ($\wedge'$), ($\exists$), ($\forall$) and (Cut$'$), working over sets of formulas is known as the Schütte-Ackermann-Tait presentation of PC.

EXERCISE.

(4) Prove that the Schütte-Ackermann-Tait rules working over *multisets* are indeed derived rules of PC, because of Contraction and Weakening.

REMARK. In the absence of contraction and weakening, but with sequents as sets, the alternative formulations of the ($\vee$) and ($\wedge$) rules lead to distinct connectives and thence to Linear Logic. Girard (1987) calls the primed rules with implicit contraction "additive" and our original rules with distinct contexts "multiplicative."

The Semantics of PC. An *interpretation* of PC gives a fixed meaning to all the formulas and consists of a structure $\mathcal{M} = \langle M, P_0^M, P_1^M, P_2^M, \ldots \rangle$ where M is some non-empty set and P_k^M is a relation on M which has the same arity as P_k and, given any list of arguments from M, is either true or false. Thus with respect to a given interpretation, and a given assignment $x_{i_1} := m_1, \ldots, x_{i_n} := m_n$ of elements of M to the free variables, a formula $A(x_{i_1}, \ldots, x_{i_n})$ makes a statement about $\mathcal{M}$ which is either true ($\boldsymbol{t}$) or false ($\boldsymbol{f}$). If it works out $\boldsymbol{t}$ under *all* possible interpretations $\mathcal{M}$ and *all* possible assignments of elements of M to its free variables, then A is said to be (logically or universally) valid.

COMPLETENESS THEOREM (GÖDEL 1930). $\vdash_{PC} \Gamma$ *iff* Γ *is valid.*

PROOF: For *soundness:* $\vdash_{PC} \Gamma \Rightarrow \Gamma$ is valid; simply note that the axioms are valid and each of the rules preserves validity.

For *adequacy:* $\not\vdash_{PC} \Gamma \Rightarrow \Gamma$ not valid; we try to construct a derivation tree for Γ by successively taking it to bits using the ($\vee$), ($\wedge$), ($\exists$), ($\forall$) rules backwards. We do not use Cut! Since we are assuming that Γ is not derivable, this procedure must fail, and out of the failure we can construct an interpretation in which Γ is false. Hence Γ is not valid. It goes thus:

First write out Γ as a sequence of formulas, starting with the atoms (if there are any). Let A denote the first non-atomic formula in the sequence and Δ the rest of Γ, thus

$$\Gamma = \text{atoms}, A, \Delta.$$

Now take A to bits using whichever one of the rules $(\vee)$, $(\wedge)$, $(\exists)$, $(\forall)$ applies. This produces one or (in the case of $\wedge$) two new sequences of formulas Γ' as follows:

$(\vee)$ If $\Gamma = \text{atoms}, (A_0 \vee A_1), \Delta$ then $\Gamma' = \text{atoms}, A_0, A_1, \Delta$;

$(\wedge)$ If $\Gamma = \text{atoms}, (A_0 \wedge A_1), \Delta$ then $\Gamma'_i = \text{atoms}, A_i, \Delta$ for each $i = 0, 1$;

$(\forall)$ If $\Gamma = \text{atoms}, \forall x A(x), \Delta$ then $\Gamma' = \text{atoms}, A(x_j), \Delta$;

$(\exists)$ If $\Gamma = \text{atoms}, \exists x A(x), \Delta$ then $\Gamma' = \text{atoms}, A(x_k), \Delta, \exists x A(x)$,

where, in $(\forall)$ x_j is any new variable not already used, and in $(\exists)$ x_k is the first variable in the list $x_0, x_1, x_2, \ldots$ which has not already been used at a previous stage to witness the same formula $\exists x A(x)$.

Repeat this process to form $\Gamma, \Gamma', \Gamma'', \ldots$ and notice that each time, Γ follows from Γ' by applying the corresponding rule. (Notice that here we are actually using the derived rule $(\wedge')$ of the Scütte-Ackermann-Tait system since we "duplicate" the context: "atoms, Δ," in each of the two sequents Γ'_i that result.) In this way we develop what looks like a derivation-tree for Γ with branching at applications of the $(\wedge)$ rule. But assuming Γ is not derivable in PC there must be at least one branch on this tree — call it $\mathcal{B}$ — which either (a) terminates in a sequence of atoms only, but is not a (Schütte-Ackermann-Tait) logical axiom, or (b) goes on forever!

From $\mathcal{B}$ we construct a "counter-interpretation",

$$\mathcal{M} = \left\langle N, P_0^M, P_1^M, P_2^M, \ldots \right\rangle$$

where $N = \{0, 1, 2, 3, \ldots\}$ and the relations P_j^M are defined as follows :

$$P_j^M(i_1, \ldots, i_n) \Leftrightarrow_{\text{Def}} \text{the atom } P_j(x_{i_1}, \ldots, x_{i_n}) \text{ does not occur on } \mathcal{B}.$$

CLAIM: *Under the interpretation $\mathcal{M}$ and the assignment $x_i := i$ to free variables, every formula A occurring on $\mathcal{B}$ is false.*

PROOF: (of CLAIM.) By induction on the build-up of formulas A occurring on $\mathcal{B}$, noticing that as the sequence $\Gamma, \Gamma', \Gamma'', \ldots$ is developed, every non-atomic formula on $\mathcal{B}$ will eventually "come under attention" as the first non-atomic formula in some stage:

(i) $A \equiv P_j(x_{i_1}, \ldots, x_{i_n})$ gets $\boldsymbol{f}$ by definition.

(ii) $A \equiv \overline{P_j}(x_{i_1}, \ldots, x_{i_n})$ gets $\boldsymbol{f}$ because its complement $P_j(x_{i_1}, \ldots, x_{i_n})$ cannot be on $\mathcal{B}$ (otherwise $\mathcal{B}$ would terminate in an axiom) and hence $P_j(x_{i_1}, \ldots, x_{i_n})$ gets $\boldsymbol{t}$ by definition.

(iii) $A \equiv A_0 \vee A_1$. Since A comes under attention at some stage in $\mathcal{B}$, both A_0 and A_1 also occur on $\mathcal{B}$. So by the induction hypothesis, both get $\boldsymbol{f}$ and hence so does A.

(iv) $A \equiv A_0 \wedge A_1$. Again, since A must come under attention at some stage, either A_0 or A_1 is on $\mathcal{B}$. So one of them gets $\boldsymbol{f}$ and hence so does A.

(v) $A \equiv \forall x A_0(x)$. In this case $A_0(x_j)$ is also on $\mathcal{B}$ for one of the variables x_j. So $A_0(x_j)$ gets $\boldsymbol{f}$ and hence so does A.

(vi) $A \equiv \exists x A_0(x)$. Then by the construction of $\mathcal{B}$, A comes under attention infinitely often and each time a "new" $A_0(x_k)$ is introduced. Therefore *every one* of

$$A_0(x_0), A_0(x_1), A_0(x_2), A_0(x_3), \ldots$$

occurs on $\mathcal{B}$, and they all get $\boldsymbol{f}$. Hence A gets $\boldsymbol{f}$.

This completes the proof of the claim. □

Now since every formula in the set Γ we started with occurs on $\mathcal{B}$, they all get $\boldsymbol{f}$ under this interpretation. Thus Γ is not valid. □

§ 3 Pure Predicate Logic—Cut-elimination

THE CUT-ELIMINATION THEOREM (GENTZEN 1936) *If Γ is derivable in PC then it is derivable without any use of the Cut-rule.*

PROOF: *(Semantic Proof.)* If $\vdash_{PC} \Gamma$ then by the Soundness of PC, Γ is valid. But the proof of adequacy actually shows that if Γ is not derivable using only the rules $\vee, \wedge, \exists, \forall$, then Γ is not valid. Since Γ is valid, it must therefore be derivable without Cut. □

In the rest of this section we shall develop a syntactic proof of the Cut-Elimination Theorem. We shall approach the result in two steps. First we shall prove the result for a subsystem of PC called MPC (standing for Multiplicative fragment of PC). This subsystem is formed by dropping the rules for contraction (C) and weakening (W) from the system given in the previous section. The importance of this subsystem of predicate logic has been stressed by Girard (1987). MPC will help us to illuminate the rôle played by the structural rules in various results like existence and disjunction properties. The Cut-Elimination result is then extended to PC.

Cut elimination in MPC takes on a particularly simple form since the reduction and elimination of cuts from a proof *decreases* the size of a proof. This is in contrast to the situation in both Classical and Intuitionistic Logic. Cut-free proofs are therefore the smallest proofs of sequents.

REMARK. This respects the idea that cuts are "indirections" in a proof. If a proof makes recourse to indirections, one should expect its size to exceed that of a "direct" proof. On the other hand, if having derived a sequent once it may nevertheless be used *more than once* within a derivation, we might expect the introduction of the indirection to lead to a decrease in size. Consequently, cuts may be used to shorten proofs in the presence of contraction.

Size, height and cut-rank of derivations. Each inference (Axiom), ($\vee$), ($\wedge$), ($\exists$) and ($\forall$), has the form:

$$\frac{\Gamma_i, \Phi_i}{\Gamma, \Theta} \quad (i < k) \quad \text{for some } k : 0 \leq k \leq 2,$$

where the $(\Phi_i)_{i<k}$ are the minor formulas of the inference, Θ the principal formula(s) and $\Gamma = \bigcup_{i<k} \Gamma_i$ (multiset union). In the sequel we shall use π_i, $i = 0, 1$, to denote the immediate subderivations of a derivation π and we shall supress mention of k. For example, $\sum_i f(\pi_i)$ will be used to denote the sum of the values of function f (from derivations to natural numbers, say) over the immediate subderivations of π; if π is an axiom, *i.e.*, $k = 0$, we have $\sum_i f(\pi_i) = 0$. Given this convention, we can define the *size*, $\boldsymbol{s}\pi$, of a derivation π inductively as follows:

$$\boldsymbol{s}\pi = 1 + \sum_i \boldsymbol{s}\pi_i.$$

Notice that if π is an axiom, $\boldsymbol{s}\pi = 1$, hence the size of a derivation equals the number of inferences that comprise it.

The *height*, $| \pi |$, of a derivation π is the length of its longest branch, *i.e.*,

$$| \pi | = 1 + \sup_i | \pi_i |.$$

Likewise, the height of a formula is the length of the longest branch in its formation tree (greatest nesting of connectives).

The *cut-rank*, $\boldsymbol{r}\pi$, of a derivation π is the height of the "tallest" cut-formula in π, *i.e.*,

$$\boldsymbol{r}\pi = \begin{cases} \sup(| C |, \sup_i \boldsymbol{r}\pi_i) & \pi \text{ ends in cut on } C; \\ \sup_i \boldsymbol{r}\pi_i, & \text{otherwise.} \end{cases}$$

If $\pi(x) \vdash \Gamma(x)$ denotes a proof π of sequent Γ with variable x free, and x' is a variable free for x in π, then $\pi(x')$ denotes the proof obtained from π by substitution of x' for x. Substitution has no effect on the size, height or cut-rank of a proof:

SUBSTITUTION LEMMA *If* $\lambda(x) \vdash \Gamma(x)$ *and* x' *is free for* x *in* π, *then* $\lambda(x') \vdash \Gamma(x')$ *with* $\boldsymbol{r}\pi(x') = \boldsymbol{r}\pi(x)$, $\boldsymbol{s}\pi(x') = \boldsymbol{s}\pi(x)$ *and* $| \pi(x') | = | \pi(x) |$.

The main technical tool in the Cut-Elimination argument is the following:

CUT-REDUCTION LEMMA *If* $\lambda \vdash \Gamma, A$ *and* $\rho \vdash \Delta, \neg A$, *both with cut-rank* $< r = |A|$, *then there is a derivation* $\pi \vdash \Gamma, \Delta$ *such that*

(i) $\boldsymbol{r}\pi < r$;

(ii) $\boldsymbol{s}\pi \leq \boldsymbol{s}\lambda + \boldsymbol{s}\rho$;

(iii) $|\pi| \leq |\lambda| + |\rho|$.

PROOF: By induction on $\boldsymbol{s}\lambda + \boldsymbol{s}\rho$.

Case 1. Either A is a side formula of the last inference of λ or $\neg A$ is a side formula of the last inference of ρ.

By symmetry, we may assume the former. λ is of the form:

$$\lambda = \frac{\overset{\lambda_i}{\Gamma_i, B_i} \quad \overset{\lambda_j}{\Gamma_j, B_j, A}}{\Gamma, A} \qquad (0 \leq i \neq j < k),$$

i.e., with at least one premise, since axioms have no side formulae. Moreover, in the absence of (implicit) contraction, A is the side formula of *exactly* one premise (distinguished here as the jth).

The induction hypothesis with $\lambda_j \vdash \Gamma_j, B_j, A$ and $\rho \vdash \Delta, \neg A$ gives a proof $\pi' \vdash \Gamma_j, B_j, \Delta$ with cut-rank $< r$, size $\leq \boldsymbol{s}\lambda_j + \boldsymbol{s}\rho$ and height $\leq |\lambda_j| + |\rho|$. Consider π, given by:

$$\pi = \frac{\overset{\lambda_i}{\Gamma_i, B_i} \quad \overset{\pi'}{\Gamma_j, B_j, \Delta}}{\Gamma, \Delta} \qquad (0 \leq i \neq j < k).$$

Thus $\boldsymbol{r}\pi = \boldsymbol{r}\pi' < r$. Also we have:

$$\boldsymbol{s}\pi = 1 + \sum_{i \neq j < k} \boldsymbol{s}\lambda_i + \boldsymbol{s}\pi' \leq 1 + \sum_{i \neq j < k} \boldsymbol{s}\lambda_i + \boldsymbol{s}\lambda_j + \boldsymbol{s}\rho = \boldsymbol{s}\lambda + \boldsymbol{s}\rho,$$

and

$$|\pi| = 1 + \sup\left(\sup_{i \neq j < k} |\lambda_i|, |\pi'|\right) \leq \sup(|\lambda|, |\lambda| + |\rho|) = |\lambda| + |\rho|.$$

Case 2. A is a principal formula of λ and $\neg A$ is a principal formula of ρ. There are six cases according to the structure of A, which are reduced by symmetry to three.

(a) $A = P(x_1, \ldots, x_n)$. (Symmetrical case: $A = \bar{P}(x_1, \ldots, x_n)$.) Then λ and ρ are of the form:

$$\lambda = A, \neg A \qquad \rho = \neg A, A.$$

Consider the proof π given by

$$\pi = \neg A, A.$$

It is clear that π has the appropriate bounds on rank, height and size.

(b) $A = B \wedge C$. (Symmetrical case: $A = B \vee C$.) Then λ and ρ are of the form:

$$\lambda \quad = \quad \frac{\begin{matrix}\lambda_0 & \lambda_1 \\ \Gamma_0, B & \Gamma_1, C\end{matrix}}{\Gamma, B \wedge C} \qquad \rho \quad = \quad \frac{\begin{matrix}\rho_0 \\ \Delta, \neg B, \neg C\end{matrix}}{\Delta, \neg B \vee \neg C}$$

Consider the proof

$$\pi \quad = \quad \frac{\begin{matrix}\lambda_0 \\ \Gamma_0, B\end{matrix} \qquad \dfrac{\begin{matrix}\lambda_1 & \rho_0 \\ \Gamma_1, C & \Delta, \neg B, \neg C\end{matrix}}{\Gamma_1, \Delta, \neg B}}{\Gamma, \Delta}$$

Again the cut-rank of π is $< r$ and we have:

$$s\pi \quad = \quad s\lambda_0 + s\lambda_1 + s\rho_0 + 2 \quad = \quad s\lambda + s\rho \quad ,$$

and

$$\begin{aligned} |\, \pi \,| &= 1 + \sup(|\, \lambda_0 \,|, 1 + \sup(|\, \lambda_1 \,|, |\, \rho_0 \,|)) \\ &\leq \sup(|\, \lambda \,|, 1 + \sup(|\, \lambda \,|, |\, \rho \,|)) \\ &\leq |\, \lambda \,| + |\, \rho \,|. \end{aligned}$$

(c) $A = \forall x B$. (Symmetrical case: $A = \exists x B$.) Then λ and ρ have the form:

$$\lambda \; = \; \frac{\begin{matrix}\lambda'(y) \\ \Gamma, B(y)\end{matrix}}{\Gamma, \forall x B(x)} \qquad \rho \; = \; \frac{\begin{matrix}\rho' \\ \Delta, \neg B(x')\end{matrix}}{\Delta, \exists x \neg B(x)}$$

Consider the proof π given by:

$$\pi \;=\; \frac{\begin{array}{cc}\lambda'(x') & \rho' \\ \Gamma, B(x') & \Delta, \neg B(x')\end{array}}{\Gamma, \Delta}$$

By the Substitution Lemma, $s\lambda'(x') = s\lambda'(y)$ and $\mid \lambda'(x') \mid = \mid \lambda'(y) \mid$. Hence

$$s\pi \;=\; 1 + s\lambda'(x') + s\rho' \;=\; 1 + s\lambda' + s\rho' \;\leq\; s\lambda + s\rho;$$

and

$$\mid \pi \mid \;=\; 1 + \sup(\mid \lambda'(x') \mid, \mid \rho' \mid) \;\leq\; \sup(\mid \lambda \mid, \mid \rho \mid) \;\leq\; \mid \lambda \mid + \mid \rho \mid.$$

This ends the proof. □

CUT-RANK REDUCTION LEMMA. *If $\pi \vdash \Gamma$ with cut rank $r > 0$, there is a proof $\pi' \vdash \Gamma$ with strictly smaller cut-rank such that: $s\pi' < s\pi$ and $\mid \pi' \mid \leq 2^{\mid \pi \mid}$.*

PROOF: By induction on $s\pi$. Assume that the last inference of π is a cut of rank r (the result follows immediately from the induction hypothesis in the other cases; note that π cannot be an axiom.) The last inference is therefore of the form:

$$\frac{\begin{array}{cc}\lambda & \rho \\ \Gamma, A & \Delta, \neg A\end{array}}{\Gamma, \Delta}.$$

By the induction hypothesis on λ and ρ we get $\lambda' \vdash \Gamma, A$ and $\rho' \vdash \Delta, \neg A$ with ranks $< r$, sizes $< s\lambda$ and $< s\rho$ resp., and heights $\leq 2^{|\lambda|}$ and $\leq 2^{|\rho|}$ resp. The Cut-Reduction Lemma on λ' and ρ' yields $\pi' \vdash \Gamma, \Delta$ with rank $< r$, size $\leq s\lambda + s\rho < s\pi$ and height $\leq 2^{|\lambda|} + 2^{|\rho|} \leq 2^{1+\sup(|\lambda|,|\rho|)} = 2^{|\pi|}$. □

Define 2^k_r by:

$$2^k_r \;=\; \begin{cases} k & r = 0, \\ 2^{2^k_{r-1}} & r > 1. \end{cases}$$

we can now formulate the Cut-Elimination Theorem, namely,

CUT-ELIMINATION THEOREM FOR MPC. *If $\pi \vdash \Gamma$ with cut rank $r > 0$, there is a cut-free proof $\pi^* \vdash \Gamma$ such that $s\pi^* < s\pi$ and $\mid \pi^* \mid = 2^{|\pi|}_r$.*

From the Cut-Elimination Theorem it is clear that (in MPC) the elimination of cuts reduces the size of proofs as expected, but increases their height exponentially.

Existence property for MPC. MPC also admits a result that is more normally associated with constructive logics, namely, that proofs of existential statements yield witnesses.

EXISTENCE PROPERTY FOR MPC. *If* $\vdash_{MPC} \exists x A(x)$ *then* $\vdash_{MPC} A(t)$ *for some term (i.e., variable)* t.

PROOF: Suppose $\pi \vdash \exists x A(x)$. The Cut-Elimination Theorem gives cut-free $\pi^* \vdash \exists x A(x)$, the last inference of which must be an $(\exists)$ inference. The result follows immediately. □

Extending Cut-Elimination to PC. To extend the Cut-Elimination Theorem to PC, we must reconsider the structural rules of contraction and weakening. At first glance these rules appear to add a new case to the Cut-Reduction Lemma, namely (in the notation of the Lemma):

Case 3. Both A and $\neg A$ are principal formulas in the proofs $\lambda \vdash \Gamma, A$ and $\rho \vdash \Gamma, \neg A$ respectively, but (at least) one, say ρ, ends with a contraction or weakening on $\neg A$. (The other case is symmetrical.)

(a) (Contraction.) Then ρ is of the form:

$$\rho \quad = \quad \frac{\begin{array}{c}\rho_0 \\ \Delta, \neg A, \neg A\end{array}}{\Delta, \neg A} \quad .$$

The induction hypothesis with λ and ρ_0 gives $\pi' \vdash \Gamma, \Delta, \neg A$ with rank $< r$, size $\leq s\lambda + s\rho_0$ and height $\leq |\lambda| + |\rho_0|$. But how do we deal with the residual $\neg A$? The natural step is to apply the induction hypothesis again to get a proof $\pi'' \vdash \Gamma, \Gamma, \Delta$, but the resulting proof does not satisfy either the size or the height bound: *i.e., contraction causes the duplication of subproofs!* Moreover, we need to follow this construction with contractions to obtain a proof $\pi \vdash \Gamma, \Delta$; the number of contractions depending on the size of Γ. We shall leave the case at this stage and investigate the effect of weakening...

(b) (Weakening.) Then ρ is of the form:

$$\rho \quad = \quad \frac{\begin{array}{c}\rho_0 \\ \Delta\end{array}}{\Delta, \neg A}$$

A suitable proof π is then just:

$$\pi \quad = \quad \frac{\begin{array}{c}\dfrac{\begin{array}{c}\rho_0 \\ \Delta\end{array}}{\vdots}\end{array}}{\Gamma, \Delta}$$

i.e., apply weakening using the formulas of Γ to obtain $\pi \vdash \Gamma, \Delta$! The size bound is clearly met, since

$$s\pi \;=\; s\rho_0 + \text{No. of formulas in } \Gamma$$

and $s\lambda \geq$ No. of formulas in Γ.

So Contraction and Weakening make the change in size and height of a derivation under cut-elimination highly dependent on the combination and placing of individual inferences within the derivation. The traditional approach to this is to *ignore* the structural rules when calculating size and height, *i.e.*, to count only the logical inferences. With this change in definition it is possible to prove the following:

CUT-ELIMINATION THEOREM FOR PC. *If* $\pi \vdash \Gamma$ *with cut-rank* $r > 0$, *there is a cut-free proof* $\pi^* \vdash \Gamma$ *such that* $|\pi^*| = 2_r^{|\pi|}$.

EXERCISE.

(5) Prove a Cut-Reduction Lemma for PC. Hints: the induction must be on $|\lambda| + |\rho|$ since the change in size of derivations under cut-elimination is less uniform. The only part that differs from the proof for MPC is that we must maintain the height bound when both formulas A and $\neg A$ are principal (in the last inferences) but one inference, introducing A, say, is a Contraction.

$$\frac{\begin{matrix}\rho_0\\ \Gamma, A, A\end{matrix}}{\Gamma, A}$$

There are two cases:

1. An ancestor of one occurrence of A is introduced by weakening higher up in ρ_0.

   In this case we can eliminate the Weakening and delete all ancestors of A throughout ρ_0. The Contraction can then be eliminated and the result follows from the induction hypothesis.

2. Ancestors of both occurrences of A are principal formulas of some (non-Weakening) inference in ρ_0. There are two subcases:

   (a) These inferences occur on the same branch of ρ. In this case we can use the induction hypothesis on the highest occurrence and introduce the remaining formulas by Weakening.

   (b) The inferences occur on different branches. Here the induction hypothesis is applied twice; but notice that the height bound is met despite the inclusion of two copies of (a distinguished subproof of) ρ_0.

Cut-Elimination for theories. Suppose one wanted to make PC-derivations from certain additional *non-logical* axioms $NLAX$.

$$NLAX \vdash_{PC} A.$$

This would be equivalent to requiring

$$\vdash_{PC} NLAX \to A.$$

Although this latter derivation has a cut-free proof in PC, we nevertheless need Cut in order to derive A from $NLAX$ as follows:

$$\dfrac{NLAX \quad \begin{matrix}\vdots \\ NLAX \to A\end{matrix}}{A}$$

Thus in the presence of non-logical axioms, we cannot expect to have (full) Cut-Elimination. Often, however, we will be able to use Cut-Elimination methods in order to keep the Cuts down to "manageable levels" as we shall see in § 6.

§ 4 Natural deduction for $\wedge$, $\to$, $\forall$. Lambda Expressions with Formulas as Types.

In Natural Deduction (ND) a single formula is proved at a time, rather than a finite (multi)set of them as in the previous section. One starts with assumptions and builds derivations using the ND-rules which now come in pairs — an introduction and an elimination rule for each logical symbol. Thus for example the $\wedge$-rules are labelled $\wedge$I and $\wedge$E. In the $\to$ I-rule, one or more occurrences of an assumption A used in proving B, may be discharged or cancelled upon deriving $A \to B$. The discharge of A is denoted by enclosing it in brackets thus $[A]$.

Each ND-derivation of a formula A in the logic based on $\wedge$, $\to$, $\forall$ has an associated "constructive" representation as a typed λ-expression t^A built up according to the rules below, where the individual variables z and terms a of the logic have ground-type 0. This association between ND-derivations and typed λ-expressions is called *The Curry-Howard correspondence* and is displayed in Figure 1.

EXAMPLE. The ND-derivation

$$\to\mathrm{I.}\dfrac{\to\mathrm{I.}\dfrac{\forall\mathrm{I.}\dfrac{\to\mathrm{E.}\dfrac{\forall\mathrm{E.}\dfrac{[\forall z.(A(z) \to B(z))] \quad z}{A(z) \to B(z)} \qquad \forall\mathrm{E.}\dfrac{[\forall z.A(z)] \quad z}{A(z)}}{B(z)}}{\forall z.B(z)}}{\forall z.A(z) \to \forall z.B(z)}}{\forall z.(A(z) \to B(z)) \to (\forall z.A(z) \to \forall z.B(z))}$$

	ND-Rules	C-H Correspondence	λ-Expressions
Ass.	A	Var	x^A
$\wedge$I.	$\dfrac{\overset{\vdots t_0}{A} \quad \overset{\vdots t_1}{B}}{A \wedge B}$	Pair	$\left\langle t_0^A, t_1^B \right\rangle^{A \wedge B}$
$\wedge$E.	$\dfrac{\overset{\vdots t}{A \wedge B}}{A}\ ,\ \dfrac{\overset{\vdots t}{A \wedge B}}{B}$	Projn.	$(t^{A \wedge B}0)^A\ ,\ (t^{A \wedge B}1)^B$
$\rightarrow$ I.	$\dfrac{\overset{[A]}{\overset{\vdots t}{B}}}{A \rightarrow B}$	λ-I.	$(\lambda x^A.t^B)^{A \rightarrow B}$
$\rightarrow$ E.	$\dfrac{\overset{\vdots t}{A \rightarrow B} \quad \overset{\vdots s}{A}}{B}$	Appn.	$(t^{A \rightarrow B} s^A)^B$
$\forall$I.	$\dfrac{\overset{\vdots t}{A(z)}}{\forall x.A(z)}$	λ^0-I.	$(\lambda z^0.t^{A(z)})^{\forall z.A}$
$\forall$E.	$\dfrac{\overset{\vdots t}{\forall z.A(z)} \quad a}{A(a)}$	Appn.	$(t^{\forall z.A} a^0)^{A(a)}$

In $\forall$I the variable z should not be free in any uncancelled assumptions.

Figure 1: The Curry-Howard Correspondence.

has corresponding λ-expression:

$$\lambda x^{\forall z(A(z) \rightarrow B(z))}.\lambda y^{\forall z A(z)}.\lambda z^0.((xz)(yz))^{B(z)}.$$

Note how, in the example, each representation can be decoded from the other.

EXERCISES. Construct ND-derivations for the following formulas and write out the λ-expressions that correspond to your derivations.

(6) $((A \rightarrow B) \wedge (B \rightarrow C)) \rightarrow (A \rightarrow C)$.

(7) $\forall z.A(z) \rightarrow (\forall z.B(z) \rightarrow \forall z.(A(z) \wedge B(z)))$.

Embedding classical logic in ND. First introduce a new symbol $\perp$ for falsity and define negation by $\neg A \equiv A \rightarrow \perp$, disjunction by $A \vee B \equiv \neg(\neg A \wedge \neg B)$, and existence by $\exists z.A \equiv \neg \forall z.\neg A$.

The system CND is then obtained by adding the classical falsity rule:

$$\begin{array}{c}[\neg A]\\ \vdots \\ \bot \\ \hline A\end{array}$$

Note that this is equivalent to adding all "stability axioms" $\neg\neg A \to A$. It is in fact sufficient to add these axioms just for atomic A.

Lemma. *The following are derived rules of CND:*

$$\vee I.\frac{A_i}{A_0 \vee A_1} \qquad\qquad \exists I.\frac{A(a)}{\exists z.A(z)}$$

$$\vee E.\frac{A_0\vee A_1 \quad \begin{array}{c}[A_0]\\ \vdots\\ C\end{array} \quad \begin{array}{c}[A_1]\\ \vdots \\ C\end{array}}{C} \qquad\qquad \exists E.\frac{\exists z.A(z) \quad \begin{array}{c}[A(z)]\\ \vdots\\ C\end{array}}{C}$$

where in $\exists E.$ the variable z is not free in any other assumptions upon which C depends.

Proof: For the $\exists$-introduction rule:

$$\to E.\frac{\forall E.\dfrac{[\forall z.\neg A(z)] \quad a}{\neg A(a)} \qquad A(a)}{\to I.\dfrac{\bot}{\neg\forall z.\neg A(z)}}$$

and for the $\exists$-elimination rule:

$$\to E.\frac{\neg\forall z.\neg A(z) \qquad \forall I.\dfrac{\dfrac{\to E.\dfrac{\neg C \quad \begin{array}{c}[A(z)]\\ \vdots\\ C\end{array}}{\bot}}{\neg A(z)}}{\forall z.\neg A(z)}}{\dfrac{\bot}{C}}$$

The $\vee$-rules are treated similarly. □

Lemma. *If $\vdash_{PC} A_1, A_2, \ldots, A_n$ then $\vdash_{CND} A_1 \vee A_2 \vee \ldots \vee A_n$, that is, $\vdash_{CND} \neg(\neg A_1 \wedge \neg A_2 \wedge \ldots \wedge \neg A_n)$.*

Proof: is left as a laborious exercise! (Check all of the ways in which $\vdash_{PC} A_1, A_2, \ldots, A_n$.) □

§ 4.1 Normalization for ND

Notice that an introduction followed immediately by the corresponding elimination is an unnecessary detour. The derivation may be "reduced" to an equivalent one in which the introduction/elimination pair is removed. Normalization is the process of continued reduction which eliminates all such unnecessary detours from a proof.

We consider typed λ-expressions rather than their corresponding ND-derivations. The "one-step" reduction rules are:

$$\begin{array}{lll} (\wedge) & \left\langle t_0^{A_0}, t_1^{A_1} \right\rangle i & \Rightarrow \; t_i^{A_i} \\ (\rightarrow) & (\lambda x^A . t^B)^{A \rightarrow B} s^A & \Rightarrow \; t[s/x]^B \\ (\forall) & (\lambda z^0 . t^{A(z)})^{\forall z A} a^0 & \Rightarrow \; t^{A(a)} \end{array}$$

where, in the $\wedge$-reduction $i = 0, 1$.

The expressions which can be reduced in one step as above are called *redexes*. A λ-expression (or ND-derivation) is said to be in *normal form* if it contains no redexes (or introduction/elimination pairs).

THE NORMALIZATION THEOREM. *Every λ-expression or ND-derivation reduces to a normal form.*

Define the *rank* of a typed λ-expression to be the maximum of all the heights of formulas/types A such that there is a redex $r^A s$ occurring in it. If the expression contains no redexes its rank is 0.

The Normalization Theorem follows from:

THE REDUCTION LEMMA. *Every λ-expression t of rank $k+1$ can be reduced to another one t_1 of rank $\leq k$.*

PROOF: By induction on the "height" of the expression t:

Variables: $t \equiv x^A$. Nothing to do.

Introductions: $t \equiv \langle t', t'' \rangle$ or $\lambda x^A . t'$ or $\lambda z^0 . t'$.
Then t reduces to $t_1 \equiv \langle t_1', t_1'' \rangle$ or $\lambda x^A . t_1'$ or $\lambda z^0 . t_1'$.
By the induction hypothesis, t has rank $\leq k$.

Eliminations: $t \equiv r^A s$.

First reduce r to r_1 with rank $\leq k$ and reduce s to s_1 with rank $\leq k$, using the induction hypothesis. Then t reduces to $r_1^A s_1$. If this is not a redex it has rank $\leq k$. If it is a redex it falls under one of the following cases:

1. $r_1^A \equiv \langle r_{10}^{A_0}, r_{11}^{A_1} \rangle$ and $s \equiv i$ $\quad (i = 0 \text{ or } 1)$.
   Therefore $r_1^A s_1 \Rightarrow r_{1i}^{A_i}$ with rank $\leq k$ and t reduces to $t_1 \equiv r_{1i}^{A_i}$ with rank $\leq k$.

2. $r_1^A \equiv \lambda z^0 . r_2^{B(z)}$ and $s_1 \equiv a^0$.
   Therefore $r_1^A s_1 \Rightarrow r_2^{B(a)}$ with rank $\leq k$ and t reduces to $t_1 \equiv r_2^{B(a)}$ with rank $\leq k$.

3. $r_1^A \equiv \lambda x^B . r_2^C$ and $s_1 \equiv s_1^B$.
   Therefore $r_1^A s_1 \Rightarrow r_2[s_1/x]^C$ with rank $\leq k(?)$
   Hence t reduces to $t_1 \equiv r_2[s_1/x]$ with rank $\leq k$.

To complete the proof, we must answer (?) in part 3: why is $r_2[s_1/x]$ of rank $\leq k$? The situation is this

(i) r_2^C has rank $\leq k$ and contains x^B free.

(ii) s_1^B has rank $\leq k$.

(iii) $A \equiv B \to C$ has height $\leq k+1$ so B has height $\leq k$.

Now to check that $r_2[s_1/x]$ has rank $\leq k$, we consider all possible forms of r_2. But the only way in which the rank of r_2 could possibly be *changed* by substitution of s_1 for x, would be if new redexes were thus created. This could only happen if r_2 contained an applicative subterm of the form $(x^B u)$ and s_1^B were of the form $\langle , \rangle$ or λ or λ^0. But then the rank of such a new redex is just the height of B which is still $\leq k$ by (iii) above! □

The Complexity of Reduction $t \mapsto t_1$. Let $|\, t \,|$ denote the height of the λ-expression t, or (equivalently) the height of its corresponding ND-derivation tree.

We want to estimate a function F such that

$$|\, t_1 \,| \leq F(|\, t \,|).$$

Notice that the worst that can happen in reducing t to t_1 occurs in case 3 where s_1 is substituted for x in r_2.

Obviously $|\, r_2[s_1/x] \,| \leq |\, r_2 \,| + |\, s_1 \,|$. So as $|\, t \,|$ increases from n to $n+1$, in the worst case $|\, t_1 \,|$ might be doubled. Thus F must have the property

$$F(n) + F(n) \leq F(n+1)$$

i.e., F is exponential $F(n) = 2^n$.

Consequently if t has rank k then it reduces to normal form t^* after k applications of the Reduction Lemma and hence the complexity of normalization is super-exponential :

$$|t^*| \leq 2^{2^{2^{\cdot^{\cdot^{2^{|t|}}}}}} \Big\} \; k \text{ times} \qquad i.e., \qquad |t^*| \;\leq\; 2_k^{|t|}.$$

This should be compared with the Cut-Elimination result of the previous section. Cut-Elimination and Normalization for the $(\wedge)$, $(\rightarrow)$, $(\forall)$ fragment of PC are analogues.

§ 4.2 Consequences of Normalization

Normal forms of ND-Derivations. A *branch* of an ND-derivation starts with any assumption, and traces down until it hits either the "end" formula (main branch), or the "minor" premise of an $\rightarrow$-elimination (side branch).

In a normal derivation each branch consists of a sequence of Eliminations followed by a sequence of Introductions.

Subformula Property. In a normal derivation of a formula A from assumptions $A_1, A_2, \ldots, A_n$, every formula which occurs must be a subformula of A or of one of the A_i.

HERBRAND'S THEOREM. *Given any ND-derivation of a Σ_1-formula of the form $\exists z.A(z) \equiv \forall z.\neg A(z) \rightarrow \perp$, where A is quantifier-free, we can find individual terms $a_1, a_2, \ldots, a_n$ such that:*

$$\vdash_{ND} A(a_1) \vee A(a_2) \vee \ldots \vee A(a_n).$$

PROOF: Normalize the given derivation of $\forall z.\neg A(z) \rightarrow \perp$. This yields a normal derivation of $\perp$ from (say n) assumptions $\forall z.\neg A(z)$. Each branch must start with an $\forall$E:

$$\frac{\forall z.\neg A(z) \quad a_i}{\neg A(a_i)}$$

Replace each one of these by an $\wedge$-elimination:

$$\frac{\neg A(a_1) \wedge \neg A(a_2) \wedge \cdots \wedge \neg A(a_n)}{\neg A(a_i)}$$

to obtain a derivation of $\perp$ from the assumption $\neg A(a_1) \wedge \cdots \wedge \neg A(a_n)$. Then by $\rightarrow$-introduction we get $A(a_1) \vee A(a_2) \vee \cdots \vee A(a_n) \;\equiv\; \neg A(a_1) \wedge \cdots \wedge \neg A(a_n) \rightarrow \perp$. □

§ 5 Gentzen's sequent calculus

Let the "sequent" $\underline{A} \vdash B$ stand for *there is a ND-derivation of B from the assumptions* $\underline{A} = A_1, A_2, ..., A_k$. Note that $\underline{A}$ now stands for a finite *sequence* of formulas, possibly with repetitions, possibly empty, and for the time being B is either a *single* formula or nothing. $B =$ "empty" means "false".

Under this interpretation, the rules for forming ND-derivations translate quite straightforwardly into the rules of Gentzen's "Sequent Calculus" LJ as shown in Figure 2, where introduction rules introduce formulas on the right of $\vdash$ and elimination rules introduce formulas on the left of $\vdash$.

The cut-rule corresponds in ND to an introduction of C followed by its use (elimination) in deriving B. Thus normalization for ND corresponds to cut-elimination for LJ.

The system described above (axioms, logical rules, structural rules and cut-rule) constitutes Gentzen's System LJ for *intuitionistic* logic. The restriction that at most one formula occurs on the right of $\vdash$ is crucial and prevents derivations of sequents such as $\neg\neg B \vdash B$. A cut-free derivation of a sequent $\vdash B$ must have a right-introduction as its final rule. Thus cut-elimination yields the following properties of intuitionistic logic:

DISJUNCTION PROPERTY. *If* $\vdash B_0 \vee B_1$ *then either* $\vdash B_0$ *or* $\vdash B_1$.

EXISTENCE PROPERTY. *If* $\vdash \exists z.B(z)$ *then* $\vdash B(a)$ *for some term a.*

Classical Sequent Calculus (LK). LK is obtained by allowing sequences of formulas $\underline{B}$ to occur also on the right hand side of $\vdash$. Thus a sequent is now of the form

$$A_1, A_2, \ldots, A_k \vdash B_1, B_2, \ldots, B_m$$

and has the intended meaning (A_1 and ... and A_k) implies (B_1 or ... or B_m).

The rules of LK are generalized versions of the LJ-rules, but now weakening, contraction and exchange are allowed on the right as well, and (for example) the left ($\vee$) rule is generalized to

$$\frac{\underline{A}, C_0 \vdash \underline{B} \quad \underline{A}', C_1 \vdash \underline{B}'}{\underline{A}, \underline{A}', (C_0 \vee C_1) \vdash \underline{B}, \underline{B}'}$$

Since more than one formula can occur on the right of $\vdash$ in a LK-derivation, notice that we can now derive :

$$\cfrac{\cfrac{\cfrac{B \vdash B}{\vdash \neg B, B}}{\neg\neg B \vdash B}}{\vdash \neg\neg B \to B}$$

Axioms

$$B \vdash B$$

Logical rules

$$(\wedge I).\frac{\underline{A} \vdash B_0 \quad \underline{A}' \vdash B_1}{\underline{A}, \underline{A}' \vdash (B_0 \wedge B_1)} \qquad (\wedge E).\frac{\underline{A}, C_i \vdash B}{\underline{A}, (C_0 \wedge C_1) \vdash B}$$

$$(\vee I).\frac{\underline{A} \vdash B_i}{\underline{A} \vdash (B_0 \vee B_1)} \qquad (\vee E).\frac{\underline{A}, C_0 \vdash B \quad \underline{A}', C_1 \vdash B}{\underline{A}, \underline{A}', (C_0 \vee C_1) \vdash B}$$

$$(\rightarrow I).\frac{\underline{A}, B_0 \vdash B_1}{\underline{A} \vdash (B_0 \rightarrow B_1)} \qquad (\rightarrow E).\frac{\underline{A} \vdash C_0 \quad \underline{A}', C_1 \vdash B}{\underline{A}, \underline{A}', (C_0 \rightarrow C_1) \vdash B}$$

$$(\neg I).\frac{\underline{A}, B \vdash}{\underline{A} \vdash \neg B} \qquad (\neg E).\frac{\underline{A} \vdash C}{\underline{A}, \neg C \vdash}$$

$$(\forall I).\frac{\underline{A} \vdash B}{\underline{A} \vdash \forall z.B} \qquad (\forall E).\frac{\underline{A}, C(a) \vdash B}{\underline{A}, \forall z.C \vdash B}$$

$$(\exists I).\frac{\underline{A} \vdash B(a)}{\underline{A} \vdash \exists z.B} \qquad (\exists E).\frac{\underline{A}, C \vdash B}{\underline{A}, \exists z.C \vdash B}$$

Structural rules

Exchange. $$\frac{\underline{A}, C_0, C_1, \underline{A}' \vdash B}{\underline{A}, C_1, C_0, \underline{A}' \vdash B}$$

Contraction. $$\frac{\underline{A}, C, C, \underline{A}' \vdash B}{\underline{A}, C, \underline{A}' \vdash B}$$

Weakenings. $$\frac{\underline{A} \vdash B}{\underline{A}, C \vdash B} \qquad \frac{\underline{A} \vdash}{\underline{A} \vdash B}$$

Transitivity/Cut rule

$$\frac{\underline{A} \vdash C \quad \underline{A}', C \vdash B}{\underline{A}, \underline{A}' \vdash B}$$

In $(\forall I)$ and $(\exists E)$ the variable z must not appear free in the conclusion.

Figure 2: Gentzen's system LJ.

We can no longer guarantee that in a cut-free derivation $\vdash B$ in LK, the last rule applied is a logical one. It might just as well have been a contraction from $\vdash B, B$, etc. Thus, for example, the Existence Property is lost in classical logic, and gets replaced by versions of Herbrand's Theorem.

From LK to PC. The system PC of classical predicate logic used in §1 is really a simplified version of LK and is easily obtained from it as follows:

1. Using the $\neg$-rules we can pass from $\underline{A} \vdash \underline{B}$ to $\vdash \neg\underline{A}, \underline{B}$.

2. Using De Morgan's Laws we can remove $\neg$ and $\rightarrow$ in favour of their "definitions" as in §1.

3. We thus obtain a system of right sequents $\vdash \underline{A}', \underline{B}$ with only right-hand introduction rules for $(\vee)$, $(\wedge)$, $(\exists)$ and $(\forall)$.

4. Finally, remove the structural rule of exchange by interpreting sequences $\underline{A}$ instead as finite multisets Γ.

   What remains is PC.

From LK to Linear Logic. Go to PC as detailed above (writing $A^{\perp}$ instead of $\neg A$), then remove the structural rules of weakening and contraction by simply omitting them and remove exchange by interpreting sequents as multisets. What remains is MPC. The reader should consult Girard (1987) and Girard et al. (1989).

§ 6 Arithmetic with Σ_1-Induction

Herbrand's Theorem provides a method for extracting or synthesizing algorithms (the terms $a_1, ..., a_n$) which "witness" existential theorems of logic. Program synthesis is concerned with this process, but in the more general context of applied logics such as Formal (Peano) Arithmetic PA.

PA can be formalized in PC by adding a distinguished constant 0 and function symbol S (successor), together with additional non-logical axioms defining given "elementary" relations and functions. For example the axioms for $+$ would be:

$$\begin{array}{llll} \Gamma, & (x+y \neq z), & (x+Sy=Sz) & \\ \Gamma, & (x+0=x) & & \\ \Gamma, & (x+y\neq z), & (x+y\neq z'), & (z=z') \end{array}$$

Finally the Induction Rule is added:

$$\frac{\Gamma, A(0) \quad \Gamma, \neg A(x), A(Sx)}{\Gamma, A(y)}$$

where x is not free in Γ and y may be any term.

We shall concern ourselves here, only with a certain *subsystem* of PA, in which the Induction Rule is restricted to Σ_1-*formulas:*

$$A(x) \equiv \exists z_1, \ldots, \exists z_n . B(x, z_1, \ldots, z_n)$$

where B is quantifier-free or, at worst, contains only "bounded" universal quantifiers. This subsystem is denoted $(\Sigma_1 - IND)$.

Cut-Elimination. In $(\Sigma_1 - IND)$ we can carry out Cut-Reduction, but only down as far as Σ_1-formulas, because then the new rule of induction gets in the way so that Cut-Reduction comes unstuck at the point:

$$\frac{\Gamma, \neg A(y) \qquad \dfrac{\Gamma, A(0) \quad \Gamma, \neg A(x), A(Sx)}{\Gamma, A(y)}}{\Gamma}$$

Henceforth we assume this Cut-Reduction to have been completed, so at worst, only Σ_1 cut-formulas C remain.

Semantics. Let $A(x_1, \ldots, x_k)$ be a Σ_1-formula:

$$A(x_1, \ldots, x_k) \equiv \exists z_1, \ldots, \exists z_\ell \, .B(x_1, \ldots, x_k, z_1, \ldots, z_\ell)$$

i.e., a specification that, given inputs $x_1, \ldots, x_k$ there are outputs $z_1, \ldots, z_\ell$ satisfying B.

Then given an assignment of numbers $m_1, \ldots, m_k$ to the free variables $x_1, \ldots, x_k$, write

$$m \models A(m_1, \ldots, m_k)$$

to mean there are numbers $n_1, \ldots, n_\ell < m$ such that $B(m_1, \ldots m_k, n_1, \ldots, n_\ell)$ is true in the standard model $\mathcal{N}$ of arithmetic.

If $\Gamma(x_1, \ldots, x_k) = \{A_1, \ldots, A_n\}$ is a set of Σ_1-formulas containing the free variables $x_1, \ldots, x_k$, write

$$m \models \Gamma(m_1, \ldots, m_k)$$

to mean that $m \models A_i(m_1, \ldots, m_k)$ for some $i = 1, .., n$.

Then, given a function $F : N^k \to N$, write $F \models \Gamma$ to mean that for all assignments $x_1 := m_1, x_2 := m_2, \ldots, x_k := m_k$,

$$F(m_1, \ldots, m_k) \models \Gamma(m_1, \ldots, m_k).$$

A note on "persistence."

1. $m \le m'$ and $m \models A(m_1, \ldots, m_k) \Rightarrow m' \models A(m_1, \ldots, m_k)$.

2. $F \le F'$ and $F \models \Gamma(x_1, \ldots, x_k) \Rightarrow F' \models \Gamma(x_1, \ldots, x_k)$.

THEOREM (KREISEL, PARSONS, MINTS, ...) *If Γ is a set of Σ_1 -formulas and $(\Sigma_1 - IND) \vdash \Gamma$ then there is an increasing "primitive recursive" function F such that $F \models \Gamma$.*

COROLLARY *If $(\Sigma_1 - IND) \vdash \forall x.\exists z.B(x,z)$ then there is a primitive recursive function f such that $B(n, f(n))$ holds for every $n \in N$.*

COROLLARY (INCOMPLETENESS) *The non-primitive recursive Ackermann Function is not provably "specifiable" in $(\Sigma_1 - IND)$.*

PROOF: (of the THEOREM.) Proceed by induction on the length of the $(\Sigma_1 - IND)$-derivation of Γ, with a case-distinction according to which rule is applied last:

The axioms are true and quantifier-free, so any F will do for them.

The $(\vee)$, (C) and (W) rules are trivial; for example, suppose

$$\frac{\Gamma, A_0, A_1}{\Gamma, (A_0 \vee A_1)}.$$

Then by the induction hypothesis we have $F' \models \Gamma, A_0, A_1$. Choose $F = F'$.

The $(\wedge)$ rule is equally trivial; suppose

$$\frac{\Gamma, A_0 \quad \Gamma, A_1}{\Gamma, (A_0 \wedge A_1)}.$$

Then by the induction hypothesis we have $F_i \models \Gamma, A_i$ for each $i = 0, 1$, so it suffices to choose $F = \max(F_0, F_1)$.

The $\forall$-rule is also trivial since Γ contains only Σ_1-formulas and hence the universal quantifier will not occur unbounded. This case is then immediate since the rule preserves truth.

For the $\exists$-rule:

$$\frac{\Gamma, A(t)}{\Gamma, \exists z A(z)},$$

we have an F_0 such that $F_0 \models \Gamma, A(t)$ by the induction hypothesis. So in this case we can choose $F = F_0 + t$.

For the Cut-rule we can assume that the cut-formula C is in Σ_1-form, say $C \equiv \exists z.B$. Then $\neg C \equiv \forall z.\neg B$ and so the application of Cut looks like this with the free variables displayed:

$$\frac{\Gamma(\underline{x}),\ \forall z.\neg B(\underline{x}, z) \quad \Gamma(\underline{x}),\ \exists z.B(\underline{x}, z)}{\Gamma(\underline{x})}$$

But the left premise now contains a $\forall z$ which must be removed in order to continue the proof. Fortunately, Exercise (3) on $\forall$-inversion comes to our aid, allowing the proof of $\Gamma(\underline{x}), \forall z.\neg B(\underline{x}, z)$ to be replaced by a proof of $\Gamma(\underline{x}), \neg B(\underline{x}, y)$ which is no longer than the original proof, but contains a new variable y. Applying the induction hypothesis to this and the right premise of the Cut, we obtain primitive recursive functions F_0 and F_1 such that

$$\begin{aligned} F_0(\underline{x}, y) &\models \Gamma(\underline{x}),\ \neg B(\underline{x}, y) \\ F_1(\underline{x}) &\models \Gamma(\underline{x}),\ \exists z.B(\underline{x}, z) \end{aligned}$$

So define by composition:

$$F(\underline{x}) \quad = \quad F_0(\underline{x}, F_1(\underline{x})).$$

We now have to verify that $F(\underline{x}) \models \Gamma(\underline{x})$ for all values of $\underline{x}$. Suppose that under a given assignment $\underline{x} := \underline{m}$ we have $F(\underline{m}) \not\models \Gamma(\underline{m})$. Then by persistence, since $F_1(\underline{m}) \leq F(\underline{m})$ we have $F_1(\underline{m}) \not\models \Gamma(\underline{m})$ and therefore (i) $F_1(\underline{m}) \models B(\underline{m}, k)$ for some $k < F_1(\underline{m})$. Similarly, since $F_0(\underline{m}, k) \leq F(\underline{m})$ we must also have (ii) $F_0(\underline{m}, k) \models \neg B(\underline{m}, k)$. But $B(\underline{m}, k)$ and $\neg B(\underline{m}, k)$ cannot both be true - contradiction! Hence $F(\underline{m}) \models \Gamma(\underline{m})$ for all assignments $\underline{m}$.

Finally, consider an application of the Σ_1-Induction Rule:

$$\frac{\Gamma, A(0) \quad \Gamma, \neg A(x), A(Sx)}{\Gamma, A(y)}.$$

where $A(x, \underline{x}) \equiv \exists z.B(x, \underline{x}, z)$ with x and the other parameters $\underline{x} = x_1, \ldots, x_r$ free. Then we have a proof of

$$\Gamma(\underline{x}),\ \exists z.B(0, \underline{x}, z)$$

and, using $\forall$-inversion, of

$$\Gamma(\underline{x}),\ \neg B(x, \underline{x}, y),\ \exists z.B(Sx, \underline{x}, z)\,.$$

By the induction hypothesis we have increasing primitive recursive F_0, F_1 such that:

$$\begin{aligned} F_0(\underline{x}) &\models \Gamma(\underline{x}),\ \exists z.B(0, \underline{x}, z) \\ F_1(x, \underline{x}, y) &\models \Gamma(\underline{x}),\ \neg B(x, \underline{x}, y),\ \exists z.B(Sx, \underline{x}, z). \end{aligned}$$

Now define F by primitive recursion from F_0 and F_1:

$$\begin{cases} F(0, \underline{x}) & = \quad F_0(\underline{x}) \\ F(x+1, \underline{x}) & = \quad F_1(x, \underline{x}, F(x, \underline{x})). \end{cases}$$

Then we must verify $F(x,\underline{x}) \models \Gamma(\underline{x}), \exists z.B(x,\underline{x},z)$ for all values of $x, \underline{x}$. To do this, fix $\underline{x} := \underline{m}$ and proceed by induction on n to show that for all n,

$$F(n,\underline{m}) \models \Gamma(\underline{m}), \exists z.B(n,\underline{m},z).$$

The basis $n = 0$ is immediate and the induction step from n to $n+1$ is very similar to the verification in the Cut-case above. It is left as a final exercise! □

Note the relationships between Cut and Composition and between Induction and Recursion. For further details see for example Schwichtenberg (1977), Wainer (1992).

References and Further Reading

J.Y. Girard. Linear Logic. *Theor. Comp. Sci.* Vol. 50 (1987), pp.1–102.

J.Y. Girard, Y. Lafont, P. Taylor. Proofs and Types. Cambridge Tracts in Theoretical Computer Science Vol. 7 (1989), CUP.

W.A. Howard. The Formulae-as-Types Notion of Construction. In J.R. Hindley and J.P. Seldin (Eds): To H.B. Curry - Essays on Combinatory Logic, Lambda Calculus and Formalism, Academic Press (1980).

G. Mints. Quantifier-Free and One-Quantifier Systems. *J. Soviet Math.* Vol. 1 (1973), 71-84.

C. Parsons. On n-Quantifier Induction. *J. Symb. Logic* Vol. 37 (1972), 466-482.

D. Prawitz. Natural Deduction. Almqvist and Wiksell, Stockholm (1965).

H. Schwichtenberg. Proof Theory - Some Applications of Cut Elimination. In J. Barwise (Ed) : Handbook of Mathematical Logic, North-Holland Studies in Logic Vol. 90, North-Holland (1977), 867-896.

W. Sieg. Herbrand Analyses. *Arch. Math. Logic*, 30 (1991), pp. 409–441.

W.W. Tait. Normal Derivability in Classical Logic. In J. Barwise (Ed) : The Syntax and Semantics of Infinitary languages, Springer lecture Notes in Math. Vol. 72, Springer-Verlag (1968), 204-236.

S.S. Wainer. Four Lectures on Primitive Recursion. In H. Schwichtenberg (Ed) Logic and Algebra of Specification, NATO ASI Series F, Springer-Verlag (1992), to appear.

A short course in ordinal analysis

W. POHLERS

A Short Course in Ordinal Analysis

W. POHLERS

Münster

Abstract

By ordinal analysis we understand the computation of the proof theoretic ordinal of an axiom system. The intention of the present paper is to give a quick introduction to the techniques of ordinal analysis. In section 1 we first explain the notion of the proof theoretic ordinal of an axiom system and study some of its basic properties.

Part I of the paper is devoted to the example of an ordinal analysis for a predicative axiom system, while part II gives an introduction to the ordinal analysis of impredicative axiom systems.

Contents

1 Basic Observations

Let $\mathcal{L}_{\mathcal{N}}$ be the language of the structure $\mathcal{N}$ of natural numbers. For convenience we may well assume that $\mathcal{N}$ is a rich structure which contains all primitive recursive functions and relations. In the language $\mathcal{L}_{\mathcal{N}}$ we allow constants for all natural numbers as well as set parameters which will usually be denoted by capital Roman letters $X, Y, \ldots$.
Abusing the usual definition we call a first-order formula of $\mathcal{L}_{\mathcal{N}}$ which does not contain free number variables but may contain set parameters a Π^1_1-sentence. This abuse is justified by Lemma 1 below. To obtain a satisfaction relation for Π^1_1-sentences we define

$$\mathcal{N} \models \phi(X_1, \ldots, X_n) \;:\Longleftrightarrow (\mathcal{N}, S_1, \ldots, S_n) \models \phi(X_1, \ldots, X_n) \text{ for } all \text{ interpretations } S_1, \ldots, S_n \text{ for the parameters } X_1 \ldots, X_n. \quad (1)$$

Here $(\mathcal{N}, S_1, \ldots, S_n)$ denotes the expansion of the structure N by the sets $S_i \subseteq \mathcal{N}$ and $\models$ on the right side of definition (1) means the usual satisfaction relation of first order logic. Then the following lemma is an immediate consequence of this definition.

Lemma 1 *Let $\vec{X}$ be the a list containing all set parameters occurring in the Π^1_1-sentence ϕ. Then $\mathcal{N} \models \phi(\vec{X})$ iff $\mathcal{N} \models (\forall \vec{X})\phi(\vec{X})$ in the sense of second-order logic.*

Let Ax be a set of Π^1_1-sentences and ϕ a Π^1_1-sentence. We define

$$\mathrm{Ax} \models \phi :\Longleftrightarrow (\mathcal{M}, S_1, \ldots, S_n) \models \mathrm{Ax} \Rightarrow (\mathcal{M}, S_1, \ldots, S_n) \models \phi \textit{ for all } \mathcal{L}_{\mathcal{N}}\textit{-structures } \mathcal{M} \textit{ and all interpretations } S_1, \ldots, S_n \subseteq \mathrm{dom}(\mathcal{M}) \textit{ for the parameters } X_1, \ldots, X_n \textit{ occurring in } \phi.$$

$\mathrm{Ax} \models \phi$ expresses that ϕ is a logical consequence of the set Ax. One should observe that $\mathrm{Ax} \models \phi$ is the usual notion of logical consequence in the sense of two sorted first order logic. By the soundness and completeness theorems of first-order logic there is a syntactical calculus – say $\vdash$, its precise formalization does not matter, – such that

$$\mathrm{Ax} \models \phi \iff \mathrm{Ax} \vdash \phi.$$

This entails that for a recursive (or even recursively enumerable) set Ax of Π^1_1-sentences the set

$$\mathrm{Con}_{\Pi^1_1}(\mathrm{Ax}) := \{\phi \mid \phi \text{ is a } \Pi^1_1\text{-sentence and } \mathrm{Ax} \models \phi\} \quad (2)$$

is recursively enumerable (r.e.). In dealing with the structure of natural numbers, however, our interest is its *theory*, which is defined by

$$\mathrm{Th}_{\Pi^1_1}(\mathcal{N}) := \{\phi \mid \phi \text{ is a } \Pi^1_1\text{-sentence and } \mathcal{N} \models \phi\}. \quad (3)$$

The only way one can imagine proving that ϕ belongs to $\mathrm{Th}_{\Pi^1_1}(\mathcal{N})$ is to show that ϕ is a logical consequence of some axiom system Ax (for which we a priori have

$\mathrm{Ax} \subseteq \mathrm{Th}_{\Pi^1_1}(\mathcal{N})$), i.e. to show $\phi \in \mathrm{Con}_{\Pi^1_1}(\mathrm{Ax})$. But, since $\mathrm{Th}_{\Pi^1_1}(\mathcal{N})$ is a proper Π^1_1-set, there is a tremendous gap between its complexity and that of the r.e. set $\mathrm{Con}_{\Pi^1_1}(\mathrm{Ax})$.

Proof theory is concerned with the study of axiom systems. A natural question is whether there is a measure for the size of the gap between the complexities of $\mathrm{Con}_{\Pi^1_1}(\mathrm{Ax})$ and $\mathrm{Th}_{\Pi^1_1}(\mathcal{N})$. We know from descriptive set theory that there are norms for Π^1_1-sentences. Thus we may hope that considering the norms of the Π^1_1-sentences provable from Ax could provide such a measure. This turns out to be true. Indeed, any of the common norms would give us a measure. In this paper, however, it will be convenient to introduce a special norm, the *truth complexity* $\mathrm{tc}(\phi)$ of a Π^1_1-sentence ϕ. It will turn out that the truth complexity for a Π^1_1-sentence is an ordinal below ω_1^{CK}, the first nonrecursive ordinal, which differs only inessentially from that of the more common norms (cf. [Columbus 1990]). The ordinal ω_1^{CK} is the recursive counterpart of ω_1, the first uncountable ordinal. Just as ω_1 can be characterized as the least ordinal which cannot be represented by a well-ordering of the natural numbers, so ω_1^{CK} may be characterized as the least ordinal which cannot be represented by a recursive well-ordering of the natural numbers. We have

$$\sup\{\mathrm{tc}(\phi) \mid \phi \in \mathrm{Th}_{\Pi^1_1}(\mathcal{N})\} = \omega_1^{CK}$$

and for an axiom system Ax we define

$$|\mathrm{Ax}| := \sup\{\mathrm{tc}(\phi) \mid \phi \in \mathrm{Con}_{\Pi^1_1}(\mathrm{Ax})\} \tag{4}$$

and call $|\mathrm{Ax}|$ the *proof theoretic* ordinal of Ax. Since $\mathrm{Con}_{\Pi^1_1}(\mathrm{Ax})$ is r.e. (provided that Ax was r.e.) and an upper bound for $\mathrm{tc}(\phi)$ can be effectively computed from ϕ, it follows that for a decidable axiom system Ax the ordinal $|\mathrm{Ax}|$ is strictly less than ω_1^{CK}. This makes us hope that $|\mathrm{Ax}|$ may indeed tell us something about Ax. The branch of proof theory which is concerned with the computation of the ordinals $|\mathrm{Ax}|$ is commonly called *ordinal analysis*. We will see later what kind of information is provided by ordinal analysis.

Since $|\mathrm{Ax}|$ is an ordinal $< \omega_1^{CK}$ there are recursive, even primitive recursive, well-orderings which represent $|\mathrm{Ax}|$. We call a well-ordering $\prec$ a *good representation for* $|\mathrm{Ax}|$ if it satisfies the following conditions:

1. $\prec$ is a primitive recursive well-ordering of the natural numbers,
2. the order type $\mathrm{otyp}(\prec)$ of $\prec$ is $|\mathrm{Ax}|$,
3. $\mathrm{Ax} \models \phi \iff \mathrm{PA} + \mathrm{TI}(\prec_{in}) \models \phi$ for all arithmetical sentences ϕ,

where PA denotes the axiom system of Peano arithmetic and $\mathrm{TI}(\prec_{in})$ is the scheme

$$\forall x\ ((\forall y \prec_{in} x)\phi(y) \to \phi(x)) \longrightarrow (\forall x \in \mathrm{field}(\prec_{in}))\phi(x)$$

of induction along all *proper* initial segments $\prec_{in}$ of $\prec$. We call an ordinal analysis *profound* if it not only computes $|\mathrm{Ax}|$ but also yields a good representation for $|\mathrm{Ax}|$. Until today all known ordinal analyses are profound ones. A profound ordinal analysis tells us more than a mere ordinal analysis. For instance it allows us to characterize the provably recursive functions of an axiom system Ax. A partial recursive function with index e is a provably recursive function of Ax if

$$\text{Ax} \models \forall x \exists y T(e, x, y),$$

where $T(e, x, y)$ denotes the KLEENE predicate. Characterizing the provably recursive functions of Ax is thus part of the more general task of characterizing the Π_2^0-Skolem functions of Ax. A function f is a Skolem function of a formula $\forall \vec{x} \exists y \phi(\vec{x}, y)$ iff for every tuple $\vec{n}$ of natural numbers we have $\mathcal{N} \models \phi(\vec{n}, f(\vec{n}))$. The class of Π_2^0-Skolem functions of Ax contains exactly the Skolem functions of formulas $\forall \vec{x} \exists y \phi(\vec{x}, y)$ – where $\phi(\vec{x}, y)$ is quantifier free and contains only the indicated variables – with $\text{Ax} \models \forall \vec{x} \exists y \phi(\vec{x}, y)$. The key role in characterizing the Π_2^0-Skolem functions of an axiom system is played by the axiom system (Σ_1^0-*IND*). The nonlogical axioms of (Σ_1^0-*IND*) are the defining equations for primitive recursive functions and relations together with the scheme

$$\phi(\underline{0}) \wedge \forall x(\phi(x) \rightarrow \phi(x + \underline{1})) \longrightarrow \forall x \phi(x)$$

of mathematical induction restricted to Σ_1^0-formulas $\phi(x)$, i.e. to formulas $\phi(x) \equiv \exists y \psi(x, y)$ for $\psi(x, y)$ quantifier free. It is well known (and was first observed by C. PARSONS) that the Π_2^0-Skolem functions of (Σ_1^0-*IND*) are exactly the primitive recursive ones. To sketch a proof of this fact we introduce the TAIT calculus for first-order logic. A peculiarity of the TAIT calculus is that its language uses no negation symbol. The negation of a formula ϕ is definable by the following clauses:

- $\neg R(t_1, \ldots, t_n) :\equiv \overline{R}(t_1, \ldots, t_n)$, where $\overline{R}$ is a symbol for the complement of the primitive recursive relation denoted by R,
- $\neg(\phi \vee \psi) :\equiv (\neg\phi \wedge \neg\psi)$,
- $\neg(\phi \wedge \psi) :\equiv (\neg\phi \vee \neg\psi)$,
- $\neg(\forall x \psi(x)) :\equiv (\exists x \neg\psi(x))$,
- $\neg(\exists x \psi(x)) :\equiv (\forall x \neg\psi(x))$.

The TAIT calculus is a straightforward simplification of GENTZEN's sequent calculus eliminating the distinction between antecedent and succedent formulas. A sequent

$$\phi_1, \ldots, \phi_m \vdash \psi_1, \ldots, \psi_n$$

in GENTZEN's sequent calculus may be interpreted as the formula

$$\neg\phi_1 \vee \ldots \vee \neg\phi_m \vee \psi_1 \vee \ldots \vee \psi_n.$$

Thus formulas marked as negated take over the role of antecedent formulas while nonnegated formulas correspond to succedent formulas. In our language, however, in which the negation symbol is a defined symbol, we cannot really distinguish between negated and nonnegated formulas. So there is indeed no distinction between antecedent and succedent formulas and therefore also no need to distinguish between left and right inferences as in the original sequent calculus. The TAIT calculus takes advantage of this and, instead of sequents, derives finite sets of formulas which are to be interpreted as finite disjunctions. We denote finite sets of formulas by capital Greek letters $\Gamma, \Delta, \Lambda, \ldots$ and write Γ, Δ instead of $\Gamma \cup \Delta$. We also write $\phi_1, \ldots, \phi_n$ instead of $\{\phi_1, \ldots, \phi_n\}$.

The logical axioms of (Σ_1^0-*IND*) are

(AxL) $\quad \vdash \Delta, \phi, \neg\phi \quad$ for atomic formulas ϕ.

The equality axioms are

(AxE_1) $\quad \vdash \Delta, s = s \quad$ for arbitrary terms s,

(AxE_2) $\quad \vdash \Delta, s \neq t, t = s \quad$ for arbitrary terms s and t.

The compatibility of equality is guaranteed by the rule

(RE) $\quad \vdash \Delta, s \neq t, \phi(s) \Rightarrow \vdash \Delta, \phi(t) \quad$ for atomic formulas $\phi(s)$.

The mathematical axioms are

(AxM) $\quad \vdash \Delta, \phi$ where ϕ is an atomic formula defining a primitive recursive function or relation.

The logical symbols are defined by the rules

($\wedge$) $\quad \vdash \Delta, \phi$ and $\vdash \Delta, \psi \Rightarrow \vdash \Delta, \phi \wedge \psi$,

($\vee$) $\quad \vdash \Delta, \phi_i \Rightarrow \vdash \Delta, \phi_1 \vee \phi_2, \quad$ for $i \in \{1, 2\}$

($\exists$) $\quad \vdash \Delta, \phi(s) \Rightarrow \vdash \Delta, \exists x \phi(x)$,

($\forall$) $\quad \vdash \Delta, \phi(x) \Rightarrow \vdash \Delta, \forall x \phi(x) \quad$ with the condition that x must not be free in any of the formulas of Δ.

Then there are the additional rules for cut

(CUT) $\quad \vdash \Delta, \phi$ and $\vdash \Delta, \neg\phi \Rightarrow \vdash \Delta$

and mathematical induction

(CI) $\quad \vdash \Delta, \phi(\underline{0})$ and $\vdash \Delta, \neg\phi(x), \phi(x + \underline{1}) \Rightarrow \vdash \Delta, \phi(s) \quad$ for arbitrary terms s. Here too, we have the condition that x must not be free in any of the formulas of $\Delta, \phi(\underline{0})$.

The important feature of (Σ_1^0-*IND*) is that it allows the elimination of cuts whose cut formulas are more complex than Σ_1^0. To make this precise we introduce the Σ_1^0-complexity $\mathrm{cp}_{\Sigma_1^0}(\phi)$ of a formula ϕ by the following clauses:

- If ϕ is Σ_1^0 or Π_1^0, then $\mathrm{cp}_{\Sigma_1^0}(\phi) := 0$.
- $\mathrm{cp}_{\Sigma_1^0}(\phi \circ \psi) := \max\{\mathrm{cp}_{\Sigma_1^0}(\phi), \mathrm{cp}_{\Sigma_1^0}(\psi)\} + 1 \quad$ for $\circ \in \{\wedge, \vee\}$.
- $\mathrm{cp}_{\Sigma_1^0}(\mathsf{Q}x\psi(x)) := \mathrm{cp}_{\Sigma_1^0}(\psi(x)) + 1 \quad$ for $\mathsf{Q} \in \{\forall, \exists\}$.

The Σ_1^0-degree of a cut is the Σ_1^0-complexity of its cut formula. Let us denote by

$$(\Sigma_1^0\text{-}IND) \mid\!\frac{n}{r}\, \phi$$

that there is a proof tree for the formula ϕ whose depth is less or equal to n and whose cuts are all of Σ_1^0-degree strictly less than r. Then we may formulate the Hauptsatz for (Σ_1^0-*IND*) as follows.

Theorem 2 (Σ_1^0-*IND*) $\frac{n}{1+m}\Delta$ *entails* (Σ_1^0-*IND*) $\vdash^{2^{(m)}(n)}_{1} \Delta$ *where* $2^{(0)}(n) := n$ *and* $2^{(k+1)}(n) := 2^{2^{(k)}(n)}$.

We will not give a proof of the theorem since there will be a similar proof in a later section. It follows literally the proof for cut elimination in pure first-order logic. The schema of mathematical induction, which usually spoils cut elimination, will do no harm because of its restriction to Σ_1^0-formulas.
The Hauptsatz, Theorem 2, enables us to characterize the Π_2^0-Skolem functions of (Σ_1^0-*IND*).

Theorem 3 (Parsons) *If* (Σ_1^0-*IND*) $\vdash \forall\vec{x}\exists y\phi(\vec{x},y)$ *for a quantifier-free formula* $\phi(\vec{x},y)$ *containing only the indicated variables free, then there is a primitive recursive function* f *such that* $\mathcal{N} \models \phi(\vec{n}, f(\vec{n}))$ *for any tuple* $\vec{n}$ *of natural numbers.*

The theorem is a consequence of the following more general lemma.

Lemma 4 *If* (Σ_1^0-*IND*) $\vdash^{n}_{1} \Delta(\vec{x}), \exists y_1\psi_1(\vec{x},y_1), \ldots, \exists y_k\psi_k(\vec{x},y_k)$, *for a finite set* $\Delta(\vec{x}), \psi_1(\vec{x},y_1), \ldots, \psi_k(\vec{x},y_k)$ *of quantifier-free formulas, containing only the indicated variables, then there are primitive recursive functions* $f_1, \ldots, f_k$ *such that* $\mathcal{N} \models \forall\vec{x}\bigvee\{\Delta(\vec{x}), \psi_1(\vec{x}, f_1(\vec{x}), \ldots, \psi_k(\vec{k}, f(\vec{x}))\}$.

The proof is by induction on n. If $\Delta(\vec{x}), \exists y_1\psi_1(\vec{x},y_1), \ldots, \exists y_2\psi_k(\vec{x},y_k)$ is an axiom then $\Delta(\vec{x})$ is already an axiom and this makes the claim trivial. If the last inference in the derivation was a sentential one, i.e. one according to ($\wedge$) or ($\vee$), then we obtain the claim immediately from the induction hypothesis using, in the case of an inference ($\wedge$), the fact that the primitive recursive functions are closed under definition by cases.
So the only cases which are left are those of an ($\exists$)-rule, a cut, and an inference for mathematical induction. In the case of an ($\exists$)-rule we have the premise

$$\vdash^{n-1}_{1} \Delta(\vec{x}), \exists y_1\psi_1(\vec{x},y_1), \ldots, \exists y_k\psi_k(\vec{x},y_k), \psi_i(\vec{x}, s(\vec{x},\vec{y}))$$

for some $i \in \{1, \ldots, k\}$ and a (possibly empty) list $\vec{y}$ of variables which is disjoint from that of $\vec{x}$. By the induction hypothesis there are primitive recursive functions $\hat{f}_1, \ldots, \hat{f}_k$ such that

$$\mathcal{N} \models \forall\vec{x}\forall\vec{y}\bigvee\{\Delta(\vec{x}), \psi_1(\vec{x}, \hat{f}_1(\vec{x},\vec{y})), \ldots, \psi_k(\vec{x}, \hat{f}_k(\vec{x},\vec{y})), \psi_i(\vec{x}, s(\vec{x},\vec{y}))\}.$$

Letting

$$f_j(\vec{x}) := \hat{f}_j(\vec{x},\vec{0}) \qquad \text{for} \quad j \neq i$$

and

$$f_i(\vec{x}) := \begin{cases} \hat{f}_i(\vec{x},\vec{0}) & \text{if } \mathcal{N} \models \neg\psi_i(\vec{x}, s(\vec{x},\vec{0})), \\ s(\vec{x},\vec{0}) & \text{otherwise,} \end{cases}$$

we conclude that

$$\mathcal{N} \models \forall\vec{x}\bigvee\{\Delta(\vec{x}), \psi_1(\vec{x}, f_1(\vec{x})), \ldots, \psi_k(\vec{x}, f_k(\vec{x}))\}.$$

But, since the terms of the language of (Σ_1^0-*IND*) are built up from variables and number constants by symbols for primitive recursive functions only, the function

$$\vec{x} \mapsto s(\vec{x}, \vec{0})^{\mathcal{N}},$$

is primitive recursive. Because $\psi_i(\vec{x}, s(\vec{x}, \vec{0}))$ is quantifier-free, it is a boolean expression in primitive recursive relations which entails that $\mathcal{N} \models \neg\psi_i(\vec{x}, s(\vec{x}, \vec{0}))$ can be primitive recursively decided. Thus f_i is primitive recursive.
In case of a cut we have the premises

$$\vdash_1^{n-1} \Delta(\vec{x}), \exists y_1 \psi_1(\vec{x}, y_1), \ldots, \exists y_k \psi_k(\vec{x}, y_k), \chi(\vec{x}, \vec{y}) \tag{5}$$

and

$$\vdash_1^{n-1} \Delta(\vec{x}), \exists y_1 \psi_1(\vec{x}, y_1), \ldots, \exists y_k \psi_k(\vec{x}, y_k), \neg\chi(\vec{x}, \vec{y})\,. \tag{6}$$

This cut is of Σ_1^0-complexity 0. Since all variables in the list $\vec{y}$ which do not also occur in $\vec{x}$ can be replaced by 0 we may, without loss of generality, assume

$$\chi(\vec{x}, \vec{y}) \equiv \exists y \chi_0(\vec{x}, y).$$

Thus we obtain from (6)

$$\vdash_1^{n-1} \Delta(\vec{x}), \exists y_1 \psi_1(\vec{x}, y_1), \ldots, \exists y_k \psi_k(\vec{x}, y_k), \neg\chi_0(\vec{x}, y). \tag{7}$$

By the induction hypothesis for (7) we therefore have primitive recursive functions $\hat{f}_1, \ldots, \hat{f}_k$ such that

$$\mathcal{N} \models \forall\vec{x}\forall y(\chi_0(\vec{x}, y) \to \bigvee\{\Delta(\vec{x}), \psi_1(\vec{x}, \hat{f}_1(\vec{x}, y)), \ldots, \psi_k(\vec{x}, \hat{f}_k(\vec{x}, y))\})$$

and by that for (5) primitive recursive functions $g_1, \ldots, g_k$ and h such that

$$\mathcal{N} \models \forall\vec{x}(\neg\chi_0(\vec{x}, h(\vec{x})) \to \bigvee\{\Delta(\vec{x}), \psi_1(\vec{x}, g_1(\vec{x})), \ldots, \psi_k(\vec{x}, g_k(\vec{x}))\}).$$

If we let

$$f_j(\vec{x}) := \begin{cases} g_k(\vec{x}) & \text{if } \mathcal{N} \models \neg\chi_0(\vec{x}, h(\vec{x})) \\ \hat{f}_j(\vec{x}, h(\vec{x})) & \text{if } \mathcal{N} \models \chi_0(\vec{x}, h(\vec{x})), \end{cases}$$

we obtain

$$\mathcal{N} \models \forall\vec{x} \bigvee\{\Delta(\vec{x}), \psi_1(\vec{x}, f_1(\vec{x})), \ldots, \psi_k(\vec{k}, f_k(\vec{x}))\}$$

and, since primitive recursive functions are closed under composition, $f_1, \ldots, f_k$ are primitive recursive.
In the case of mathematical induction there are two subcases. First we assume that the induction formula is a formula $\phi(s(\vec{x}), \vec{x})$ belonging to the set $\Delta(\vec{x})$. Then we have the premises

$$\vdash_1^{n-1} \Delta_0(\vec{x}), \phi(\underline{0}, \vec{x}) \tag{8}$$

and

$$\vdash_1^{n-1} \Delta_0(\vec{x}), \neg\phi(z, \vec{x}), \phi(z + \underline{1}, \vec{x})\,, \tag{9}$$

where we have used the obvious abbreviation

$$\Delta_0(\vec{x}) :\equiv \Delta(\vec{x}), \exists y_1\psi_1(\vec{x}, y_1), \ldots, \exists y_k\psi_k(\vec{x}, y_k).$$

By the induction hypothesis for (8) there are primitive recursive functions $g_1, \ldots, g_k$ such that ($\mathcal{N}$ satisfies – we will not emphasize this any longer –)

$$\forall\vec{x} \bigvee\{\Delta(\vec{x}), \psi_1(\vec{x}, g_1(\vec{x})), \ldots, \psi_k(\vec{x}, g_k(\vec{x})), \phi(0, \vec{x})\} \tag{10}$$

and by that for (9) primitive recursive functions $h_1, \ldots, h_k$ such that

$$\forall z\forall\vec{x} \bigvee\{\Delta(\vec{x}), \psi_1(\vec{x}, h_1(\vec{x}, z)), \ldots, \psi_k(\vec{x}, h_k(\vec{x}, z)), \neg\phi(z, \vec{x}), \phi(z + 1, \vec{z})\}. \tag{11}$$

Choose an arbitrary tuple $\vec{x}$ of natural numbers. Put $m := s(\vec{x})$. If $m = 0$ or $\mathcal{N} \not\models \phi(0, \vec{x})$ we let

$$f_i(\vec{x}) := g_i(\vec{x}) \text{ for } i = 1, \ldots, k.$$

Now let $m > 0$ and

$$\phi(0, \vec{x}). \tag{12}$$

Then there must be a natural number $l < m$ such that

$$\bigvee\{\Delta(\vec{x}), \psi_1(\vec{x}, h_1(\vec{x}, l)), \ldots, \psi_k(\vec{x}, h_k(\vec{x}, l))\}, \tag{13}$$

because assuming the contrary and noting that $\phi(m, \vec{x}) \in \Delta(\vec{x})$ we conclude from (12) and (11) that

$$\phi(0, \vec{x}) \wedge \ldots \wedge \phi(m, \vec{x}),$$

contradicting our assumption. In this case we let

$$f_i(\vec{x}) := h_i(r, \vec{x}) \text{ for } i = 1, \ldots, k$$
$$\text{where } r := \min\{l < m \mid \bigvee\{\Delta(\vec{x}), \psi_1(\vec{x}, h_1(l, \vec{x})), \ldots, \psi_k(\vec{x}, h_k(l, \vec{x}))\}\}.$$

It is obvious that the functions $f_1, \ldots, f_k$ are primitive recursive and have the required properties.
For the second case of mathematical induction we have to assume that the induction formula is one of the existential formulas, say $\exists y_i\psi_i(s(\vec{x}), \vec{x}, y_i)$. Then we have the premises

$$\vdash_1^{n-1} \Delta(\vec{x}), \exists y_1\psi_1(\vec{x}, y_1), \ldots, \exists y_k\psi_k(\vec{x}, y_k), \exists y_i\psi_i(\underline{0}, \vec{x}, y_i) \tag{14}$$

and

$$\vdash_1^{n-1} \Delta(\vec{x}), \exists y_1\psi_1(\vec{x}, y_1), \ldots, \exists y_k\psi_k(\vec{x}, y_k), \forall y_i\neg\psi_i(z, \vec{x}, y_i), \exists y_i\psi_i(z + \underline{1}, \vec{x}, y_i), \tag{15}$$

where z is a 'new' variable not belonging to the list $\vec{x}$. By the induction hypothesis for (14) there are primitive recursive functions $\hat{f}_1, \ldots, \hat{f}_k, g$ such that

$$\forall\vec{x} \bigvee\{\Delta(\vec{x}), \psi_1(\vec{x}, \hat{f}_1(\vec{x})), \ldots, \psi_k(\vec{x}, \hat{f}_k(\vec{x})), \psi_i(0, \vec{x}, g(\vec{x}))\}, \tag{16}$$

and by that for (15) primitive recursive functions $\check{f}_1, \ldots, \check{f}_k, h$ such that

$$\forall y \forall z \forall \vec{x} \bigvee\{\Delta(\vec{x}), \psi_1(\vec{x}, \check{f}_1(z, \vec{x}, y)), \ldots, \psi_k(\vec{x}, \check{f}_k(z, \vec{x}, y)), \neg\psi_i(z, \vec{x}, y), \psi_i(z+1, \vec{x}, h(z, \vec{x}, y))\}. \tag{17}$$

Choose any tuple $\vec{x}$ of natural numbers and put $m := s(\vec{x})$. If

$$\bigvee\{\Delta(\vec{x}), \psi_1(\vec{x}, \hat{f}_1(\vec{x})), \ldots, \psi_k(\vec{x}, \hat{f}_k(\vec{x}))\}$$

we let

$$f_j(\vec{x}) := \hat{f}_j(\vec{x}) \text{ for } j = 1, \ldots, k.$$

Otherwise we have by (16) that

$$\psi_i(0, \vec{x}, g(\vec{x})). \tag{18}$$

Let

$$\tilde{f}_i(0, \vec{x}) := g(\vec{x})$$

and

$$\tilde{f}_i(z+1, \vec{x}) := \begin{cases} \check{f}_i(z, \vec{x}, \tilde{f}_i(z, \vec{x})) & \text{if } \bigvee\{\Delta(\vec{x}), \psi_1(\vec{x}, \check{f}_1(z, \vec{x}, \tilde{f}_i(z, \vec{x}))), \ldots, \\ & \quad \psi_k(\vec{x}, \check{f}_k(z, \vec{x}, \tilde{f}_i(z, \vec{x})))\}, \\ h((z, \vec{x}, \tilde{f}_i(z, \vec{x}))) & \text{otherwise.} \end{cases}$$

Then $\tilde{f}_i$ is primitive recursive. Either there is an $l < m$ such that

$$\bigvee\{\Delta(\vec{x}), \psi_1(\vec{x}, \check{f}_1(l, \vec{x}, \tilde{f}_i(l, \vec{x}))), \ldots, \psi_k(\vec{x}, \check{f}_k(l, \vec{x}, \tilde{f}_i(l, \vec{x})))\}$$

and we define

$$f_j(\vec{x}) := \check{f}_j(l, \vec{x}, \tilde{f}_i(l, \vec{x}))$$

for $j = 1, \ldots, k$ and a minimal such l,
or we obtain from (18) and (17)

$$\psi_j(z, \vec{x}, \tilde{f}_j(z, \vec{x}))$$

for all $z \leq m$ and define

$$f_i(\vec{x}) := \tilde{f}_i(m, \vec{x}).$$

In any case we have

$$\bigvee\{\Delta(\vec{x}), \psi_1(\vec{x}, f_1(\vec{x})), \ldots, \psi_k(\vec{x}, f_k(\vec{x}))\}.$$ □

It follows from Theorem 3 that the Π^0_2-Skolem functions of (Σ^0_1-*IND*) are exactly the primitive recursive functions. This entails that the provably recursive functions of (Σ^0_1-*IND*) are exactly the primitive recursive functions. For that reason one often calls (Σ^0_1-*IND*) the system of *primitive recursive arithmetic* and denotes it by *PRA*. We will follow this convention for the rest of this paper. Because of its simple Π^0_2-Skolem functions, *PRA* seems to be a canonical choice for a basic system. This evidence will be confirmed by our further observations. These, however, require some further preparations. We introduce the schema

$(PRWO(\prec))$ $\qquad \forall\vec{z}\exists y(\neg f(\vec{z}, y+1) \prec f(\vec{z}, y))$

where f varies over all primitive recursive functions. Thus $PRWO(\prec)$ states that every primitive recursive $\prec$-descending chain is finite. Let $PRA(\prec)$ denote the theory $PRA + PRWO(\prec)$. We will see that the Π^0_2-Skolem functions of $PRA(\prec)$ are as easy to characterize as those of PRA itself.
$PRWO(\prec)$, in its open form, is still a Σ^0_1-statement. Thus Theorem 2 extends to $PRA(\prec)$ as follows.

Theorem 5 *$PRA(\prec) \frac{n}{1+m}\Delta$ entails $PRA(\prec) \frac{2^{(m)}(n)}{1}\Delta$.*

The modification of the proof of Theorem 3, however, needs an extra case. There we have also to consider that we have an axiom of the form

$$\vdash^{n}_{1} \Delta, \exists y(\neg f(\vec{z}, y+1) \prec f(\vec{z}, y)).$$

Of course there is in general no primitive recursive function witnessing

$$\exists y(\neg f(\vec{z}, y+1) \prec f(\vec{z}, y)). \tag{19}$$

But, if we extend the class of primitive recursive functions by introducing a $\prec$-descending search operator $\mu_\prec$ which is defined by

$$(\mu_\prec f)(\vec{x}) := \min\{y : \neg f(\vec{x}, y+1) \prec f(\vec{x}, y)\},$$

i.e. $\mu_\prec$ searches for the length of a minimal $\prec$-descending sequence

$$f(\vec{x}, 0) \succ f(\vec{x}, 1) \succ \ldots,$$

then $(\mu_\prec f)(\vec{z})$ witnesses (19). The class $\prec$-*REC* of $\prec$-descending recursive functions is the smallest class which contains the constant functions, all projection functions and is closed under substitution, primitive recursion and the $\prec$-descending search operator $\mu_\prec$. Theorem 3 can be extended to the following result.

Theorem 6 *The class of Π^0_2-Skolem functions for $PRA(\prec)$ is exactly the class $\prec$-REC of $\prec$-descending recursive functions.*

Thus the missing link in the determination of the provably recursive functions of an arbitrary axiom system Ax is the connection between Ax and $PRA(\prec)$. To establish this let us assume that

$$\mathrm{Ax} \vdash \forall\vec{x}\exists y\phi(\vec{x}, y) \tag{20}$$

and that there is a profound ordinal analysis for Ax, i.e. that for every arithmetical sentence ψ there is an initial segment $\prec_{in}$ of a primitive recursive well-ordering $\prec$ representing $|\mathrm{Ax}|$ such that

$$\mathrm{Ax} \vdash \psi \iff PA + TI(\prec_{in}) \vdash \psi. \tag{21}$$

Let us abbreviate $PA + TI(\prec)$ to $PA(\prec)$. Then by (20) and (21) we have for any choice of tuples $\vec{x}$ of numerals a $PA(\prec_{in})$-proof of $\exists y\phi(\vec{x}, y)$ and may unravel it into an infinitary one using the ω-rule. In the environment of a Tait calculus the ω-rule has the form

$$\vdash \Delta, \phi(\underline{n}) \text{ for all } n \in \omega \quad \Rightarrow \quad \vdash \Delta, \forall x\phi(x).$$

This rule, in some variations, will play *the* key role throughout this paper. The uniformity of the unraveled proof is such that it can be coded by a primitive recursive function, which means that we can talk about it within *PRA*. Moreover, we may assume that the nodes of this infinitary proof tree are labeled by elements of the field of the order relation $\prec$ increasingly from top to bottom (i.e. in the usual tree order). Of course *PRA* does not know that this tree is well-founded. But there is a powerful tool discovered by G. MINTS known as MINTS' continuous cut elimination procedure. There is no space to go into the details of this procedure. However, all we need here is, that it works also for non-well-founded primitive recursive proof trees and finally delivers a primitive recursive cut-free proof tree. [1] Applying it, we thus obtain a primitive recursive cut-free proof tree T of $\phi(\vec{x})$ and all that we have done until now is formalizable in PRA. A cut-free proof tree has the subformula property, i.e. all formulas occurring in T are subformulas of its end-formula. The end-formula $\exists y\phi(\vec{x}, y)$ is Σ^0_1 and thus does not contain $\forall$-quantifiers. So there are no $\forall$-quantifiers at all in T and this entails that there are no applications of the ω-rule in T. Thus T is a finitely branching primitive recursive tree and this implies that every path in T is primitive recursively definable. But every primitive recursive path induces a primitive recursive $\prec$-descending sequence via its labels in the field of $\prec$. Therefore $PRWO(\prec)$ entails that every path in T is finite, i.e. T is well-founded, and we show the truth of $\phi(\vec{x})$ by induction on T. Since all this is formalizable in $PRA + PRWO(\prec_{in})$ we finally get an n such that

$$PRA + PRWO(\prec_{in}) \vdash True_n\left(\ulcorner \exists y\phi(\dot{\vec{x}}, y)\urcorner\right), \tag{22}$$

where $True_n$ is a local truth predicate for formulas of complexities $\leq n$. By the familiar techniques (e.g. cf. [Troelstra 1973], in which you will also find an explanation for the dot notation $True_n\left(\ulcorner\phi(\dot{\vec{x}}, y)\urcorner\right)$) this finally yields

$$PRA + PRWO(\prec_{in}) \vdash \forall\vec{x}\exists y\phi(\vec{x}, y). \tag{23}$$

This together with Theorem 6 yields the following result.

Theorem 7 *Let $\prec$ be a good representation for the proof-theoretic ordinal* $|\mathrm{Ax}|$ *of an axiom system* Ax. *Then the class of Π^0_2-Skolem functions for* Ax *is* $\bigcup\{\prec_{in}\text{-}REC \mid \prec_{in}$ *is an initial segment of* $\prec\}$.

If

$$f \in \bigcup\{\prec_{in}\text{-}REC \mid \prec_{in} \text{ is an initial segment of } \prec\},$$

[1] This, of course, makes the proof rather sketchy. However, since we we will deal quite a lot with the ω-rule and cut-elimination in this paper, it might be worthwhile to reread the sketch after having studied the rest of the paper.

we sloppyly call f a $\prec_{in}$-*descending recursive* function. Using this terminology we reformulate Theorem 7 as follows.

Corollary 8 *If $\prec$ is as in Theorem 7 then the provably recursive functions of* Ax *are exactly the $\prec_{in}$-descending recursive functions.*

We want to mention that there are much nicer descriptions of the $\prec_{in}$-descending recursive functions than that given here. They may be characterized as the class of functions obtainable by extending ordinary recursion to recursion along $\prec_{in}$. If the order relation allows the primitive recursive definition of some basic ordinal functions then we may arrange the the $\prec$-descending recursive functions in a nice subrecursive hierarchy indexed by ordinals. Examples of that can be found in TAKEUTI's book on proof theory.
It was the aim of these introductory remarks to emphasize that ordinal analysis, and especially a profound ordinal analysis, indeed gives us a good deal of information about an axiom system Ax. In the following sections we are going to sketch how to obtain ordinal analyses.

Part I
Predicative Ordinal Analysis

2 The Truth Complexity of Π^1_1-sentences

The usual definition of the satisfaction relation $\mathcal{N} \models \phi$ uses implicitly an infinitary language at the meta-language level. Making this explicit we get the following definition:

- $\mathcal{N} \models \phi :\iff \phi \in \mathcal{D}(\mathcal{N})$ for atomic ϕ. Here $\mathcal{D}(\mathcal{N})$ denotes the *diagram* of $\mathcal{N}$, i.e. the set of atomic sentences true in $\mathcal{N}$..
- $\mathcal{N} \models \phi \land \psi :\iff \bigwedge\{\mathcal{N} \models \phi, \mathcal{N} \models \psi\}$.
- $\mathcal{N} \models \phi \lor \psi :\iff \bigvee\{\mathcal{N} \models \phi, \mathcal{N} \models \psi\}$.
- $\mathcal{N} \models \forall x \phi(x) :\iff \bigwedge\{\mathcal{N} \models \phi(\underline{n}) \mid n \in \omega\}$.
- $\mathcal{N} \models \exists x \phi(x) :\iff \bigvee\{\mathcal{N} \models \phi(\underline{n}) \mid n \in \omega\}$.

We will use this and define the truth complexity directly for infinitary sentences. Thus we first we have to fix the infinitary language.

Definition 9 (The infinitary languages $\mathcal{L}_\infty$ and $\mathcal{L}_\infty(X, Y, \ldots)$)
The nonlogical symbols of both languages are the same as those of the language $\mathcal{L}_{\mathcal{N}}$.
$\mathcal{L}_\infty$ and $\mathcal{L}_\infty(X, Y, \ldots)$ do not contain number variables (since they don't make sense in the definition of a satisfaction relation).
$\mathcal{L}_\infty(X, Y, \ldots)$, however, contains (finitely many) free set parameters (denoted by

$X, Y, \ldots$).
Due to the absence of number variables all terms of both languages are built up from number constants by constants for primitive recursive functions and are thus primitive recursively evaluable.

Formulas are defined by the following clauses:

1. *The atomic formulas of $\mathcal{L}_\infty$ are of the form*
$$R(t_1, \ldots, t_n),$$
where R is a symbol for an n-ary primitive recursive relation and $t_1, \ldots, t_n$ are terms. In $\mathcal{L}_\infty(X, Y, \ldots)$ we have the additional atomic formulas
$$t \in X \quad \text{and} \quad t \notin X,$$
where t is a term and X a set parameter.
2. *If Φ is a set of formulas then $\bigvee \Phi$ and $\bigwedge \Phi$ are formulas, too.*

If we restrict the sets Φ occurring in clause 2 to countable ones we obtain the languages $\mathcal{L}_{\omega_1}$ and $\mathcal{L}_{\omega_1}(X, Y, \ldots)$, respectively.

The satisfaction relation for the language $\mathcal{L}_\infty$ is now obvious. However we want to give a more formal definition of a satisfaction relation $\models^{\alpha} \phi$ which says that there is a 'satisfaction tree' for ϕ whose depth is bounded by the ordinal α. A precise definition can be given as follows.

Definition 10 (The satisfaction relation $\models^{\alpha} \phi$)
1. *If $\phi \in \mathcal{D}(\mathcal{N})$, then $\models^{\alpha} \phi$ for any ordinal α.*
2. *If $\models^{\alpha_\phi} \phi$ and $\alpha_\phi < \alpha$ for all $\phi \in \Phi$, then $\models^{\alpha} \bigwedge \Phi$.*
3. *If $\models^{\alpha_\phi} \phi$ and $\alpha_\phi < \alpha$ for some $\phi \in \Phi$, then $\models^{\alpha} \bigvee \Phi$.*

We can then trivially conclude the following result.

Theorem 11 *$\mathcal{N} \models \phi$ iff there is an ordinal α such that $\models^{\alpha} \phi$.*

For the language $\mathcal{L}_\infty(X, Y, \ldots)$ we define the satisfaction relation in a way similar to that in which we did it for the Π^1_1-sentences in $\mathcal{L}_{\mathcal{N}}$. We say that

$$\mathcal{N} \models \phi(X_1, \ldots, X_n)$$

iff

$$(\mathcal{N}, S_1, \ldots, S_n) \models \phi(X_1, \ldots, X_n)$$

for any choice of subsets $S_1, \ldots, S_n$ of ω. It is much harder to define a satisfaction relation $\models^{\alpha} \phi$ for ϕ in $\mathcal{L}_\infty(X, Y, \ldots)$ for which there is a counterpart of Theorem 11. This will not be possible in full generality but only for the countable language $\mathcal{L}_{\omega_1}$. We prefer to define the satisfaction relation in the form of a TAIT calculus (which has technical advantages and also lays the groundwork for our later applications of the definition of truth complexity). Again we denote finite sets of $\mathcal{L}_\infty(X, Y, \ldots)$-formulas by capital Greek letters $\Delta, \Gamma, \Lambda, \ldots$.

Definition 12 (The satisfaction relation $\models^{\alpha} \Delta$)

(AxL) *If s and t are terms such that $t^{\mathcal{N}} = s^{\mathcal{N}}$ (recall that this is primitive recursively decidable) then $\models^{\alpha} \Delta, s \in X, t \notin X$ for all ordinals α.*

(AxM) *If $\phi \in \mathcal{D}(\mathcal{N})$ then $\models^{\alpha} \Delta, \phi$ for all ordinals α.*

($\bigwedge$) *If $\models^{\alpha_\phi} \Delta, \phi$ and $\alpha_\phi < \alpha$ for all $\phi \in \Phi$ then $\models^{\alpha} \Delta, \bigwedge\Phi$*

($\bigvee$) *If $\models^{\alpha_\phi} \Delta, \phi$ and $\alpha_\phi < \alpha$ for some $\phi \in \Phi$ then $\models^{\alpha} \Delta, \bigvee\Phi$.*

The soundness of the relation $\models^{\alpha} \Delta$ is easily proven by induction on α, i.e.

Lemma 13 *If $\models^{\alpha} \phi_1, \ldots, \phi_n$ then $\mathcal{N} \models \phi_1 \vee \ldots \vee \phi_n$.*

The converse direction of Lemma 13 is much harder to show and holds only for fragments of the countable language $\mathcal{L}_{\omega_1}(X, Y, \ldots)$. To obtain a proof of it we define *search trees* inversely to the rules ($\bigvee$) and ($\bigwedge$). To do this we interpret a finite set Δ of $\mathcal{L}_{\omega_1}(X, Y, \ldots)$-formulas as a sequence. Such a sequence Δ is called *reducible* if it contains a non atomic formula. The leftmost non atomic formula is the *distinguished redex* of Δ. The *reductum* Δ^r of a reducible sequence Δ is obtained by cancelling the distinguished redex in Δ. The *search tree* S_Δ for a sequence Δ is a tree (i.e. a set of sequences of natural numbers which is closed under initial segments) together with a label function δ which assigns a finite formula sequence $\delta(\sigma)$ to every node $\sigma \in S_\Delta$ satisfying the following clauses:

(Btm) $\langle\rangle \in S_\Delta$ and $\delta(\langle\rangle) = \Delta$.

(Top) If $\sigma \in S_\Delta$ and $\delta(\sigma)$ is irreducible or an axiom according to (AxL) or (AxM) then σ is the topmost node of S_Δ.

Thus assume for the following clauses that $\delta(\sigma)$ is reducible and not an axiom.

($\bigwedge$) Let $\sigma \in S_\Delta$ and assume that the distinguished redex in $\delta(\sigma)$ is $\bigwedge\Phi$. Assume that $\Phi = \{\phi_i : i \in I \subseteq \omega\}$ (which is possible since $\bigvee\Phi \in \mathcal{L}_{\omega_1}(X, Y, \ldots)$). Then $\sigma^\frown\langle i\rangle \in S_\Delta$ for all $i \in I$ and $\delta(\sigma^\frown\langle i\rangle) := \delta(\sigma)^r, \phi_i$.

($\bigvee$) If $\sigma \in S_\Delta$ and the distinguished redex in $\delta(\sigma)$ is $\bigvee\Phi = \bigvee\{\phi_i \mid i \in I \subseteq \omega\}$ then $\sigma^\frown\langle 0\rangle \in S_\Delta$ and $\delta(\sigma^\frown\langle 0\rangle) := \delta(\sigma)^r, \phi_{i_0}$ where $i_0 \in I$ is the first index such that the formula ϕ_{i_0} does not occur in the set $\delta(S_\Delta \cap \sigma) := \{\delta(\tau) \mid \tau \in S_\Delta \wedge \tau \subset \sigma\}$. If there is no such i_0 then $\delta(\sigma^\frown\langle 0\rangle) := \delta(\sigma)^r$.

Clause (Top) in the definition of S_Δ ensures that a search tree in which every path contains an axiom is well-founded. Since the clauses ($\bigwedge$) and ($\bigvee$) are inverse to the corresponding rules in the definition of $\models^{\alpha} \Delta$, an easy induction along S_Δ (taking into account that ω_1 is a regular ordinal) shows:

Lemma 14 (Syntactical Main Lemma) *If Δ is a finite sequence of $\mathcal{L}_{\omega_1}(X, Y, \ldots)$-formulas such that every path in the search tree S_Δ contains an axiom, then there is an ordinal $\alpha < \omega_1$ such that $\models^{\alpha} \Delta$.*

The semantical counterpart of Lemma 14 is given by the following lemma.

Lemma 15 (Semantical Main Lemma) *Let Δ be a finite sequence of $\mathcal{L}_{\omega_1}(X, Y, \ldots)$-formulas. If there is a path in S_Δ which does not contain an axiom, then there is an assignment $S_1, \ldots, S_n$ of subsets of ω to the set parameters $X_1, \ldots, X_n$ occurring in Δ such that*

$$(\mathcal{N}, S_1, \ldots, S_n) \not\models \bigvee\{\phi \mid \phi \in \Delta\}.$$

The combination of the Semantical and the Syntactical Main Lemmas shows the completeness of the $\models^{\alpha}$-relation for formulas in the countable language $\mathcal{L}_{\omega_1}(X, Y, \ldots)$.

Theorem 16 (Soundness and Completeness for $\models^{\alpha} \phi$) *For an $\mathcal{L}_{\omega_1}(X, Y, \ldots)$-formula ϕ we have*

$$\mathcal{N} \models \phi \text{ iff there is an } \alpha < \omega_1 \text{ such that } \models^{\alpha} \phi\,.$$

The proof is obvious. If $\not\models^{\alpha} \phi(X_1, \ldots, X_n)$ for all $\alpha < \omega_1^{CK}$ then, according to the Syntactical Main Lemma, no path of S_Δ contains an axiom. By the Semantical Main Lemma this entails the existence of sets $S_1, \ldots, S_n$ of natural numbers such that $(\mathcal{N}, S_1, \ldots, S_n) \not\models \phi(X_1, \ldots, X_n)$, i.e. $\mathcal{N} \not\models \phi(X_1, \ldots, X_n)$. This is the completeness part. The soundness part is given by Lemma 13. □

To prove the Semantical Main Lemma let f be a path in S_Δ which does not contain an axiom and define the assignment by

$$S_i := \{t^{\mathcal{N}} \mid (t \notin X_i) \in \bigcup_{\sigma \in f} \delta(\sigma)\}.$$

This defines a correct assignment because f does not contain axioms according to (AxL) and it is not very hard to show $(\mathcal{N}, S_1, \ldots, S_n) \not\models \psi$ for all $\psi \in \bigcup_{\sigma \in f} \delta(\sigma)$. For details cf. [Pohlers 1989]. □

We use Theorem 16 to define the truth complexity for $\mathcal{L}_{\omega_1}(X, Y, \ldots)$-formulas as follows.

Definition 17 *Let ϕ be an $\mathcal{L}_{\omega_1}(X, Y, \ldots)$ formula. Then*

$$\mathrm{tc}(\phi) := \begin{cases} \min\{\alpha \mid \models^{\alpha} \phi\} & \textit{if this exists,} \\ \omega_1 & \textit{otherwise.} \end{cases}$$

Using the notion of truth complexity Theorem 16 takes the form

$$\mathcal{N} \models \phi \quad \text{iff} \quad \mathrm{tc}(\phi) < \omega_1. \tag{24}$$

The intention of introducing the infinitary language was to get a formalization of the satisfaction relation for the language $\mathcal{L}_{\mathcal{N}}$. This is obtained by the obvious translation of the language $\mathcal{L}_{\mathcal{N}}$ into $\mathcal{L}_\infty$. Both languages have the same nonlogical symbols. Thus we put:

- $\phi^\infty :\equiv \phi$ for atomic sentences ϕ.

- For $\phi \equiv \phi_1 \wedge \phi_2$ let $\phi^\infty :\equiv \bigwedge\{\phi_1^\infty, \phi_2^\infty\}$ and dually $(\phi_1 \vee \phi_2)^\infty :\equiv \bigvee\{\phi_1^\infty, \phi_2^\infty\}$.
- For $\phi \equiv \forall x \psi(x)$ let $\phi^\infty :\equiv \bigwedge\{\psi(\underline{n}) \mid n \in \omega\}$ and dually $(\exists x \psi(x))^\infty :\equiv \bigvee\{\psi(\underline{n}) \mid n \in \omega\}$.

It is no problem to prove that $\phi^\infty \in \mathcal{L}_{\omega_1}$ for $\phi \in \mathcal{L}_\mathcal{N}$ and therefore we may well regard $\mathcal{L}_\mathcal{N}$ as a sublanguage of $\mathcal{L}_{\omega_1}$ (and will do so in the future without emphasizing it any longer). Therefore we will talk about Π^1_1-sentences of $\mathcal{L}_{\omega_1}$ which of course are to be understood as $^\infty$ translations of Π^1_1-sentences of $\mathcal{L}_\mathcal{N}$. It is easy to see that for a finite sequence Δ of Π^1_1-sentences the search tree S_Δ is recursive. Therefore we may sharpen Theorem 16 to

Theorem 18 *For a Π^1_1-sentence ϕ we have $\mathcal{L}_\mathcal{N} \models \phi$ iff there is an ordinal $\alpha < \omega_1^{CK}$ such that $\mathcal{L}_\mathcal{N} \models^{\alpha} \phi$.*

We think it is worthwhile mentioning that the truth complexity for Π^1_1-sentences is closely connected to the usual norms defined on Π^1_1-relations. More precisely this means that we may define a norm $|m|$ on the elements m of a Π^1_1-set $R = \{x \mid \phi(x)\}$ by

$$|m| := \mathrm{tc}(\phi(\underline{m}))$$

and this norm will only inessentially diverge from the norm as obtained, for example, by the tree of unsecured sequences (or any other of the current definitions). The usefulness of the notion of truth complexity will be clarified by the following theorem. There we will use the abbreviations

$$Prog(\prec, X) :\equiv \forall x(\forall y(y \prec x \rightarrow y \in X) \longrightarrow x \in X)$$

and

$$TI(\prec) :\equiv Prog(\prec, X) \longrightarrow \forall x \in \mathrm{field}(\prec)(x \in X)$$

expressing induction along the relation $\prec$.

Theorem 19 (Boundedness Theorem) *If* $\mathrm{tc}(TI(\prec)) \leq \alpha$, *then* $\mathrm{otyp}(\prec) \leq 2^\alpha$.

To prove the theorem one shows the more general claim

$$\models^{\alpha} \neg Prog(\prec, X), s_1 \notin X, \ldots, s_n \notin X, \Delta(X) \Rightarrow (\mathcal{L}_\mathcal{N}, \{k \in \omega \mid \mathrm{otyp}_\prec(k) \leq \beta + 2^\alpha\}) \models \bigvee\{\phi \mid \phi \in \Delta(X)\}, \quad (\star)$$

where X is supposed to occur only positively in $\Delta(X)$ (i.e., not in the form $t \notin X$ for any term t) and $\beta := \max\{\mathrm{otyp}_\prec(s_1^\mathcal{N}), \ldots, \mathrm{otyp}_\prec(s_n^\mathcal{N})\}$. The theorem follows from $(\star)$ because $\models^{\alpha} TI(\prec)$ entails $\models^{\alpha} \neg Prog(\prec, X), \forall x \in \mathrm{field}(\prec)(x \in X)$.
The claim $(\star)$ itself is proven by a straightforward induction on α. Details can be found in [Pohlers 1989]. □

The name 'boundedness theorem' is usually associated with the theorem in generalized recursion theory stating that every Σ^1_1-definable well-ordering has order type less than ω_1^{CK}. It is easy to see that this theorem is indeed a corollary of

Theorem 19. If $\prec$ is a Σ_1^1-definable well-ordering then $TI(\prec)$ is obviously a Π_1^1-sentence. Hence $\mathrm{tc}(TI(\prec)) < \omega_1^{CK}$ by Theorem 18. Since $\mathrm{otyp}(\prec) \leq 2^{\mathrm{tc}(TI(\prec))}$ by the boundedness theorem 19 and ω_1^{CK} is closed under exponentiation we obtain $\mathrm{otyp}(\prec) < \omega_1^{CK}$. In a similar way one may also deduce that there are no Σ_1^1-paths through KLEENE's $\mathcal{O}$ and the other versions of the boundedness theorem.

The boundedness theorem is also the link to the more common definition of the proof-theoretic ordinal of an axiom system Ax as the sup of the order types of primitive recursive well-orderings whose well-foundedness can be proven in Ax. By the boundedness theorem this sup must be less than or equal to $|\mathrm{Ax}|$.

Before we start to sketch the technicalities of an ordinal analysis we want to give an outline of the problems which arise.
Whenever we have an axiom system Ax we can assume that the axioms ϕ in Ax are so obvious that we more or less know $\mathrm{tc}(\phi)$. If we assume that we have $\mathrm{Ax} \models \psi$ then we know by the completeness theorem for first-order logic that there are finitely many formulas $\phi_1, \ldots, \phi_n$ in Ax such that

$$\frac{|n}{|0} \neg\phi_1, \ldots, \neg\phi_n, \psi,$$

where $\frac{|m}{|0}$ denotes any TAIT-like calculus for first-order logic. Thus, if we put $\alpha_1 := \mathrm{tc}(\phi_1), \ldots, \alpha_n := \mathrm{tc}(\phi_n)$, we have

$$\models^{\alpha_1} \phi_1, \ldots, \models^{\alpha_n} \phi_n \tag{25}$$

and

$$\models^{m} \neg\phi_1, \ldots, \neg\phi_n, \psi \tag{26}$$

and want to compute $\mathrm{tc}(\psi)$ from these data. Certainly, we know from (25) and (26) that there must be some $\alpha < \omega_1^{CK}$ such that

$$\models^{\alpha} \psi,$$

but yet it cannot be seen how to get α from the given data. Up to now there is no possibility to link (25) and (26). The obvious idea to get the link is of course to extend the infinitary calculus which is given by the $\models^{\alpha}$ -relation by a cut rule

$$\models^{\beta_1} \Delta, \phi \text{ and } \models^{\beta_2} \Delta, \neg\phi \quad \Longrightarrow \quad \models^{\delta} \Delta$$

for $\delta > \sup\{\beta_1, \beta_2\}$. This would allow us to link (25) and (26), but of course we have to keep track of the complexity of the involved cuts and – what is most important – to get rid again of all these cuts without losing the information about the involved ordinals. To make this precise we are going to introduce an infinitary calculus with cut.

Definition 20 (The infinitary calculus $\vdash^{\alpha}_{\rho} \Delta$)
(AxM) If $\phi \in \mathcal{D}(\mathcal{N})$, then $\vdash^{\alpha}_{\rho} \Delta, \phi$ for all ordinals α and ρ.

(AxL) *If s and t are terms such that* $s^{\mathcal{N}} = t^{\mathcal{N}}$, *then* $\vdash^{\alpha}_{\rho} \Delta, t \in X, t \notin X$ *for all ordinals* α *and* ρ.

($\bigwedge$) *If* $\vdash^{\alpha_\phi}_{\rho} \Delta, \phi$ *and* $\alpha_\phi < \alpha$ *for all* $\phi \in \Phi$, *then* $\vdash^{\alpha}_{\rho} \Delta, \bigwedge \Phi$

($\bigvee$) *If* $\vdash^{\alpha_\phi}_{\rho} \Delta, \phi$ *and* $\alpha_\phi < \alpha$ *for some* $\phi \in \Phi$, *then* $\vdash^{\alpha}_{\rho} \Delta, \bigvee \Phi$.

(cut) *If* $\vdash^{\alpha_1}_{\rho} \Delta, \phi$, $\vdash^{\alpha_2}_{\rho} \Delta, \neg\phi$, $\alpha_1 < \alpha$, $\alpha_2 < \alpha$, *and* $\mathrm{rk}(\phi) < \rho$ *(where* $\mathrm{rk}(\phi)$ *denotes the rank of* ϕ, *i.e. the depth of its defining tree), then* $\vdash^{\alpha}_{\rho} \Delta$.

From Definition 20 we get immediately

$$\vdash^{\alpha}_{0} \Delta \iff \models^{\alpha} \Delta. \tag{27}$$

The infinitary calculus which is given by the $\vdash^{\alpha}_{\rho}$-relation is obviously sound. Thus we conclude from (27), the Soundness and the Completeness Theorem the following theorem.

Theorem 21 (Eliminability of Cuts) *Let* Δ *be a set of* $\mathcal{L}_{\omega_1}$*-formulas such that* $\vdash^{\alpha}_{\rho} \Delta$. *Then there is a countable ordinal* β *such that* $\vdash^{\beta}_{0} \Delta$.

This theorem, however, is of no use for ordinal analysis since we do not yet know how β depends on α and ρ. Thus the problem of ordinal analysis reduces to finding a function, say f, which maps pairs of ordinals into ordinals such that

$$\vdash^{\alpha}_{\rho} \Delta \implies \vdash^{f(\alpha,\rho)}_{0} \Delta.$$

In order to define such a function we need to take a closer look at the sequence of ordinal numbers.

3 Ordinals

Ordinals are supposed to represent magnitudes which allow us to continue the process of counting into the transfinite. Counting a set means to order it. On the other hand not every ordering enables us to count a set. To use an order relation $\prec$ as a counter for a set it has to be guaranteed that, after having counted arbitrarily many elements, there is a $\prec$-least member among the remaining elements (provided that we are not already done with the counting, i.e. that there are no remaining elements). Orderings $\prec$ in which every nonempty subset of the field has a $\prec$-least element are called *well-orderings*. Thus ordinals were originally understood as equivalence classes of well-orderings. Within a framework of nonnaive set theory, however, this leads directly to difficulties because these equivalence classes will become proper classes. Ordinals, however, should be sets. This makes it necessary to represent ordinals by some canonical well-ordering. There are intrinsic reasons to opt for the membership relation $\in$, i.e. to represent ordinals by sets which are well-ordered by the $\in$-relation. This entails that an ordinal is the set of its predecessors. Nowadays one commonly understands ordinals in this set theoretic sense and, since one usually assumes a well-founded universe of sets, defines an ordinal as a hereditarily transitive set. In this paper we will follow this convention. There are three types of ordinals

- The ordinal 0,
- Successor ordinals, i.e. ordinals of the form $\beta \cup \{\beta\}$,
- Limit ordinals, i.e. ordinals which are neither 0 nor successors.

The least limit ordinal is denoted by ω. Thus all ordinals less than ω are 0 or sucessors and can thus be accessed from 0 by finitely many Successor steps. Ordinals less than ω are called *finite*. We will identify natural numbers and finite ordinals (as we already have been doing in the previous sections). The Successor $\alpha \cup \{\alpha\}$ of an ordinal α will be usually denoted by α'. An ordinal α is *countable* iff there is a 1–1 mapping from α into ω. The first uncountable ordinal is denoted by ω_1 (also this notation has already been used). We denote the class of ordinals (which is indeed a proper class) by *On*. The important properties of ordinals are *transfinite induction* and *transfinite recursion*. Transfinite induction means

$$\forall \xi (\forall \eta < \xi \phi(\eta) \rightarrow \phi(\xi)) \longrightarrow \forall \xi \phi(\xi)$$

where we use the convention that small Greek letters denote ordinals and $\phi(\xi)$ denotes any 'property' of the ordinal ξ (usually described by some formula in the language of set theory).
Transfinite recursion (in the special formulation which we we need in this paper) assures the existence of a uniquely determined (class-) function F whose domain is the class *On* of ordinals and which satisfies the recursion equations

$$F(0) = \alpha,$$

$$F(\alpha') = G(F(\alpha), \alpha),$$

$$F(\lambda) = \bigcup_{\xi < \lambda} F(\xi) \quad \text{for limit ordinals } \lambda.$$

More generally, transfinite recursion assures the unique existence of a class-function F satisfying

$$F(\alpha) = G(F|\alpha),$$

where in both formulations G means a previously given class-function mapping sets into sets and $F|\alpha$ is the restriction of F to α.
The *supremum* $\sup M$ of a set $M \subset On$ is the least ordinal σ such that $\xi \leq \sigma$ holds for all $\xi \in M$, i.e.

$$\sup M = \bigcup M.$$

The *cardinality* $\text{card}(M)$ of a set M is the least ordinal κ such that there exists a 1-1 mapping from M onto κ.
Cardinals are ordinals which cannot be mapped onto a smaller ordinal by a 1-1 mapping, i.e. cardinals are ordinals κ such that $\text{card}(\kappa) = \kappa$.
An ordinal ρ is called *regular* iff every subset $M \subset \rho$ of cardinality $< \rho$ is bounded by some ordinal $< \rho$.
A class $M \subseteq On$ is a *segment* if it contains with an ordinal α also all its predecessors,

i.e. if $\alpha \in M$ entails $\alpha \subseteq M$. Thus segments are hereditarily transitive classes and therefore either ordinals or the class On itself.
For any class $M \subseteq On$ there is a uniquely defined function en_M whose domain is a segment of On and which enumerates the elements of M in increasing order. The domain of en_M is an ordinal iff M is a set. Otherwise $\mathrm{dom}(en_M)$ is On. As before we call $\mathrm{dom}(en_M)$ the order-type of the class M and denote it by $\mathrm{otyp}(M)$.
If $f\colon M \longrightarrow On$ is a strictly increasing function whose domain M is a segment then $\alpha \leq f(\alpha)$ for all $\alpha \in M$.
A strictly increasing function is *continuous* if

$$f(\sup M) = \sup_{\xi \in M} f(\xi)$$

for all $M \subseteq \mathrm{dom} f$ such that $\sup M \in \mathrm{dom} f$.
A class is *unbounded* (in some ordinal κ) if for any ordinal ξ ($< \kappa$) there is an η ($< \kappa$) such that $\xi \leq \eta$. It is *closed* if it contains all its limit points. The following theorem is folklore in the theory of closed and unbounded classes.

Theorem 22 *A class $M \subseteq On$ ($M \subseteq \kappa$) is closed unbounded (in κ) iff* $\mathrm{otyp}(M) = On$ ($\mathrm{otyp}(M) = \kappa$) *and en_M is continuous.*

Another folklore result is that the derivative,

$$M' := \{\xi \mid en_M(\xi) = \xi\},$$

of a closed unbounded set M is closed unbounded, too. The third result we have to borrow from set theory is:

> *if $\{M_\xi \mid \xi < \lambda < \kappa\}$ is a family of in κ closed unbounded sets M_ξ, then $\bigcap\{M_\xi \mid \xi < \lambda < \kappa\}$ is also closed unbounded in κ.*

The 'arithmetical' operations $+$, $\cdot$ and exponentiation are canonically lifted to ordinals by the following recursion equations:

$$\alpha + 0 = \alpha, \quad \alpha + \beta' = (\alpha + \beta)', \quad \alpha + \lambda = \sup_{\xi < \lambda}(\alpha + \xi) \quad \text{for limit ordinals } \lambda$$

$$\alpha \cdot 0 = 0, \quad \alpha \cdot \beta' = (\alpha \cdot \beta) + \alpha, \quad \alpha \cdot \lambda = \sup_{\xi < \lambda}(\alpha \cdot \xi) \quad \text{for limit ordinals } \lambda$$

$$\alpha^0 = 0', \quad \alpha^{\beta'} = (\alpha^\beta) \cdot \alpha, \quad \alpha^\lambda = \sup_{\xi < \lambda}(\alpha^\xi) \quad \text{for limit ordinals } \lambda$$

An ordinal α is *additively indecomposable* if it cannot be decomposed into the sum of smaller ordinals, i.e. if $\xi, \eta < \alpha$ entail $\xi + \eta < \alpha$. It is easy to see that the class $\mathbb{H}$(for German Hauptzahl) of additively indecomposable ordinals is closed unbounded in any regular ordinal. It is not hard to show that

$$en_{\mathbb{H}}(\alpha) = \omega^\alpha. \tag{28}$$

By induction on α we get easily that for every ordinal α there are uniquely determined ordinals $\{\alpha_1, \ldots, \alpha_n\} \subset \mathbb{H}$ such that $\alpha_1 \geq \ldots \geq \alpha_n$ and $\alpha = \alpha_1 + \ldots + \alpha_n$.

Together with (28) this gives the Cantor normal-form theorem for ordinals stating that

for every ordinal α there are uniquely determined ordinals $\alpha_1, \ldots, \alpha_n$ such that $\alpha = \omega^{\alpha_1} + \ldots + \omega^{\alpha_n}$ and $\alpha_1 \geq \ldots \geq \alpha_n$.

If we define

$$\varepsilon_0 := \min\{\xi \mid \omega^\xi = \xi\}$$

then it follows from the Cantor normal form theorem that every ordinal less than ε_0 can be uniquely denoted by a term which is built up from the symbols $0, +, \omega$ solely. Such a term system is called a *notation system* for the ordinals below ε_0. Using the above results on closed unbounded classes, we obtain a hierarchy of classes $Cr(\alpha)$ which are closed unbounded in any regular ordinal κ. We define

$$Cr(0) := \mathbb{H},$$

$$Cr(\alpha') := Cr(\alpha)'$$

and

$$Cr(\lambda) := \bigcap_{\xi<\lambda} Cr(\xi) \quad \text{for limit ordinals } \lambda.$$

We put $\varphi_\alpha := en_{Cr(\alpha)}$, i.e. φ_α enumerates the elements of $Cr(\alpha)$. Since the classes $Cr(\alpha)$ form a descending chain we always have

$$\varphi_\alpha(\varphi_\beta(\gamma)) = \varphi_\beta(\gamma) \quad \text{for } \alpha < \beta. \tag{29}$$

One easily checks that (29) entails

Lemma 23 *$\varphi_{\alpha_1}(\beta_1) = \varphi_{\alpha_2}(\beta_2)$ or $\varphi_{\alpha_1}(\beta_1) < \varphi_{\alpha_2}(\beta_2)$ hold iff one of the following conditions is satisfied*

1. *$\alpha_1 < \alpha_2$ and $\beta_1 = \varphi_{\alpha_2}(\beta_2)$ or $\beta_1 < \varphi_{\alpha_2}(\beta_2)$, respectively*
2. *$\alpha_1 = \alpha_2$ and $\beta_1 = \beta_2$ or $\beta_1 < \beta_2$, respectively*
3. *$\alpha_1 > \alpha_2$ and $\varphi_{\alpha_1}(\beta_1) = \beta_2$ or $\varphi_{\alpha_1}(\beta_1) < \beta_2$, respectively.*

For the moment this is all of the theory of ordinals we need although we will have to revisit it later. In the next section we will learn that the functions φ_α play an important role in the ordinal analysis of axiom systems.

4 Predicative Cut Elimination

At the end of Section 2 we introduced the infinitary calculus $\vdash^{\alpha}_{\rho} \Delta$ and raised the problem of finding an ordinal function which computes the depth of a cut-free infinitary proof tree out of the length and the cut rank of a given derivation. In this section we will show that the function $\varphi = \lambda\xi\eta.\varphi_\xi(\eta)$ already does the job.

We start by looking closer at the properties of the infinitary calculus. First we observe that we may as well raise the ordinal bounds as enlarge the derived formula set, i.e.

$$\vdash^{\alpha}_{\rho} \Delta,\ \alpha \leq \beta,\ \rho \leq \sigma \text{ and } \Delta \subseteq \Gamma \implies \vdash^{\beta}_{\sigma} \Gamma \tag{30}$$

As a word of warning we want to emphasize that besides the weakening property, as expressed in (30), there is also a contraction rule tacitly built into the TAIT-calculus. For example, if we assume that $\vdash^{\alpha_\phi}_{\rho} \Delta, \bigwedge\Phi, \phi$ for all $\phi \in \Phi$ then we obtain $\vdash^{\alpha}_{\rho} \Delta, \bigwedge\Phi, \bigwedge\Phi$ by an $(\bigwedge)$-inference which, in view that this calculus derives formula sets, is the same as $\vdash^{\alpha}_{\rho} \Delta, \bigwedge\Phi$. In proofs by induction along infinitary proof trees we will sometimes have to take care of this. The crucial situation during the cut elimination procedure is the following:
Assume that we have

$$\vdash^{\alpha}_{\rho} \Delta, \phi \quad \text{and} \quad \vdash^{\beta}_{\rho} \Gamma, \neg\phi,$$

where ϕ is a formula of rank ρ, and want to conclude Δ, Γ. The usual way is to use (30) to get $\vdash^{\alpha}_{\rho+1} \Delta, \Gamma, \phi$ and $\vdash^{\beta}_{\rho+1} \Delta, \Gamma, \neg\phi$ and then derive Δ, Γ by a cut. The next lemma, however, tells us that we may avoid this cut – at the cost of an increasing derivation length.

Lemma 24 (Elimination Lemma) *Let* $\mathrm{rk}(\phi) = \rho$ *and assume* $\vdash^{\alpha}_{\rho} \Delta, \phi$ *and* $\vdash^{\beta}_{\rho} \Gamma, \neg\phi$. *Then* $\vdash^{\alpha \# \beta}_{\rho} \Delta, \Gamma$.

The term $\alpha \# \beta$ denotes the *natural sum* of α and β, which is obtained by decomposing $\alpha = \alpha_1 + \ldots + \alpha_n$ with $\{\alpha_1 + \ldots \alpha_n\} \subset \mathbf{H}$ and $\alpha_1 \geq \ldots \geq \alpha_n$ – we are going to denote this by $\alpha =_{NF} \alpha_1 + \ldots + \alpha_n$ – and $\beta =_{NF} \alpha_{n+1} + \ldots \alpha_m$. Then we put

$$\alpha \# \beta := \alpha_{\pi(1)} + \ldots + \alpha_{\pi(m)},$$

where π is a permutation of the numbers $1, \ldots, m$ such that $\alpha_{\pi(1)} \geq \ldots \geq \alpha_{\pi(m)}$.
The proof of the theorem is by induction on $\alpha \# \beta$. The situation is easy if either ϕ or $\neg\phi$ is not the main formula of the last inference in one of both derivations, i.e. the formula on which this inference depends. Then we obtain the claim immediately from the induction hypotheses. So let us assume that both formulas are main formulas of the last inferences. Then there are only two possibilities. Either ϕ is atomic and $\vdash^{\alpha}_{\rho} \Delta, \phi$ as well as $\vdash^{\beta}_{\rho} \Gamma, \neg\phi$ are axioms depending on ϕ and $\neg\phi$, respectively or ϕ is a formula $\bigwedge\Phi$, say. (The case that $\phi = \bigvee\Phi$ is symmetrical since then $\neg\phi$ is a conjunction.) In the first case ϕ must be a formula $t \in X$ because we cannot simultaneously have $\phi \in \mathcal{D}(\mathcal{N})$ and $\neg\phi \in \mathcal{D}(\mathcal{N})$. But then there are formulas $(s_1 \notin X)$ in Δ and $(s_2 \in X)$ in Γ with $s_1^{\mathcal{N}} = t^{\mathcal{N}} = s_2^{\mathcal{N}}$. Thus we have $\vdash^{\alpha \# \beta}_{\rho} \Delta, \Gamma$ by (AxL). In the second case we have the premises

$$\vdash^{\alpha_\psi}_{\rho} \Delta, \bigwedge\Phi, \psi \tag{i}$$

for all $\psi \in \Phi$ and

$$\vdash^{\beta_0}_{\rho} \Delta, \bigvee\Phi, \neg\psi_0 \tag{ii}$$

for some $\psi_0 \in \Phi$. From the hypotheses and (i) or (ii), respectively, we get by the induction hypothesis

$$\vdash^{\alpha_{\psi_0} \# \beta}_{\rho} \Delta, \Gamma, \psi_0 \tag{iii}$$

and

$$\vdash_{\rho}^{\alpha \# \beta_0} \Delta, \Gamma, \neg\psi_0, \qquad (iv)$$

respectively. Since $\alpha_{\psi_0} \# \beta < \alpha \# \beta$, $\alpha \# \beta_0 < \alpha \# \beta$, and $\mathrm{rk}(\psi) < \mathrm{rk}(\phi)$ we obtain

$$\vdash_{\rho}^{\alpha \# \beta} \Delta, \Gamma$$

from (iii) and (iv) by a cut. □

As an immediate consequence of the elimination lemma we can decrease the cut rank of a derivation by one. We get

Theorem 25 (First Elimination Theorem) $\vdash_{\rho+1}^{\alpha} \Delta$ *entails* $\vdash_{\rho}^{2^\alpha} \Delta$.

The proof is simply by induction on α. The only interesting case is that of a cut with cut-formula ϕ of rank ρ, since in all other cases the claim is immediate from the induction hypothesis. Then, however, we have

$$\vdash_{\rho}^{2^{\alpha_1}} \Delta, \phi \qquad (i)$$

and

$$\vdash_{\rho}^{2^{\alpha_2}} \Delta, \neg\phi \qquad (ii)$$

by induction hypothesis and, since $2^{\alpha_1} \# 2^{\alpha_2} \leq 2^\alpha$, we may apply the elimination lemma and (30) to obtain

$$\vdash_{\rho}^{2^\alpha} \Delta .$$

□

Iterated application of Theorem 25 already enables us to transform derivations with finite cut rank into cut-free ones. It is of course obvious that the $^\infty$-translation of Section 2 applied to a Π_1^1-sentence always yields an $\mathcal{L}_\infty$-formula of finite rank. Thus Theorem 25 already suffices for an ordinal analysis of PEANO ARITHMETIC or equivalent axiom systems. Let us again assume an axiomatization of number theory in which we have the defining axioms for all primitive recursive relations and functions together with the schema of mathematical induction. If $\forall\vec{x}\phi(\vec{x})$ is a defining equation for a primitive recursive relation or function, then we have $\phi(\underline{\vec{n}}) \in \mathcal{D}(\mathcal{N})$ for all tuples $\vec{n}$ of natural numbers. Thus $\mathrm{tc}(\forall\vec{x}\phi(\vec{x}))$ is some finite ordinal. To check the truth complexity of mathematical induction we prove

$$\models^{2(\mathrm{rk}(\phi)+n)} \neg\phi(\underline{0}), \neg\forall x(\phi(x) \to \phi(x+\underline{1})), \phi(\underline{n}) \qquad (31)$$

for all $n \in \omega$ and all formulas ϕ. The proof is by induction on n and needs the observation that

$$\models^{2\mathrm{rk}(\phi)} \Delta, \phi, \neg\phi \qquad (32)$$

holds for any $\mathcal{L}_\infty$-formula ϕ. Statement (32) is easily proven by induction on $\mathrm{rk}(\phi)$. For atomic ϕ it is either an axiom (AxM) or (AxL). For $\phi = \bigwedge \Phi$ we have

$$\models^{2\mathrm{rk}(\psi)} \Delta, \psi, \neg\psi$$

for all $\psi \in \Phi$ by the induction hypothesis. This first yields $\overset{2\mathrm{rk}(\psi)+1}{\models} \Delta, \psi, \neg\phi$ for all $\psi \in \Phi$ by ($\bigvee$) and, since $2\mathrm{rk}(\psi) + 1 < 2\mathrm{rk}(\phi)$, then $\overset{2\mathrm{rk}(\phi)}{\models} \Delta, \phi, \neg\phi$ by ($\bigwedge$).
A special case of (32) is

$$\overset{2\mathrm{rk}(\phi)}{\models} \neg\phi(\underline{0}), \neg\forall x(\phi(x) \to \phi(x+\underline{1})), \phi(\underline{0})$$

which is the basis of the induction for (31). For the induction step we have the induction hypothesis

$$\overset{2(\mathrm{rk}(\phi)+n)}{\models} \neg\phi(\underline{0}), \bigvee\{\phi(\underline{m}) \wedge \neg\phi(\underline{m}+\underline{1}) \mid m \in \omega\}, \phi(\underline{n}) \tag{i}$$

Together with $\overset{2\mathrm{rk}(\phi)}{\models} \neg\phi(\underline{n}+\underline{1}), \phi(\underline{n}+\underline{1})$ this yields by applications of inferences ($\bigwedge$) and ($\bigvee$)

$$\overset{2(\mathrm{rk}(\phi+n))+2}{\models} \neg\phi(\underline{0}), \bigvee\{\phi(\underline{m}) \wedge \neg\phi(\underline{m}+\underline{1}) \mid m \in \omega\}, \phi(\underline{n}+\underline{1})$$

which is the claim. □

From (31) we easily obtain

$$\mathrm{tc}\,(\phi(\underline{0}) \wedge \forall x(\phi(x) \to \phi(x+1)) \to \forall x\phi(x)) \le \omega + 3. \tag{33}$$

Now we have all the data for an ordinal analysis of PEANO ARITHMETIC. If $PA \vdash \phi$ then we have axioms $\psi_1, \ldots, \psi_n \in PA$ such that, according to (33) and (27),

$$\overset{\alpha_1}{\underset{0}{\models}} \psi_1\,, \ \ldots\ ,\overset{\alpha_n}{\underset{0}{\models}} \psi_n$$

and

$$\overset{m}{\underset{0}{\models}} \neg\psi_1, \ldots, \neg\psi_n, \phi$$

for $\alpha_1, \ldots, \alpha_n \le \omega + 3$ and m finite. Since all the axioms $\psi_1, \ldots, \psi_n$ have finite rank we obtain by some cuts

$$\overset{\alpha}{\underset{k}{\models}} \phi$$

for $\alpha < \omega + \omega$ and $k < \omega$. Iterated applications of Theorem 25 and (27) then yield

$$\mathrm{tc}(\phi) \le 2^{(k)}(\alpha) < \varepsilon_0.$$

This entails that $|PA| \le \varepsilon_0$ and it can be shown (cf., e.g. [Pohlers 1989]) that this bound is indeed the best possible one.

This seems to be a good place for a remark concerning the profoundness of ordinal analyses obtained in the above manner. We start with the assumption that there is a primitive recursive well-ordering representing $|\mathrm{Ax}|$ on the natural numbers. If we have $\mathrm{Ax} \models \phi$ then there are sentences $\psi_1, \ldots, \psi_n$ in Ax such that $\vdash \neg\psi_1, \ldots, \neg\psi_n, \phi$ is a theorem of first-order logic. If we can show that there are recursive proof trees $\overset{\alpha_1}{\underset{0}{\models}} \psi_1\,, \ldots ,\overset{\alpha_n}{\underset{0}{\models}} \psi_n$ then we can get a recursive proof tree (whose index is e, say) such that $e \overset{\alpha}{\underset{\rho}{\models}} \phi$, where the latter notation means that $\{e\}$ is the characteristic function of a tree whose nodes are labeled by finite formula sets and notations for ordinals in such a way that the tree becomes locally correct with respect to the axioms and inference rules in Definition 20. As long as our manipulations during the cut elimination procedure are locally recursive we may use the recursion lemma[2] to obtain a global partial recursive function g such that (cf., e.g. [Pohlers 1981])

$$e \,\frac{|^{\alpha}}{\rho}\, \Delta \quad\Longrightarrow\quad g(e)\downarrow \text{ and } g(e) \,\frac{|^{\bar{g}(\alpha,\rho)}}{0}\, \Delta\,. \tag{†}$$

Since basic recursion theory (including the recursion theorem, which is the basis for the recursion lemma) can be developed within PA we just need $TI(\prec_{in})$, where $\prec_{in}$ represents all ordinals occurring in $g(e)$, to apply the recursion lemma to obtain (†). Induction along $\prec_{in}$ will also prove the soundness of the end formula in (†). Since all the formulas in a cut-free proof tree are of bounded complexity and a partial truth predicate for formulas of restricted complexity can be formalized within PEANO ARITHMETIC we may formalize this soundness proof in $PA + TI(\prec_{in})$ and obtain the following reflection principle

$$PA + TI(\prec_{in}) \vdash Proof_{\infty}^{CF}(e, \ulcorner\phi\urcorner) \to \phi \tag{34}$$

where $Proof_{\infty}^{CF}(e, \ulcorner\phi\urcorner)$ formalizes

'e is the index of a cut-free infinitary proof with end formula ϕ'.

Putting these facts together we obtain from Ax $\vdash \phi$

$$PA + TI(\prec_{in}) \vdash Proof_{\infty}^{CF}(e, \ulcorner\phi\urcorner)$$

for some e which in fact can be computed from the formal proof Ax $\vdash \phi$. This together with (34) entails

$$PA + TI(\prec_{in}) \vdash \phi\,.$$

The opposite direction is obtained by showing

$$\text{Ax} \vdash TI(\prec_{in})$$

for every initial segment $\prec_{in}$ of $\prec$. But this is part of the definition of '$\prec$ is a good representation for $|\text{Ax}|$'.
Summing up, we see that an ordinal analysis will always be a profound one provided that the following conditions are met:

- $\prec$ is a primitive recursive representation for $|\text{Ax}|$ such that Ax $\vdash TI(\prec_{in})$ for all proper initial segments $\prec_{in}$ of $\prec$.

[2] The recursion lemma says that if for a well-founded relation $\prec$ and a binary relation R there is a local recursive function h satisfying

$$\forall n \forall e\,[(\forall m \prec n) R(m, \{e\}(m)) \to R(n, h(e,n))],$$

then there is a global recursive function g such that

$$(\forall n \in fld(\prec)) R(n, g(n)).$$

- For every $\psi \in \mathrm{Ax}$ we can compute a proof tree $e \,\frac{\alpha}{0}\, \psi$ primitive recursively.
- The proof predicate $e \,\frac{\alpha}{\rho}\, \phi$ (for fixed α) is formalizable in $PA + TI(\prec_{in})$ and the cut elimination procedure for the infinitary calculus $\frac{\alpha}{\rho}\, \Delta$ is locally recursive, i.e. if $R(x, y)$ formalizes one reduction step in the procedure then there is a recursive function h such that

$$(\forall m \prec n)\,(R(m, \{e\}(m)) \to R(n, h(e, n)))$$

  holds for all indices e of partial recursive functions.

Commonly these requirements are satisfied. So we will not have to bother too much about getting a profound ordinal analysis and can concentrate on the computation of the proof-theoretic ordinal.
So let us return to that. We did not yet answer the question for the function which computes the length of a cut-free derivation out of the length and the cut rank of the original derivation. Theorem 25, however, is already the key to answer this question, too.

Theorem 26 (Second Elimination Theorem) $\frac{\alpha}{\beta+\omega^\rho}\, \Delta$ *implies* $\frac{\varphi_\rho(\alpha)}{\beta}\, \Delta$

We prove this by induction on ρ with a side induction on α.
Since $2^\alpha \le \omega^\alpha = \varphi_0(\alpha)$ the case $\rho = 0$ is already covered by the First Elimination Theorem. Thus assume $\rho > 0$. If the last inference in $\frac{\alpha}{\beta+\omega^\rho}\, \Delta$ is not a cut of rank $\sigma \in [\beta, \beta + \omega^\rho)$ then we get the claim easily from the induction hypothesis and the fact that the function φ_ρ is order preserving. Otherwise we have the premises

$$\frac{\alpha_1}{\beta+\omega^\rho}\, \Delta, \psi \quad \text{and} \quad \frac{\alpha_2}{\beta+\omega^\rho}\, \Delta, \neg\psi \tag{i}$$

with $\beta \le \mathrm{rk}(\psi) =: \sigma < \beta + \omega^\rho$. But then $\sigma = \beta + \omega^{\sigma_1} + \ldots + \omega^{\sigma_n}$ with $\rho > \sigma_1 \ge \ldots \ge \sigma_n$. Hence

$$\sigma < \beta + \omega^{\sigma_1} \cdot (n+1). \tag{ii}$$

By the side induction hypothesis we have

$$\frac{\varphi_\rho(\alpha_1)}{\beta}\, \Delta, \psi \quad \text{and} \quad \frac{\varphi_\rho(\alpha_2)}{\beta}\, \Delta, \neg\psi, \tag{iii}$$

which by (ii), (30), and cut yield

$$\frac{\varphi_\rho(\alpha_1)+\varphi_\rho(\alpha_2)}{\beta+\omega^{\sigma_1}\cdot(n+1)}\, \Delta. \tag{iv}$$

Since $\sigma_1 < \rho$ we obtain

$$\frac{\varphi_{\sigma_1}^{(n+1)}(\varphi_\rho(\alpha_1)+\varphi_\rho(\alpha_2))}{\beta}\, \Delta \tag{v}$$

by $n+1$ applications of the main induction hypothesis. From $\alpha_i < \alpha$ for $i = 1, 2$ and $\varphi_\rho(\alpha) \in \mathbb{H}$ we get $\varphi_\rho(\alpha_1) + \varphi_\rho(\alpha_2) < \varphi_\rho(\alpha)$, and this together with $\sigma_1 < \rho$ yields

$$\varphi_{\sigma_1}^{(n+1)}(\varphi_\rho(\alpha_1) + \varphi_\rho(\alpha_2)) < \varphi_\rho(\alpha) \tag{vi}$$

by Lemma 23. The claim now follows from (v), (vi), and (30). □

As a simple example of an application of Theorem 26 we want to show how to compute (an upper bound for) the proof-theoretic ordinal of second order PEANO ARITHMETIC with the schema of ARITHMETICAL COMPREHENSION.
This theory is a second-order theory (to stay within the realm of first-order logic for which we developed our notions we regard second-order logic as two sorted first-order logic) with the comprehension schema

$$(\Delta^1_0\text{-}CA) \qquad \exists X \forall x(x \in X \leftrightarrow \phi(x))$$

where $\phi(x)$ is an arithmetical formula, i.e. a formula without occurrences of second-order quantifiers. To extend the definition of the $^\infty$ translation to this language we assume that $\{\psi_n \mid n \in \omega\}$ is an enumeration of all the arithmetical sentences and define

$$(\exists X \phi(X))^\infty :\equiv \bigvee \{\phi(\psi_n(.)) \mid n \in \omega\}$$

and

$$(\forall X \phi(X))^\infty :\equiv \bigwedge \{\phi(\psi_n(.)) \mid n \in \omega\},$$

where $\phi(\psi(.))$ means that any occurrence of $t \in X$ or $t \notin X$ in $\psi(X)$ is replaced by $\psi(t)$ or $\neg\psi(t)$ respectively.
Then we have

$$(\Delta^1_0\text{-}CA)^\infty :\equiv \bigvee \{\forall x(\psi_n(x) \leftrightarrow \phi(x)) \mid n \in \omega\}$$

and obtain easily

$$\vdash^{\omega}_{0} (\Delta^1_0\text{-}CA)^\infty .$$

Hence $\mathrm{tc}((\Delta^1_0\text{-}CA)^\infty) \leq \omega$ but $\mathrm{rk}((\Delta^1_0\text{-}CA)^\infty) = \omega$ which, on its side, entails that there might be instances of mathematical induction with rank $\omega + k$. A look at (31) tells us that this will increase the truth complexity of the schema of mathematical induction to something below $\omega \cdot 3$. Thus we get

$$(\mathbf{\Delta^1_0\text{-}CA}) \vdash \phi \quad \Longrightarrow \quad \vdash^{\alpha}_{\omega+k} \phi^\infty \tag{35}$$

for $\alpha < \omega \cdot 3$ and finite k. By Theorem 26, the Second Elimination Theorem, and (27) we therefore obtain

$$(\mathbf{\Delta^1_0\text{-}CA}) \vdash \phi \quad \Longrightarrow \quad \mathrm{tc}(\phi) < \varphi_1(\varepsilon_0). \tag{36}$$

This in turn entails

$$|(\mathbf{\Delta^1_0\text{-}CA})| \leq \varphi_1(\varepsilon_0) \tag{37}$$

and again it can be proven that we have equality. Of course this is a simple example. More complex examples will certainly need more subtle considerations. (See, for example, the paper by M. RATHJEN [Rathjen 1991] in this volume.)

5 The Limits of Predicativity

If we choose $\beta = 0$ in the Second Elimination Theorem we obtain the special case

$$\vdash^{\alpha}_{\rho} \Delta \Longrightarrow \vdash^{\varphi_\rho(\alpha)}_{0} \Delta. \tag{38}$$

As a consequence we have that $\vdash^{\alpha}_{\rho} \phi$ always entails $\mathrm{tc}(\phi) \leq \varphi_\rho(\alpha)$. If we apply this to the Π^1_1-sentence $TI(\prec)$, expressing transfinite induction along the relation $\prec$ (which we assume to be arithmetically definable), then we get by Theorem 19

$$\vdash^{\alpha}_{\rho} TI(\prec) \Longrightarrow \mathrm{otyp}(\prec) \leq \varphi_\rho(\alpha). \tag{39}$$

This shows that the first ordinal which is closed under the function $\lambda\xi\eta.\,\varphi_\xi(\eta)$ represents a limit for the order type of well-orderings which can be "accessed from below". To make this a bit more precise we first study the class of ordinals which are closed under $\lambda\xi\eta.\,\varphi_\xi(\eta)$. Define the class of strongly critical ordinals by

$$SC := \{\alpha \mid \alpha \in Cr(\alpha)\}. \tag{40}$$

It is easy to see that this class is closed and unbounded. It follows easily from Lemma 23 that $\lambda\xi.\varphi_\xi(0)$ is order preserving. For $\alpha \in SC$ there is a ξ such that $\alpha = \varphi_\alpha(\xi)$ and we get

$$\alpha \leq \varphi_\alpha(0) \leq \varphi_\alpha(\xi) = \alpha,$$

which yields

$$SC = \{\alpha \mid \alpha = \varphi_\alpha(0)\}. \tag{41}$$

Thus for $\alpha \in SC$ and $\xi, \eta < \alpha$ we have $\varphi_\xi(\eta) < \varphi_\alpha(0) = \alpha$ by Lemma 23. The SCHÜTTE - FEFERMAN ordinal

$$\Gamma_0 := \min SC \tag{42}$$

is known as the limit of predicativity. We call a notion *predicative* iff it can be defined without referring to itself. A good example of a predicative definition is that of the collection Def(A) of sets which are *definable* from a given set A. We say $x \in \mathrm{Def}(A)$ iff there is a formula ϕ in the language of set theory, i.e. the only nonlogical symbol occurring in ϕ is the membership symbol $\in$, and a list $\vec{a}$ of elements of A such that

$$x = \{z \in A \mid A \models \phi(z, \vec{a})\}.$$

Thus in order to determine the elements of Def(A) we only need to know A. So we may say that definition of Def(A) is predicative in A. The stages of the constructible hierarchy are given by

$$\mathsf{L}_\alpha = \begin{cases} \emptyset & \text{if } \alpha = 0, \\ \mathrm{Def}(\mathsf{L}_\beta) & \text{if } \alpha = \beta + 1, \\ \bigcup_{\xi<\alpha} \mathsf{L}_\xi & \text{for limit ordinals } \alpha. \end{cases} \tag{43}$$

The constructible hierachy

$$\mathsf{L} := \bigcup_{\xi \in On} \mathsf{L}_\xi$$

is then *locally predicative*, i.e. each level is predicative in its preceding levels. Globally, however, the definition of the stages L_α still refers to the sequence of the ordinal numbers up to α which must be assumed to exist independently. If we really want to construct a universe in a predicative manner we will also have to bother about the ordinals we need in its construction. We might say that we can accept a countable ordinal α once we have a representation for it, i.e. a well-ordering $\prec$ on the natural numbers of order type α for which we know that $TI(\prec)$ is true. However, we should be able to recognize the truth of $TI(\prec)$ within our universe constructed thus far. We may say that we are able to recognize the truth of a sentence within L_α if the tree, representing $\models^{\xi}_{\eta} \phi$, belongs to L_α. For ξ, η and $\mathrm{rk}(\phi)$ less than α this will always be the case. Thus accepting an ordinal β in L_α can be made precise by requiring to have $\models^{\xi}_{\eta} TI(\prec)$ for $\xi, \eta < \alpha$ and a order relation $\prec$ of order type β. The construction of the sets in L_α is so simple that we we can accept L_α as soon as we have accepted the ordinal α. So we may start the following bootstrapping process. We begin with some ordinal, say α, and then try to secure larger ordinals by proving $\models^{\xi}_{\eta} TI(\prec)$ for ordinals $\xi, \eta < \alpha$ and relations $\prec$ such that $\mathrm{rk}(TI(\prec))$ is still less than α. If $\mathrm{otyp}(\prec) = \beta$ we accept the ordinal β and construct L_β. If we begin with some finite α we conclude from the First Elimination Theorem and the Boundedness Theorem that we will secure only finite ordinals. This shows the impossibility of creating infinite domains out of finite ones. Anyhow, even if we accept an infinity axiom postulating the existence of ω we see from the Second Elimination Theorem and the Boundedness Theorem that Γ_0 is inaccessible by this bootstrapping process. On the other hand S. FEFERMAN and K. SCHÜTTE have independently shown that every ordinal $\xi < \Gamma_0$ is accessible by the bootstrapping process. Therefore one commonly calls the ordinal Γ_0 the *limit of predicativity*.

There are many axioms systems having proof theoretic ordinal Γ_0. One of the systems investigated by S. FEFERMAN was $(\mathbf{\Delta^1_1\text{-}CA}) + \mathbf{BR}$. This again is second-order PEANO ARITHMETIC with the schema of mathematical induction, the Δ^1_1-comprehension schema

$$(\Delta^1_1\text{-}CA) \qquad \forall x(\psi(x) \leftrightarrow \phi(x)) \longrightarrow \exists X \forall x(x \in X \leftrightarrow \phi(x))$$

where $\psi(x)$ and $\phi(x)$ are supposed to be Π^1_1- and Σ^1_1-formulas, respectively, and the *bar rule*

$$(\mathrm{BR}) \qquad \begin{array}{l} \vdash \forall X(\exists x(x \in X) \to \exists x \in X(\forall y \in X)(\neg y \prec x)) \Longrightarrow \\ \vdash \forall x((\forall y \prec x)\phi(y) \to \phi(x)) \longrightarrow \forall x \phi(x)) . \end{array}$$

Let us abbreviate the first line in (BR), which expresses that every nonempty *set* has a $\prec$-least element, by $Wf(\prec)$ and the second line, which expresses the principle of transfinite induction along $\prec$ and is equivalent to the fact that the *class* $\{x \mid \phi(x)\}$ possesses a $\prec$-least element provided it is not empty, by $TI(\prec, \phi)$. The schema

$$(\mathrm{BI}) \qquad Wf(\prec) \longrightarrow TI(\prec, \phi)$$

is known as the schema of *bar induction*. The schema (BI) is usually much stronger than the rule (BR). The reasons for the weakness of the rule in comparison to the schema (BI) have been investigated by M. RATHJEN in [Rathjen 1989], where he showed that (BR) has the same strength as $(\mathrm{BI})^-$ in which we require that the definition of the relation $\prec$ must not contain parameters (not even number parameters).
Another nowadays prominent axiom system with proof-theoretic ordinal Γ_0 is the system $\mathbf{ATR_0}$ of autonomous transfinite recursions. This system has an axiom

$$\text{(TR)} \qquad Wf(\prec) \longrightarrow \exists X \mathcal{J}(\prec, X)$$

stating that, whenever there is a arithmetically definable well-ordered relation $\prec$, then we can construct the jump hierarchy over the field of this relation. The subscript $_0$ indicates that we have the *single axiom*

$$\text{(IA)} \qquad \forall X(\underline{0} \in X \wedge \forall x(x \in X \to x + \underline{1} \in X) \longrightarrow \forall x(x \in X))$$

instead of the *full schema* of mathematical induction.
Another more recent example is a subsystem of set theory introduced by G. JÄGER axiomatizing a set universe which is the admissible limit of admissibles (which means that its least standard model in the constructible hierarchy appears at the stage of the first recursively inaccessible ordinal) but requires no foundation at all. This system incorporates an infinity axiom and allows the proof of *axiom* β, which states that for every well-ordering there is an ordinal representing the order type of this well-ordering. Therefore it allows the construction of the stages of the constructible hierarchy below Γ_0 from the ordinal ω.

Part II

Towards Impredicative Proof Theory

Predicative axiom systems, i.e. axiom systems having proof-theoretic ordinals $\leq \Gamma_0$, allow the development of a good deal of mathematics as has been shown in the program of reverse mathematics by H. FRIEDMAN, S. SIMPSON, and others. However, these axioms systems form only a small portion of the commonly considered systems.
The definition of the proof-theoretic ordinal of an axiom system Ax is closely connected to the construction of partial models of Ax in the constructible hierarchy. The basic observation here is the SPECTOR-GANDY theorem, by which for every Π^1_1-sentence ϕ there is a Σ_1-sentence ψ in the language of set theory[3] such that

$$\mathcal{N} \models \phi \iff (\exists \alpha < \omega_1^{CK}) \mathsf{L}_\alpha \models \psi. \qquad (\dagger)$$

Indeed, we have nearly proven $(\dagger)$ by showing

$$\mathcal{N} \models \phi \iff (\exists \alpha < \omega_1^{CK}) \models^{\alpha} \phi$$

[3] A Σ_1-sentence is a sentence of the form $\exists x \psi(x)$ where $\psi(x)$ contains no unbounded quantifiers.

in theorem 18. All that is lacking is a proof that $\models^{\alpha} \phi$ can be described by an Σ_1-formula in set theory. But this is not too hard to do. Thus determining the proof-theoretic ordinal for Ax is closely connected to the determination of the least model for the $\Sigma_1(\mathsf{L}_{\omega_1^{CK}})$-sentences provable from Ax. The exact connection is controlled by the Second Elimination Theorem 26 which gives the proof-theoretic ordinal $\varphi_{\alpha_1}(\ldots(\varphi_{\alpha_n}(0)\ldots))$ if $\alpha =_{NF} \omega^{\alpha_1} + \ldots + \omega^{\alpha_n}$ is the least stage at which L_α is a model for the $\Sigma_1(\mathsf{L}_{\omega_1^{CK}})$-sentences provable from Ax. Sufficiently strong systems, however, have strongly critical proof-theoretic ordinals which implies that for them the proof-theoretic ordinal and the stage of the least $\Sigma_1(\mathsf{L}_{\omega_1^{CK}})$ model in the constructible hierarchy coincide. The proof-theoretic ordinal of an axiom system Ax thus tells us how much of the universe is used by Ax.
Call a function $f\colon \mathsf{L} \longrightarrow \mathsf{L}$ a provable ω_1^{CK}-recursive function of an axiom system Ax, iff the graph of f is Σ_1-definable and

$$\mathrm{Ax} \vdash (\forall x \in \mathsf{L}_{\omega_1^{CK}})(\exists y \in \mathsf{L}_{\omega_1^{CK}})(f(x) = y).$$

It is not hard to show that the $\Sigma_1(\mathsf{L}_{\omega_1^{CK}})$ and the $\Pi_2(\mathsf{L}_{\omega_1^{CK}})$ models of Ax coincide and we thus get

$$|\mathrm{Ax}| = \min\{\alpha \mid f[\mathsf{L}_\alpha] \subseteq \mathsf{L}_\alpha \ \text{ for all provably } \omega_1^{CK}\text{-recursive functions } f \text{ of Ax}\}.$$

On the other hand, building a model in the constructible hierarchy L along a 'constructively given' well-ordering may be considered as a 'constructive' process. Thus we are back at the roots of proof theory, which started with 'constructive' consistency proofs.
What we can see thus far is that for impredicative axiom systems the least $\Sigma_1(\mathsf{L}_{\omega_1^{CK}})$-model cannot be produced by a bootstrapping process, because any such process will, as we have seen in the previous section, stop below Γ_0. Thus in order to build 'constructive' $\Sigma_1(\mathsf{L}_{\omega_1^{CK}})$-models we need points from outside. The addition of these 'outer points' will later require a completely new technique in the ordinal analysis of impredicative systems which is sloppily described by the term *collapsing*. Collapsing will 'collapse' the 'outer points' into the manageable part of the 'constructive' $\Sigma_1(\mathsf{L}_{\omega_1^{CK}})$-model. A more precise description of collapsing will appear in a later section of this paper.
Of course it will be necessary to have 'outer points' already in the construction of the ordinals – although, from the point of view of pure definability, it is possible to *define* ordinals larger than Γ_0, the problem is to justify their well-foundedness by a bootstrapping process.
In the next sections we will give a simple example of an ordinal analysis for an impredicative system. Since ordinal analysis and determination of weak models in the constructible hierarchy are closely connected problems, we will choose an example which is a subsystem of set theory for which we have models in L directly. Subsystems of second-order PEANO ARITHMETIC are canonically embeddable into subsystems of set theory. Thus ordinal analyses for subsystems of set theory in general also produce upper bounds for the proof-theoretic ordinals of subsystems of second-order PEANO ARITHMETIC.

6 Subsystems of Set Theory

Our example of a simple impredicative subsystem of set theory will be the axiom system **KP**ω of KRIPKE-PLATEK set theory with the axiom of infinity (indicated by adding the letter ω). The theory **KP** has been studied in full detail in BARWISE's book [Barwise 1969]. The reader who wants to know more about the model theory and the models of **KP** is referred to this book.
KRIPKE-PLATEK set theory is formulated in the language of set theory, i.e. its only nonlogical symbol is the membership symbol $\in$. It is very close to a predicative axiom system because of the care which has been taken in choosing its axioms. From the proof-theoretic point of view only those axioms are critical which incorporate either the existence of possibly impredicatively defined sets or the possibility of strong inductions. Possible impredicative axioms are comprehension scheme and collection scheme. Therefore one restricts comprehension to Δ_0-formulas and collection to collections which can be defined by Δ_0-formulas. Since Δ_0-formulas contain only bounded quantifiers, they are absolute with respect to transitive models. This implies that enlarging (or shrinking) the universe does not change the meaning of Δ_0-formulas. Therefore sets defined by Δ_0-formulas are ideal objects in a bootstrapping process because they will not change their extension during the construction process. Using this as the basic idea, it has been shown by FEFERMAN (and later reproved in a more direct way by JÄGER) that **KP**$\mathcal{N}$ – a system with the structure of natural numbers as urelement structure – becomes predicative if the foundation axiom is only required for sets (and not for classes).

The axioms of **KP** are the universal closures of the following formulas.

(Extensionality) $\forall x(x \in a \leftrightarrow x \in b) \longrightarrow a = b.$

(Foundation) $\exists x\phi(x) \longrightarrow \exists x\,(\phi(x) \wedge (\forall y{\in}x)\neg\phi(y)),$
which says that any class $\{x \mid \phi(x)\}$ definable by an arbitrary formula $\phi(x)$ in the language of set theory has an $\in$-least element.

(Pair) $\forall x\forall y\exists a(x \in a \wedge y \in a),$
which expresses the existence of a set containing $\{x, y\}$.

(Union) $\exists b(\forall y{\in}a)(\forall x{\in}y)(x \in b),$
which expresses the existence of a set including $\bigcup a$.

(Δ_0-Separation) $\exists b\forall x\,(x \in b \leftrightarrow x \in a \wedge \phi(x))\,,$
for Δ_0-formulas $\phi(x)$, which allows one to separate out as a set the elements of a satisfying $\phi(x)$.

(Δ_0-Collection) $(\forall x{\in}a)\exists y\phi(x,y) \longrightarrow \exists z(\forall x{\in}a)(\exists y{\in}z)\phi(x,y)$
which assures the existence of a set containing all elements of the collection $\{y_x \mid \phi(x, y_x)\}_{x\in a}$ for a Δ_0-formula $\phi(x, y)$.

The theory **KP** is already astonishingly rich. It allows the introduction of most of the important notions of set theory. So we may talk about ordinals and define the notions of limit and successor ordinals. We introduce a further axiom,

(Infinity) $\exists\xi\,\mathrm{Lim}(\xi)$,

assuring the existence of at least one limit ordinal. We call the theory with infinity axiom $\mathbf{KP}\omega$. The least standard model of $\mathbf{KP}\omega$ in the constructible hierarchy is at level ω_1^{CK}. Thus any Σ_1-formula provable in $\mathbf{KP}\omega$ is a $\Sigma_1(\mathsf{L}_{\omega_1^{CK}})$-formula. Ordinal analysis for $\mathbf{KP}\omega$ is therefore equivalent to the determination of the least level at which the constructible hierarchy is a model for the Σ_1-sentences provable in $\mathbf{KP}\omega$. We will determine these levels with the help of an infinitary system similar to that we used in the determination of the proof-theoretic ordinal of PEANO ARITHMETIC and the limits of predicativity. But, as already pointed out in the beginning of the previous section, the construction will need 'outer points'. Thus it is first necessary to develop a segment of the ordinals based on an 'outer point'. This will be done in the following section.

7 More Ordinals

Let us return to the material of Section 3 in which we developed a segment of the ordinals below the first strongly critical ordinal Γ_0. There is an alternative way to access this segment. We could have defined the *additive hull* $\tilde{C}(\beta)$ ($\tilde{C}$ for closure) of an ordinal β inductively by the following clauses:

- $\beta \cup \{0\} \subseteq \tilde{C}(\beta)$.
- If $\{\xi,\eta\} \subseteq \tilde{C}(\beta)$ then $\xi+\eta \in \tilde{C}(\beta)$.

It is obvious that

$$\mathbb{H} = \{\xi \mid \xi \notin \tilde{C}(\xi)\}. \tag{44}$$

This implies that $\tilde{C}(\beta)$ is always the first additively indecomposable ordinal $\geq \beta$. Let $\tilde{\vartheta}_0$ denote the enumerating function of $\mathbb{H}$. Then

$$\tilde{\vartheta}_0(\alpha) = \phi_0(\alpha) = \omega^\alpha.$$

We can iterate the concept of additive hulls by closing a hull also under all enumerating functions $\tilde{\vartheta}_\xi$ of previously defined additive hulls $\tilde{C}_\xi(\beta)$. This suggests to define the *autonomously α^{th}-iterated additive hull of an ordinal β* inductively by the following clauses:

($\tilde{C}_0$) $\beta \cup \{0\} \subseteq \tilde{C}_\alpha(\beta)$.
($\tilde{C}_1$) *If* $\{\xi,\eta\} \subseteq \tilde{C}_\alpha(\beta)$ *then* $\xi+\eta \in \tilde{C}_\alpha(\beta)$.
($\tilde{C}_2$) *If* $\{\xi,\eta\} \subseteq \tilde{C}_\alpha(\beta)$ *and* $\xi < \alpha$ *then* $\tilde{\vartheta}_\xi(\eta) \in \tilde{C}_\alpha(\beta)$.
($\tilde{\vartheta}_\alpha$) $\tilde{\vartheta}_\alpha$ *is the enumerating function of the class* $In(\alpha) := \{\xi \mid \xi \notin \tilde{C}_\alpha(\xi)\}$ *of α-inaccessible ordinals.*

From the above definition we obtain immediately the following consequences:

$$\alpha \leq \xi \text{ and } \beta \leq \eta \;\Rightarrow\; \tilde{C}_\alpha(\beta) \subseteq \tilde{C}_\xi(\eta) \text{ and } \tilde{\vartheta}_\alpha(\beta) \leq \tilde{\vartheta}_\xi(\eta). \tag{45}$$

$$\beta < \gamma \;\Rightarrow\; \tilde{\vartheta}_\alpha(\beta) < \tilde{\vartheta}_\alpha(\gamma). \tag{46}$$

$$\beta \leq \tilde{\vartheta}_\alpha(\beta). \tag{47}$$

$$[\alpha,\delta) \cup \tilde{C}_\alpha(\beta) = \emptyset \;\Rightarrow\; \tilde{C}_\alpha(\beta) = \tilde{C}_\delta(\beta). \tag{48}$$

$$\tilde{C}_\lambda(\beta) = \bigcup_{\xi<\lambda} \tilde{C}_\xi(\beta) \quad \text{for limit ordinals } \lambda. \tag{49}$$

Choose some $\beta < \omega_1$ and let η be $\min\{\xi \mid \beta \leq \xi \notin \tilde{C}_\alpha(\beta)\}$. Then $\eta \subseteq \beta$ which implies $\tilde{C}_\alpha(\eta) = \tilde{C}_\alpha(\beta)$. Hence $\eta \notin \tilde{C}_\alpha(\beta) = \tilde{C}_\alpha(\eta)$ which entails $\beta \leq \eta \in In(\alpha)$. So we have proven that

$$\textit{the class } In(\alpha) \textit{ is cofinal in } \omega_1. \tag{50}$$

As an obvious consequence of that we get:

$$\begin{array}{ll} (i) & \tilde{\vartheta}_\alpha \textit{ maps the ordinals below } \omega_1 \textit{ into } \omega_1. \\ (ii) & \tilde{C}_\alpha(\beta) \subset \omega_1 \textit{ for } \beta < \omega_1. \end{array} \tag{51}$$

To establish the connection with the φ-functions of Section 3 we observe that

$$In(\alpha+1) = In(\alpha)' \cup \{\tilde{\vartheta}_\alpha(\eta) \mid \alpha \notin \tilde{C}_\alpha(\tilde{\vartheta}_\alpha(\eta))\} \tag{52}$$

and

$$In(\lambda) = \bigcap_{\xi<\lambda} In(\xi) \quad \textit{for limit ordinals } \lambda. \tag{53}$$

Statement (53) is obvious and the proof of (52) is easy because $\eta < \tilde{\vartheta}_\alpha(\eta)$ and $\alpha \in \tilde{C}_\alpha(\tilde{\vartheta}_\alpha(\eta)) \subseteq \tilde{C}_{\alpha+1}(\tilde{\vartheta}_\alpha(\eta))$ entail $\tilde{\vartheta}_\alpha(\eta) \in \tilde{C}_{\alpha+1}(\tilde{\vartheta}_\alpha(\eta))$, i.e. $\tilde{\vartheta}_\alpha(\eta) \notin In(\alpha+1)$, which gives the direction from left to right. On the other hand $\alpha \notin \tilde{C}_\alpha(\tilde{\vartheta}_\alpha(\eta))$ entails $\tilde{C}_\alpha(\tilde{\vartheta}_\alpha(\eta)) = \tilde{C}_{\alpha+1}(\tilde{\vartheta}_\alpha(\eta))$ and thus $\tilde{\vartheta}_\alpha(\eta) \notin \tilde{C}_{\alpha+1}(\tilde{\vartheta}_\alpha(\eta))$, i.e. $\tilde{\vartheta}_\alpha(\eta) \in In(\alpha+1)$. If $\tilde{\vartheta}_\alpha(\eta) = \eta$ the assumption $\tilde{\vartheta}_\alpha(\eta) \notin In(\alpha+1)$, i.e. $\tilde{\vartheta}_\alpha(\eta) \in \tilde{C}_{\alpha+1}(\tilde{\vartheta}_\alpha(\eta))$ implies $\tilde{\vartheta}_\alpha(\eta) = \tilde{\vartheta}_\mu(\xi)$ for some $\mu \leq \alpha$ and $\xi < \eta$ and thus leads to the contradiction $\eta = \tilde{\vartheta}_\mu(\xi) < \tilde{\vartheta}_\mu(\eta) \leq \tilde{\vartheta}_\alpha(\eta) = \eta$. □

Another observation, which we don't want to prove in detail right now, is

$$\tilde{C}_\alpha(0) = \tilde{\vartheta}_\alpha(0). \tag{54}$$

The ordinals in $\tilde{C}_\alpha(0)$ have as notations terms which are built up solely from 0, $+$, and $\tilde{\vartheta}$. Since $\tilde{C}_\alpha(0)$ is countable for all ordinals α, there is an ordinal σ_0 such that the hierarchy of sets $\tilde{C}_\alpha(0)$ becomes stationary for all $\alpha \geq \sigma_0$. Thus $\tilde{C}_{\sigma_0}(0) = \tilde{C}_{\omega_1}(0)$ is the largest set we can obtain and it is again not too hard to show that $\alpha \in \tilde{C}_\alpha(\tilde{\vartheta}_\alpha(\eta))$ holds for all $\alpha \in \tilde{C}_{\omega_1}(0)$. Thus by (52)

$$In(\alpha+1) = In(\alpha)',$$

which together with (44) and (53) entails that the $In(\alpha)$-hierarchy and the $Cr(\alpha)$-hierarchy from Section 3 coincide. This can be extended to a proof that $\Gamma_0 = \sigma_0 = \tilde{\vartheta}_{\omega_1}(0)$ and $\tilde{\vartheta}_\alpha(\beta) = \varphi_\alpha(\beta)$ for all ordinals $\alpha, \beta < \Gamma_0$.

To make the autonomously iterated additive hulls more powerful we will have to start with more ordinals from the beginning, i.e. we will have to put ordinals as parameters into $\tilde{C}_\alpha(\beta)$ already at step $\tilde{C}_0$. To obtain a segment whose size suffices for the ordinal analysis of **KP**ω it will be enough to use just one parameter. However, to get the full strength of the iteration, we have to be sure that this additional parameter is indeed an 'outer point', i.e. that it is outside the segment which we will eventually obtain. But all we know of this segment so far is that it is countable. Thus to be on the safe side we will use ω_1 as parameter. Therefore we alter clause $(\tilde{C}_0)$ to

(C_0) $\beta \cup \{0\} \cup \{\omega_1\} \subseteq C_\alpha(\beta)$.

This will not change properties (45) – (49). Moreover (50) as well as (52) can be obtained with the same proof, while (52) and (53) remain true as well. Thus we still have

$$In(\alpha+1) = In(\alpha)' \cup \{\tilde{\vartheta}_\alpha(\eta) \mid \alpha \notin C_\alpha(\tilde{\vartheta}_\alpha(\eta))\},$$

but in contrast to the previous situation the set $\{\xi \mid \alpha \notin C_\alpha(\xi)\}$ will no longer be empty (we have for instance $\tilde{\vartheta}_{\omega_1}(0) \notin C_{\tilde{\vartheta}_{\omega_1}(0)}(0)$). Therefore we define sets

$$\overline{In}(\alpha) := \{\xi \mid \xi \notin C_\alpha(\xi)\} \cap \{\xi \mid \alpha \in C_\alpha(\xi)\} \tag{55}$$

and new functions ϑ_α by altering clause $(\tilde{\vartheta}_\alpha)$ to

(ϑ_α) ϑ_α is the enumerating function of the class $\overline{In}(\alpha)$.

Summing up, we have

Definition 27 *(The autonomously iterated additive hull of an ordinal β)*
(C_0) $\beta \cup \{0\} \cup \{\omega_1\} \subseteq C_\alpha(\beta)$.
(C_1) If $\{\xi,\eta\} \subseteq C_\alpha(\beta)$ then $\xi+\eta \in C_\alpha(\beta)$.
(C_2) If $\{\xi,\eta\} \subseteq C_\alpha(\beta)$ and $\xi < \alpha$ then $\vartheta_\xi(\eta) \in C_\alpha(\beta)$.
(ϑ_α) ϑ_α is the enumerating function of the class $\overline{In}(\alpha) := \{\xi \mid \xi \notin C_\alpha(\xi) \wedge \alpha \in C_\alpha(\xi)\}$.

We do, however, emphasize that even with these alterations the new definition "endextends" the previous one, i.e. we still have $\Gamma_0 = \vartheta_{\omega_1}(0)$ and $\vartheta_\alpha(\eta) = \varphi_\alpha(\eta)$ for $\alpha, \xi < \Gamma_0$. But now the hierarchy of autonomously iterated additive hulls no longer collapses at ω_1 but we have $C_{\omega_1}(0) \neq C_{\omega_1+1}(0)$ because $\omega_1 \in C_{\omega_1}(0)$. For cardinality reasons it is clear that the hierachy collapses at $C_{\omega_2}(\beta)$, where ω_2 is the first regular ordinal larger than ω_1. Thus the largest class which can be denoted by terms using only the parameters 0 and ω_1 is $C_{\omega_2}(0)$. Properties (45) – (49) also hold for the sets $C_\alpha(\beta)$ and the functions ϑ_α with the exception of the weak monontonicity in the argument α as it is stated in (45). Not so easy to check is the revised version of (50).

Lemma 28 *For $\alpha \in C_{\omega_2}(0)$ the class $\overline{In}(\alpha)$ is cofinal in ω_1 as well as in ω_2.*

The proof follows that of (50). We define $\eta := \min\{\xi \mid \beta \leq \xi \notin C_\alpha(\beta) \wedge \alpha \in C_\alpha(\xi)\}$ and have to assure that $\beta < \omega_i$ entails $\eta < \omega_i$ for $i \in \{1,2\}$. For this it is sufficient to have

$$\alpha \in C_\alpha(\omega_1) \text{ for all } \alpha \in C_{\omega_2}(0). \tag{56}$$

To assure this we first prove the following lemma.

Lemma 29 *If $\eta \notin C_\xi(\eta)$, $\alpha \in C_\alpha(\eta)$, $\alpha < \xi$, and $\beta < \eta$ then $\vartheta_\alpha(\beta) < \eta$.*

This is easily obtained by induction on β. We have $\vartheta_\alpha(\rho) < \eta$ for all $\rho < \beta$ by the induction hypothesis. Since $\eta \in \overline{In}(\alpha)$, this entails $\vartheta_\alpha(\beta) \leq \eta$. But $\alpha \in C_\alpha(\eta) \subseteq C_\xi(\eta)$ and $\beta < \eta \subseteq C_\xi(\eta)$ imply $\vartheta_\alpha(\beta) \in C_\xi(\eta)$, which excludes equality. □

As a consequence we get

$$\omega_1 \leq \gamma \notin C_\alpha(\gamma) \quad \Longrightarrow \quad C_\alpha(\gamma) = \gamma. \tag{57}$$

Now $\gamma \subseteq C_\alpha(\gamma)$ holds by definition and

$$\xi \in C_\alpha(\gamma) \quad \Longrightarrow \quad \xi < \gamma$$

follows immediately by induction on the definition of $\xi \in C_\alpha(\gamma)$ and Lemma 29. □

Since we always have $\xi \in C_\xi(\vartheta_\xi(\eta))$ we get by (57) that

$$\omega_1 < \vartheta_\xi(\eta) \Longrightarrow \xi < \vartheta_\xi(\eta). \tag{58}$$

This already enables us to prove (56) by induction on the definition of $\alpha \in C_{\omega_2}(0)$. If $\alpha \leq \omega_1$ or if α is additively decomposable then the claim is either obvious or immediate from the induction hypothesis. Thus let $\omega_1 < \alpha = \vartheta_\xi(\eta)$ with $\{\xi, \eta\} \subseteq C_{\omega_2}(0)$. Then we have $\xi \in C_\alpha(\omega_1) \cap \alpha$ by the induction hypothesis, (58), and (45) and $\eta \in C_\alpha(\omega_1)$ by induction hypothesis and $\eta \leq \alpha$. Hence $\alpha \in C_\alpha(\omega_1)$ by (C_2). This also completes the proof of Lemma 28. □

Corollary 30 *For any ordinal $\alpha \in C_{\omega_2}(0)$ the function ϑ_α maps ω_1 into ω_1.*

All the ordinals in $C_{\omega_2}(0)$ can be denoted by terms which are built up from 0, ω_1, $+$, and ϑ. However, this notation is not unique. For additively decomposable terms we already introduced a notion in normal form which is $\alpha =_{NF} \alpha_1 + \ldots + \alpha_n$. For additively indecomposable ordinals in $C_{\omega_2}(0)$ of the form $\vartheta_\xi(\eta)$ we define

$$\alpha =_{NF} \vartheta_\xi(\eta) \quad :\Longleftrightarrow \quad \alpha = \vartheta_\xi(\eta) \text{ and } \eta < \alpha.$$

This *normal form* denotation of an additively indecomposable ordinal is obviously uniquely determined. Furthermore we can show that

$$\text{if } \alpha =_{NF} \vartheta_\xi(\eta) \text{ and } \alpha =_{NF} \vartheta_\mu(\nu), \text{ then } \mu = \xi \text{ and } \nu = \eta. \tag{59}$$

To check (59) by reductio ad absurdum assume $\mu < \xi$. Since $\mu \in C_\mu(\alpha) \subseteq C_\xi(\alpha)$ and $\nu < \alpha \subseteq C_\xi(\alpha)$ we obtain $\vartheta_\xi(\eta) = \vartheta_\mu(\nu) \in C_\xi(\vartheta_\xi(\eta))$, which is a contradiction. Thus $\mu = \xi$, which in turn implies $\nu = \eta$ because of the strict monotonicity of the functions ϑ_ξ. □

We have the following four types of ordinal terms in $C_{\omega_2}(0)$:

- 0
- ω_1

- additively decomposable ordinals $\alpha =_{NF} \alpha_1 + \ldots + \alpha_n$
- additively indecomposabel ordinals $\alpha =_{NF} \vartheta_\xi(\eta)$

In the following we will not distinguish between ordinals and their notations as ordinal terms. Whenever we use an ordinal term denoting an ordinal we tacitly assume that this term is in normal form. The set $AC(\alpha)$ of *additively indecomposable components* of an ordinal α is defined in the obvious way by

$$AC(\alpha) := \begin{cases} \emptyset & \text{if } \alpha = 0; \\ AC(\alpha_1) \cup \ldots \cup AC(\alpha_n) & \text{if } \alpha =_{NF} \alpha_1 + \ldots + \alpha_n; \\ \{\alpha\} & \text{if } \alpha \in \mathbb{H}. \end{cases}$$

Of more importance, however, are the sets $AC_{\omega_1}(\alpha)$ of *additively indecomposable components hereditarily less than* ω_1. These are given by

$$AC_{\omega_1}(\alpha) := \begin{cases} \emptyset & \text{if } \alpha = 0 \text{ or } \alpha = \omega_1; \\ AC_{\omega_1}(\alpha_1) \cup \ldots \cup AC_{\omega_1}(\alpha_n) & \text{if } \alpha =_{NF} \alpha_1 + \ldots + \alpha_n; \\ \{\alpha\} & \text{if } \alpha \in \mathbb{H} \cap \omega_1; \\ AC_{\omega_1}(\xi) \cup AC_{\omega_1}(\eta) & \text{if } \omega_1 < \alpha =_{NF} \vartheta_\xi(\eta). \end{cases}$$

Then we obtain for ordinals $\alpha \in C_{\omega_2}(0)$ that

$$\alpha \in C_\xi(\eta) \implies AC(\alpha) \cup AC_{\omega_1}(\alpha) \subseteq C_\xi(\eta) \tag{60}$$

and

$$AC_{\omega_1}(\alpha) \subseteq C_\xi(\eta) \text{ and } \alpha \leq \xi \implies \alpha \in C_\xi(\eta). \tag{61}$$

While (60) is obvious, the proof of (61) makes use of (58). We prove (61) by induction on the definition of $\alpha \in C_{\omega_2}(0)$. The only nontrivial case is $\omega_1 < \alpha =_{NF} \vartheta_{\alpha_1}(\alpha_2)$. Here we obtain $\{\alpha_1, \alpha_2\} \subseteq C_\xi(\eta)$ by the induction hypothesis. Since $\alpha_1 \lessdot \alpha$ by (58) and $\alpha \leq \xi$ we obtain $\alpha \in C_\xi(\eta)$ by (C_2). □

We may strengthen (60) to

$$\text{if } \eta \notin C_\xi(\eta) \text{ and } \alpha \in C_\xi(\eta) \text{ then } AC_{\omega_1}(\alpha) \subseteq \eta. \tag{62}$$

The proof is by induction on the definition of $\alpha \in C_\xi(\eta)$. The claim is trivial for $\alpha \in \{0, \omega_1\}$ and immediate from the induction hypothesis if α is additively decomposable or $\omega_1 < \alpha =_{NF} \vartheta_\mu(\nu)$. If $\alpha =_{NF} \vartheta_\mu(\nu) < \omega_1$ then we have $\mu < \xi$ and by the induction hypothesis that $AC_{\omega_1}(\mu) \cup AC_{\omega_1}(\nu) \subseteq \eta$. So we obtain $\mu \in C_\mu(\eta)$ by (61) and thus $\vartheta_\mu(\nu) < \eta$ by Lemma 29. □

Since $\vartheta_\xi(\eta) \notin C_\xi(\vartheta_\xi(\eta))$ it follows from Corollary 30, (58), and (62) that

$$C_\xi(\vartheta_\xi(\eta)) \cap \eta^+ = \vartheta_\xi(\eta), \tag{63}$$

where α^+ denotes the least regular ordinal which is bigger than α, i.e. $\alpha^+ = \omega_1$ for $\alpha < \omega_1$ and $\alpha^+ = \omega_2$ otherwise.
From (63) and (57) we can conclude that

$$\text{if } \alpha^+ = \eta^+ \text{ then } \alpha < \vartheta_\alpha(\eta). \tag{64}$$

We observe that from (56) we obtain for $\omega_1 \leq \xi$ that

$$\xi \in \overline{In}(\alpha+1) \iff \xi \in \overline{In}(\alpha)' \tag{65}$$

and

$$\xi \in \overline{In}(\lambda) \iff \xi \in \bigcap_{\mu<\lambda} \overline{In}(\mu) \quad \text{for limit } \lambda. \tag{66}$$

For $\eta \geq \omega_1$ we therefore have $\vartheta_\xi(\eta) = \varphi_\xi(\eta)$ and hence $\vartheta_0(\eta) = \omega^\eta$. As an exercise the reader may check that $\Gamma_0 = \vartheta_{\omega_1}(0)$ and $\varphi_\xi(\eta) = \vartheta_\xi(\eta)$ for $\xi, \eta < \Gamma_0$.
Another consequence of (61) and Lemma 29 is that

$$\text{if } \xi < \alpha \text{ and } AC_{\omega_1}(\xi) \cap \{\eta\} \subseteq \vartheta_\alpha(\beta) \text{ then } \vartheta_\xi(\eta) < \vartheta_\alpha(\beta). \tag{67}$$

Putting these together yields the following lemma.

Lemma 31 $\vartheta_\xi(\eta) < \vartheta_\alpha(\beta)$ *holds iff at least one of the following conditions is satisfied:*

$\xi < \alpha$ *and* $AC_{\omega_1}(\xi) \cap \{\eta\} \subseteq \vartheta_\alpha(\beta)$.
$\xi = \alpha$ *and* $\eta < \beta$.
$\alpha \leq \xi$ *and* $(\exists \nu \in AC_{\omega_1}(\alpha) \cup \{\beta\})(\vartheta_\xi(\eta) \leq \nu)$.

□

If we assume $\alpha \in C_\alpha(0)$ and define $\eta := \min\{\xi \mid \xi \notin C_\alpha(0)\}$ then we get $\eta \subseteq C_\alpha(0)$, which entails $\eta \leq \vartheta_\alpha(0)$ and $C_\alpha(\eta) = C_\alpha(0)$. Hence $\eta \in \overline{In}(\alpha)$ and thus also $\vartheta_\alpha(0) \leq \eta$. So we can conclude that

$$\text{if } \alpha \in C_\alpha(0) \text{ then } C_\alpha(0) = C_\alpha(\vartheta_\alpha(0)) \tag{68}$$

and hence that

$$C_\alpha(\vartheta_\alpha(\beta)+1) = C_\alpha(\vartheta_\alpha(\beta+1)) \tag{69}$$

by analogous considerations.
Without going into the details we just mention that by an arithmetization of the ordinal terms in normal form which denote the ordinals in $C_{\omega_2}(0)$ we obtain a primitive recursive set of codes on which the less than relation which is induced by the order relation on the denoted ordinals is primitive recursive.
According to (69) the segment of ordinals contained in $C_{\omega_2}(0)$ could be $\vartheta_{\omega_2}(0)$, if we had $\omega_2 \in C_{\omega_2}(0)$. We did not put ω_2 in the additive hulls since there is no need for a system of this strength in this paper. So we just let $\vartheta_{\omega_2}(0)$ denote the segment in $C_{\omega_2}(0)$.
Let us recall that the reason to opt for ω_1 as an additional parameter in the definition of the autonomously iterated additive hulls was the fact that this ordinal is safely outside the eventually obtained segment. Now, after having finished the development of the ordinal system, one would easily guess that any ordinal greater than $\vartheta_{\omega_2}(0)$ would work equally well. This is in fact true. A proof for a somewhat different but closely related system is given in [Pohlers 1989]. To emphasize that ω_1 might be replaced by ordinals greater than $\vartheta_{\omega_2}(0)$ we will hereafter use the

symbol Ω in all places where we first used ω_1. Thus Ω is an ordinal constant whose standard interpretation is ω_1. Taking into account that the set $C_{\omega_2}(0)$ and the order relation on it are primitive recursive we can conclude that $\vartheta_{\omega_2}(0) < \omega_1^{CK}$. Thus ω_1^{CK} is a possible interpretation for the symbol Ω. In the following sections one should always think of ω_1^{CK} as the intended interpretation for Ω.
Finally let us once more emphasize the facts which will play the key roles in the ordinal analysis of $KP\omega$:

- $\vartheta_\alpha(\eta)$ is defined for all α and η below ω_2.
- For $\eta < \omega_1$ the function $\lambda\xi.\vartheta_\xi(\eta)$ is a collapsing function, i.e. $\vartheta_\xi(\eta) < \omega_1$ holds for $\eta < \omega_1$.

We close this section by a remark which indicates the connection of the ϑ_α-functions to other – perhaps more familiar – ordinal functions. The functions ϑ_α are very close to the functions $\overline{\theta}_\alpha$ developed by BUCHHOLZ (and described, for example, in [Schütte 1977]) which in turn are obtained from the FEFERMAN-ACZEL functions θ_α. The $\overline{\theta}_\alpha$–functions are exactly the fixed-point-free versions of the ϑ_α-functions. Both families of functions are also closely connected to the ψ-functions as they have been used in [Pohlers 1989]. The precise connection is in general not so simple to state but for characteristic ordinals it is often easier. So, for example, we have $\psi(\varepsilon_{\Omega+1}) = \vartheta_{\varepsilon_{\Omega+1}}(0)$ for the HOWARD-ordinal.

8 A Satisfaction Relation for Ramified Set Theory

In this section we will first develop a satisfaction relation for the constructible hierarchy L. Since the constructible hierarchy comes in stages, we refer to its language as the language $\mathcal{L}_{RS}$ of *ramified set theory.*
By $\mathcal{L}_\in$ we denote the language of set theory. An $\mathcal{L}_\in$-formula ϕ is called a Δ_0-formula iff all of its quantifiers are bounded, i.e. quantifiers of the form $(\forall x{\in}u)$ or $(\exists x{\in}u)$. A Σ_1-formula (Π_1-formula) is a formula $\exists x\phi(x)$ $(\forall x\phi(x))$, where $\phi(x)$ is a Δ_0-formula. The class of Σ-formulas is the smallest class which contains all Δ_0-formulas and is closed under the positive boolean operations $\wedge$ and $\vee$, bounded quantification and unbounded $\exists$-quantification. The class of Π-formulas is defined dually. For an $\mathcal{L}_\in$-formula ϕ let ϕ^u be the formula obtained from ϕ by restricting all its quantifiers to u.
The stages L_α of the constructible hierarchy L have been defined in (43).
The definition of the set terms of the language $\mathcal{L}_{RS}$ follows the same pattern.

Definition 32 (The RS-terms and their stages)
1. For every ordinal α $\check{\mathsf{L}}_\alpha$ is an RS-term of stage α.
2. If $\phi(x_1,\ldots,x_n)$ is an $\mathcal{L}_\in$-formula in which no variables other than $x_1,\ldots,x_n$ occur free and $s_1,\ldots,s_n$ are RS-terms of stages less than α then $\{x{\in}\check{\mathsf{L}}_\alpha \mid \phi(s_1,\ldots,s_n)^{\check{\mathsf{L}}_\alpha}\}$ is an RS-term of stage α.
We denote the stage of an RS-term s by $|s|$.

For every set $a \in \mathsf{L}$ we have an corresponding RS-term $\check{a}$ which is defined in the obvious way such that

$$(\check{a})^{\mathsf{L}} = a.$$

Vice versa we also have an interpretation s^{L} for every RS-term s which is given by

- $(\check{\mathsf{L}}_\alpha)^{\mathsf{L}} := \mathsf{L}_\alpha$,
- $\{x\in\check{\mathsf{L}}_\alpha \mid \phi(x, s_1 \ldots, s_n)\}^{\mathsf{L}} := \{x\in\mathsf{L}_\alpha \mid \mathsf{L}_\alpha \models \phi(x, s_1^{\mathsf{L}}, \ldots, s_n^{\mathsf{L}}\}$.

In view of this correspondence we will not longer distinguish between sets in the constructible hierarchy and their corresponding RS-terms. It should always be clear from the context which one is meant.
The $\mathcal{L}_{RS}$-formulas are obtained from $\mathcal{L}_\in$-formulas by restricting all quantifiers to some $\check{\mathsf{L}}_\alpha$ and replacing ıall free variables by RS-terms of stages $< \alpha$. By the stage $\mathsf{stg}(\phi)$ of an $\mathcal{L}_{RS}$ formula ϕ we understand the maximum stage of RS-terms occurring in ϕ.
An $\mathcal{L}_{RS}$-formula is $\Sigma_1(\mathsf{L}_\alpha)$, $\Sigma(\mathsf{L}_\alpha)$, $\Pi_1(\mathsf{L}_\alpha), \ldots$ iff $\phi \equiv \psi(s_1, \ldots, s_n)^{\mathsf{L}_\alpha}$ for some Σ_1-, Σ-, Π_1-, ...-formula $\psi(x_1, \ldots, x_n)$ and RS-terms $s_1, \ldots, s_n \in RS_\alpha$.
Again we assume that $\mathcal{L}_{RS}$ is formulated in a TAIT language, i.e. we have $\in$ and $\notin$ as basic symbols and consider $\neg\phi$ as defined. The equality symbol will not be counted among the basic symbols but is considered to be defined by

$$a = b \quad :\Longleftrightarrow \quad (\forall x\in a)(x \in b) \wedge (\forall x\in b)(x \in a).$$

We let RS_α be the set of RS-terms of stages $< \alpha$.
To define the satisfaction relation for $\mathcal{L}_{RS}$ as similarly as possible to that for $\mathcal{L}_\infty$ we introduce *infinity types* for $\mathcal{L}_{RS}$-formulas.

Definition 33 (The infinity type of an RS-formula) *The infinity type of a formula ϕ will be defined as the set* it(ϕ) *of RS formulas such that formulas ϕ of $\bigvee$-type will be semantically equivalent to $\bigvee$*it(ϕ) *and formulas of $\bigwedge$-type to $\bigwedge$*it(ϕ)*. For formulas ϕ of $\bigvee$-type* it(ϕ) *is given recursively by the following clauses:*

- $\mathrm{it}(a \in \check{\mathsf{L}}_\alpha) = \{(s = a) \mid s \in RS_\alpha\}$.
- $\mathrm{it}(a \in \{x\in\check{\mathsf{L}}_\alpha \mid \phi(x)\}) = \{(s = a) \wedge \phi(s) \mid s \in RS_\alpha\}$.
- $\mathrm{it}(\phi \vee \psi) = \{\phi, \psi\}$.
- $\mathrm{it}\,((\exists x\in\mathsf{L}_\alpha)\phi(x)) = \{\phi(s) \mid s \in RS_\alpha\}$.
- $\mathrm{it}\,((\exists x\in b)\phi(x)) = \{\psi(s) \wedge \phi(s) \mid s \in RS_\alpha\}$ *if* $b = \{x\in\mathsf{L}_\alpha \mid \psi(x)\}$

These are all the formulas of $\bigvee$-type. If $\neg\phi$ is a formula of $\bigvee$-type then ϕ is a formula of $\bigwedge$-type and we put

- $\mathrm{it}(\phi) = \{\neg\psi \mid \psi \in \mathrm{it}(\neg\phi)\}$.

It is obvious that

$$\mathsf{L} \models \phi \quad \text{iff} \quad \mathsf{L} \models \bigvee \mathrm{it}(\phi) \tag{70}$$

for $\mathcal{L}_{RS}$-formulas ϕ having $\bigvee$-type and

$$\mathsf{L} \models \phi \quad \text{iff} \quad \mathsf{L} \models \bigwedge \mathrm{it}(\phi) \tag{71}$$

for formulas of $\bigwedge$-type. This immediately suggests the following definition of the satisfaction relation.

Definition 34 (The satisfaction relation $\models^{\alpha} \Delta$ for finite sets Δ of RS-formulas)

($\bigvee$) *If ϕ is of $\bigvee$-type, $\alpha_0 < \alpha$, and $\models^{\alpha_0} \Delta, \psi$ for some $\psi \in \mathrm{it}(\phi)$, then $\models^{\alpha} \Delta, \phi$.*

($\bigwedge$) *If ϕ is of $\bigwedge$-type, $\alpha_\psi < \alpha$, and $\models^{\alpha_\psi} \Delta, \psi$ for all $\psi \in \mathrm{it}(\phi)$, then $\models^{\alpha} \Delta, \phi$.*

The proof that

$$\mathsf{L} \models \phi \ \text{ iff } \ \exists\alpha \left(\models^{\alpha} \phi\right) \tag{72}$$

becomes immediate from (70) and (71) as soon as we know that the formulas in $\mathrm{it}(\phi)$ are of lower complexity than ϕ. Then we may just perform an induction on the complexity of ϕ. Therefore we assign a rank $\mathrm{rk}(\phi)$ to every $\mathcal{L}_{RS}$-formula ϕ.

Definition 35 (The rank of an $\mathcal{L}_{RS}$-formula)

- $\mathrm{rk}(s \in t) = \mathrm{rk}(s \notin t) := \max\{\omega \cdot (3|s| + 2),\ \omega \cdot (3|t| + 1)\}$.
- $\mathrm{rk}(\psi \wedge \phi) = \mathrm{rk}(\psi \vee \phi) := \max\{\mathrm{rk}(\psi),\ \mathrm{rk}(\phi)\} + 1$.
- $\mathrm{rk}((\mathsf{Q} \in t)\phi(x)) := \begin{cases} \max\{\omega \cdot 3|t|,\ \mathrm{rk}(\phi(\emptyset)) + 2\} & \textit{if } t \textit{ is } \mathsf{L}_\alpha, \\ \max\{\omega \cdot (3|t| + 1),\ \mathrm{rk}(\phi(\emptyset)) + 2\} & \textit{otherwise} \end{cases}$

  for $\mathsf{Q} \in \{\forall, \exists\}$.

The following lemma, which is easy but tedious to prove, is left as an exercise.

Lemma 36 *If $\psi \in \mathrm{it}(\phi)$ then $\mathrm{rk}(\psi) < \mathrm{rk}(\phi)$.*

By Lemma 36 we also get (72) and we define the truth complexity for $\mathcal{L}_{RS}$-formulas ϕ by

$$\mathrm{tc}(\phi) := \begin{cases} \min\{\alpha : \models^{\alpha} \phi\} & \text{if this exists,} \\ \mathsf{stg}(\phi)^+ & \text{otherwise.} \end{cases}$$

With a little effort we can then prove the following lemma.

Lemma 37 *Let ϕ be an $\mathcal{L}_{RS}$-formula such that $\mathrm{tc}(\phi) \leq \alpha$. Then $\mathsf{L}_\alpha \models \phi$.*

Due to some silly technical details this proof is a bit awkward. It becomes, however, trivial by strengthening the conditions for the ordinals in clause ($\bigvee$) of the satisfaction relation. To do so we observe that the infinity type of an $\mathcal{L}_{RS}$-formula ϕ is either of the form

$$\bigwedge_{s \in RS_\alpha} \psi(s) \quad \text{or} \quad \bigvee_{s \in RS_\alpha} \psi(s) \tag{†}$$

or else ϕ is a finite disjunction or conjunction. So we assign the ordinal

$$\mathcal{O}(\phi) := \begin{cases} \alpha & \text{if } \phi \text{ has one of the forms displayed in (†),} \\ 2 & \text{otherwise,} \end{cases}$$

to ϕ and

$$\mathcal{O}_\phi(\psi) := \begin{cases} |s| & \text{if } \phi \text{ is as in (†) and } \psi = \psi(s), \\ i & \text{if } \phi = \psi_0 \overset{\wedge}{\vee} \psi_1 \text{ and } \psi = \psi_i, \end{cases}$$

to formulas $\psi \in \mathrm{it}(\phi)$.

We alter clause ($\bigvee$) to the following one.

($\bigvee$) *If ϕ is of $\bigvee$-type, $\{\alpha_0, \mathcal{O}_\phi(\psi)\} \subseteq \alpha$ and $\models^{\alpha_0} \Delta, \psi$ for some $\psi \in \mathrm{it}(\phi)$, then $\models^{\alpha} \Delta, \phi$.*

This does not spoil (72) and turns Lemma 37 into a triviality.
For $\mathcal{L}_\in$-formulas ϕ the formula $\phi^{\mathsf{L}_{\omega_1^{CK}}}$ becomes an $\mathcal{L}_{RS}$-formula. Thus we may let

$$|\mathbf{KP}\omega| := \sup\{\mathrm{tc}(\phi^{\mathsf{L}_{\omega_1^{CK}}}) \mid \phi \text{ is a } \Sigma_1\text{-formula and } \mathbf{KP}\omega \vdash \phi\} \tag{73}$$

and call $|\mathbf{KP}\omega|$ the proof-theoretic ordinal of $\mathbf{KP}\omega$.[4] This definition 'end extends' the classical one, which defines the proof-theoretic ordinal as the sup of the order types of primitive recursive well-orderings whose well-foundedness is provable in $\mathbf{KP}\omega$. Arguments similar to those used in the proof of Theorem 19 show that $\mathrm{tc}(Wf(\prec)) \le \alpha$ entails $\mathrm{otyp}(\prec) \le 2^\alpha$ for Δ_0-definable well-orderings $\prec$. On the other hand it is not too hard to see that for a Σ_1-definable well-ordering $\prec$ we have $\overset{\beta}{\models} Wf(\prec)$ for some $\beta < otype(\prec) + \omega$ and that for $\beta < \alpha$ this infinitary proof tree can be constructed within $\mathbf{KP}\omega$.
Moreover, using Lemma 37 we can show that, if $|\mathbf{KP}\omega| = \alpha$ then L_α is a model of all Σ_1-theorems of $\mathbf{KP}\omega$.

9 The Infinitary Calculus $RS(\Omega)$

The aim of the current section is to modify the satisfaction relation for $\mathcal{L}_{RS}$ to an infinitary calculus which is based on the ordinals in $C_{\omega_2}(0)$. Since the only constant needed in the development of $C_{\omega_2}(0)$ is Ω we like to call this calculus $RS(\Omega)$. The language of $RS(\Omega)$ is obtained from $\mathcal{L}_{RS}$ by restricting all ordinals to $C_{\omega_2}(0)$. This implies also that the infinity types may become smaller. E.g. it is

$$\mathrm{it}_\Omega(\forall x \in \check{\mathsf{L}}_\Omega \phi(x)) = \{\phi(s) \mid |s| \in C_{\omega_2}(0) \cap \Omega\},$$

which is a proper subset of $\mathrm{it}(\forall x \in \check{\mathsf{L}}_\Omega \phi(x))$. We think that this example makes sufficiently clear how to define it_Ω in general. Following the pattern of predicative ordinal analysis, we should now define an infinitary calculus, say $RS(\Omega) \overset{\alpha}{\underset{\rho}{\vdash}}$, by adding a cut rule. A moment of consideration, however, tells us that this cannot be sufficient. For the following two reasons:
First, the ordinal Ω, viewed from $C_{\omega_2}(0)$, is $C_{\omega_2}(0) \cap \Omega = \vartheta_{\omega_2}(0) < \omega_1^{CK}$, which tells us that using only ordinals from $C_{\omega_2}(0)$ we never can prove that

$$RS(\Omega) \overset{\alpha}{\underset{\rho}{\vdash}} (\forall x \in a)(\exists y \in \mathsf{L}_\Omega)\phi(x,y) \longrightarrow (\exists z \in \mathsf{L}_\Omega)(\forall x \in a)(\exists y \in z)\phi(x,y), \tag{Cl}$$

even for Δ_0-formulas $\phi(x,y)$, because this would imply that $\omega_1^{CK} \le \Omega \cap C_{\omega_2}(0)$. But because Δ_0-collection is an axiom of $\mathbf{KP}\omega$ we will be forced to add an axiom to $RS(\Omega)$ which allows us to get (Cl). This will be done by adding the closure rule (Cl_Ω) given below.
Second, we have $\mathrm{tc}(\phi) \ge \omega_1^{CK}$ for formulas ϕ which are not $\Sigma_1(\mathsf{L}_{\omega_1^{CK}})$. This means that for those formulas we only can have $RS(\Omega) \overset{\alpha}{\underset{0}{\vdash}} \phi$ for $\alpha \ge \Omega$. But the truth

[4] As a word of warning we want to emphasize that for stronger theories this definition needs to be put in more precise terms. There we have to replace Σ_1-formulas by $\Sigma_1(\mathsf{L}_{\omega_1^{CK}})$-formulas. This becomes superfluous for $\mathbf{KP}\omega$ because $\mathsf{L}_{\omega_1^{CK}}$ is its least standard model.

complexities of Σ_1-formulas – which are the things we are really interested in – are $< \omega_1^{CK}$. So we need a 'collapsing' procedure which allows us to collapse the ordinal of an $RS(\Omega)$ proof tree whose end formula is Σ_1 to an ordinal $< \Omega$. To make a collapsible ordinal assignment possible we introduce the relation

$$\alpha \ll \beta \quad :\Longleftrightarrow \quad \alpha < \beta \text{ and } \vartheta_\alpha(0) < \vartheta_\beta(0) \tag{74}$$

and read $\alpha \ll \beta$ as '*α is collapsibly less than β*'. It follows from Lemma 31, (61), and (60) that

$$\alpha \ll \beta \text{ iff } (\alpha < \beta \wedge AC_\Omega(\alpha) \subseteq \vartheta_\beta(0)) \text{ iff } \alpha \in C_\beta(\vartheta_\beta(0)) \cap \beta. \tag{75}$$

Our plan is to assign ordinals to the derivations of $RS(\Omega)$ which are collapsibly increasing instead of just increasing. In case of an formula ϕ of $\bigwedge$-type for which we have $\mathcal{O}(\phi) = \Omega$, however, this won't work because there are only $\Gamma_0 = \vartheta_\Omega(0)$ many ordinals $\ll \Omega$. In this case we will have to enumerate the ordinals of the premises by a function, which of course cannot be completely arbitrary. For this purpose we introduce the concept of an '*α-controlled function*' given by

$$f \ll \alpha :\Longleftrightarrow (\forall \xi \in \mathrm{dom}(f))(\forall \eta)(\forall \delta)(\alpha, \xi \in C_\delta(\eta) \Rightarrow f(\xi) \in C_\delta(\eta) \cap \alpha), \tag{76}$$

which means that at most the parameters already used for ξ and α can occur in an ordinal term denoting $f(\xi)$. For $f \ll \alpha$ and $\xi \in \mathrm{dom}(f)$ we have always

$$f(\xi) \in C_\alpha(\vartheta_\alpha(\xi) + 1) \cap \alpha$$

which entails

$$AC_\Omega(f(\xi)) \subseteq \vartheta_\alpha(\xi + 1). \tag{77}$$

We observe easily that

$$\alpha \ll \beta \quad \text{implies} \quad \alpha \# \gamma \ll \beta \# \gamma \text{ and } \omega^{\alpha+1} \ll \omega^{\beta+1} \tag{78}$$

and

$$f \ll \beta \quad \text{implies} \quad \lambda\xi . f(\xi) \# \gamma \ll \beta \# \gamma \text{ and } \lambda\xi . \omega^{f(\xi)+1} \ll \omega^{\beta+1}. \tag{79}$$

The α-controlled functions will serve to enumerate the premises of a formula of $\bigwedge$-type, say ϕ. To simplify the notation we write $f(\psi)$ instead of $f(\mathcal{O}_\phi(\psi))$ or even simply $f(s)$ in case that $\mathrm{it}_\Omega(\phi) = \{\psi(s) \mid |s| < \mathcal{O}(\phi)\}$.
For an $\mathcal{L}_{RS}$-formula ϕ we denote by $\phi \ll \alpha$ that, whenever L_ξ occurs in ϕ, we have $\xi \ll \alpha$.

Definition 38 (The proof relation $RS(\Omega) \overset{\alpha}{\underset{\rho}{\vdash}} \Delta$ for finite sets Δ of $RS(\Omega)$-formulas)

- ($\bigvee$) *If ϕ is of $\bigvee$-type, $RS(\Omega) \overset{\alpha_0}{\underset{\rho}{\vdash}} \Delta, \psi$, and $\mathcal{O}_\phi(\psi), \alpha_0 \ll \alpha$ for some $\psi \in \mathrm{it}_\Omega(\phi)$, then $RS(\Omega) \overset{\alpha}{\underset{\rho}{\vdash}} \Delta, \phi$.*
- ($\bigwedge$) *If ϕ is of $\bigwedge$-type, $\mathrm{dom}(f) = \mathcal{O}(\phi) \leqq \alpha$, $f \ll \alpha$, and $RS(\Omega) \overset{f(\psi)}{\underset{\rho}{\vdash}} \Delta, \psi$ for all $\psi \in \mathrm{it}_\Omega(\phi)$, then $RS(\Omega) \overset{\alpha}{\underset{\rho}{\vdash}} \Delta, \phi$.*

(Cl_Ω) *If* $RS(\Omega) \mathrel{|\!\!\frac{\alpha_0}{\rho}} \Delta, (\forall x \in a)(\exists y \in \mathsf{L}_\Omega)\phi(x,y)$ *for a* Δ_0*-formula* $\phi(\emptyset,\emptyset)$ *and* $\Omega, \alpha_0 \ll \alpha$ *then* $RS(\Omega) \mathrel{|\!\!\frac{\alpha}{\rho}} \Delta, (\exists z \in \mathsf{L}_\Omega)(\forall x \in a)(\exists y \in z)\phi(x,y)$.

(*cut*) *If* $RS(\Omega) \mathrel{|\!\!\frac{\alpha_0}{\rho}} \Delta, \phi$, $RS(\Omega) \mathrel{|\!\!\frac{\alpha_1}{\rho}} \Delta, \neg\phi$, $\phi, \alpha_0, \alpha_1 \ll \alpha$, *and* $\mathrm{rk}(\phi) < \rho$, *then* $RS(\Omega) \mathrel{|\!\!\frac{\alpha}{\rho}} \Delta$.

First we observe that for $\beta < \Omega$ we have

$$\alpha \ll \beta \text{ iff } \alpha < \beta$$

and

$$f \ll \beta \text{ iff } (\forall \xi \in \mathrm{dom}(f))(f(\xi) < \beta).$$

This, together with the condition that the conclusions of (Cl_Ω) inferences must have ordinals above Ω, ensures that for $\alpha < \Omega$ we have

$$RS(\Omega) \mathrel{|\!\!\frac{\alpha}{0}} \phi \quad \text{iff} \quad \models^{\alpha} \phi \tag{80}$$

and thus also

$$\alpha < \Omega \text{ and } RS(\Omega) \mathrel{|\!\!\frac{\alpha}{0}} \phi \quad \text{imply} \quad \mathrm{tc}(\phi) \leq \alpha. \tag{81}$$

Likewise it follows that for $\alpha, \rho < \Omega$ the relation $RS(\Omega) \mathrel{|\!\!\frac{\alpha}{\rho}} \Delta$ is essentially the same as that for the infinitary system of Section 2. Thus we have all the properties we proved in Section 2 in this situation. Obviously we have

$$RS(\Omega) \mathrel{|\!\!\frac{\alpha}{\rho}} \Delta, \ \alpha \leqq \beta, \ \rho \leq \sigma \text{ and } \Delta \subseteq \Gamma \quad \text{imply } RS(\Omega) \mathrel{|\!\!\frac{\beta}{\sigma}} \Gamma. \tag{82}$$

The first observation is that it is possible to invert the $\bigwedge$-rules.

Lemma 39 (Inversion Lemma) *Let* ϕ *be of* $\bigwedge$*-type and assume* $RS(\Omega) \mathrel{|\!\!\frac{\alpha}{\rho}} \Delta, \phi$, *then*

$$RS(\Omega) \mathrel{|\!\!\frac{\alpha \# \mathcal{O}_\phi(\psi)}{\rho}} \Delta, \psi$$

for all $\psi \in \mathrm{it}_\Omega(\phi)$.

The proof is an easy induction on α. The only interesting case is that of an $\bigwedge$-inference with main formula ϕ. Then there is a function $f \ll \alpha$ and we have among the premises

$$RS(\Omega) \mathrel{|\!\!\frac{f(\psi)}{\rho}} \Delta, \phi, \psi.$$

This yields

$$RS(\Omega) \mathrel{|\!\!\frac{f(\psi) \# \mathcal{O}_\phi(\psi)}{\rho}} \Delta, \psi$$

by the induction hypothesis. We have to check $f(\psi) \# \mathcal{O}_\phi(\psi) \ll \alpha \# f(\psi)$. It is obvious that $f(\psi) \# \mathcal{O}_\phi(\psi) < \alpha \# \mathcal{O}_\phi(\psi)$ and we obtain $AC_\Omega(f(\psi)) \cup AC_\Omega(\mathcal{O}_\phi(\psi)) < \vartheta_{\alpha \# \mathcal{O}_\phi(\psi)}(0)$ from $AC_\Omega(f(\psi)) < \vartheta_\alpha(\mathcal{O}_\phi(\psi)+1) < \vartheta_{\alpha \# \mathcal{O}_\phi(\psi)}(0)$ and the observation that $AC_\Omega(\delta) < \vartheta_\delta(0)$ holds for any δ. □

The elimination lemma needs a slight modification.

Lemma 40 *Let ϕ be of $\bigwedge$-type. If $RS(\Omega) \mid\frac{\alpha}{\rho} \Delta, \phi$, $RS(\Omega) \mid\frac{\beta}{\rho} \Gamma, \neg\phi, \phi \ll \alpha$ and $\mathrm{rk}(\phi) = \rho \neq \Omega$, then $RS(\Omega) \mid\frac{\alpha \# \beta}{\rho} \Delta, \Gamma$.*

This time we prove the lemma by induction on β. In the case that $\neg\phi$ is not the main formula of the last inference, we obtain the claim immediately from the induction hypothesis using (78) and (79).
If $\neg\phi$ is the main formula of the last inference, $\mathrm{rk}(\phi) \neq \Omega$ excludes the possibility of an (Cl_Ω)-inference. Thus we have the premise

$$RS(\Omega) \mid\frac{\beta_0}{\rho} \Gamma, \neg\phi, \neg\psi \tag{i}$$

for some $\psi \in \mathrm{it}_\Omega(\phi)$ and obtain

$$RS(\Omega) \mid\frac{\alpha \# \beta_0}{\rho} \Delta, \Gamma, \neg\psi \tag{ii}$$

by the induction hypothesis. From the first hypothesis we get

$$RS(\Omega) \mid\frac{\alpha \# \mathcal{O}_\phi(\psi)}{\rho} \Delta, \Gamma, \psi \tag{iii}$$

by inversion and the structural rule (82). We want to apply a cut to (*ii*) and (*iii*) and have to check the ordinal conditions. By the ordinal condition for $\bigvee$-inferences we have $\mathcal{O}_\phi(\psi) \ll \beta$ which implies $\alpha \# \mathcal{O}_\phi(\psi) \ll \alpha \# \beta$ and together with the hypothesis $\phi \ll \alpha$ also $\psi \ll \alpha \# \beta$. Finally $\beta_0 \ll \alpha$ implies $\alpha \# \beta_0 \ll \alpha \# \beta$. So we obtain

$$RS(\Omega) \mid\frac{\alpha \# \beta}{\rho} \Delta, \Gamma$$

by a cut. □

As an immediate consequence of Lemma 40 we obtain the next result by nearly literally the proof of Theorem 25.

Theorem 41 (First Elimination Theorem) *$RS(\Omega) \mid\frac{\alpha}{\rho+1} \Delta$ and $\rho \neq \Omega$ imply $RS(\Omega) \mid\frac{\omega^{\alpha+1}}{\rho} \Delta$.*

The only new point in the proof is that in case of a cut

$$RS(\Omega) \mid\frac{\alpha_1}{\rho+1} \Delta, \phi, \quad RS(\Omega) \mid\frac{\alpha_2}{\rho+1} \Delta, \neg\phi \quad \Longrightarrow \quad RS(\Omega) \mid\frac{\alpha}{\rho} \Delta$$

we have $\phi \ll \alpha \leqq \omega^\alpha$. From the induction hypothesis and $\omega^{\alpha_i+1} \leqq \omega^\alpha$ we obtain

$$RS(\Omega) \mid\frac{\omega^\alpha}{\rho} \Delta, \phi, \quad RS(\Omega) \mid\frac{\omega^\alpha}{\rho} \Delta, \neg\phi$$

from which we obtain the claim by a cut. □

As an exercise the reader may now infer the general Second Elimination Theorem for $RS(\Omega)$ derivations. We skip it because in the ordinal analysis of **KP**ω we will just need the Second Elimination Theorem for RS-derivations below Ω.
A very important feature of the system $RS(\Omega)$ is the boundedness property stated below. It's proof is a completely straightforward induction on α.

Lemma 42 (Boundedness) *Let* $RS(\Omega) \vdash^{\alpha}_{\rho} \Delta[(\exists x{\in}\mathsf{L}_{\gamma})\phi(x)]$ *and* $\alpha \leq \beta < \Omega$. *Then* $RS(\Omega) \vdash^{\alpha}_{\rho} \Delta[(\exists x{\in}\mathsf{L}_{\beta})\phi(x)]$.

The next lemma provides the essential step in the ordinal analysis of $\mathbf{KP}\omega$. For a finite set Γ of formulas we let $\Gamma^{\forall\vec{\xi}}$ be the set which is obtained by replacing all quantifiers $(\forall x{\in}\mathsf{L}_{\Omega})$ by $(\forall x{\in}\mathsf{L}_{\xi_i})$. This of course tatcitly implies that the length of the tuple $\vec{\xi}$ coincides with the number of quantifiers $(\forall x{\in}\mathsf{L}_{\Omega})$ occuring in Γ. Let moreover $\vartheta_{\alpha}(\vec{\xi}+1)$ stand for $\vartheta_{\alpha}(\xi_1 \# \ldots \# \xi_n + 1)$ if $n > 0$ and $\vartheta_{\alpha}(0)$ otherwise.

Lemma 43 (Collapsing) *Let* Δ *be a set of* $\Sigma(\mathsf{L}_{\Omega})$ *and* Γ *a set of* $\Pi(\mathsf{L}_{\Omega})$ *sentences. Assume* $RS(\Omega) \vdash^{\alpha}_{\Omega+1} \Delta, \Gamma$. *Then* $RS(\Omega) \vdash^{\vartheta_{\alpha}(\vec{\xi}+1)}_{\Omega} \Delta, \Gamma^{\forall\vec{\xi}}$ *for any tuple* $\vec{\xi}$ *of ordinals* $< \Omega$ *of the appropriate length.*

The proof is by induction on α.[5] There are several interesting cases. Let us start with the most interesting one, a cut of rank Ω. There we have the premises

$$RS(\Omega) \vdash^{\alpha_1}_{\Omega+1} \Delta, \Gamma, (\exists y{\in}\mathsf{L}_{\Omega})\psi(y) \qquad (i)$$

and

$$RS(\Omega) \vdash^{\alpha_2}_{\Omega+1} \Delta, \Gamma, (\forall y{\in}\mathsf{L}_{\Omega})\neg\psi(y). \qquad (ii)$$

From (i) we obtain by the induction hypothesis and boundedness

$$RS(\Omega) \vdash^{\vartheta_{\alpha_1}(\vec{\xi}+1)}_{\Omega} \Delta, \Gamma^{\forall\vec{\xi}}, (\exists y{\in}\mathsf{L}_{\vartheta_{\alpha_1}(\vec{\xi}+1)})\psi(y) \qquad (iii)$$

and from (ii)

$$RS(\Omega) \vdash^{\vartheta_{\alpha_2}(\vec{\xi} \# \vartheta_{\alpha_1}(\vec{\xi}+1)+1)}_{\Omega} \Delta, \Gamma^{\forall\vec{\xi}}, (\forall y{\in}\mathsf{L}_{\vartheta_{\alpha_1}(\vec{\xi}+1)})\psi(x). \qquad (iv)$$

Now we have $(\exists y{\in}\mathsf{L}_{\Omega})\psi(y) \ll \alpha$. From $\alpha_1 \ll \alpha$ we obtain $\vartheta_{\alpha_1}(\vec{\xi}+1) \ll \vartheta_{\alpha}(\vec{\xi}+1)$. This and $\alpha_2 \ll \alpha$ entail $\vartheta_{\alpha_2}(\vec{\xi} \# \vartheta_{\alpha_1}(\vec{\xi}+1)+1) \ll \vartheta_{\alpha}(\vec{\xi}+1)$ and we obtain

$$RS(\Omega) \vdash^{\vartheta_{\alpha}(\vec{\xi}+1)}_{\Omega} \Delta, \Gamma^{\forall\vec{\xi}}$$

from (iii) and (iv) by a cut.
The next interesting case is that of an application of the $(\bigwedge)$-rule. There we have the premises

$$RS(\Omega) \vdash^{f(s)}_{\Omega+1} \Delta, \Gamma, \phi(s) \qquad (v)$$

for all $|s| < \mathrm{dom}(f)$. By the induction hypothesis we obtain

$$RS(\Omega) \vdash^{\vartheta_{f(s)}(\vec{\xi}+1)}_{\Omega} \Delta, \Gamma^{\forall\vec{\xi}}, \phi(s) \qquad (vi)$$

[5]This proof presents yet another simplification of the method of local predicativity. For more background see [Pohlers 1990] and [Buchholz 1991].

for all $|s| < \mathrm{dom}(f)$. If $\mathrm{dom}(f) = \Omega$ then there is a formula $(\forall x \in \mathsf{L}_\Omega)\phi(x) \in \Gamma$ and we let μ be a member of the list $\vec{\xi}$. Otherwise we put $\mu := \mathrm{dom}(f) \leqq \alpha$. In order to get

$$RS(\Omega) \mid\frac{\vartheta_\alpha(\vec{\xi}+1)}{\Omega} \Delta, \Gamma^{\forall\vec{\xi}} \qquad (vii)$$

by an application of an $(\bigwedge)$-clause we have to check

$$\lambda s < \mu . \vartheta_{f(s)}(\vec{\xi}+1) \ll \vartheta_\alpha(\vec{\xi}+1). \qquad (\dagger)$$

Let $|s| < \mu$ and assume $|s|, \vartheta_\alpha(\vec{\xi}+1) \in C_\delta(\eta)$. We have to show that

$$\vartheta_{f(s)}(\vec{\xi}+1) \in C_\delta(\eta) \cap \vartheta_\alpha(\vec{\xi}+1).$$

Since $\vartheta_\alpha(\vec{\xi}+1) < \Omega$ it suffices to show

$$\vartheta_{f(s)}(\vec{\xi}+1) < \vartheta_\alpha(\vec{\xi}+1).$$

We have $f(s) < \alpha$ and $\vec{\xi}+1 < \vartheta_\alpha(\vec{\xi}+1)$. So it remains to show that $AC_\Omega(f(s)) < \vartheta_\alpha(\vec{\xi}+1)$. For this, however, it suffices to have $f(s) \in C_\alpha(\vartheta_\alpha(\vec{\xi}+1))$. But we have $\alpha \in C_\alpha(\vartheta_\alpha(\vec{\xi}+1))$ and either $|s| < \mu < \vartheta_\alpha(\vec{\xi}+1) \subseteq C_\alpha(\vartheta_\alpha(\vec{\xi}+1))$ or $|s| < \mu \leqq \alpha$ which in turn entails $|s| < \vartheta_\alpha(0) \subseteq C_\alpha(\vartheta_\alpha(\vec{\xi}+1))$. Since $f \ll \alpha$ these facts imply $f(s) \in C_\alpha(\vartheta_\alpha(\vec{\xi}+1))$ and we are done.
Much simpler is the case of a clause $(\bigvee)$ in which we have the premise

$$RS(\Omega) \mid\frac{\alpha_0}{\Omega+1} \Delta, \Gamma, \psi \qquad (viii)$$

for some $\phi \in \Delta$ and $\psi \in \mathrm{it}_\Omega(\phi)$. By the induction hypothesis we have

$$RS(\Omega) \mid\frac{\vartheta_{\alpha_0}(\vec{\xi}+1)}{\Omega} \Delta, \Gamma^{\forall\vec{\xi}}, \psi \qquad (ix)$$

and obtain

$$RS(\Omega) \mid\frac{\vartheta_\alpha(\vec{\xi}+1)}{\Omega} \Delta, \Gamma^{\forall\vec{\xi}} \qquad (x)$$

from (ix) by an inference $(\bigvee)$ as soon as we have checked $\mathcal{O}_\phi(\psi) \ll \vartheta_\alpha(\vec{\xi}+1)$ and $\vartheta_{\alpha_0}(\vec{\xi}+1) \ll \vartheta_\alpha(\vec{\xi}+1)$. But since $\mathcal{O}_\phi(\psi) < \Omega$ the first follows from $\mathcal{O}_\phi(\psi) \ll \alpha$ and the latter from $\alpha_0 \ll \alpha$.
A bit more interesting is the case of a clause (Cl_Ω). It is obvious that we have to get rid of this inference because derivations with length less than Ω cannot contain such rules. We have the premise

$$RS(\Omega) \mid\frac{\alpha_0}{\Omega+1} \Delta, \Gamma, (\forall x \in a)(\exists y \in \mathsf{L}_\Omega)\phi(x,y) \qquad (xi)$$

with $\alpha_0 \ll \alpha$, and $(\exists z \in \mathsf{L}_\Omega)(\forall x \in a)(\exists y \in z)\phi(x,y) \in \Delta$. By the induction hypothesis and boundedness we get

$$RS(\Omega) \mid\frac{\vartheta_{\alpha_0}(\vec{\xi}+1)}{\Omega} \Delta, \Gamma^{\forall\vec{\xi}}, (\forall x \in a)(\exists y \in \mathsf{L}_{\vartheta_{\alpha_0}(\vec{\xi}+1)})\phi(x,y). \qquad (xii)$$

Since $\vartheta_{\alpha_0}(\vec{\xi}+1) \ll \vartheta_\alpha(\vec{\xi}+1)$ we may apply an inference according to $(\bigvee)$ to (xii) and get

$$RS(\Omega) \,\Big|\!\frac{\vartheta_\alpha(\vec{\xi}+1)}{\Omega}\, \Delta, \Gamma^{\forall \vec{\xi}} \qquad \square$$

As a consequence we obtain the following proposition.

Corollary 44 *If $RS(\Omega) \,|\!\frac{\alpha}{\Omega+1}\, \Delta$ for a finite set Δ of $\Sigma(\mathsf{L}_\Omega)$-formulas, then $RS(\Omega) \,|\!\frac{\vartheta_\alpha(0)}{\vartheta_\alpha(0)}\, \Delta$.*

By Lemma 43 we first get $RS(\Omega) \,|\!\frac{\vartheta_\alpha(0)}{\Omega}\, \Delta$ and prove

$$RS(\Omega) \,|\!\frac{\beta}{\Omega}\, \Delta \ \text{ for } \beta \leq \vartheta_\alpha(0) \Longrightarrow RS(\Omega) \,|\!\frac{\beta}{\vartheta_\alpha(0)}\, \Delta \tag{83}$$

by induction on β. The only noteworthy case is a cut in which we have the premises

$$RS(\Omega) \,|\!\frac{\beta_1}{\Omega}\, \Delta, \psi \quad \text{and} \quad RS(\Omega) \,|\!\frac{\beta_2}{\Omega}\, \Delta, \neg\psi$$

with $\psi \ll \beta \leq \vartheta_\alpha(0)$. Due to the closure properties of ordinals like $\vartheta_\alpha(0)$ this entails $\mathrm{rk}(\psi) < \vartheta_\alpha(0)$. Thus we obtain the claim from the induction hypotheses by a cut. $\square$

We can now prove the following result by a slight modification of the proof of (83).

Theorem 45 *Let Δ be a set of $\Sigma(\mathsf{L}_\Omega)$ formulas. Then $RS(\Omega) \,|\!\frac{\alpha}{\Omega}\, \Delta$ implies $\mathsf{L}_{\vartheta_\alpha(0)} \models \bigvee_{\phi\in\Delta} \phi$.*

$\square$

Now we have all the facts we need for the proof of the major result of this section.

Theorem 46 (Cut Elimination) *Let Δ be a finite set of $\Sigma(\mathsf{L}_\Omega)$-formulas, and let α and β be ordinals such that $\Omega \leq \beta$ and $\alpha \ll \beta$. If $RS(\Omega) \,|\!\frac{\alpha}{\Omega+1}\, \Delta$, then $RS(\Omega) \,|\!\frac{\vartheta_\beta(0)}{0}\, \Delta$.*

To see this apply first Corollary 44 and obtain $RS(\Omega) \,|\!\frac{\vartheta_\alpha(0)}{\vartheta_\alpha(0)}\, \Delta$. This, however, is a derivation below Ω which means that Theorem 26, the Second Elimination Theorem, applies. Thus we get $|\!\frac{\vartheta_{\vartheta_\alpha(0)}(\vartheta_\alpha(0))}{0}\, \Delta$ and $\vartheta_{\vartheta_\alpha(0)}(\vartheta_\alpha(0)) < \vartheta_\beta(0)$ follows from $\vartheta_\alpha(0) < \Omega < \beta$ and $\vartheta_\alpha(0) < \vartheta_\beta(0)$. $\square$

To obtain an ordinal analysis for $\mathbf{KP}\omega$ we show

$$RS(\Omega) \,|\!\frac{\alpha}{0}\, \phi^{\mathsf{L}_\Omega} \ \text{ and } \ \alpha \ll \varepsilon_{\Omega+1} \tag{84}$$

for every axiom ϕ of $\mathbf{KP}\omega$. Since for every $\mathcal{L}_{\in}$ formula ϕ there is a finite ordinal m such that $\mathrm{rk}(\phi^{\mathsf{L}_\Omega}) = \Omega + m$, it follows from (84) that

$$RS(\Omega) \,|\!\frac{\alpha}{\Omega+m}\, \phi^{\mathsf{L}_\Omega} \ \text{ for } \alpha \ll \varepsilon_{\Omega+1} \text{ and } m < \omega \tag{85}$$

for all theorems ϕ of $\mathbf{KP}\omega$. By the First Elimination Theorem this implies

$$RS(\Omega) \mid\frac{\alpha}{\Omega+1} \phi^{\mathsf{L}_\Omega} \tag{86}$$

for another ordinal α still collapsibly less than $\varepsilon_{\Omega+1}$. Using the Cut Elimination Theorem this yields

$$RS(\Omega \mid\frac{\vartheta_{\varepsilon_{\Omega+1}}(0)}{0} \phi^{\mathsf{L}_\Omega} \tag{87}$$

for all Σ_1-theorems of $\mathbf{KP}\omega$. We can now set an upper bound on $|\mathbf{KP}\omega|$.

Theorem 47 $|\mathbf{KP}\omega| \leq \vartheta_{\varepsilon_{\Omega+1}}(0)$.

Indeed we have equality in Theorem 47 but we will not prove it here. A proof of it could for instance be obtained by embedding the theory $\mathbf{ID_1}$ in $\mathbf{KP}\omega$ – which is very easy – and then referring to [Pohlers 1989]. A direct proof follows from [Rathjen 1991] in this volume.
We will also not check (84) in full detail. Some of the axioms (e.g. those involving equality) are technically awkward to check. We will restrict ourselves to the essential axioms, which are Δ_0-collection and foundation. First we observe

$$RS(\Omega) \mid\frac{\omega^\phi \# 2\cdot \mathrm{rk}(\phi)}{0} \phi, \neg\phi, \tag{88}$$

where $\omega^\phi := \omega^{\xi_1} \# \ldots \# \omega^{\xi_n}$ if $\mathsf{L}_{\xi_1}, \ldots, \mathsf{L}_{\xi_n}$ is the complete list of constants L_ξ occurring in ϕ. For a set term s we define ω^s analogously. By (88) we thus have

$$RS(\Omega) \mid\frac{\omega^s \# \Omega+4}{0} \neg(\forall x{\in}s)(\exists y{\in}\mathsf{L}_\Omega)\phi(x,y), (\forall x{\in}s)(\exists y{\in}\mathsf{L}_\Omega)\phi(x,y), \tag{89}$$

which by clauses (Cl_Ω), two times $(\bigvee)$ and $(\bigwedge)$ entails

$$\mid\frac{\Omega\cdot 2}{0} (\forall u{\in}\mathsf{L}_\Omega)[\neg(\forall x{\in}u)(\exists y{\in}\mathsf{L}_\Omega)\phi(x,y) \vee (\exists z{\in}\mathsf{L}_\Omega)(\forall x{\in}u)(\exists y{\in}\mathsf{L}_\Omega)\phi(x,y)].$$

For foundation we show

$$RS(\Omega) \mid\frac{2\cdot\mathrm{rk}(\phi) \# \omega^{|s|+2}}{0} \neg\phi(s), (\exists x{\in}\mathsf{L}_\Omega)[\phi(x) \wedge (\forall y{\in}x)\neg\phi(y)], \tag{90}$$

where we may assume that ϕ does not contain additional set parameters, by induction on $|s| < \Omega$. By the induction hypothesis we have

$$RS(\Omega) \mid\frac{2\cdot\mathrm{rk}(\phi) \# \omega^{|t|+2}}{0} \neg\phi(t), (\exists x{\in}\mathsf{L}_\Omega)[\phi(x) \wedge (\forall y{\in}x)\neg\phi(y)]$$

for all $|t| < |s|$. In case that $s = \{x{\in}\mathsf{L}_\alpha \mid \psi(x)\}$ we may weaken this to

$$RS(\Omega) \mid\frac{2\cdot\mathrm{rk}(\phi) \# \omega^{|t|+4}}{0} \neg\psi(t) \vee \neg\phi(t), (\exists x{\in}\mathsf{L}_\Omega)[\phi(x) \wedge (\forall y{\in}x)\neg\phi(y)].$$

Using $(\bigwedge)$ this yields

$$RS(\Omega) \mid\frac{2\cdot\mathrm{rk}(\phi) \# \omega^{|s|}}{0} (\forall y{\in}s)\neg\phi(y), (\exists x{\in}\mathsf{L}_\Omega)[\phi(x) \wedge (\forall y{\in}x)\neg\phi(y)].$$

This together with (88) implies by an $(\bigwedge)$-inference

$$RS(\Omega) \mid\!\frac{2\cdot \mathrm{rk}(\phi)\,\#\,\omega^{|s|+1}}{0} \neg\phi(s), (\forall y\in s)\neg\phi(y) \wedge \phi(s), (\exists x\in \mathsf{L}_\Omega)[\phi(x) \wedge (\forall y\in x)\neg\phi(y)].$$

Since $|s| < \Omega$ we infer (90) by an $(\bigvee)$-inference. □

From (90), however, we obviously obtain

$$RS(\Omega) \mid\!\frac{2\cdot \mathrm{rk}(\phi)\,\#\,\Omega}{0} \neg(\exists x\in \mathsf{L}_\Omega)\phi(x), (\exists x\in \mathsf{L}_\Omega)[\phi(x) \wedge (\forall y\in y)\neg\phi(y)]$$

which gives us the required translation of the foundation scheme.

References

[Barwise 1969] J. Barwise *Admissible Sets and Structures* Springer (1969)

[Buchholz 1975] W. Buchholz *Normalfunktionen und konstruktive Systeme von Ordinalzahlen* Springer LNM 500 (1975)

[Buchholz 1991] W. Buchholz *A simplified version of local predicativity* This volume.

[Columbus 1990] J. Columbus *Normen der deskriptiven Mengenlehre als Wahrheitskomplexitäten* Thesis Münster (1990)

[Jäger 1986] G. Jäger *Theories for Admissible Sets: A Unifying Approach to Proof Theory* Bibliopolis (1986)

[Pohlers 1981] W. Pohlers *Proof-theoretical analysis of* $\mathbf{ID}_\nu$ *by the method of local predicativity* in W. Buchholz, S. Feferman, W. Pohlers, W. Sieg *Iterated Inductive Definitions and Subsystems of Analysis: Recent Proof-Theoretical Studies* Springer LNM 897 (1981)

[Pohlers 1989] W. Pohlers *Proof Theory. An Introduction* Springer LNM 1407 (1989)

[Pohlers 1990] W. Pohlers *Proof theory and ordinal analysis* Arch. Math. Log.30 (1991) 311-376

[Rathjen 1989] M. Rathjen *The role of parameters in bar induction* Preprint Münster (1989)

[Rathjen 1991] M. Rathjen *Fragments of Kripke-Platek set theory with infinity* This volume

[Schütte 1977] K. Schütte *Proof Theory* Springer (1977)

[Takeuti 1975] G. Takeuti *Proof Theory* North Holland (1975)

[Troelstra 1973] A. S. Troelstra (ed.) *Metamathematical Investigations of Intuitionistic Arithmetic* Springer LNM 344 (1973)

A more comprehensive list of references can be found in [Pohlers 1989]

Proofs as programs

H. SCHWICHTENBERG

Proofs as Programs

HELMUT SCHWICHTENBERG

Mathematisches Institut, Universität München

Suppose a formal proof of $\forall x \exists y \, \mathrm{Spec}(x, y)$ is given, where $\mathrm{Spec}(x, y)$ is an atomic formula expressing some specification for natural numbers x, y. For any particular number n we then obtain a formal proof of $\exists y \, \mathrm{Spec}(n, y)$. Now the proof–theoretic normalization procedure yields another proof of $\exists y \, \mathrm{Spec}(n, y)$ which is in normal form. In particular, it does not use induction axioms any more, and it also does not contain non–evaluated terms. Hence we can read off, linearly in the size of the normal proof, an instance m for y such that $\mathrm{Spec}(n, m)$ holds. In this way a formal proof can be seen as a program, and the central part in implementing this programming language consists in an implementation of the proof–theoretic normalization procedure.

There are many ways to implement normalization. As usual, a crucial point is a good choice of the data structures. One possibility is to represent a term as a function (i.e. a SCHEME–procedure) of its free variables, and similarly to represent a derivation (in a Gentzen–style system of natural deduction) as a function of its free assumption and object variables. Then substitution is realized as application, and normalization is realized as the built–in evaluation process of SCHEME (or any other language of the LISP–family). We presently experiment with an implementation along these lines, and the results up to now are rather promising. Some details are given in an appendix.

It is not the prime purpose of the present paper to discuss this implementation. Rather, we want to explore the theoretical possibilities and limitations of a programming language based on formal proofs. The notion of proof is taken here in a quite basic sense: the formal language is supposed to talk about algebraic data structures (i.e. free algebras), and structural recursion as well as structural induction is allowed. Hence we discuss systems of the strength of ordinary arithmetic. We will measure the strength of our proofs/programs in terms of the so–called slow growing hierarchy G_α introduced by Wainer and studied by Girard. We will give a new proof of the following result of Kreisel and (Girard 1981): Any function defined by a proof of $\forall x \exists y\, \mathrm{Spec}(x,y)$ is bounded by a function G_α of the hierarchy with α below the Bachmann–Howard ordinal, and conversely that for any such G_α there is an atomic formula $\mathrm{Spec}_\alpha(x,y)$ such that $G_\alpha(n) \leq$ the least m with $\mathrm{Spec}_\alpha(n,m)$, and $\forall x \exists y\, \mathrm{Spec}_\alpha(x,y)$ is provable, and hence for any proof of this fact the function computed by that proof (considered as a program) grows at least as fast as G_α.

On the more technical side, our work builds heavily on earlier work of (Buchholz 1987) and (Arai 1989). In particular, the material in Sections 1–3 on trees, tree notations and the slow growing hierarchy is taken from Buchholz. Also, the ω^+–Rule below is derived from (a special case of) the Ω–Rule in (Buchholz 1987) (or more precisely of its "slow–growing" variant in (Arai 1989)), which in turn is based on earlier work of (Howard 1972). The new twist here is that we make use of a technique of (Howard 1980) to measure the complexity of a (finite) term/proof by (transfinite) trees; for this to go through it is essential to use a natural deduction system and not a Tait calculus as in (Buchholz 1987) or (Buchholz and Wainer 1987).

More precisely, we inductively define what it means for a (finite) term/proof involving recursion/induction constants to be SDH–generated (for Sanchis–Diller–Howard) with measure α (a transfinite tree) and rank m. One clause of this inductive definition is called ω^+–rule and introduces uncountable trees. In this setup it is easy to provide relatively perspicious and complete proofs of the relations mentioned above between the slow growing hierarchy and the functions computed by proofs/programs in arithmetical systems.

1. TREES

We give an informal treatment of the *tree classes* $\mathcal{T}_\sigma$ with $\sigma \leq \nu$, for some fixed $\nu < \omega$. For our later applications it will suffice to take $\nu = 2$. The material developed here will later (in Section 2) give rise to a system of (finitary, or algebraic) notations for such trees.

Let $\sigma < \omega$, and assume that $\mathcal{T}_\varrho$ for all $\varrho < \sigma$ is defined already. We then define the *tree class* $\mathcal{T}_\sigma$ inductively by the clause

$\mathcal{T}_\sigma$. If $\alpha: I \to \mathcal{T}_\sigma$ is a function with $I = \emptyset, \{0\}$ or $\mathcal{T}_\varrho$ for some $\varrho < \sigma$, then $\alpha \in \mathcal{T}_\sigma$.

If $I = \emptyset$, then $\alpha: I \to \mathcal{T}_\sigma$ is denoted by 0. If $I = \{0\}$, then $\alpha: I \to \mathcal{T}_\sigma$ is determined by $\alpha(0) =: \beta$ and denoted by β^+. If $I = \mathcal{T}_\varrho$, then $\alpha: I \to \mathcal{T}_\sigma$ is denoted by $(\alpha_\zeta)_{\zeta \in \mathcal{T}_\varrho}$ with $\alpha_\zeta := \alpha(\zeta)$.

$\mathcal{T}_0$ consists of $0, 0^+, 0^{++}, \dots$ and hence is identified with the set $\mathbf{N}$ of natural numbers. $\mathcal{T}_1$ is the set of countable trees. For example,

$$\omega := (n)_{n\in\mathbf{N}} \in \mathcal{T}_1$$

and more generally

$$\Omega_\sigma := (\zeta)_{\zeta\in\mathcal{T}_\sigma} \in \mathcal{T}_{\sigma+1},$$

hence $\omega = \Omega_0$.

Note that, since $\mathcal{T}_\sigma$ is defined inductively, the following principle of transfinite (or Noetherian) induction on $\mathcal{T}_\sigma$ holds.

$$(\forall\alpha \in \mathcal{T}_\sigma.\forall\zeta \in \mathrm{dom}(\alpha) : \varphi(\alpha_\zeta) \to \varphi(\alpha)) \to \forall\alpha \in \mathcal{T}_\sigma : \varphi(\alpha).$$

Here φ is an arbitrary property of elements of $\mathcal{T}_\sigma$.

Addition, multiplication and exponentiation of trees are defined as follows.

i. $\alpha + 0 = \alpha$

ii. $\alpha + \beta^+ = (\alpha + \beta)^+$

iii. $\alpha + (\beta_\zeta)_{\zeta\in\mathcal{T}_\sigma} = (\alpha + \beta_\zeta)_{\zeta\in\mathcal{T}_\sigma}$.

Then $(\alpha + \beta) + \gamma = \alpha + (\beta + \gamma)$; this can be proved easily by induction on γ.

i. $\alpha \cdot 0 = 0$.

ii. $\alpha \cdot (\beta + 1) = (\alpha \cdot \beta) + \alpha$.

iii. $\alpha \cdot (\beta_\zeta)_{\zeta\in\mathcal{T}_\sigma} = (\alpha \cdot \beta_\zeta)_{\zeta\in\mathcal{T}_\sigma}$.

Then $\alpha \cdot (\beta + \gamma) = \alpha \cdot \beta + \alpha \cdot \gamma$, and also $(\alpha \cdot \beta) \cdot \gamma = \alpha \cdot (\beta \cdot \gamma)$.

i. $\alpha^0 = 1$.

ii. $\alpha^{\beta+1} = \alpha^\beta \cdot \alpha$.

iii. $\alpha^{(\beta_\zeta)_{\zeta\in\mathcal{T}_\sigma}} = (\alpha^{\beta_\zeta})_{\zeta\in\mathcal{T}_\sigma}$.

Then $\alpha^{(\beta+\gamma)} = \alpha^\beta \cdot \alpha^\gamma$, and also $(\alpha^\beta)^\gamma = \alpha^{\beta\cdot\gamma}$.

Using these arithmetical operations we can now give some more examples of trees.

$$\omega \cdot 2 = \omega + \omega = (\omega + n)_{n\in\mathbf{N}},$$

$$\omega^2 = \omega \cdot \omega = (\omega \cdot n)_{n\in\mathbf{N}},$$

$$\omega^\omega = (\omega^n)_{n\in\mathbf{N}}$$

and similarly, for $\Omega := \Omega_1$,

$$\Omega \cdot 2 = \Omega + \Omega = (\Omega + \zeta)_{\zeta\in\mathcal{T}_1},$$

$$\Omega^2 = \Omega \cdot \Omega = (\Omega \cdot \zeta)_{\zeta \in \mathcal{T}_1},$$

$$\Omega^\Omega = (\Omega^\zeta)_{\zeta \in \mathcal{T}_1}.$$

From now on we restrict attention to the tree class $\mathcal{T}_\nu$ for some fixed $\nu < \omega$. We define *collapsing functions* $\mathcal{D}_\sigma : \mathcal{T}_\nu \to \mathcal{T}_{\sigma+1}$ for all $\sigma < \nu$, by induction on $\mathcal{T}_\nu$.

i. $\mathcal{D}_\sigma 0 := \Omega_\sigma$

ii. $\mathcal{D}_\sigma(\alpha + 1) := (\mathcal{D}_\sigma(\alpha) \cdot (n+1))_{n \in \mathbf{N}}$

iii. If $\varrho \leq \sigma$, then $\mathcal{D}_\sigma((\alpha_\zeta)_{\zeta \in \mathcal{T}_\varrho}) := (\mathcal{D}_\sigma \alpha_\zeta)_{\zeta \in \mathcal{T}_\varrho}$.

iv. If $\sigma < \mu + 1$, then $\mathcal{D}_\sigma((\alpha_\zeta)_{\zeta \in \mathcal{T}_{\mu+1}}) := (\mathcal{D}_\sigma \alpha_{\zeta_n})_{n \in \mathbf{N}}$ where $\zeta_0 := \Omega_\mu$, $\zeta_{n+1} := \mathcal{D}_\mu \alpha_{\zeta_n}$.

For $\alpha \in \mathcal{T}_{\sigma+1}$, $\mathcal{D}_\sigma \alpha$ is similar to $\Omega_\sigma \cdot \omega^\alpha$; the only difference is that in ii we have $n+1$ instead of n (for technical reasons; cf. the proof of the Cut Elimination Lemma in Section 4). However, the crucial clause in the definition of $\mathcal{D}_\sigma$ is iv, which makes $\mathcal{D}_\sigma$ defined for trees beyond $\mathcal{T}_{\sigma+1}$, and hence makes it a collapsing function.

For example, $\mathcal{D}_0 \Omega_1 = (\mathcal{D}_0 \zeta_n)_{n \in \mathcal{T}_0}$ where $\zeta_0 = \omega$, $\zeta_{n+1} = \mathcal{D}_0 \zeta_n$. Since $\mathcal{D}_0 \alpha$ for $\alpha \in \mathcal{T}_1$ is similar to the exponential ω^α, we can conclude that $\mathcal{D}_0 \Omega_1$ is similar to the tree $(1, \omega, \omega^\omega, \omega^{\omega^\omega}, \ldots)$, which is usually denoted by ε_0.

From now on we restrict attention to trees built up from $0, 1$ by $+$ and $\mathcal{D}_\sigma$, for $\sigma < \nu$. Such trees can clearly be denoted by elements of an appropriate free algebra, hence by finitary notations.

2. TREE NOTATIONS

Let D_σ for $\sigma < \nu$ be unary function symbols; again $\nu < \omega$ is a fixed number (and $\nu = 2$ in Sections 4 and 5). We define a set T of terms and simultaneously a set HT of principal terms inductively by

i. $1 \in \mathrm{HT}$.

ii. If $a \in \mathrm{T}$ and $\sigma < \nu$, then $D_\sigma a \in \mathrm{HT}$.

iii. If $a_1, \ldots, a_k \in \mathrm{HT}$ with $k \geq 0$, then $(a_1, \ldots, a_k) \in \mathrm{T}$.

The empty list $()$ is denoted by 0. For the one element list (a) we often write a; in this sense we have $\mathrm{HT} \subset \mathrm{T}$.

The elements of T are called *tree notations*, since for any $a \in \mathrm{T}$ we can define its *value* $\mathrm{val}(a) \in \mathcal{T}_\nu$ by

i. $\mathrm{val}(1) = 1$,

ii. $\mathrm{val}(D_\sigma a) = \mathcal{D}_\sigma(\mathrm{val}(a))$,

iii. $\mathrm{val}(a_1, \ldots, a_k) = \mathrm{val}(a_1) + \cdots + \mathrm{val}(a_k)$.

For $a, b \in \mathrm{T}$ we define $a + b$ to be the concatenation of the lists a and b. Then clearly $a+b \in \mathrm{T}$, and also $a+0 = 0+a = a$, $a+(b+c) = (a+b)+c$. We abbreviate $a + \cdots + a$ by $a \cdot n$.

The subsets $\mathrm{T}_\sigma \subseteq \mathrm{T}$ and $\mathrm{HT}_\sigma \subseteq \mathrm{HT}$ are to consist of those terms containing D_μ with $\sigma \leq \mu$ only in a context $D_\rho a$ with $\rho < \sigma$. More precisely, for any $\sigma < \nu$ the sets T_σ and HT_σ are defined by

i. $1 \in \mathrm{HT}_\sigma$.

ii. If $a \in \mathrm{T}$ and $\rho < \sigma$, then $D_\rho a \in \mathrm{HT}_\sigma$.

iii. If $a_1, \ldots, a_k \in \mathrm{HT}_\sigma$ with $k \geq 0$, then $(a_1, \ldots, a_k) \in \mathrm{T}_\sigma$.

Clearly $\mathrm{val}(a) \in \mathcal{T}_\sigma$ for $a \in \mathrm{T}_\sigma$.

T_0 consists of $0, 1, 1+1, 1+1+1, \ldots$ and hence is identified with the set $\mathbf{N}$ of natural numbers. Let $\omega := D_0 0, \Omega := D_1 0$ and generally $\Omega_\sigma := D_\sigma 0$. The Ω_σ's as well as 1 are called *regular* tree notations.

For any $a \in \mathrm{T}$ we have $\mathrm{val}(a) \in \mathcal{T}_\nu$, i.e. $\mathrm{val}(a)\colon I \to \mathcal{T}_\nu$ with $I = \emptyset, \{0\}$ or $\mathcal{T}_\sigma$ for some $\sigma < \nu$. We now want to recover from a its *type* $\tau(a)$, which is to be $0, 1$ or Ω_σ if I is $\emptyset, \{0\}$ or $\mathcal{T}_\sigma$, respectively. In the case $\tau(a) = \Omega_\sigma$, we also want to recover from a its *fundamental sequence*, i.e. notations $a[z] \in \mathrm{T}$ with value $\mathrm{val}(a)(\mathrm{val}(z))$, for all $z \in \mathrm{T}_\sigma$.

Let $|0| := \emptyset, |1| := \{0\}$ and $|\Omega_\sigma| := \mathrm{T}_\sigma$. For $a \in \mathrm{T}$ we define $\tau(a) \in \{0,1\} \cup \{\Omega_\sigma : \sigma < \nu\}$ and $a[z] \in \mathrm{T}$ for $z \in |\tau(a)|$ by induction on a, as follows.

i. For $a \in \{0,1\} \cup \{\Omega_\sigma : \sigma < \nu\}$ let $\tau(a) := a$ and $a[z] := z$.

ii. For $D_\sigma a$ with $\tau(a) = 1$ let $\tau(D_\sigma a) := \omega$ and $(D_\sigma a)[n] := (D_\sigma a[0]) \cdot (n+1)$.

iii. For $D_\sigma a$ with $\tau(a) = \Omega_\varrho$ with $\varrho \leq \sigma$ let $\tau(D_\sigma a) := \Omega_\varrho$ and $(D_\sigma a)[z] := D_\sigma a[z]$.

iv. For $D_\sigma a$ with $\tau(a) = \Omega_{\mu+1}$ with $\sigma < \mu+1$ let $\tau(D_\sigma a) := \omega$ and $(D_\sigma a)[n] := D_\sigma a[z_n]$ with $z_0 := \Omega_\mu$, $z_{n+1} := D_\mu a[z_n]$.

v. $\tau(a_1, \ldots, a_k) := \tau(a_k)$ and $(a_1, \ldots, a_k)[z] := (a_1, \ldots, a_{k-1}, a_k[z])$.

Then clearly $\tau(a) = 0 \iff a = 0$ and $\tau(a) = 1 \iff a = a[0] + 1$. Also, if $a \in \mathrm{T}_\sigma$ and $\tau(a) \neq 0, 1$, then $\tau(a) = \Omega_\varrho$ for some $\varrho < \sigma$, and in this case we have $a[z] \in \mathrm{T}_\sigma$ for all $z \in \mathrm{T}_\varrho = |\tau(a)|$.

Lemma 2.1. *If* $a \in \mathrm{T}$ *and* $z \in |\tau(a)|$, *then* $\mathrm{val}(z) \in \mathrm{dom}(\mathrm{val}(a))$ *and* $\mathrm{val}(a[z]) = \mathrm{val}(a)(\mathrm{val}(z))$.

Proof. First note that if $\tau(a) = 0, 1$ or Ω_σ, then $\mathrm{dom}(\mathrm{val}(a)) = \emptyset, \{0\}$ or $\mathcal{T}_\sigma$. We prove the Lemma by induction on a, and treat only Case iv, i.e. $D_\sigma a$ with

$\tau(a) = \Omega_{\mu+1}$ and $\sigma < \mu+1$. Let $\mathrm{val}(a) = (\alpha_\zeta)_{\zeta \in \mathcal{T}_{\mu+1}}$. Then by induction hypothesis

$$\mathrm{val}((D_\sigma a)[n]) = \mathrm{val}(D_\sigma a[z_n]) = \mathcal{D}_\sigma(\mathrm{val}(a[z_n])) = \mathcal{D}_\sigma \alpha_{\mathrm{val}(z_n)}$$

with $z_0 = \Omega_\mu, z_{n+1} = D_\mu a[z_n]$, and

$$\mathrm{val}(D_\sigma a)(n) = \mathcal{D}_\sigma(\mathrm{val}(a))(n) = \mathcal{D}_\sigma \alpha_{\zeta_n}$$

with $\zeta_0 = \Omega_\mu, \zeta_{n+1} = \mathcal{D}_\mu \alpha_{\zeta_n}$. Hence it suffices to prove $\mathrm{val}(z_n) = \zeta_n$. This follows by induction on n from $\mathrm{val}(\Omega_\mu) = \Omega_\mu$ and

$$\mathrm{val}(z_{n+1}) = \mathcal{D}_\mu \mathrm{val}(a[z_n]) = \mathcal{D}_\mu \alpha_{\mathrm{val}(z_n)} = \mathcal{D}_\mu \alpha_{\zeta_n} = \zeta_{n+1}. \square$$

As a consequence, we can infer the principle of *transfinite induction on* T_σ, i.e.

$$(\forall a \in \mathrm{T}_\sigma . \forall z \in |\tau(a)| : \varphi(a[z]) \to \varphi(a)) \to \forall a \in \mathrm{T}_\sigma : \varphi(a),$$

from the principle of transfinite induction on $\mathcal{T}_\sigma$ in Section 1. To see this, assume the premise and let $a \in \mathrm{T}_\sigma$. We use transfinite induction on $\mathrm{val}(a) \in \mathcal{T}_\sigma$. It suffices to prove $\forall z \in |\tau(a)| : \varphi(a[z])$. So let $z \in |\tau(a)|$. By Lemma 2.1 $\mathrm{val}(z) \in \mathrm{dom}(\mathrm{val}(a))$ and $\mathrm{val}(a[z]) = \mathrm{val}(a)(\mathrm{val}(z))$. Hence $\mathrm{val}(a[z])$ comes before $\mathrm{val}(a)$ in the sense of the inductive generation of $\mathcal{T}_\sigma$. So $\varphi(a[z])$ by induction hypothesis.

3. THE SLOW GROWING HIERARCHY

Given a tree notation $a \in \mathrm{T}_1$ and a natural number n, we may decide to climb down the tree (which grows downwards), using n as a parameter. This is done as follows. If the node we are at is formed by the successor operation, then we have to do some work to climb down one step. If on the other hand the node is formed as a sequence (which must be of length ω, since $a \in \mathrm{T}_1$), then we don't have to work but just slip down to the n-th element of the sequence.

If we count the pieces of work we have done until we reach a bottom node, we get a natural number $G_a(n)$. These functions $G_a : \mathbf{N} \to \mathbf{N}$ for $a \in \mathrm{T}_1$ form the so-called *slow growing hierarchy*; the formal definition is by transfinite induction on $a \in \mathrm{T}_1$, as follows

i. $G_0(n) = 0$,

ii. $G_{a+1}(n) = G_a(n) + 1$,

iii. $G_a(n) = G_{a[n]}(n)$ if $\tau(a) = \omega$.

Note that $G_{a+b}(n) = G_a(n) + G_b(n)$; this can be proved easily by transfinite induction on $b \in \mathrm{T}_1$.

For example,

$$
\begin{aligned}
G_k(n) &= k,\\
G_\omega(n) &= G_{\omega[n]}(n) = G_n(n) = n,\\
G_{D_0 1}(n) &= G_{\omega\cdot(n+1)}(n) = (n+1)\cdot G_\omega(n) = (n+1)\cdot n,\\
G_{D_0 2}(n) &= G_{(D_0 1)\cdot(n+1)}(n) = (n+1)\cdot G_{D_0 1}(n) = (n+1)^2\cdot n,\\
G_{D_0\omega}(n) &= G_{D_0 n}(n) = (n+1)^n\cdot n.
\end{aligned}
$$

Hence, the functions G_a with a built up from $0, 1$ by $+$ and D_0 but without nesting of D_0 are all polynomials.

The functions G_a with a of the form $D_0 D_1^m 0$ will be used in Section 4 to estimate the instances provided by existential proofs in arithmetic. We will also show in Section 5 that this result is best possible, since any such G_a is bounded by a function provably total in arithmetic.

In order to achieve these results we need some monotonicity properties of the G_a. Since $G_k n = k$ and $G_\omega n = n$, we cannot have that $\mathrm{val}(a) < \mathrm{val}(b)$ implies $G_a n \le G_b n$, for all n. Hence we introduce appropriate relations $<_k$ such that $a <_k b$ implies $G_a n \le G_b n$ for all $n \ge k$.

For $a \ne 0$ let $a^- := a[0]$ if $\tau(a) = 1$ or $\tau(a) = \omega$, and $a^- := a[\Omega_\mu]$ if $\tau(a) = \Omega_{\mu+1}$. Let $a <_k b$ iff we have a finite sequence $a = a_0, a_1, \ldots, a_n = b$ with $n > 0$ such that for all $i < n$ either $a_i = a_{i+1}^-$ or $\tau(a_{i+1}) = \omega$ and $a_i = a_{i+1}[j]$ for some j with $1 \le j \le k$. Note that from $a <_k b$ and $k \le l$ we can obviously conclude that $a <_l b$. We write $a \le_k b$ for $a <_k b$ or $a = b$.

Some of our later arguments will be by induction on $\mathrm{length}(a)$, which is defined by

$$
\begin{aligned}
\mathrm{length}(0) &= 0,\\
\mathrm{length}(1) &= 1,\\
\mathrm{length}(D_\sigma a) &= \mathrm{length}(a) + \sigma + 1,\\
\mathrm{length}(a_1, \ldots, a_k) &= \mathrm{length}(a_1) + \cdots + \mathrm{length}(a_k).
\end{aligned}
$$

Note that $\mathrm{length}(a+b) = \mathrm{length}(a) + \mathrm{length}(b)$.

Lemma 3.1.

i. *If $a \ne 0$, then $(D_\sigma a)^- = D_\sigma a^-$.*
ii. *If $b \ne 0$, then $(a+b)^- = a + b^-$.*
iii. *If $a \ne 0$, then $\mathrm{length}(a^-) < \mathrm{length}(a)$.*

Proof. i. If $\tau(a) = 1$ or ω, then $\tau(D_\sigma a) = \omega$ and

$$(D_\sigma a)^- = (D_\sigma a)[0] = (D_\sigma a[0]) \cdot 1 = D_\sigma a^-.$$

If $\tau(a) = \Omega_{\mu+1}$ with $\mu + 1 \leq \sigma$, then $\tau(D_\sigma a) = \Omega_{\mu+1}$ and

$$(D_\sigma a)^- = (D_\sigma a)[\Omega_\mu] = D_\sigma a[\Omega_\mu] = D_\sigma a^- .$$

If $\tau(a) = \Omega_{\mu+1}$ with $\sigma < \mu + 1$, then $\tau(D_\sigma a) = \omega$ and

$$(D_\sigma a)^- = (D_\sigma a)[0] = D_\sigma a[\Omega_\mu] = D_\sigma a^- .$$

ii. The claim follows from $\tau(a+b) = \tau(b)$ and $(a+b)[z] = a + b[z]$.
iii. By induction on a. Case $1, \omega$. Then $a^- = a[0] = 0$ and the claim is immediate. Case $D_\sigma a$. For $a = 0$ this is clear. For $a \neq 0$ we have by i

$$\begin{aligned} \text{length}((D_\sigma a)^-) &= \text{length}(D_\sigma a^-) \\ &= \text{length}(a^-) + \sigma + 1 \\ &< \text{length}(a) + \sigma + 1 \\ &= \text{length}(D_\sigma a). \end{aligned}$$

Case $a + b$. Similarly, using ii. □

Lemma 3.2.

i. If $b_0 <_k b$, then $a + b_0 <_k a + b$.
ii. If $c \neq 0$, then $1 \leq_1 c$.
iii. If $b <_k a$, then $D_\sigma b <_k D_\sigma a$.
iv. $(D_\sigma^m a) + 1 \leq_1 D_\sigma^m (a+1)$.

Proof. i. The claim follows from Lemma 3.1 ii together with $\tau(a+b) = \tau(b)$ and $(a+b)[z] = a + b[z]$.
ii. By induction on $\text{length}(c)$. Case 1. $1 \leq_1 1$. Case ω. $1 = \omega[1] <_1 \omega$. Case $\Omega_{\mu+1}$. $1 \leq_1 \Omega_\mu <_1 \Omega_{\mu+1}$; here $1 \leq \Omega_\mu$ holds by induction hypothesis. Case $D_\sigma a$ with $a \neq 0$. $1 \leq_1 D_\sigma a^- = (D_\sigma a)^- <_1 D_\sigma a$; here the first inequality follows by induction hypothesis, since $\text{length}(a^-) < \text{length}(a)$. Case $a + b$ with $a, b \neq 0$. $1 \leq_1 a <_1 a + 1 \leq_1 a + b$; in the last inequality we have used i and the induction hypothesis.
iii. This follows from $(D_\sigma a)^- = D_\sigma a^-$ and the fact that, if $\tau(a) = \omega$, then $\tau(D_\sigma a) = \omega$ and $(D_\sigma a)[n] = D_\sigma a[n]$.
iv. By induction on m. For 0 there is nothing to show, and in the induction step we have $(D_\sigma^{m+1} a) + 1 \leq_1 (D_\sigma^{m+1} a) \cdot 2 = (D_\sigma((D_\sigma^m a) + 1))[1] <_1 D_\sigma((D_\sigma^m a) + 1) \leq_1 D_\sigma^{m+1}(a+1)$, where in the first inequality we have used ii, and in the last one we have used the induction hypothesis and iii. □

Lemma 3.3.

i. If $\tau(c) = \Omega_{\mu+1}$ and $x, y \in |\tau(c)|$ and $x <_k y$, then $c[x] <_k c[y]$.
ii. If $\tau(c) = \Omega_{\mu+1}$ and $x \in |\tau(c)|$, then $c[x] + 1 \leq_1 c[x+1]$.

iii. *If* $\tau(c) = \omega$, *then* $c[n] + 1 \leq_1 c[n+1]$.

Proof. i. By induction on length(c). Case $\Omega_{\mu+1}$. Obvious, since $\Omega_{\mu+1}[z] = z$. Case $D_\sigma a$. Then $\tau(a) = \Omega_{\mu+1}$ and $\mu + 1 \leq \sigma$, hence

$$(D_\sigma a)[x] = D_\sigma a[x] <_k D_\sigma a[y] = (D_\sigma a)[y],$$

by induction hypothesis and Lemma 3.2 iii. Case $a + b$. Then $\tau(b) = \Omega_{\mu+1}$ and

$$(a+b)[x] = a + b[x] <_k a + b[y] = (a+b)[y].$$

ii. By induction on length(c). Case $\Omega_{\mu+1}$. Obvious, since $\Omega_{\mu+1}[z] = z$. Case $D_\sigma a$. Then $\tau(a) = \Omega_{\mu+1}$ and $\mu + 1 \leq \sigma$, hence

$$(D_\sigma a)[x] + 1 = D_\sigma a[x] + 1 \leq_1 D_\sigma(a[x] + 1) \leq_1 D_\sigma a[x+1] = (D_\sigma a)[x+1]$$

where in the first inequality we have used Lemma 3.2 iv, and in the second one the induction hypothesis and Lemma 3.2 iii. Case $a + b$. Then $\tau(b) = \Omega_{\mu+1}$ and

$$(a+b)[x] + 1 = a + b[x] + 1 \leq_1 a + b[x+1] = (a+b)[x+1].$$

iii. By induction on length(c). Case ω. Then $\omega[n] + 1 = n + 1 = \omega[n+1]$. Case $D_\sigma a$ with $\tau(a) = 1$. Then

$$(D_\sigma a)[n] + 1 = (D_\sigma a[0]) \cdot (n+1) + 1 \leq_1 (D_\sigma a[0]) \cdot (n+2) = (D_\sigma a)[n+1].$$

Case $D_\sigma a$ with $\tau(a) = \omega$. Then

$$(D_\sigma a)[n] + 1 = (D_\sigma a[n]) + 1 \leq_1 D_\sigma(a[n] + 1) \leq_1 D_\sigma a[n+1] = (D_\sigma a)[n+1].$$

Case $D_\sigma a$ with $\tau(a) = \Omega_{\mu+1}, \sigma < \mu + 1$. Then $(D_\sigma a)[n] = D_\sigma a[z_n]$ with $z_0 = \Omega_\mu$, $z_{n+1} = D_\mu a[z_n]$. It suffices to prove

$$z_n + 1 \leq_1 z_{n+1}, \tag{1}$$

for then we obtain

$$(D_\sigma a[z_n]) + 1 \leq_1 D_\sigma(a[z_n] + 1) \leq_1 D_\sigma a[z_n + 1] \leq_1 D_\sigma a[z_{n+1}],$$

using ii, (1) and i. We prove (1) by induction on n. The base case follows from

$$\Omega_\mu + 1 \leq_1 (D_\mu 0) \cdot 2 = (D_\mu 1)[1] <_1 D_\mu 1 \leq_1 D_\mu a[\Omega_\mu],$$

and the induction step follows from

$$(D_\mu a[z_n]) + 1 \leq_1 D_\mu(a[z_n] + 1) \leq_1 D_\mu a[z_n + 1] \leq_1 D_\mu a[z_{n+1}],$$

where we have used ii, the induction hypothesis and i. Case $a+b$ with $\tau(b) = \omega$. Then

$$(a+b)[n] + 1 = a + b[n] + 1 \leq_1 a + b[n+1] = (a+b)[n+1]. \square$$

Now we can prove the monotonicity properties of the functions G_a we were looking for.

Lemma 3.4. (Monotonicity Properties of the G_a)

i. *If $b <_k a$ and $k \leq n$, then $G_b(n) \leq G_a(n)$*

ii. *$G_a(n) \leq G_a(n+1)$.*

Proof. i. By transfinite induction on $a \in T_1$. Case a^-. If $\tau(a) = 1$, we have

$$G_{a^-}(n) < G_{a^-}(n) + 1 = G_a(n).$$

If $\tau(a) = \omega$, we have $a^- = a[0]$, and by Lemma 3.3 iii we know $a[0] \leq_1 a[n]$. Hence by induction hypothesis

$$G_{a^-}(n) = G_{a[0]}(n) \leq G_{a[n]}(n) = G_a(n).$$

Case $a[j]$ with $1 \leq j \leq k$. Then again by Lemma 3.3 iii we have $a[j] \leq_1 a[n]$, hence by induction hypothesis

$$G_{a[j]}(n) \leq G_{a[n]}(n) = G_a(n).$$

ii. By transfinite induction on $a \in T_1$. Case 0. $G_0(n) = 0 = G_0(n+1)$. Case $a+1$.

$$G_{a+1}(n) = G_a(n) + 1 \leq G_a(n+1) + 1 = G_{a+1}(n+1),$$

by induction hypothesis. Case $\tau(a) = \omega$.

$$G_a(n) = G_{a[n]}(n) \leq G_{a[n]}(n+1) \leq G_{a[n+1]}(n+1) = G_a(n+1)$$

by induction hypothesis and Lemma 3.3 iii together with i. $\square$

We finally prove a Lemma on the functions G_a which enables us to shift a depence on n from the index into the argument. This will be used in Section 4.

Lemma 3.5. *Let $a = D_0(c \cdot (n+1))$ with $c = D_\sigma^m(\Omega_\sigma \cdot m)$ and $1 \leq m \leq n$, and furthermore $d = D_0 D_\sigma^{m+2} 0$. Then we have $G_a(1) \leq G_d(n)$.*

Proof. First note that

$$\begin{aligned}
c \cdot (n+1) &= (D_\sigma^m(\Omega_\sigma \cdot m)) \cdot (n+1) \\
&= (D_\sigma(D_\sigma^{m-1}(\Omega_\sigma \cdot m) + 1))[n] \\
&\leq_n D_\sigma(D_\sigma^{m-1}(\Omega_\sigma \cdot m) + 1) \\
&\leq_1 D_\sigma^m(\Omega_\sigma \cdot (m+1)) \\
&= D_\sigma^m((D_\sigma 1)[m]) \\
&\leq_m D_\sigma^{m+1} 1
\end{aligned}$$

Hence we obtain, using Lemma 3.4 i and ii

$$G_{D_0(c\cdot(n+1))}(1) \leq G_{D_0(c\cdot(n+1))}(n) \leq G_{D_0 D_\sigma^{m+2} 0}(n). \square$$

4. AN ESTIMATE OF INSTANCES IN EXISTENTIAL PROOFS

We now set up a formal system of terms involving recursion operators and on top of it a formal system of derivations involving induction axioms. It is possible and convenient to treat both simultaneously; we use r, s, t to denote terms as well as derivations.

For any term/derivation r we define inductively what it means for r to be SDH–generated with size a (a tree notation) and rank m; we write $\vdash_m^a r$ for this. Note that r is a finite term/derivation here, i.e. it is not expanded into an infinite object using some kind of ω–rule. The transfinite analysis of r comes in at the level of transfinite SDH generation trees for such r, whose size is measured by our notations for (transfinite) trees treated in Section 2. The inductive definition of $\vdash_m^a r$ involves an ω^+–Rule, which is used for an appropriate analysis of terms/derivations containing recursion/induction.

We start out with the easy observation that for any term/derivation r we can find an SHD generation tree of size Ωk and rank m, for some k and m reflecting the levels of recursion/induction operators in r. Hence we get $\vdash_m^{\Omega k} r$. Then we use a Cut Elimination Lemma to bring the rank m down to zero, at the expense of rising the size Ωk to $D_1^m(\Omega k)$; so we get

$$\vdash_0^{D_1^m(\Omega k)} r.$$

Now we can apply a First Collapsing Lemma, which says that if $\vdash_0^a r$ with r closed, then $\vdash_0^{D_0(a)} |r|$, where $|r|$ is the numeral denoting

- the value of r in case r is a term, or
- the value of some correct instance provided by r in case r is a closed derivation of an existential formula $\exists y\, \mathrm{Spec}(n, y)$ with an atomic formula Spec.

Hence we get

$$\vdash_0^{D_0 D_1^m(\Omega k)} |r|.$$

But SDH generation trees of rank 0 for numerals can be easily analysed: From $\vdash_0^a n$ with $a \in T_1$ we first get $\vdash_0^{G_a(1)} n$ by the Second Collapsing Lemma and then $n < G_a(1)$ by the Value Lemma. So altogether we have

$$|r| < G_{D_0 D_1^m(\Omega k)}(1),$$

and by Lemma 3.5 this essentially suffices for our desired estimate.

We now carry out this program. First we have to say exactly what we mean by a term and by a formal proof. Our definition is guided by the following considerations. It should be possible to

- view a formal proof as a λ-term (i.e. a SCHEME procedure) which has the derived formula as its type, such that normalization will correspond to evaluation, and to
- carry out an ordinal (or better tree) analysis of formal proofs by the SDH–technique.

Since the SDH–technique also refers to λ-terms, it seems appropriate to use the $\to\forall$–fragment of Gentzens natural deduction calculus, for then the logical rules are just introduction and elimination rules for $\to$ and $\forall$, which correspond exactly to λ-abstraction and application.

The first thing to note is that we don't loose anything by this restriction to the $\to\forall$–fragment, and in particular don't need any special axioms to recover classical arithmetic. To see this, we first show that for any atomic formula $A(\vec{x})$ we can derive its stability $\forall\vec{x}.\neg\neg A(\vec{x}) \to A(\vec{x})$. This is done as follows. Atomic formulas are taken as terms $\mathrm{atom}(r)$ of type prop, with r a term of type boole and atom a constant of type boole $\to$ prop. In particular, falsity $\bot$ is defined as $\mathrm{atom}(\mathbf{ff})$ with $\mathbf{ff}$ a constant of type boole; then $\neg\varphi$ is defined to be $\varphi \to \bot$. Using boolean induction $\varphi(\mathbf{tt}) \to \varphi(\mathbf{ff}) \to \forall p\varphi(p)$, first prove

$$\forall p, q.\, \mathrm{atom}(p \supset q) \leftrightarrow (\mathrm{atom}(p) \to \mathrm{atom}(q))$$

where $\supset$ is a constant of type boole $\to$ boole $\to$ boole corresponding to implication; here we need the truth axiom $\mathrm{atom}(\mathbf{tt})$. Using this it is easy to prove

$$\forall p.\neg\neg\,\mathrm{atom}(p) \to \mathrm{atom}(p),$$

again by boolean induction.

Now we can substitute a boolean term $r(\vec{x})$ for p, and with $A(\vec{x}) :\equiv \mathrm{atom}(r(\vec{x}))$ we obtain $\forall\vec{x}.\neg\neg A(\vec{x}) \to A(\vec{x})$.

Using induction on $\to\forall$–formulas it is easy to derive $\neg\neg\varphi \to \varphi$ from the stability of atomic formulas. Now defining

$$\begin{aligned} \varphi \vee \psi \quad &\text{by} \quad \neg\varphi \to \neg\psi \to \bot, \\ \exists x\varphi(x) \quad &\text{by} \quad \neg\forall x\neg\varphi(x). \end{aligned}$$

we can derive exactly the same formulas as in classical arithmetic.

For brevity we do not give all details of our notion (and implementation) of term/derivation, but only collect those features which are relevant for our later arguments.

1. *Terms* have *types*, built up from ground types (here, for simplicity, just nat) by $(\varrho \to \sigma)$. Particular terms are the constructor constants 0 of type nat, S of type nat $\to$ nat and the recursion constants

   R of type $\varrho \to (\mathrm{nat} \to \varrho \to \varrho) \to \mathrm{nat} \to \varrho.$

   Any type has a *level*, defined by

$$\mathrm{lev}(\tau) = 0,$$
$$\mathrm{lev}(\varrho \to \sigma) = \max(\mathrm{lev}(\varrho) + 1, \mathrm{lev}(\sigma))$$

   with τ a ground type.

2. Since formulas are for derivations what types are for terms, we also need the notion of the *level* of a formula

$$\mathrm{lev}(A) = 0,$$
$$\mathrm{lev}(\varphi \to \psi) = \max(\mathrm{lev}(\varphi) + 1, \mathrm{lev}(\psi)),$$
$$\mathrm{lev}(\forall x \varphi(x)) = \max(\mathrm{lev}(\mathrm{nat}) + 1, \mathrm{lev}(\varphi))$$

   with A atomic. Note that for simplicity we only consider formulas with quantified variables of level 0.

3. *Derivations* derive formulas. Particular derivations are the induction axioms

   R of the formula $\varphi(0) \to (\forall x.\varphi(x) \to \varphi(Sx)) \to \forall x \varphi(x),$

   the truth axiom of the formula $\top$ and possibly some other axioms (or constructor constants for derivations) of true Π–formulas, i.e. formulas with only quantifier-free premises in implications.

4. If r derives ψ, then $\lambda u^{\varphi} r$ derives $\varphi \to \psi$. Similarly, if r has type σ, then $\lambda x^{\varrho} r$ has type $\varrho \to \sigma$. If r derives $\varphi(x)$ and if no assumption variable free in r assumes a formula with x among its free variables (this is known as *variable condition*), then $\lambda x r$ derives $\forall x \varphi(x)$.

5. If r derives $\varphi \to \psi$ and s derives φ, then rs derives ψ. Similarly, if r has type $\varrho \to \sigma$ and s has type ϱ, then rs has type σ. If r derives $\forall x \varphi(x)$ and s has type nat, then rs derives $\varphi(s)$.

6. Any term/derivation has a uniquely determined long normal form, where for R we have the usual conversion rules $Rrs0 \mapsto r$ and $Rrs(St) \mapsto st(Rrst)$. For example, if F is of type (nat $\to$ nat) $\to$ (nat $\to$ nat) and g is of type nat $\to$ nat, then the long normal form of

   g is $\lambda x.gx$

F is $\lambda zx.F(\lambda y.zy)x$
Fg is $\lambda x.F(\lambda y.gy)x$

We identify terms/derivations with the same long normal form.

For any term/derivation r let $\mathrm{lev}(r)$ denote the level of its type/formula.

For terms/derivations r with $\mathrm{lev}(r) = 0$, tree notations $a \in \mathrm{T}$ (see Section 2, taken with $\nu = 2$) and $m \in \mathbf{N}$ we define inductively the relation $\vdash^a_m r$, to be read r is SDH-*generated* with size a and rank m, by the following rules.

- *Variable Rule.* If $\vdash^a_m t_i\vec{y_i}$ for $i = 1, \ldots, n$ with $n \geq 0$, then $\vdash^{a+1}_m xt_1 \ldots t_n$.
- *Closure Rule 0.* $\vdash^1_m 0$.
- *Closure Rule S.* If $\vdash^a_m r$, then $\vdash^{a+1}_m Sr$.
- *Lemma Rule.* Let L be a lemma asserting a true Π–formula φ. If $\vdash^a_m r_i\vec{y_i}$ for $i = 1, \ldots, n$ with $n \geq 0$, then $\vdash^{a+1}_m L\vec{r}$.
- ω^+*–Rule.* If $\tau(a) = \Omega, \vdash^{a^-}_m t$ and $\forall z \in \mathrm{T}_1 \forall n. \vdash^z_0 n \rightarrow \vdash^{a[z]}_m Rrsn\vec{t}$, then $\vdash^a_m Rrst\vec{t}$.
- $<_1$*–Rule.* If $\vdash^b_m r$ and $b <_1 a$, then $\vdash^a_m r$.
- *Cut Rule.* If $\vdash^a_m r\vec{y}$ with $\mathrm{lev}(r) \leq m$ and $\vdash^a_m t_i\vec{y_i}$ for $i = 1, \ldots, n$ with $n \geq 1$, then $\vdash^{a+1}_m rt_1 \ldots t_n$.

More precisely, we first inductively define $\vdash^a_m r$ for $a \in \mathrm{T}_1$ by the rules given excluding the ω^+–Rule, and based on this relation we then define $\vdash^a_m r$ for $a \in \mathrm{T}$ by all the rules given.

Variable Lemma 4.1. *If* $c \neq 0$ *and* $\mathrm{lev}(x) < k$, *then* $\vdash^{c \cdot k}_m x\vec{y}$.

Proof. By induction on $\mathrm{lev}(x)$. By induction hypothesis $\vdash^{c \cdot (k-1)}_m y_i\vec{z_i}$, hence $\vdash^{c \cdot (k-1)+1}_m x\vec{y}$ by the Variable Rule, hence $\vdash^{c \cdot k}_m x\vec{y}$ by the $<_1$–Rule. □

Substitution Lemma 4.2. *If* $\vdash^a_m r$ *and* $\vdash^b_m s_j\vec{y_j}$ *with* $\mathrm{lev}(s_j) \leq m$ *for* $j = 1, \ldots, n$, *then* $\vdash^{b+a}_m r_{\vec{x}}[\vec{s}]$.

Proof. By induction on $\vdash^a_m r$. We write t^* for $t_{\vec{x}}[\vec{s}]$. *Variable Rule.* By induction hypothesis $\vdash^{b+a}_m t^*_i\vec{y_i}$, hence $\vdash^{b+a+1}_m xt^*_1 \ldots t^*_n$ by the Variable Rule. Now if x is one of the variables x_j to be substituted by s_j, we must use the Cut Rule instead of the Variable Rule. This is possible since $\mathrm{lev}(s_j) \leq m$ by hypothesis and $\vdash^{b+a}_m s_j\vec{y_j}$ by hypothesis and the $<_1$–Rule. Then (if $n > 0$) the Cut Rule yields $\vdash^{b+a+1}_m s_jt^*_1 \ldots t^*_n$, as required. In case $n = 0$ there are no t_i's and we have used the Variable Rule to generate $\vdash^{a+1}_m x_j$. But then $\vdash^{b+a+1}_m s_j$ holds by hypothesis and the $<_1$–Rule. For all other rules the claim follows easily from the induction hypothesis and the same rule. □

Cut Elimination Lemma 4.3. *If* $\vdash^a_{m+1} r$, *then* $\vdash^{D_1 a}_m r$.

Proof. By induction on $\vdash^a_{m+1} r$. *Variable Rule.* By induction hypothesis $\vdash^{D_1 a}_m t_i \vec{y_i}$, hence $\vdash^{(D_1 a)+1}_m x t_1 \dots t_n$ by the Variable Rule, hence $\vdash^{D_1(a+1)}_m x t_1 \dots t_n$ by the $<_1$–Rule. *Closure Rule 0.* Note that $1 <_1 D_1 1$. Hence $\vdash^{D_1 1}_m 0$ by the $<_1$–Rule. *Closure Rule S.* By induction hypothesis $\vdash^{D_1 a}_m r$, hence $\vdash^{(D_1 a)+1}_m Sr$ by the Closure Rule S, hence $\vdash^{D_1(a+1)}_m Sr$ by the $<_1$–Rule. *Lemma Rule.* By induction hypothesis $\vdash^{D_1 a}_m r_i \vec{y_i}$, hence $\vdash^{(D_1 a)+1}_m L\vec{r}$ by the Lemma Rule, hence $\vdash^{D_1(a+1)}_m L\vec{r}$ by the $<_1$–Rule. *ω^+–Rule.* Then $\vdash^a_{m+1} Rrst\vec{t}$ has been inferred from $\tau(a) = \Omega$, $\vdash^{a^-}_{m+1} t$, and

$$\forall z \in \mathrm{T}_1 \forall n.\ \vdash^z_0 n \rightarrow \vdash^{a[z]}_{m+1} Rrsn\vec{t}.$$

By induction hypothesis $\vdash^{D_1 a^-}_m t$, and

$$\forall z \in \mathrm{T}_1 \forall n.\ \vdash^z_0 n \rightarrow \vdash^{D_1 a[z]}_m Rrsn\vec{t}.$$

Now $D_1 a^- = (D_1 a)^-$, and since $\tau(a) = \Omega$ we have $D_1 a[z] = (D_1 a)[z]$. Hence $\vdash^{D_1 a}_m Rrst\vec{t}$ by the ω^+–Rule. *$<_1$–Rule.* By induction hypothesis $\vdash^{D_1 b}_m r$. Since from $b <_1 a$ we can infer $D_1 b <_1 D_1 a$, we get $\vdash^{D_1 a}_m r$ by the $<_1$–Rule. *Cut Rule.* By induction hypothesis $\vdash^{D_1 a}_m r\vec{y}$ and $\vdash^{D_1 a}_m t_i \vec{y_i}$. Since $\mathrm{lev}(r) \le m+1$, we have $\mathrm{lev}(t_i) \le m$ and hence $\vdash^{D_1 a + D_1 a}_m r t_1 \dots t_n$ by the Substitution Lemma. But $(D_1(a+1))[1] = D_1 a + D_1 a$, so $\vdash^{D_1(a+1)}_m r t_1 \dots t_n$ by the $<_1$–Rule. □

We now want to prove the Collapsing Lemma mentioned above. For its formulation we need the notion of the *first instance* $|r|$ *provided by a refutation* r *of* Π*–assumptions.* So let r be such a refutation, i.e. a derivation of a closed false atomic formula from assumptons $u_i{:}\,\varphi_i$, φ_i closed Π–formulas and φ_i true if φ_i is quantifier–free. Note that we identify derivations with the same long normal form, so we can always assume r to be normal. Hence r must be of one of the two forms below. In particular, it cannot contain induction axioms any more.

Case $r \equiv u_i \vec{r}$. If all derivations r_i among $\vec{r}$ actually derive true formulas (which can be decided, since the formulas are quantifier–free and can clearly be assumed to be closed), let $|r|$ be the list of all $|r_j|$, r_j term among $\vec{r}$. Otherwise, let $|r|$ be $|r_i \vec{u}|$, where r_i is the first derivation among $\vec{r}$ deriving a false quantifier–free formula and $\vec{u}$ are lemmas or assumptions of true formulas.

Case $r \equiv L\vec{r}$ with L a lemma. Then some r_i among $\vec{r}$ must derive a false quantifier–free formula, since r derives a false formula and the lemma L is assumed to be true. Let $|r|$ be $|r_i \vec{u}|$ for the first such r_i, with $\vec{u}$ lemmas or assumptions of true formulas.

First Collapsing Lemma 4.4. *Suppose* $\vdash_0^a r$ *with* r *a closed term of type* nat *or else a refutation of* Π*–assumptions. Let* $|r|$ *be the numerical value of* r *(in case* r *is a term), or the maximum value in the first instance provided by* r *(in case* r *is a derivation). Then* $\vdash_0^{D_0 a} |r|$.

Proof. By induction on $\vdash_0^a r$. *Variable Rule.* Then $r \equiv u_i \vec{r}$, and $\vdash_0^{a+1} u_i \vec{r}$ has been inferred from $\vdash_0^a r_i \vec{y}$. If all derivations r_i among $\vec{r}$ derive true formulas, then by definition $|r|$ is the list of all $|r_j|$, r_j term among $\vec{r}$, and $\vdash_0^{D_0 a} |r_j|$ holds by induction hypothesis, hence $\vdash_0^{D_0(a+1)} |r_j|$ by the $<_1$–Rule. Otherwise, again by definition $|r| = |r_i \vec{u}|$ where r_i is the first derivation among $\vec{r}$ deriving a false quantifier–free formula and $\vec{u}$ lemmas or assumptions of true formulas. Then $\vdash_0^{D_0 a} |r_i \vec{u}|$ holds by induction hypothesis, hence $\vdash_0^{D_0(a+1)} |r_i \vec{u}|$ by the $<_1$–Rule. *Closure Rule 0.* Clear, since $\vdash_0^{D_0 1} 0$ by the $<_1$–Rule. *Closure Rule S.* By induction hypothesis $\vdash_0^{D_0 a} |r|$, hence $\vdash_0^{D_0 a+1} S|r|$ by the Closure Rule S, hence $\vdash_0^{D_0(a+1)} S|r|$ by the $<_1$–Rule, and $|Sr| = S|r|$. *Lemma Rule.* Then $r \equiv L\vec{r}$, and $\vdash_0^{a+1} L\vec{r}$ has been inferred from $\vdash_0^a r_i \vec{y}$. By definition $|r| = |r_i \vec{u}|$ for some r_i among $\vec{r}$ deriving a false quantifier–free formula with $\vec{u}$ lemmas or assumptions of true formulas. By induction hypothesis$\vdash_0^{D_0 a} |r_i \vec{u}|$, hence $\vdash_0^{D_0(a+1)} |r_i \vec{u}|$ by the $<_1$–Rule. ω^+*–Rule.* Then $\vdash_0^a R r_0 s t \vec{t}$ has been inferred from $\tau(a) = \Omega$, $\vdash_0^{a^-} t$, and

$$\forall z \in \mathrm{T}_1 \forall n. \vdash_0^z n \rightarrow \vdash_0^{a[z]} R r_0 s n \vec{t}.$$

We have to show $\vdash_0^{D_0 a} |R r_0 s k \vec{t}|$ with $k := |t|$. From $\tau(a) = \Omega$ we get $\tau(D_0 a) = \omega$ and $(D_0 a)[n] = D_0 a[z_n]$ with $z_0 = \omega$, $z_{n+1} = D_0 a[z_n]$, hence $z_1 = D_0 a[\omega] = D_0 a^-$. Since $D_0 a^- = (D_0 a)^-$, the induction hypothesis yields $\vdash_a^{(D_0 a)^-} k$. Since $(D_0 a)^- \in T_1$, we get $\vdash_0^{a[(D_0 a)^-]} |R r_0 s k \vec{t}|$ from our assumption, so again the induction hypothesis yields $\vdash_0^{D_0 a[(D_0 a)^-]} |R r_0 s k \vec{t}|$. But $D_0 a[z_1] = (D_0 a)[1]$, so the $<_1$–Rule gives $\vdash_0^{D_0 a}$ $|R r_0 s k \vec{t}|$. $<_1$*–Rule.* By induction hypothesis $\vdash_0^{D_0 b} |r|$, hence $\vdash_0^{D_0 a} |r|$ by the $<_1$–Rule. □

Second Collapsing Lemma 4.5. *If* $\vdash_0^a n$ *with* $a \in \mathrm{T}_1$, *then* $\vdash_0^{G_a(1)} n$.

Proof. By induction on $\vdash_0^a n$. *Closure Rule 0.* $\vdash_0^{G_1(1)} 0$ since $G_1(1) = 1$. *Closure Rule S.* By induction hypothesis $\vdash_0^{G_a(1)} n$, hence $\vdash_0^{G_{a+1}(1)} Sn$ by the Closure Rule S, since $G_{a+1}(1) = G_a(1) + 1$. $<_1$*–Rule.* By induction hypothesis $\vdash_0^{G_b(1)} n$, hence $\vdash_0^{G_a(1)} n$ by the $<_1$–Rule, since from $b <_1 a$ we can conclude $G_b(1) \leq G_a(1)$. □

Value Lemma 4.6. *If* $\vdash_0^k n$, *then* $n < k$.

Proof. By induction on $\vdash_0^k n$. *Closure Rule 0.* Clear, since $|0| = 0$. *Closure Rule S.* By induction hypothesis $n < k$, hence $Sn < k + 1$. $<_1$*–Rule.* Note first that from $b <_1 k$ we can conclude $b \in T_0$ and hence that b is a numeral l with $l < k$. By induction hypothesis $n < l$, hence $n < k$. □

We now construct an "initial" SDH–generation tree for any term/derivation r. The main point here is that by using the Cut Rule we can sort of "shortcut" an enormous SDH–generation tree. Consider for example an application term $(\lambda x r)s$ where s may be complex and r may contain many occurrences of x. The shortcut is achieved by considering instead of $(\lambda x r)s$, which may have a complex normal form, the two terms $(\lambda x r)y$ (with a variable y) and s separately.

Embedding Lemma 4.7. *Assume that all subterms/subderivations of r have levels $\leq m$. Then we can find k such that $\vdash_m^{\Omega\cdot k} r\vec{y}$*

Proof. By induction on r. *Case x.* The claim follows from the Variable Lemma with $k := \mathrm{lev}(x) + 1$. *Case L.* By the Variable Rule, the Lemma Rule and the $<_1$–Rule we have $\vdash_0^{\Omega(k+1)} L\vec{y}$ if $\mathrm{lev}(y_i) < k$. *Case R.* Consider $Rywx\vec{y}$. We want to apply the ω^+–Rule to get $\vdash_m^{\Omega\cdot(k+1)} Rywx\vec{y}$ with $k = \mathrm{lev}(y)$. Since trivially $\tau(\Omega\cdot(k+1)) = \Omega$ and $\vdash_0^{(\Omega\cdot(k+1))^-} x$ we only have to show

$$\forall z \in \mathrm{T}_1 \forall n. \vdash_0^z n \to \vdash_m^{\Omega\cdot k+z} Rywn\vec{y}.$$

This is done by induction on $\vdash_0^z n$. *Closure Rule 0.* Since $Ryw0\vec{y}$ is identified with $y\vec{y}$ it suffices to show $\vdash_m^{\Omega\cdot k+1} y\vec{y}$. Since $\mathrm{lev}(y_i) < k$, this follows from the Variable Lemma and the Variable Rule. *Closure Rule S.* By induction hypothesis $\vdash_m^{\Omega\cdot k+z} Rywn\vec{y}$. Since $Ryw(Sn)\vec{y}$ is identified with $wn(Rywn)\vec{y}$ it suffices to show $\vdash_m^{\Omega\cdot k+z+1} wn(Rywn)\vec{y}$. This follows from the Variable Rule, since from $\vdash_0^z n$ we get $\vdash_0^{\Omega\cdot k+z} n$ by the Substitution Lemma. *$<_1$–Rule.* The claim follows from the induction hypothesis and the $<_1$–Rule. *Case* 0. Obvious. *Case S.* By the Variable Rule $\vdash_m^1 y$, hence $\vdash_m^{\Omega} y$ by the $<_1$–Rule, hence $\vdash_m^{\Omega+1} Sy$ by the Closure Rule S, hence $\vdash_m^{\Omega\cdot 2} Sy$ again by the $<_1$–Rule. *Case $\lambda x r$.* By induction hypothesis $\vdash_m^{\Omega\cdot k} r\vec{y}$, which says $\vdash_m^{\Omega\cdot k} (\lambda x r)x\vec{y}$, since both terms have the same normal form and hence are identified. *Case ts.* By induction hypothesis $\vdash_m^{\Omega\cdot k} ty\vec{y}$ and $\vdash_m^{\Omega\cdot k} s\vec{z}$. Also $\vdash_m^{\Omega\cdot k} y_i\vec{y}_i$. Note that by the $<_1$–Rule we can assume that we have the same k in all cases. Then $\vdash_m^{\Omega\cdot k+1} ts\vec{y}$ by the Cut Rule, hence $\vdash_m^{\Omega\cdot(k+1)} ts\vec{y}$ by the $<_1$–Rule. □

Now we obtain the desired estimate of instances in existential proofs, in terms of the slow growing hierarchy.

Theorem 4.8. *Let r be a closed term of type* nat → nat. *Then there is an m such that for all $n \geq m$*

$$|rn| \leq G_{D_0 D_1^{m+2} 0}(n).$$

Similarly, let r be a closed derivation of a closed formula $\forall x \exists y\, \mathrm{Spec}(x,y)$ with $\mathrm{Spec}(x,y)$ atomic, and let $u{:}\forall y \neg \mathrm{Spec}(x,y)$ be an assumption variable. Then there is an m such that for all $n \geq m$

$$|rnu| \leq G_{D_0 D_1^{m+2} 0}(n).$$

Proof. We only treat the second part, since the proof of the first part is identical (just leave u out). Consider $r(Sx)u$. By the Embedding Lemma 4.7 we find an m such that $\vdash_m^{\Omega \cdot m} r(Sx)u$. Hence $\vdash_0^c r(Sx)u$ with $c := D_1^m(\Omega \cdot m)$ by the Cut Elimination Lemma 4.3. Since $\vdash_0^{c \cdot n}(n-1)$ (by the Closure Rules and the $<_1$–Rule) we get $\vdash_0^{c \cdot (n+1)} rnu$ by the Substitution Lemma 4.2, and then $\vdash_0^a |rnu|$ with $a := D_0(c \cdot (n+1))$ by the First Collapsing Lemma 4.4. Hence $|rnu| < G_a(1)$ by the Second Collapsing Lemma 4.5 and the Value Lemma 4.6. So by Lemma 3.5 we get $|rnu| < G_d(n)$ with $d := D_0 D_1^{m+2}0$, for all $n \geq m$. □

5. COMPLEX EXISTENTIAL PROOFS

We have just seen that for any closed derivation r of a closed formula of the form $\forall x \exists y \, \mathrm{Spec}(x, y)$ with $\mathrm{Spec}(x, y)$ atomic there is an m such that for all $n \geq m$ the instance $|rn|$ provided by the existential derivation $\exists y \, \mathrm{Spec}(n, y)$ is bounded by $G_{D_0 D_1^{m+2}0}(n)$. We now show that this bound is sharp: We consider the particular specification

$$(D_0 D_1^{m+2}0)[x]^y = 0.$$

By Section 2 we already know that

$$\forall x \exists y (D_0 D_1^{m+2}0)[x]^y = 0$$

is true; here we show that for any m this formula is actually derivable in an arithmetical system. Since by the definition of the slow growing hierarchy in Section 3 the least k such that $(D_0 D_1^{m+2}0)[n]^k = 0$ is $\geq G_{D_0 D_1^{m+2}0}(n)$ (if we let $a[n] := a[0]$ for $\tau(a) = 1$), we can conclude that the bound of Section 4 is best possible.

The arithmetical system we work with is taken to deal with tree notations directly. However, of course we do not use any kind of transfinite induction but only structural induction on the build-up of tree notations. More precisely, we take the system T of tree notations treated in Section 2 based on the fixed $\nu = 2$; let a, b, c, z range over T. Then the function $a[z]$ giving the z–th element of the fundamental sequence for a is defined by the structural recursion in Section 2. We also use $a[z]^k := a[z][z] \dots [z]$.

Let $W_n = \{a \in \mathrm{T}_1 | \exists k a[n]^k = 0\}$, and call a formula $\varphi(a)$ *n–progressive* if

$$\forall a. \forall z \in \|\tau(a)\|_n : \varphi(a[z]) \rightarrow \varphi(a)$$

where $\|\Omega\|_n := W_n$, $\|\omega\|_n := \{n\}$, $\|1\|_n := \{n\}$ and $\|0\|_n := \emptyset$.

Lemma 5.1. *Let $\varphi(a)$ be the formula $D_0 a \in W_n$. Then $\varphi(a)$ is n–progressive, i.e.*

$$\forall a. \forall z \in \|\tau(a)\|_n : D_0 a[z] \in W_n \rightarrow D_0 a \in W_n$$

Proof. Let a be fixed. Assume

$$\forall z \in \|\tau(a)\|_n : D_0 a[z] \in W_n. \tag{1}$$

We have to show that $D_0 a \in W_n$, i.e. that $\exists k (D_0 a)[n]^k = 0$. *Case* $a = 0$. The claim follows from $\omega[n] = n$ and $m[n]^k = m - k$. *Case* $\tau(a) = 1$. Note first that the set W_n clearly is closed against addition. Since $(D_0 a)[n] = (D_0 a[n]) \cdot (n+1)$, the claim follows from (1), which in our case is $D_0 a[n] \in W_n$. *Case* $\tau(a) = \omega$. Then $(D_0 a)[n] = D_0 a[n]$, and $D_0 a[n] \in W_n$ by (1). *Case* $\tau(a) = \Omega$. Then $(D_0 a)[0] = D_0 a[\omega]$, $(D_0 a)[m+1] = D_0 a[(D_0 a)[m]]$. We show $(D_0 a)[m] \in W_n$ by induction on m. For $m = 0$ we get $D_0 a[\omega] \in W_n$ by (1), since $\omega \in W_n$ (see Case $a = 0$). For the induction step we can assume $(D_0 a)[m] \in W_n$. But then $D_0 a[(D_0 a)[m]] \in W_n$ by (1). □

Lemma 5.2. *If the formula $\psi(a)$ is n–progressive, then so is*

$$\psi^*(a) :\equiv \forall c. \psi(c) \to \psi(c + D_1 a).$$

Proof. Let $\psi(a)$ be n–progressive, i.e.

$$\forall a. \forall z \in \|\tau(a)\|_n : \psi(a[z]) \to \psi(a). \tag{2}$$

We have to show that $\psi^*(a)$ is n–progressive. So let a be given and assume that

$$\forall z \in \|\tau(a)\|_n \forall c. \psi(c) \to \psi(c + D_1 a[z]). \tag{3}$$

We must show $\psi^*(a)$. So let also c be given and assume $\psi(c)$. We have to show $\psi(c + D_1 a)$. By (2) it suffices to prove

$$\forall z \in \|\tau(D_1 a)\|_n : \psi(c + (D_1 a)[z]). \tag{4}$$

Case $a = 0$. We must show $\forall z \in W_n : \psi(c + z)$, i.e. $z \in \mathrm{T}_1 \to z[n]^k = 0 \to \psi(c + z)$. This is done by induction on k. For $k = 0$ the claim follows from our assumption $\psi(c)$. For the induction step, assume $z \in \mathrm{T}_1$. Then $\|\tau(z)\|_n = \{n\}$ (if $z \neq 0$, but the case $z = 0$ is obvious). Hence by (2) with $c + z$ for a it suffices to show $\psi(c + z[n])$. But since $(z[n])[n]^k = z[n]^{k+1} = 0$ this follows from the induction hypothesis. *Case* $\tau(a) = 1$. We must show $\psi(c + (D_1 a)[n])$, i.e. $\psi(c + (D_1 a[n]) \cdot (n+1))$. We prove $\psi(c + (D_1 a[n]) \cdot m)$ by induction on m. For $m = 0$ we have $\psi(c)$ by our assumption. For the induction step, (3) with $c + (D_1 a[n]) \cdot m$ for c and the induction hypothesis yield $\psi(c + (D_1 a[n]) \cdot m + D_1 a[n])$. *Case* $\tau(a) = \omega, \Omega$. Since in this case $\tau(D_1 a) = \tau(a)$ and $(D_1 a)[z] = D_1 a[z]$ we get the claim (4) from (3) and our assumption $\psi(c)$. □

Theorem 5.3. *For any m, we can formally prove in arithmetic*

$$\forall x \exists y (D_0 D_1^m 0)[x]^y = 0.$$

Proof. We give an informal proof which can easily be formalized. Let n be fixed. Since the formula $\varphi(a) \equiv D_0 a \in W_n$ is n–progressive by Lemma 5.1, we know from Lemma 5.2 that also $\varphi^*(a)$, $\varphi^{**}(a), \dots, \varphi^m(a)$ are n–progressive. Hence we have $\varphi^m(0)$, hence $\varphi^{m-1}(D_1 0)$ by the definition of ψ^*, hence inductively $\varphi^*(D_1^{m-1}0)$, hence $\varphi(D_1^m 0)$, hence $\exists y(D_0 D_1^m 0)[n]^y = 0$. □

Note that in this proof we had to use induction axioms of complexity (alternating quantifiers) depending on m. The main idea here, i.e. the definition of $\psi^*(a)$ as a kind of "lift by an exponential of a", again goes back to early work of Gentzen.

APPENDIX: AN IMPLEMENTATION OF PROOFS

We now describe in some more detail our implementation of arithmetical terms and proofs, specifically of the proofs of the combinatorial theorems in Section 5. These proofs are of particular interest since — in spite of their simplicity — they exhaust the strength of arithmetic, in the sense that although $\forall n \exists k (D_0 D_1^m 0)[n]^k = 0$ is provable for any fixed m, the general theorem $\forall m \forall n \exists k (D_0 D_1^m 0)[n]^k = 0$ is not. We also use these implemented proofs to discuss the proofs–as–programs paradigm, and report on some experiments where we have used some of these proofs as programs. Finally we have some comments on how our implementation of proofs relates to others (like Lambda and Isabelle).

Obviously normalization of proofs is the central subject for the use of proofs as programs, and as already mentioned in the introduction, we implement normalization by the built–in evaluation mechanism of SCHEME. This is possible since we can work with the $\rightarrow\forall$–fragment of Gentzen's natural deduction calculus, for then the logical rules are just introduction and elimination rules for $\rightarrow$ and $\forall$, which correspond exactly to λ–abstraction and application.

However, to carry out this plan we have to overcome a difficulty: Derivations in natural deduction style generally contain free assumption variables $u{:}\varphi$ where φ can be any formula. Now when we want to normalize this derivation by evaluating it, we have to assign something to the variable $u{:}\varphi$. A moments reflection will show that this should be a procedure of the same "arity" $\alpha_1 \rightarrow \dots \rightarrow \alpha_n \rightarrow 0$ as the formula φ (where the arity $\alpha(\varphi)$ of a formula φ is defined by $\alpha(A) = 0$ for an atomic formula A, $\alpha(\varphi \rightarrow \psi) = \alpha(\varphi) \rightarrow \alpha(\psi)$ and $\alpha(\forall x \varphi) = 0 \rightarrow \alpha(\varphi)$), and should be such that when it is applied to argument procedures $f_1, \dots, f_n$, then the outcome should be a term $ur_1 \dots r_n$, where r_i is a lambda–term whose value is f_i. We call this procedure the result of making u self–evaluating at the arity of the formula φ attached to u. From the above description it is rather clear that a precise definition of how u is made self–evaluating will involve another operation of independent interest, which inverts evaluation in the following sense: When it is given a procedure obtained by evaluating a (typable) lambda–term, it returns a lambda–term which evaluates to this very procedure.

An implementation of such operations **make-self-evaluating** and **proc->expr** in SCHEME can be given by simultaneous recursion: (For a treatment of the same problem in the general theory of functional programming languages, which avoids SCHEME's operational **gensym**–construct for creating new bound variables, cf. (Berger and Schwichtenberg 1991)).

```
(define (mse expr arity) ;mse for make-self-evaluating
  (if (equal? 0 arity)
      expr
      (lambda (arg)
        (mse (list expr (proc->expr arg (arg-arity arity)))
             (val-arity arity)))))

(define (proc->expr proc arity)
  (if (equal? 0 arity)
      proc
      (let* ((arity0 (arg-arity arity))
             (symbol (gensym-of-arity arity0)))
        (list 'lambda (list symbol)
              (proc->expr
                (proc (mse symbol arity0))
                (val-arity arity))))))
```

Another point in our implementation of proofs is that we want to shift the “computational part” of an arithmetical proof as much as possible to a rewrite system. Hence terms occurring in formulas are always normalized according to the recursive definitions of the function symbols occurring in the term. Since normalization is done by evaluation, we have to deal with the same problem just discussed for derivations. The solution is the same: make the free variables self–evaluating. However, since we only treat first–order terms we can make a variable self–evaluating by just quoting it. So we want e.g.

```
((+-nat 2) 3) => 5
((+-nat 2) 'x) => ((+-nat 2) x)
((+-nat 'x) 0) => x
((+-nat 'x) 2) => (suc-nat (suc-nat x))
((+-nat 2) (suc-nat 'x)) => (suc-nat ((+-nat 2) x))
```

This can be achieved if we define `+-nat` by:

```
(define +-nat (lambda (m) (lambda (n)
  (cond ((zero-nat? n) m)
        ((suc-nat? n) (suc-nat ((+-nat m) (pred-nat n))))
        (else (list (list '+-nat m) n))))))
```

Here we have used

```
(define (suc-nat x) (if (and (integer? x) (not (negative? x)))
                        (+ 1 x)
                        (list 'suc-nat x)))

(define (zero-nat? x) (and (integer? x) (zero? x)))

(define (suc-nat? x)
  (or (and (integer? x) (positive? x))
      (and (pair? x) (equal? 'suc-nat (car x)))))

(define (pred-nat x)
  (cond ((and (integer? x) (positive? x)) (- x 1))
        ((and (pair? x) (equal? 'suc-nat (car x))) (cadr x))
        (else (error "can't form" 'pred-nat x))))
```

`*-nat` is defined similarly.

To implement proofs we first have to build formulas from terms. Since the formulas serve as types in derivations and in particular determine which rules are to be applied we must be careful never to "compute" say propositional formulae, since this will destroy their logical form and hence spoil the correctness of a derivation. So we distinguish between boolean objects on the one side (where the propositional connectives can be computed) and formulas or objects of type `prop` on the other side (where such computations are not allowed). Specifically, equality is taken as a binary boolean-valued function `=-nat`, i.e. `((=-nat 3) 5)` evaluates to the boolean object `#F` (also denoted by `()`), whereas the corresponding prime formula is given by `(atom ((=-nat 3) 5))` (which evaluates to `(atom ())`, our prime formula for falsity), where `atom` transforms a boolean expression into an expression of a formula. The formal definitions of `=-nat` and `atom` are

```
(define  =-nat (lambda (m) (lambda (n)
  (cond ((zero-nat? m)
         (cond ((zero-nat? n) true)
               ((suc-nat? n) false)
               (else (list (list '=-nat m) n))))
        ((suc-nat? m)
         (cond ((zero-nat? n) false)
               ((suc-nat? n)
                ((=-nat (pred-nat m)) (pred-nat n)))
               (else (list (list '=-nat m) n))))
        (else (list (list '=-nat m) n))))))

(define (atom x) (list 'atom x))
```

`<=-nat` is defined similarly.

Also, we have two versions of implication: `imp#` to build boolean terms and `imp` to build formulas, such that e.g.

```
((imp# #T) #F) => ()
(imp (atom #T) (atom #F)) => (imp (atom #T) (atom ()))
```

This is achieved by defining

```
(define imp# (lambda (p) (lambda (q)
  (cond ((false? p) true)
        ((true? p) q)
        ((true? q) true)
        (else (list (list 'imp# p) q))))))

(define (imp x y) (list 'imp x y))
```

The universal quantifier over natural numbers is taken as `all-nat` of type `(nat->prop)->prop`. For instance, the formula $\forall n : 0 + n = n$ is represented as the self–evaluating SCHEME object

```
(all-nat (lambda (n) (atom ((=-nat ((+-nat 0) n)) n))))
```

The precise SCHEME definition of **all-nat** is

```
(define (all-nat proc)
  (let ((symbol (gensym "X^0_")))
    (list 'all-nat
          (list 'lambda (list symbol) (proc symbol)))))
```

where **gensym** is used to avoid clashes of bound variables.

For the implementation of proofs first note that we can describe a proof by three objects: a context, a formula and an expression which evaluates — provided the context symbols are made self-evaluating — to itself in case formula is of level 0, and to a procedure in case the formula is not of level 0. So the expression is a (type–free) lambda term corresponding to the build–up of the derivation from axiom–constants and assumption–variables by elimination and introduction rules. A context is an association list $((x_1\varrho_1)\dots(x_m\varrho_m)(u_1\varphi_1)\dots(u_n\varphi_n))$ (not necessarily in this order) assigning types and formulas to symbols, where

- the symbols $x_1,\dots,x_m,u_1,\dots,u_n$ are distinct,
- if y is a symbol in the context of an assumption formula φ_i, then y does not appear among $x_1,\dots,x_m$, and
- the contexts of all assumption formulas are consistent; their sup is called the critical context of the given context.

$(x_1\varrho_1)\dots(x_m\varrho_m)$ is called the free context, the sup of the free context and the critical context the object context, and $(u_1\varphi_1)\dots(u_n\varphi_n)$ the assumption context of the given context.

To give an example of an implemented proof, let us see how the usual inductive proof of $\forall n: 0+n=n$ can be represented. We first write this proof in a self–explaining natural deduction notation, which in our implementation is also machine–readable.

```
(define 0+n=n-proof
  (elim (ind-axiom-at |(n)(0+n=n)|)
        truth-axiom
        (intro (var 'IH |0+n=n|)
               (list 'IH |0+n=n|)
```

```
              (list 'n nat))))
```

where the induction axiom at $\forall n : 0 + n = n$ is of course an axiom–constant of the formula

$$0 + 0 = 0 \to (\forall n.0 + n = n \to 0 + Sn = Sn) \to \forall n : 0 + n = n.$$

Note that the formula $0 + 0 = 0$, i.e. `(atom ((=-nat ((+-nat 0) 0)) 0))`, evaluates to and hence is identified with `(atom #T)`, and similarly the formula $0 + Sn = Sn$, i.e. `(atom ((=-nat ((+-nat 0) (suc-nat n))) (suc-nat n)))`, evaluates to and hence is identified with $0 + n = n$, i.e. with `(atom ((=-nat ((+-nat 0) n)) n))`. This is the reason why in the above proof the initial case of the induction is just the truth axiom of the formula `(atom #T)`, and in the induction step the induction hypothesis is identical with the claim.

The internal representation of this proof is a three–element list consisting of the context — which is empty in this case — , the derived formula and the expression

```
(((ind-at (quote ...))
    truth-axiom-symbol)
    (lambda (n) (lambda (IH) IH)))
```

where `...` is to be replaced by the internal representation of the formula $\forall n : 0 + n = n$ we make induction on.

To give an example of a proof from assumptions, let us derive $\forall mn : n \leq n + m$ from $\forall n : n \leq Sn$ and reflexivity and transitivity of $\leq$.

```
(define leq-proof ;proves (mn)(n<=n+m)
  (elim (ind-axiom-at |(mn)(n<=n+m)|)
        (var 'Refl-<= |(n)(n<=n)|) ;init
        (intro ;step
          (elim (var 'Trans-<= |(nmk)(n<=m->m<=k->n<=k)|)
                |n| |n+m| |S(n+m)|
                (elim (var 'IH |(n)(n<=n+m)|) |n|)
                (elim (var 'Lemma |(n)(n<=Sn)|) |n+m|))
          (list 'n nat)
          (list 'IH |(n)(n<=n+m)|)
          (list 'm nat))))
```

In the internal representation of this proof, the context now consists of the three pairs `(Lemma ...1)`, `(Refl-<= ...2)` and `(Trans-<= ...3)`, where `...1`, `...2` and `...3` are the internal representations of the respective formulas. The expression in this case is

```
(((IND-AT (QUOTE ...))
    REFL-<=)
   (LAMBDA (M) (LAMBDA (IH) (LAMBDA (N)
     (((((TRANS-<= N) ((+-NAT N) M)) (SUC-NAT ((+-NAT N) M)))
           (IH N))
           (LEMMA ((+-NAT N) M))))))))
```

There is one more point which can be demonstrated in this example. If from the above proof of $\forall mn : n \leq n+m$ we want to conclude $\forall n : n \leq n+2$ by the rule of ∀–elimination, we just apply the procedure defined by the expression above to 2, that is we evaluate

```
((((IND-AT (QUOTE ...))
     REFL-<=)
     step)
     2)
```

where `step` stands for the expression above. Now `(ind-at (quote ...))` is defined to be a procedure which when supplied with `init`, `step` and `arg` where arg is a natural number gives the result of applying `step` as many times as `arg` says to `init`. In our case, we get the outcome of the evaluation of

```
((step 1) ((step 0) Refl-<=))
```

that is of

```
((step 1) (LAMBDA (n) (((((TRANS-<= n) n) (SUC-NAT n))
                          (REFL-<= n))
                          (LEMMA n))))
```

that is of

```
(LAMBDA (n)
  (((((TRANS-<= n) (SUC-NAT n)) (SUC-NAT (SUC-NAT n)))
        (((((TRANS-<= n) n) (SUC-NAT n))
```

```
          (REFL-<= n))
          (LEMMA n)))
    (LEMMA (SUC-NAT n))))
```

So $\forall n : n \leq n + 2$ is derived in the indicated way by two applications of the transitivity of $\leq$ and one application of the reflexivity of $\leq$, but without an application of an induction axiom. The precise definition of `ind-at` is

```
(define (ind-at all-formula)
  (lambda (init)
    (lambda (step)
      (lambda (arg)
        (cond ((zero-nat? arg) init)
              ((suc-nat? arg)
               ((step (pred-nat arg))
                ((((ind-at all-formula)
                   init) step) (pred-nat arg))))
              (else ...))))))

(define (ind-axiom-at all-formula)
  (list (context-of-formula all-formula) ;should be empty
        (formula-of-ind-at all-formula)
        (list 'ind-at (list 'quote all-formula))))
```

Here ... describes how the expression is to be reproduced in case `arg` is neither 0 nor a successor. Written out fully ... is

```
(let* ((init-arity (arity-of-formula
                     (specialize all-formula zero-nat-term)))
       (step-arity (cons-arity 0 (cons-arity init-arity
                                              init-arity))))
  (mse (list (list (list (list 'ind-at (list 'quote
                                              all-formula))
                         (proc->expr init init-arity))
                   (proc->expr step step-arity))
             arg)
       init-arity))
```

We now treat a slightly more complex example of an arithmetical proof, which can be used to demonstrate the proofs-as-programs paradigm in an easy case.

We prove by induction on n that n can be divided by $m+1$ with some quotient q and remainder r, as follows

```
(define quot-rem-proof
  (elim
    (ind-axiom-at |(nm)(Eqr)(n=(m+1)*q+r&r<=m)|)
    (intro ;init
      (elim (var 'u1 |(qr)(0=(m+1)*q+r->r<=m->falsity)|)
            |0| |0| truth-axiom truth-axiom)
      (list 'u1 |(qr)(0=(m+1)*q+r->r<=m->falsity)|)
      (list 'm nat))
    (intro ;step
      (elim
        (var 'IV |(m)(Eqr)(n=(m+1)*q+r&r<=m)|)
        |m|
        (intro
          (elim
            (var 'Lemma-<=
                 |(mr)(r<=m->-(r+1<=m)->-(r=m)->falsity)|)
            |m| |r|
            (var 'u2 |r<=m|)
            (intro
              (elim
                (var 'u3 |(qr)(n+1=(m+1)*q+r->r<=m->falsity)|)
                |q| |r+1|
                (var 'u4 |n=(m+1)*q+r|)
                (var 'u5 |r+1<=m|))
              (list 'u5 |r+1<=m|))
            (intro
              (elim
                (var 'u3 |(qr)(n+1=(m+1)*q+r->r<=m->falsity)|)
                |q+1| |0|
                (elim
                  (var 'Lemma-=
                       |(nmqr)(r=m->n=(m+1)*q+r->n=(m+1)*q+m)|)
                  |n| |m| |q| |r|
                  (var 'u6 |r=m|)
                  (var 'u4 |n=(m+1)*q+r|))
                truth-axiom)
              (list 'u6 |r=m|)))
          (list 'u2 |r<=m|)
```

```
        (list 'u4 |n=(m+1)*q+r|)
        (list 'r nat)
        (list 'q nat)))
    (list 'u3 |(qr)(n+1=(m+1)*q+r->r<=m->falsity)|)
    (list 'm nat)
    (list 'IV |(m)(Eqr)(n=(m+1)*q+r&r<=m)|)
    (list 'n nat))))
```

This clearly formalizes the informal proof by cases: If $r < m$ let $q' = q$ and $r' = r + 1$, and if $r = m$ let $q' = q + 1$ and $r' = 0$. Note that in the formal proof above we have freely used true Π–assumptions as lemmata, since they have no computational content and hence don't affect the use of this proof as a program.

If we now specialize this proof to particular numbers (using ∀–elimination) and then normalize it, all uses of induction axioms disappear as we just have demonstrated. As described in Section 4 we can then read off the first instance provided by the resulting refutation from Π–assumptions. Formally, we can easily implement a procedure `instance-from-refutation-of-Pi-assumptions` by the same recursion as in Section 4, and with

```
(define (qr n m)
  (instance-from-refutation-of-Pi-assumptions
    (normal-form-of-proof
      (elim quot-rem-proof n m))))
```

we obtain (in a few seconds even on a PC)

```
(qr 7-term 2-term) => ((() NAT 2) (() NAT 1))
```

since 7 divided by 3 has quotient 2 and remainder 1.

Finally we come to an implementation of the proofs in Section 5. The tree notations we have to deal with are viewed as a free algebra generated from 0 by one unary constructor S and two binary constructors C_0 and C_1. Intuitively, $C_0(a,b)$ corresponds to the tree notation written $a + D_0 b$ in Section 2, and $C_1(a,b)$ corresponds to $a + D_1 b$; for example, $C_0(0,0) = \omega$ and $C_1(0,0) = \Omega$. Now `=-tree`, `+-tree` and `*-tree` can be defined in the obvious way, similarly to what we did for `nat`. The functions $\tau(a)$, $a[z]$, $a[z]^k$ and the predicate T_1 can be defined by the same recursions as in Section 2.

To implement our proofs we have to start with the initial 0–case of Lemma 5.1 and prove $D_0 0 \in W_n$, i.e. $\exists k (D_0 0)[n]^k = 0$. Note that $D_0 0$ denotes ω and is represented here as $C_0(0,0)$. We obtain this proof easily from the Lemma $(D_0 0)[n]^{n+1} = 0$. The next case of Lemma 5.1 is that of a successor tree Sa, i.e. we prove

$$D_0 a \in W_n \to D_0(Sa) \in W_n \tag{0.1}$$

or more explicitely $\exists k (D_0 a)[n]^k = 0 \to \exists k (D_0 Sa)[n]^k = 0$. Again the construction of the second k from the first one can be given explicitely with our tree functions available, and hence we can use the Π–formula $(D_0 a)[n]^k = 0 \to (D_0 Sa)[n]^{S(kn+k)} = 0$ as a lemma. The complete proof is

```
(define P-01
;proves (na)((Ek)(C00a)[n]^k=0->(Ek)(C00(Sa))[n]^k=0)
  (intro
    (elim
      (var 'u |-(k)-(C00a)[n]^k=0|)
      (intro
        (elim
          (var 'v |(k)-(C00(Sa))[n]^k=0|)
          (elim
            (var 'Lemma-01
|(nak)((C00a)[n]^k=0->(C00(Sa))[n]^(S(k*n+k))=0)|)
            |n| |a| |k|
            (var 'w |(C00a)[n]^k=0|)))
        (list 'w |(C00a)[n]^k=0|)
        (list 'k nat)))
    (list 'v |(k)-(C00(Sa))[n]^k=0|)
    (list 'u |-(k)-(C00a)[n]^k=0|)
    (list 'a tree)
    (list 'n nat)))
```

The ω–case of Lemma 5.1, i.e. the proof of

$$\tau(a) = \omega \to D_0 a[n] \in W_n \to D_0 a \in W_n \tag{0.ω}$$

is similar; we use $\tau(a) = \omega \to (D_0 a[n])[n]^k = 0 \to (D_0 a)[n]^{k+1} = 0$ as a lemma. More interesting is the final Ω–case of Lemma 5.1, i.e. the proof of

$$\tau(a) = \Omega \to (\forall z \in W_n : D_0 a[z] \in W_n) \to D_0 a \in W_n \tag{0.Ω}$$

or somewhat more explicitely of

$$\tau(a) = \Omega \to (\forall kz . z \in \mathrm{T}_1 \to z[n]^k = 0 \to \exists k (D_0 a[z])[n]^k = 0) \to \exists k (D_0 a)[n]^k = 0.$$

As in the proof of Lemma 5.1 we use here an auxiliary theorem

$$\tau(a) = \Omega \to (\forall kz. z \in \mathrm{T}_1 \to z[n]^k = 0 \to \exists k (D_0 a[z])[n]^k = 0) \to \exists k (D_0 a)[m][n]^k = 0,$$

which is proved separately by induction on m, using the lemmata

$$\tau(a) = \Omega \to (D_0 a)[m] \in \mathrm{T}_1$$

$$\tau(a) = \Omega \to (D_0 a)[0] = D_0 a[\omega]$$

$$\tau(a) = \Omega \to (D_0 a)[m+1] = D_0 a[(D_0 a)[m]]$$

$$(D_0 0)[n]^{n+1} = 0$$

Note that we do not give an explicit form of our theorem (i.e. with open premises), as in the previous cases. The reason is that the resulting k is obtained roughly by n-fold iteration of the function given by the premise

$$\forall kz. z \in \mathrm{T}_1 \to z[n]^k = 0 \to \exists k (D_0 a[z])[n]^k = 0$$

and our term language does not contain a construct for function-iteration. Rather, we use the proofs-as-programs paradigm here to provide such a construct.

The last proof we have implemented is that of the initial 0–case (which in fact is the most complex case) of Lemma 5.2 for the formula $D_0 a \in W_n$, which was proved to be n–progressive in Lemma 5.1. So we have to prove

$$D_0 c \in W_n \to D_0(c + \Omega) \in W_n. \tag{1.0}$$

This is obtained from (0.Ω) with $c + \Omega$ for a. So we have to prove its second premise from the assumption $D_0 c \in W_n$, i.e.

$$\exists k (D_0 c)[n]^k = 0 \to z \in \mathrm{T}_1 \to z[n]^k = 0 \to \exists k (D_0(c + z))[n]^k = 0. \qquad (1.0 - \mathrm{aux1})$$

This is done by induction on k, where in the induction step we need the lemma $z \in \mathrm{T}_1 \to z[n] \in \mathrm{T}_1$ and

$$z \in \mathrm{T}_1 \to \exists k (D_0(c + z[n]))[n]^k = 0 \to \exists k (D_0(c + z))[n]^k = 0. \qquad (1.0 - \mathrm{aux2})$$

This is proved by cases on z (formally by tree-induction on z), using our previous theorems (0.1), (0.ω) and also the lemma $((c + a) + D_0 b)[n] = c + (a + D_0 b)[n]$. Note that we do not give an explicit form of (1.0-aux2), since this would require a lazy if-then-else-construct in our term language, which we don't have. In fact, addition of such a construct to our term language is impossible in our present SCHEME-implementation, since SCHEME employs eager evaluation. Rather, we again use the proofs-as-programs paradigm here to provide such a construct.

Now when we come to actually use these proofs as programs, there is the obvious practical difficulty that the proofs were just designed to require very fast growing functions to instantiate the existential quantifier. For instance, already the proof of $D_0\omega \in W_n$ requires an exponential function (roughly n^n) for its instantiation. So only very small initial cases like $D_0 2 \in W_n$ can actually be tested, and we have successfully done so.

Now let us look back and ask ourselves what we have achieved by our implementation of these proofs. First, of course, we have machine–checked them and can be sure that we have not overlooked some cases or assumptions; this has been the motivation for de Bruijn's Automath–project (cf. (de Bruijn 1990) for a recent survey). On the other hand, since we have the whole proof available (without eating up too much space, since we don't need to code formulas in the proof, but just the build-up from introduction and elimination rules for $\to$ and $\forall$, i.e. just a type–free lambda term), we can use it e.g. as a program, as done here.

A further possibility is to modify the proof if the specification is changed, or else to "prune" it (this is the terminology of (Goad 1980)) when we have some additional knowledge on the input data and use this knowledge to derive some of the assumptions in case distinctions, making these case distinctions superfluous and hence the whole proof prunable. Note that the new pruned proof can yield an extensionally different program for the same specification; hence we have a program transformation here which in fact changes the function computed by the program.

All this is a sufficient reason for us to actually carry the whole proof along in an interactive proof system. This is in contrast to e.g. Paulson's Isabelle (cf. Paulson 1990) or Fourman's Lambda system (cf. Finn, Fourman, Francis and Harris 1990), who do the opposite and only save theorems, throwing their proofs away.

BIBLIOGRAPHY

1. Abelson, H., Sussman, G.J. (1985) Structure and interpretation of computer programs. MIT Press, Cambridge.
2. Arai, T. (1989) A Slow Growing Analogue of Buchholz' Proof. Nagoya University, Department of Mathematics. To appear in Annals Pure Appl. Logic.

3. Berger, U., Schwichtenberg, H. (1991) An inverse of the evaluation functional for typed lambda calculus. Proc. 6th IEEE Symp. on Logic in Computer Science, pp. 203–211.

4. Buchholz, W. (1987) An independence result for $(\Pi_1^1 - CA) + BI$. Annals Pure Appl. Logic *33*, 131–155.

5. Buchholz, W., Wainer, S. (1987) Provably computable functions and the fast growing hierarchy. Logic and Combinatorics. Contemp. Math. 65, AMS, pp. 179–198.

6. Constable, R. et al. (1986) Implementing mathematics with the Nuprl proof development system. Prentice Hall, Englewood Cliffs, New Jersey.

7. de Bruijn, N.G. (1990) A plea for weaker frameworks. In: BRA Logical Frameworks Workshop, Sophia Antipolis.

8. Finn, S., Fourman, M.P., Francis, M., Harris, R. (1990) Formal System Design — Interactive Synthesis Based on Computer–Assisted Formal Reasoning. In: L.J.M Claasen (ed.). Formal VLSI Specification and Synthesis, I, North-Holland, Amsterdam, pp. 139–152.

9. Girard, J.Y. (1981) Π_2^1-Logic. Annals Math. Logic *21*, 75–219.

10. Goad, C. (1980) Computational uses of the manipulation of formal proofs. Stanford Dept. of Computer Science, Report No. STAN-CS-80-819.

11. Howard, W.A. (1972) A system of abstract constructive ordinals. J. Symbolic Logic 37, *2*, 355–374.

12. Howard, W.A. (1980) Ordinal analysis of terms of finite type. J. Symbolic Logic *45*, 3, 493–504.

13. Martin–Löf, P. (1980) Constructive mathematics and computer programming. In: Logic, Methodology and the Philosophy of Science VI. North Holland, Amsterdam, pp. 153–175

14. Paulson, L.P. (1990) Isabelle: the Next 700 Theorem Provers. In: P. Oddifreddi (editor), Logic and Computer Science. Academic Press, London, pp. 361–386.

15. Rees, J., Clinger, W. (eds) (1986) Revised^3 report on the algorithmic language Scheme. AI Memo 848a, MIT, Cambridge.

16. Schmerl, U. (1982) Number theory and the Bachmann/Howard ordinal. In: J. Stern (ed.) Proc. Herbrand Symposium. North Holland, Amsterdam, pp. 287–298.

17. Schwichtenberg, H. (1986) A normal form for natural deductions in a type theory with realizing terms. Atti del Congresso Logica e Filosofia della Scienza, oggi. San Gimignano 1983. Vol. I - Logica, CLUEB, Bologna, pp. 95–138.

A simplified version of local predicativity

W. BUCHHOLZ

A Simplified Version of Local Predicativity

W. BUCHHOLZ

Mathematisches Institut der Universität München [1]

The method of local predicativity as developed by Pohlers in [10],[11],[12] and extended to subsystems of set theory by Jäger in [4],[5],[6] is a very powerful tool for the ordinal analysis of strong impredicative theories. But up to now it suffers considerably from the fact that it is based on a large amount of very special ordinal theoretic prerequisites. This is true even for the most recent (very polished) presentation of local predicativity in (Pohlers [15]). The purpose of the present paper is to expose a simplified and conceptually improved version of local predicativity which — besides some very elementary facts on ordinal addition, multiplication, and exponentiation — requires only amazingly little ordinal theory. (All necessary nonelementary ordinal theoretic prerequisites can be developed from scratch on just two pages, as we will show in section 4.) The most important feature of our new approach however seems to be its conceptual clarity and flexibility, and in particular the fact that its basic concepts (i.e. the infinitary system RS^{∞} and the notion of an $\mathcal{H}$-controlled RS^{∞}-derivation) are in no way related to any system of ordinal notations or collapsing functions. Our intention with this paper is to make the fascinating field of 'admissible proof theory' (created by Jäger and Pohlers) more easily accessible for non-prooftheorists, and to provide a technically and conceptually well developed basis for further research in this area. We think a good way to accomplish this goal is to apply our method to one particularly interesting (and strong) theory, namely the system KPi first analyzed by Jäger and Pohlers in [9], and to carry out the ordinal analysis for this theory in full detail. Accordingly the whole paper is devoted to the proof of the following

[1]The final version of this paper was written while the author was visiting Carnegie Mellon University during the academic year 1990/91. I would like to express my sincere thanks to Wilfried Sieg (who invited me) and all members of the Philosophy Department of CMU for their generous hospitality.

MAIN THEOREM

If ϕ *is a* Σ_1*-sentence (in the language* $\mathcal{L}$ *of set theory) such that* KPi *proves* $\forall x(\,Ad(x) \rightarrow \phi^x\,)$ *then* $L_\upsilon \models \phi$, *where* $\upsilon := \psi_{\Omega_1}(\varepsilon_{I+1})$.

We assume that the reader has some familiarity with Kripke-Platek set theory and with theories for iterated admissible sets like KPi. Therefore here we only add two short remarks concerning the significance of the above theorem. For extensive background information we refer the reader to [6],[8],[13],[15],[16].

1. The meaning of the formula $\forall x(Ad(x) \rightarrow \phi^x)$ is "$L_{\omega_1^{CK}} \models \phi$", and the ordinal υ is in fact less than ω_1^{CK}. So the theorem gives a specific ordinal $\upsilon < \omega_1^{CK}$ such that L_υ is a model of each Σ_1-sentences ϕ for which KPi proves that $L_{\omega_1^{CK}}$ is a model of ϕ.

2. As shown in (Rathjen [19]) the above theorem implies that υ is an upper bound for |KPi|, the *proof-theoretic ordinal* of KPi defined by

$$|\text{KPi}| := \sup\{|\prec| : \prec \text{ prim.rec.wellord. with KPi} \vdash \text{“} \prec \text{ is wellfounded”}\},$$

where $|\prec|$ denotes the ordertype of $\prec$.

(For the readers convenience we repeat the proof given in [19]. Suppose that $\prec$ is a primitive recursive wellordering of ω such that KPi$\vdash$ "$\prec$ is wellfounded", and let $\phi_\prec$ be the Σ_1-sentence expressing that there is a function $f : \omega \rightarrow \text{On}$ with $f(n) = \{f(m) : m \prec n\}$ $(\forall n \in \omega)$. Then by [8](Theorem 4.6) we have KPi$\vdash \forall x(Ad(x) \rightarrow \phi_\prec^x)$, and the Main Theorem yields $L_\upsilon \models \phi_\prec$, i.e. there exists a function $f \in L_\upsilon$ with $\text{dom}(f) = \omega$ and $f(n) = \{f(m) : m \prec n\}$ $(\forall n \in \omega)$. But this implies $|\prec| = \text{ran}(f) \in L_\upsilon$, i.e. $|\prec| < \upsilon$.)

Remark

The method introduced in this paper can also be used to simplify considerably Rathjen's [19] ordinal analysis of KPM, a theory much stronger than KPi. This will be carried out in a forthcoming paper [3]. For the sake of completeness we want to mention that another ordinal analysis of KPM has been obtained independently by T. Arai [1].

1 The language $\mathcal{L}_{RS}$ of ramified set theory

Let $\mathcal{L}$ denote the usual first order language of set theory whose only nonlogical symbol is the binary predicate constant $\in$. The language $\mathcal{L}_{Ad}$ is obtained from $\mathcal{L}$ by adding the unary predicate constant Ad. The *language $\mathcal{L}_{RS}$ of ramified set theory* is obtained from $\mathcal{L}_{Ad}$ by adding a certain class $\mathcal{T}$ of individual constants, the so-called *set terms* or *RS-terms*. The definition of $\mathcal{T}$ will be given below. Before that we introduce some technical notions and abbreviations. In this context we use the letters u, v to denote both, individual variables and RS-terms. Individual variables are indicated by w, x, y, z.

The *atomic formulas* of $\mathcal{L}_{RS}$ are $u \in v$, $\neg(u \in v)$, $Ad(u)$, $\neg Ad(u)$. The *formulas* of $\mathcal{L}_{RS}$ are built up from atomic formulas by means of $\wedge, \vee, \forall, \exists$. The *negation* $\neg A$ of an $\mathcal{L}_{RS}$-formula A is *defined* via de Morgan's laws. A quantifier (occurrence) $\forall x$ $[\exists x]$ in a formula A is called *restricted* (or *bounded*) if its range (i.e. the subformula following that quantifier) is of the form $x \in v \rightarrow B(x)$ $[x \in v \wedge B(x)]$ with $x \not\equiv v$. A formula A is called a Δ_0-*formula* if it contains no unrestricted quantifier. The Δ_0-formulas of the language $\mathcal{L}_{RS}$ are called *RS-formulas.* As usual the formula obtained from A by *restricting every unrestricted quantifier to u* is denoted by A^u.

From now on we use A, B, C to denote *RS-sentences* (i.e. *closed* RS-formulas), and $A(x_1, \ldots, x_n)$, etc. to denote RS-formulas which have all their free variables among $x_1, \ldots, x_n$. Correspondingly we use $\phi, \psi, \phi(x_1, \ldots, x_n)$, etc. to denote sentences and formulas of the language $\mathcal{L}_{Ad}$. Finite sequences of variables are abbreviated by $\vec{x}, \vec{y}, \ldots$.

Abbreviations

$A(\vec{x}) \rightarrow B(\vec{x}) :\equiv \neg A(\vec{x}) \vee B(\vec{x})$

$\forall x{\in}v B(x, \vec{y}) :\equiv \forall x(x \in v \rightarrow B(x, \vec{y})) \quad (x \not\equiv v)$

$\exists x{\in}v B(x, \vec{y}) :\equiv \exists x(x \in v \wedge B(x, \vec{y})) \quad (x \not\equiv v)$

$u \subseteq v :\equiv \forall x{\in}u(x \in v)$

$u = v :\equiv u \subseteq v \wedge v \subseteq u$

$u \notin v :\equiv \neg(u \in v)$

$u \neq v :\equiv \neg(u = v)$

$\mathsf{tran}(u) :\equiv \forall x{\in}u \forall y{\in}x(y \in u)$

$\mathsf{infinite}(u) :\equiv \exists x{\in}u(x \subseteq x) \wedge \forall x{\in}u \exists y{\in}u(x \in y)$

Definition 1.1 (RS-terms and their levels)

1. For every ordinal α the constant L_α is an *RS-term of level* α.

2. If $\phi(x, y_1, \ldots, y_n)$ is an $\mathcal{L}_{Ad}$-formula which contains at least one free occurrence of x, and if $a_1, \ldots, a_n$ are RS-terms of levels $< \alpha$ (where $\alpha > 0$), then

$$[x \in \mathsf{L}_\alpha : \phi^{\mathsf{L}_\alpha}(x, a_1, \ldots, a_n)]$$

is an *RS-term of level* α.

We denote the class of all RS-terms by $\mathcal{T}$, and the class of all RS-terms of level less than α by $\mathcal{T}_\alpha$.

In the following RS-terms are denoted by the letters a, b, c, s, t.
Note that all variables occurring in an RS-term are bound.

Definition 1.2 (Definition of $\mathrm{k}(\theta)$ and $|\theta|$)
If θ is an RS-term or RS-formula we set

$\mathrm{k}(\theta) := \{\alpha \in \mathrm{On} : \mathsf{L}_\alpha \text{ occurs in } \theta\}$ and $|\theta| := \max(\mathrm{k}(\theta) \cup \{0\})$

Here *all* occurrences of L_α, i.e. also those inside of subterms of θ are counted.
(Example: $\mathrm{k}([x \in \mathsf{L}_\alpha : \mathsf{L}_\beta \in x] \in \mathsf{L}_\gamma) = \{\alpha, \beta, \gamma\}$.)
For technical reasons we also define $\mathrm{k}(0) := \mathrm{k}(1) := \emptyset$, $|0| := |1| := 0$.

Remark
For each $t \in \mathcal{T}$ we have *level of* $t = |t| \in \mathrm{k}(t)$.
Hence $\mathcal{T}_\alpha = \{t \in \mathcal{T} : |t| < \alpha\}$.

Definition 1.3
For RS-terms a, b with $|a| < |b|$ we set

$$a \mathrel{\mathring{\in}} b :\equiv \begin{cases} B(a) & \text{if } b \equiv [x \in \mathsf{L}_\beta : B(x)] \\ a \notin \mathsf{L}_0 & \text{if } b \equiv \mathsf{L}_\beta \end{cases} \quad \text{and} \quad a \mathrel{\mathring{\notin}} b :\equiv \neg(a \mathrel{\mathring{\in}} b).$$

We now are going to intoduce a semantics for the language $\mathcal{L}_{RS}$. For this we fix some class R of ordinals which will then be used for defining the meaning of the predicate constant *Ad*. The intended interpretation of *Ad* is the class $\{\mathsf{L}_\kappa : \omega < \kappa \text{ admissible }\}$. Therefore we should take R as the class $\{\kappa : \omega < \kappa \text{ admissible }\}$. But for the purpose of this paper it is much more convenient to define R as a class of uncountable regular *cardinals* as we will do in section 4. For the meantime it suffices to make the following

Assumption: R *is a nonempty class of* ε*-numbers.*

In the following the letters κ, π, τ *always denote elements of* R.

Definition 1.4 (Semantics of $\mathcal{L}_{RS}$)

By recursion on $|a|$ we define, for each $a \in \mathcal{T}$, a set $\mathsf{s}(a)$ as follows:

1. $\mathsf{s}(\mathsf{L}_\alpha) := \mathsf{s}[\mathcal{T}_\alpha] := \{\mathsf{s}(t) : t \in \mathcal{T}_\alpha\}$
2. $\mathsf{s}([x \in \mathsf{L}_\alpha : \phi^{\mathsf{L}_\alpha}(x, a_1, \ldots, a_n)]) :=$
   $\{\mathsf{s}(t) : t \in \mathcal{T}_\alpha \ \& \ (\mathsf{s}(\mathsf{L}_\alpha), \in, \underline{Ad}_\alpha) \models \phi(\mathsf{s}(t), \mathsf{s}(a_1), \ldots, \mathsf{s}(a_n))\}$,
   where $\underline{Ad}_\alpha := \{\mathsf{s}(\mathsf{L}_\kappa) : \kappa < \alpha\}$,
   and $\in$ is the standard membership relation.

Now let $\mathcal{M}$ be the first order structure for $\mathcal{L}_{RS}$ consisting of

- the universe $\mathsf{s}[\mathcal{T}] := \{\mathsf{s}(t) : t \in \mathcal{T}\}$,
- the membership relation $\in$,
- the class $\underline{Ad} := \{\mathsf{s}(\mathsf{L}_\kappa) : \kappa \in \mathrm{R}\}$,
- the family $(\mathsf{s}(a))_{a \in \mathcal{T}}$.

Then for each $\mathcal{L}_{RS}$-sentence Φ we set: $\quad \models \Phi :\Longleftrightarrow \mathcal{M} \models \Phi$.

Obviously $\mathsf{s}[\mathcal{T}]$ as well as all $\mathsf{s}(\mathsf{L}_\alpha)$ ($\alpha \in \mathrm{On}$) are transitive, and one easily verifies the following equivalences:

$(\models 1) \quad \models Ad(a) \iff \exists \kappa \leq |a| (\models \mathsf{L}_\kappa = a)$

$(\models 2) \quad \models a \in b \iff \exists t \in \mathcal{T}_{|b|} (\models t \mathring{\in} b \wedge t = a)$

$(\models 3) \quad \models \exists x \in b A(x) \iff \exists t \in \mathcal{T}_{|b|} (\models t \mathring{\in} b \wedge A(t))$

(For the proof of ($\models 1$) one has to use the fact that $|a| < \kappa$ implies $\mathsf{s}(a) \in \mathsf{s}(\mathsf{L}_\kappa)$ and thus $\mathsf{s}(a) \neq \mathsf{s}(\mathsf{L}_\kappa)$.)

Lemma 1.5

Let $(L_\alpha)_{\alpha \in \mathrm{On}}$ *be the constructible hierarchy.*

Then for each $\mathcal{L}$*-sentence* ϕ *and each* $\beta \leq \min(\mathrm{R})$ *we have*

$\models \phi^{\mathsf{L}_\beta} \iff L_\beta \models \phi.$

Proof.

For $\beta \leq \min(\mathrm{R})$ let $\mathcal{T}_\beta^- := \{t \in \mathcal{T}_\beta : Ad \text{ does not occur in } t\}$. Using $\forall \beta \leq \min(\mathrm{R}) (\underline{Ad}_\beta = \emptyset)$ we obtain $\mathsf{s}[\mathcal{T}_\beta] = \mathsf{s}[\mathcal{T}_\beta^-]$, for all $\beta \leq \min(\mathrm{R})$. Now

by induction on β it follows that $L_\beta = \mathsf{s}[\mathcal{T}_\beta] = \mathsf{s}(\mathsf{L}_\beta)$. Hence
$\models \phi^{\mathsf{L}_\beta} \Leftrightarrow \mathsf{s}[\mathcal{T}] \models \phi^{\mathsf{L}_\beta} \Leftrightarrow \mathsf{s}(\mathsf{L}_\beta) \models \phi \Leftrightarrow L_\beta \models \phi$.

The next definition is motivated by ($\models 1$) – ($\models 3$).

Definition 1.6 [2]
To each RS-sentence A we assign a certain (infinitary) conjunction $\bigwedge(A_\iota)_{\iota\in J}$ or disjunction $\bigvee(A_\iota)_{\iota\in J}$ of RS-sentences and we indicate this assignment by writing $A \simeq \bigwedge(A_\iota)_{\iota\in J}$, $A \simeq \bigvee(A_\iota)_{\iota\in J}$, resp.

1. $Ad(a) :\simeq \bigvee(t = a)_{t\in J}$ with $J := \{\mathsf{L}_\kappa : \kappa \in \mathrm{R} \ \& \ \kappa \leq |a|\}$
2. $a \in b :\simeq \bigvee(t \mathring{\in} b \wedge t = a)_{t\in J}$ with $J := \mathcal{T}_{|b|}$
3. $\exists x{\in}b\, A(x) :\simeq \bigvee(t \mathring{\in} b \wedge A(t))_{t\in J}$ with $J := \mathcal{T}_{|b|}$
4. $(A_0 \vee A_1) :\simeq \bigvee(A_\iota)_{\iota\in\{0,1\}}$
5. $\neg A :\simeq \bigwedge(\neg A_\iota)_{\iota\in J}$, if A is one of the formulas under 1.–4.

As an immediate consequence of ($\models 1-\models 3$) we obtain the following lemma.

Lemma 1.7
(*i*) $\models \bigwedge(A_\iota)_{\iota\in J} \iff \forall\iota{\in}J(\models A_\iota)$
(*ii*) $\models \bigvee(A_\iota)_{\iota\in J} \iff \exists\iota{\in}J(\models A_\iota)$

In the formulation of the above lemma we have already used the following notational convention to which we stick through the whole paper.

Notational convention
By writing $\bigwedge(A_\iota)_{\iota\in J}$ [$\bigvee(A_\iota)_{\iota\in J}$, *resp.*] *we indicate a certain RS-sentence* A *such that* $A \simeq \bigwedge(A_\iota)_{\iota\in J}$ [$A \simeq \bigvee(A_\iota)_{\iota\in J}$, *resp.*].

We now define a rank-function for RS-sentences in such a way that
$\forall\iota{\in}J(\mathrm{rk}(A_\iota) < \mathrm{rk}(A))$ whenever $A \simeq \substack{\bigwedge \\ \bigvee}(A_\iota)_{\iota\in J}$.

Definition 1.8 (the rank of RS-sentences and RS-terms)
The rank $\mathrm{rk}(\theta)$ of an RS-sentence or RS-term θ is defined by induction on the

[2] this elegant way of turning a formal language into a fragment of infinitary propositional logic I have first seen in an unpublished manuscript by W.W.Tait

number of symbols occurring in θ as follows:

1. $\mathrm{rk}(\mathsf{L}_\alpha) := \omega \cdot \alpha$
2. $\mathrm{rk}([x \in \mathsf{L}_\alpha : A(x)]) := \max\{\omega \cdot \alpha + 1, \mathrm{rk}(A(\mathsf{L}_0)) + 2\}$
3. $\mathrm{rk}(Ad(a)) := \mathrm{rk}(\neg Ad(a)) := \mathrm{rk}(a) + 5$
4. $\mathrm{rk}(a \in b) := \mathrm{rk}(a \notin b) := \max\{\mathrm{rk}(a) + 6, \mathrm{rk}(b) + 1\}$
5. $\mathrm{rk}(\exists x{\in}b\, A(x)) := \mathrm{rk}(\forall x{\in}b\, A(x)) := \max\{\mathrm{rk}(b), \mathrm{rk}(A(\mathsf{L}_0)) + 2\}$
6. $\mathrm{rk}(A \wedge B) := \mathrm{rk}(A \vee B) := \max\{\mathrm{rk}(A), \mathrm{rk}(B)\} + 1$

Lemma 1.9

Let $A \simeq \bigvee(A_\iota)_{\iota \in J}$ or $A \simeq \bigwedge(A_\iota)_{\iota \in J}$. Then the following holds.

a) $\mathrm{rk}(A) = \omega \cdot |A| + n$, *for some* $n \in \omega$

b) $\mathrm{rk}(A_\iota) < \mathrm{rk}(A)$, *for all* $\iota \in J$

c) $\mathrm{k}(\iota) \subseteq \mathrm{k}(A_\iota) \subseteq \mathrm{k}(A) \cup \mathrm{k}(\iota)$, *for all* $\iota \in J$.

d) $\mathrm{rk}(A) = \omega \cdot \alpha \implies A \equiv \exists x{\in}\mathsf{L}_\alpha B(x)$ *or* $A \equiv \forall x{\in}\mathsf{L}_\alpha B(x)$

e) $\mathrm{rk}(A) = \mathrm{rk}(\neg A)$

Proof.

The easy proofs of a),c),d),e) are left to the reader. The proof of b) is obtained by successively verifying the following propositions.

(1) $|c| < |A(\mathsf{L}_0)| \implies \mathrm{rk}(A(c)) = \mathrm{rk}(A(\mathsf{L}_0))$

(2) $|c| < \beta \implies \mathrm{rk}(A(c)) < \max\{\omega\beta, \mathrm{rk}(A(\mathsf{L}_0)) + 1\}$

(3) $|c| < |b| \implies \mathrm{rk}(c \mathrel{\mathring{\in}} b) + 1 < \mathrm{rk}(b)$

(4) $\mathrm{rk}(\mathsf{L}_0 \in \mathsf{L}_0) = 6$ and $\mathrm{rk}(\mathsf{L}_0 \in b) = \mathrm{rk}(b) + 1$ for $b \not\equiv \mathsf{L}_0$

(5) $\mathrm{rk}(\mathsf{L}_0 = \mathsf{L}_0) = 9$ and

$\mathrm{rk}(a = b) = \max\{\mathrm{rk}(a), \mathrm{rk}(b)\} + 4$, if $a \neq \mathsf{L}_0$ or $b \neq \mathsf{L}_0$

(6) $|c| < |b| \implies \mathrm{rk}(c \mathrel{\mathring{\in}} b \wedge c = a) < \mathrm{rk}(a \in b)$ and

$\mathrm{rk}(c \mathrel{\mathring{\in}} b \wedge A(c)) < \mathrm{rk}(\exists x{\in}b A(x))$

(7) $\kappa \leq |a| \implies \mathrm{rk}(\mathsf{L}_\kappa = a) = \mathrm{rk}(a) + 4$

We close this section by some additional definitions and abbreviations.

Definition 1.10

1. A formula which contains no unrestricted universal quantifier is called a Σ_1-*formula*.

2. The set of all RS-sentences $A \equiv \phi^{\mathsf{L}_\kappa}(\vec{a})$ with $\phi(\vec{x}) \in \Sigma_1$ and $\vec{a} \in \mathcal{T}_\kappa$ is denoted by $\Sigma(\kappa)$.

3. For $A \equiv \phi^{\mathsf{L}_\kappa}(\vec{a}) \in \Sigma(\kappa)$ we set $A^{(u,\kappa)} :\equiv \phi^u(\vec{a})$, and we abbreviate A^{L_β} by A^β, and $A^{(\mathsf{L}_\beta,\kappa)}$ by $A^{(\beta,\kappa)}$.

Definition 1.11
1. $\mathcal{T}^{0,1} := \mathcal{T} \cup \{0,1\}$ and $J|\alpha := \{\iota \in J : |\iota| < \alpha\}$ for $J \subseteq \mathcal{T}^{0,1}$.
2. We use Θ to denote finite sequences consisting of RS-sentences and elements of $\mathcal{T}^{0,1}$, and for $\Theta = (\theta_1, \dots, \theta_n)$ we set $\mathrm{k}(\Theta) := \mathrm{k}(\theta_1) \cup \dots \cup \mathrm{k}(\theta_n)$.
3. Finite sequences of RS-sentences are called *RS-sequents* and indicated by the letters Γ, Γ'. For $\Gamma = (A_0, \dots, A_n)$ we set $\models \Gamma :\Longleftrightarrow \models A_0 \vee \dots \vee A_n$.

Definition 1.12

For each ordinal α we set $\alpha^{\mathrm{R}} := \begin{cases} \min\{\kappa \in \mathrm{R} : \alpha < \kappa\} & \text{if } \exists\kappa{\in}\mathrm{R}(\alpha < \kappa) \\ \alpha & \text{otherwise} \end{cases}$

The letters $\alpha, \beta, \gamma, \delta, \mu, \sigma, \xi, \eta, \zeta$ always denote ordinals. On denotes the class of all ordinals, Lim the class of all limit numbers, and $\mathcal{P}(\mathrm{On})$ the class of all subsets of On. Every ordinal α is identified with the set $\{\xi \in \mathrm{On} : \xi < \alpha\}$ of its predecessors. For $\alpha \leq \beta$ we set $[\alpha, \beta] := \{\xi : \alpha \leq \xi \leq \beta\}$ and $[\alpha, \beta[:= \{\xi : \alpha \leq \xi < \beta\}$. An ordinal α with $\omega^\alpha = \alpha$ is called an *ε-number*. $\alpha \# \beta$ denotes the *natural sum* of α and β, in particular $\omega^{\alpha_1} \# \dots \# \omega^{\alpha_n} = \omega^{\alpha_{p(1)}} + \dots + \omega^{\alpha_{p(n)}}$, where p is a permutation of $\{1, \dots, n\}$ with $\alpha_{p(1)} \geq \dots \geq \alpha_{p(n)}$.

2 An intermediate Proof System

In this section we introduce an intermediate infinitary proof system RS* which is just strong enough to prove all axioms of KPi. In section 3 we will embed RS* into another infinitary system RS$^\infty$ which so to speak is the main system of this paper and for which we will prove a cut-elimination and collapsing theorem. The main advantage of RS* is that here we need not to keep control over the lengths of derivations, since the complexity of the endsequent of a derivation d always provides a sufficiently good upper bound for the length of d. Before starting with RS* let's give the complete list of KPi-axioms.

Axioms of KPi

(Ext) $\forall x \forall y \forall z[x = y \rightarrow (x \in z \rightarrow y \in z) \wedge (Ad(x) \rightarrow Ad(y))]$
(Found) $\forall \vec{z}[\forall x(\forall y{\in}x\, \phi(y, \vec{z}) \rightarrow \phi(x, \vec{z})) \rightarrow \forall x \phi(x, \vec{z})]$
(Pair) $\forall x \forall y \exists z(x \in z \wedge y \in z)$
(Union) $\forall x \exists z \forall y{\in}x \forall u{\in}y(u \in z)$

(Δ_0-Sep) $\forall\vec{z}\forall w\exists y[\forall x{\in}y(x\in w\wedge\phi(x,\vec{z}))\wedge\forall x{\in}w(\phi(x,\vec{z})\rightarrow x\in y)](\phi\in\Delta_0)$
(Δ_0-Col) $\forall\vec{z}\forall w[\forall x{\in}w\exists y\phi(x,y,\vec{z})\rightarrow\exists w_1\forall x{\in}w\exists y{\in}w_1\,\phi(x,y,\vec{z})]\quad(\phi\in\Delta_0)$
(Ad.1) $\forall x[Ad(x)\rightarrow \mathsf{tran}(x)\wedge\exists w{\in}x\ \mathsf{infinite}(w)]$
(Ad.2) $\forall x\forall y[Ad(x)\wedge Ad(y)\rightarrow(x\in y\vee x=y\vee y\in x)]$
(Ad.3) $\forall x[Ad(x)\rightarrow\psi^x]$, for every instance ψ of (Pair),(Union), (Δ_0-Sep),(Δ_0-Col)
(Lim) $\forall x\exists y(Ad(y)\wedge x\in y)$

The system KPi without (Δ_0-Col) is called KPℓ.

Definition 2.1
1. For each sequent $\Gamma=(A_1,\ldots,A_n)$ we define its *norm* $\|\Gamma\|$ by

$$\|\Gamma\|:=\omega^{\mathrm{rk}(A_1)}\#\ldots\#\omega^{\mathrm{rk}(A_n)}.$$

2. For $X\subseteq\mathrm{On}$ we set $X^\star:=X\cup\{\omega\}\cup\{\xi+1:\xi\in X\}\cup\{\xi^{\mathrm{R}}:\xi\in X\}$.

Definition 2.2 (The infinitary system RS*)
We define RS* as the collection of all derivations (i.e. wellfounded trees of RS-sequents Γ) generated by the following five inference rules (where the last two are just axiom schemes):

$$(\bigwedge)^\star\quad\frac{\ldots\Gamma,A_\iota\ldots(\iota\in J)}{\Gamma,\bigwedge(A_\iota)_{\iota\in J}}$$

$$(\bigvee)^\star\quad\frac{\Gamma,A_{\iota_0},\ldots,A_{\iota_n}}{\Gamma,\bigvee(A_\iota)_{\iota\in J}}\quad\text{if }\iota_0,\ldots,\iota_n\in J\text{ and }\mathrm{k}(\iota_0,\ldots,\iota_n)\subseteq\mathrm{k}(\Gamma,\bigvee(A_\iota)_{\iota\in J})^\star$$

$$(\mathrm{Ad})^\star\quad\frac{\ldots\Gamma,B(\mathsf{L}_\kappa)\ldots(\kappa\le|a|)}{\Gamma,Ad(a)\rightarrow B(a)}$$

(Ref)* $\Gamma,A\rightarrow\exists z{\in}\mathsf{L}_\kappa A^{(z,\kappa)}$ if $A\in\Sigma(\kappa)$ and $\kappa\in\mathrm{R}$

(Found)* $\Gamma,\exists x{\in}\mathsf{L}_\alpha(\forall y{\in}x A(y)\wedge\neg A(x)),\forall x{\in}\mathsf{L}_\alpha A(x)$

In RS* we identify sequents which differ only with respect to the order of their elements. So actually we are working with multisets of RS-sentences. The formula $B(a)$ in (Ad)* is called the *principal formula* of the respective inference.

Remarks

1. Note that every formula $A \simeq \bigwedge(A_\iota)_{\iota\in J}$ with $J = \emptyset$ (e.g. $A \equiv a \not\in \mathsf{L}_0$) is derivable in RS* simply by an application of $(\bigwedge)^\star$.

2. Note that in $(\bigvee)^\star$ some of the formulas $A_{\iota_0}, \ldots, A_{\iota_n}$ may be identical, so that for example $\frac{\Gamma,A,A,B,B,B}{\Gamma,A\vee B}$ and $\frac{\Gamma,B,B}{\Gamma,A\vee B}$ are instances of $(\bigvee)^\star$.

3. If Γ' is a premise of an RS*-inference with conclusion Γ then $\|\Gamma'\| < \|\Gamma\|$.

Definition 2.3

$$\mathrel{\vert\!\frac{\star}{\rho}}\Gamma :\Longleftrightarrow \begin{cases} \text{there exists an RS}^\star\text{-derivation } d \text{ of } \Gamma \text{ such that} \\ \text{i) } \mathrm{rk}(B(a)) < \rho \text{ holds for every} \\ \quad \text{principal formula } B(a) \text{ of an (Ad)}^\star\text{-inference in } d \\ \text{ii) if } \rho = 0 \text{ then } d \text{ contains no application of (Ref)}^\star \text{ or (Found)}^\star \end{cases}$$

$$\mathrel{\vert\!\frac{\star}{}}\Gamma :\Longleftrightarrow \mathrel{\vert\!\frac{\star}{0}}\Gamma$$

(So $\mathrel{\vert\!\frac{\star}{}}\Gamma$ means that Γ is derivable by means of $(\bigwedge)^\star$ and $(\bigvee)^\star$ alone.)

Lemma 2.4 (Derived rules of RS*)

(Weak) $\mathrel{\vert\!\frac{\star}{\rho}}\Gamma \implies \mathrel{\vert\!\frac{\star}{\rho}}\Gamma, C$

$(\bigwedge/\bigvee)$ $\forall\iota{\in}J(\mathrel{\vert\!\frac{\star}{\rho}}\Gamma, A_\iota, B_\iota) \;\&\; J \subseteq J' \implies \mathrel{\vert\!\frac{\star}{\rho}}\Gamma, \bigwedge(A_\iota)_{\iota\in J}, \bigvee(B_\iota)_{\iota\in J'}$.

(TND) $\mathrel{\vert\!\frac{\star}{}}\neg A, A$

(TND') $\mathrel{\vert\!\frac{\star}{\rho}}\Gamma, B \implies \mathrel{\vert\!\frac{\star}{\rho}}\Gamma, \neg A, A \wedge B$

$(\forall^\beta)$ $\forall t{\in}\mathcal{T}_\beta(\mathrel{\vert\!\frac{\star}{\rho}}\Gamma, A(t)) \implies \mathrel{\vert\!\frac{\star}{\rho}}\Gamma, \forall x{\in}\mathsf{L}_\beta A(x)$

$(\exists^\beta)$ $\mathrel{\vert\!\frac{\star}{\rho}}\Gamma, A(t) \;\&\; t \in \mathcal{T}_\beta \;\&\; \mathrm{k}(t) \subseteq \mathrm{k}(\Gamma, A(x))^\star \implies \mathrel{\vert\!\frac{\star}{\rho}}\Gamma, \exists x{\in}\mathsf{L}_\beta A(x)$

Proof. The proofs are almost trivial. We just give some short hints.
ad $(\bigwedge/\bigvee)$: Here one uses the fact that $\mathrm{k}(\iota) \subseteq \mathrm{k}(A_\iota)$.
ad (TND): This is proved by transfinite induction on $\mathrm{rk}(A)$ using $(\bigwedge/\bigvee)$.
ad $(\exists^\beta)$: We have $\exists x{\in}\mathsf{L}_\beta A(x) \simeq \bigvee(t \mathrel{\mathring{\in}} \mathsf{L}_\beta \wedge A(t))_{t\in\mathcal{T}_\beta}$ with
$(t \mathrel{\mathring{\in}} \mathsf{L}_\beta) \equiv (t \not\in \mathsf{L}_0) \simeq \bigwedge(\ldots)_{\iota\in\emptyset}$.

Lemma 2.5

a) $\mathrel{\vert\!\frac{\star}{}} b \not\in b$

b) $\mathrel{\vert\!\frac{\star}{}} a \subseteq a$

c) $\mathrel{\vert\!\frac{\star}{}} b \mathrel{\mathring{\not\in}} a, b \in a,$ *if* $|b| < |a|$.

d) $\mathrel{\vert\!\frac{\star}{}} a \neq b, b = a$

e) $\models^{\star} a \mathring{\in} \mathsf{L}_\beta$ *and* $\models^{\star} a \in \mathsf{L}_\beta$, *if* $|a| < \beta$

f) $\models^{\star} \mathsf{tran}(\mathsf{L}_\alpha)$

g) $\models^{\star} \exists x{\in}\mathsf{L}_\alpha \mathsf{infinite}(x)$, *if* $\alpha > \omega$

h) $\models^{\star} Ad(\mathsf{L}_\kappa)$, *for every* $\kappa \in \mathrm{R}$.

Proof.

a) This is proved by transfinite induction on rk(b) as follows. By I.H. (induction hypothesis) we have $\models^{\star} t \notin t$ for all $t \in \mathcal{T}_{|b|}$. From this we obtain $\models^{\star} t \mathring{\notin} b, t \mathring{\in} b \wedge t \notin t$ (by (TND')) and then $\models^{\star} t \mathring{\notin} b, \exists x{\in}b(x \notin t)$ (by $(\bigvee)^{\star}$). Now by two more applications of $(\bigvee)^{\star}$ we get $\models^{\star} t \mathring{\in} b \rightarrow t \neq b \quad (\forall t \in \mathcal{T}_{|b|})$, and then (by $(\bigwedge)^{\star}$) $\models^{\star} b \notin b$.

From now on such simple proofs will be given in a more condensed form, namely just by a (horicontal or vertical) sequence of statements '$\models^{\star}_{(\rho)} \Gamma$' such that every but the first statement in the sequence follows from its immediate predecessor(s) by means of one or two instances of the rules $(\bigwedge)^{\star}, (\bigvee)^{\star}, (\mathrm{Ad})^{\star}$, $(\mathrm{Ref})^{\star}$, (Weak), $(\bigwedge/\bigvee)$, (TND), (TND'), $(\forall^\beta)$, $(\exists^\beta)$. The above proof would then look like this:

(I.H.)$\models^{\star} t \notin t \quad \models^{\star} t \mathring{\notin} b, t \mathring{\in} b \wedge t \notin t \quad \models^{\star} t \mathring{\notin} b, \exists x{\in}b(x \notin t) \quad \models^{\star} t \mathring{\notin} b, t \neq b$

$\models^{\star} t \mathring{\in} b \rightarrow t \neq b \ (\forall t \in \mathcal{T}_{|b|}) \quad \models^{\star} b \notin b$.

b) Induction on rk(a): (I.H.) $\models^{\star} b \subseteq b \quad \models^{\star} b = b \quad \models^{\star} b \mathring{\notin} a, b \mathring{\in} a \wedge b = b$

$\models^{\star} b \mathring{\notin} a, b \in a \quad (\forall b \in \mathcal{T}_{|a|}) \quad \models^{\star} \forall x{\in}a(x \in a)$.

c) This follows from the above proof of b).

d) Obvious.

e) Since $(a \notin \mathsf{L}_0) \simeq \bigwedge(A_\iota)_{\iota \in \emptyset}$, we have $\models^{\star} a \notin \mathsf{L}_0$, i.e. $\models^{\star} a \mathring{\in} \mathsf{L}_\beta$. From this and b) we obtain $\models^{\star} a \mathring{\in} \mathsf{L}_\beta \wedge a = a$ and then by $(\bigvee)^{\star}$ $\models^{\star} a \in \mathsf{L}_\beta$.

f) $\models^{\star} t \in \mathsf{L}_\alpha \ (\forall b{\in}\mathcal{T}_\alpha,\ t{\in}\mathcal{T}_{|b|}) \quad \models^{\star} \forall x{\in}\mathsf{L}_\alpha \forall y{\in}x(y \in \mathsf{L}_\alpha)$.

g) $\models^{\star} b \in \mathsf{L}_{|b|+1} \models^{\star} \exists z{\in}\mathsf{L}_\omega(b \in z) \ (\forall b{\in}\mathcal{T}_\omega) \models^{\star} \forall y{\in}\mathsf{L}_\omega \exists z{\in}\mathsf{L}_\omega(y \in z)$

$\models^{\star} \mathsf{infinite}(\mathsf{L}_\omega) \models^{\star} \exists w{\in}\mathsf{L}_\alpha \mathsf{infinite}(w)$. Note that $\mathrm{k}(\mathsf{L}_\omega) = \{\omega\} \subseteq \mathrm{k}(\ldots)^{\star}$.

h) $\models^{\star} \mathsf{L}_\kappa = \mathsf{L}_\kappa \quad \models^{\star} Ad(\mathsf{L}_\kappa)$.

Abbreviation

$\Gamma, [a \neq b] \ :\equiv\ \Gamma, \neg a \subseteq b, \neg b \subseteq a$

Lemma 2.6

$\models^{\star} [a \neq b]\ ,\ [\mathsf{L}_\gamma \neq a],\ if\ |b| < \gamma$

Proof by induction on γ. Let $\alpha := |a|\ ,\ \beta := |b| < \gamma$.

$\models^{\star} [s \neq t]\ ,\ [\mathsf{L}_\beta \neq s]$ (by I.H.)

$\models^{\star} t \mathring{\in} b \rightarrow t \neq s\ ,\ [\mathsf{L}_\beta \neq s]$ $(\forall t \in \mathcal{T}_\beta)$

$\models^{\star} s \notin b\ ,\ [\mathsf{L}_\beta \neq s]$

$\models^{\star} s \mathring{\in} a \wedge s \notin b\ ,\ s \mathring{\notin} a\ ,\ s \neq \mathsf{L}_\beta$

$\models^{\star} \exists x \in a (x \notin b)\ ,\ s \mathring{\notin} a\ ,\ s \neq \mathsf{L}_\beta$ $(\forall s \in \mathcal{T}_\alpha)$

$\models^{\star} [a \neq b]\ ,\ \mathsf{L}_\beta \notin a$

$\models^{\star} [a \neq b]\ ,\ \exists x \in \mathsf{L}_\gamma (x \notin a)$

$\models^{\star} [a \neq b]\ ,\ [\mathsf{L}_\gamma \neq a]$

Lemma 2.7

If $A(x_1, \ldots, x_n)$ *is an RS-formula such that every* x_i $(i = 1, \ldots, n)$ *has at most one free occurrence in* $A(\vec{x})$ *then*

$$\models^{\star} [s_1 \neq t_1], \ldots, [s_n \neq t_n], \neg A(s_1, \ldots, s_n), A(t_1, \ldots, t_n)$$

Corollary

$\models^{\star} s \neq t, \neg A(s), A(t)$, *for every RS-formula* $A(x)$.

Proof of the corollary.

Given $A(x)$, there is a formula $B(x_1, \ldots, x_n)$ such that $A(x) \equiv B(x, \ldots, x)$ and every x_i occurs at most once in $B(x_1, \ldots, x_n)$. By the lemma we have $\models^{\star} [s \neq t], \ldots, [s \neq t]\ ,\ \neg B(s, \ldots, s)\ ,\ B(t, \ldots, t)$, and from this we get $\models^{\star} s \neq t\ ,\ \neg A(s)\ ,\ A(t)$ by $(\bigvee)^{\star}$.

Proof of the lemma by induction on $\mathrm{rk}(A(\vec{s}))\#\mathrm{rk}(A(\vec{t}))$

(CASE 1) $A(x_1, x_2) \equiv x_1 \in x_2$.

$\models^{\star} [s_1 \neq t_1]\ ,\ [s \neq t]\ ,\ s \neq s_1\ ,\ t = t_1$ (by I.H.)

$\models^{\star} [s_1 \neq t_1]\ ,\ t \mathring{\notin} t_2 \vee t \neq s\ ,\ s \neq s_1\ ,\ t \mathring{\in} t_2 \wedge t = t_1$ $(\forall t \in \mathcal{T}_{|t_2|})$

$\models^{\star} [s_1 \neq t_1]\ ,\ s \notin t_2\ ,\ s \neq s_1\ ,\ t_1 \in t_2$

$\models^{\star} [s_1 \neq t_1]\ ,\ s \mathring{\in} s_2 \wedge s \notin t_2\ ,\ s \mathring{\notin} s_2 \vee s \neq s_1\ ,\ t_1 \in t_2 \quad (\forall s {\in} \mathcal{T}_{|s_2|})$

$\models^{\star} [s_1 \neq t_1]\ ,\ [s_2 \neq t_2]\ ,\ s_1 \notin s_2\ ,\ t_1 \in t_2$

(CASE 2) $A(x) \equiv Ad(x)$.

$\models^{\star} [s \neq t]\ ,\ \mathsf{L}_\kappa \neq s\ ,\ \mathsf{L}_\kappa = t \quad (\forall \kappa \leq \min\{|s|, |t|\}) \quad$ (by I.H.)

$\models^{\star} [s \neq t]\ ,\ \mathsf{L}_\kappa \neq s\ ,\ Ad(t) \quad (\forall \kappa \leq \min\{|s|, |t|\})$

$\models^{\star} [s \neq t]\ ,\ \mathsf{L}_\kappa \neq s\ ,\ Ad(t) \quad (\forall \kappa \leq |s|)$ [by 2.6 $\models^{\star} [s \neq t], \mathsf{L}_\kappa \neq s\ (\forall \kappa > |t|)$]

$\models^{\star} [s \neq t]\ ,\ \neg Ad(s)\ ,\ Ad(t)$.

(CASE 3) $A(\vec{x}) \equiv \exists y {\in} x_1 B(x_2, \ldots, x_n, y)$: similar to CASE 1 .

The remaining cases are easy.

Lemma 2.8

$\models^{\star} b \notin a, b \mathring{\in} a.$

Proof.

$\models^{\star} t \mathring{\notin} a\ ,\ t \neq b\ ,\ b \mathring{\in} a \quad$ (by 2.7)

$\models^{\star} t \mathring{\notin} a \vee t \neq b\ ,\ b \mathring{\in} a \quad (\forall t {\in} \mathcal{T}_{|a|})$

$\models^{\star} b \notin a\ ,\ b \mathring{\in} a$

Theorem 2.9

a) *For every limit ordinal* λ *we have*
$\models^{\star} (\mathrm{Ext})^\lambda \wedge (\mathrm{Found})^\lambda \wedge (\mathrm{Pair})^\lambda \wedge (\mathrm{Union})^\lambda \wedge (\Delta_0\text{-Sep})^\lambda$.

b) *For every* $\kappa \in \mathrm{R}$ *we have* $\models^{\star}_{1} (\Delta_0\text{-Col})^\kappa$.

c) *For every limit ordinal* λ *such that* $\forall \alpha {<} \lambda \exists \kappa {\in} \mathrm{R} (\alpha {<} \kappa {<} \lambda)$ *we have*
$\models^{\star}_{\lambda} (\mathrm{KP}\ell)^\lambda$, *i.e.* $\models^{\star}_{\lambda} \phi^\lambda$ *holds for every axiom* ϕ *of* KPℓ.

Proof.

a) (Ext):

By 2.7 we have $\models^{\star} a \neq b, a \notin c, b \in c$ and $\models^{\star} a \neq b, \neg Ad(a), Ad(b)$, for all $a, b, c \in \mathcal{T}$. Hence $\models^{\star} (\mathrm{Ext})^\lambda$.

(Found): trivial.

(Pair):

Let $a, b \in \mathcal{T}_\lambda$ and $\delta := \max\{|a|, |b|\} + 1$

Then $\models^{\star} a \in \mathsf{L}_\delta \wedge b \in \mathsf{L}_\delta$ from which we get $\models^{\star} \exists z {\in} \mathsf{L}_\lambda (a \in z \wedge b \in z)$, since

$\delta \in (\mathrm{k}(a) \cup \mathrm{k}(b))^\star$ and $\delta < \lambda$.

(Union):

For every $a \in \mathcal{T}_\lambda$ we have

$\models^\star s \in \mathsf{L}_{|a|} \quad (\forall s{\in}\mathcal{T}_{|a|})$

$\models^\star \forall x{\in}t(x \in \mathsf{L}_{|a|}) \quad (\forall t{\in}\mathcal{T}_{|a|})$

$\models^\star \forall y{\in}a\forall x{\in}y(x \in \mathsf{L}_{|a|})$

$\models^\star \exists z{\in}\mathsf{L}_\lambda\forall y{\in}a\forall x{\in}y(x \in z)$

(Δ_0-Sep):

Let $\phi(x, z_1, \ldots, z_n) \in \Delta_0$ and $a, c_1, \ldots, c_n \in \mathcal{T}_\lambda$. We have to prove

$\models^\star \exists y{\in}\mathsf{L}_\lambda(\psi_1(y, a, \vec{c}) \land \psi_2(y, a, \vec{c}))$,

where $\psi_1(y, a, \vec{c}) :\equiv \forall x{\in}y(x \in a \land \phi(x, \vec{c}))$

and $\psi_2(y, a, \vec{c}) :\equiv \forall x{\in}a(\phi(x, \vec{c}) \to x \in y)$.

For this let $\delta := \max\{|a|, |c_1|, \ldots, |c_n|\} + 1$, and $d := [x \in \mathsf{L}_\delta : x \in a \land \phi(x, \vec{c})]$.

Then $d \in \mathcal{T}_\lambda$ and $\mathrm{k}(d) \subseteq \mathrm{k}(\psi_1(y, a, \vec{c}))^\star$.

Therefore it suffices to prove (1) $\models^\star \psi_1(d, a, \vec{c})$ and (2) $\models^\star \psi_2(d, a, \vec{c})$.

But (1) follows immediately from the fact that $t \mathrel{\mathring{\in}} d \equiv t \in a \land \phi(t, \vec{c})$ and therefore $\models^\star t \mathrel{\mathring{\in}} d \to t \in a \land \phi(t, \vec{c}) \quad (\forall t{\in}\mathcal{T}_\delta)$.

And (2) is obtained as follows:

$\models^\star t \mathrel{\mathring{\notin}} a\, ,\, t \in a$

$\models^\star t \mathrel{\mathring{\notin}} a\, ,\, \neg\phi(t, \vec{c})\, ,\, t \in a \land \phi(t, \vec{c})$

$\models^\star t \mathrel{\mathring{\notin}} a\, ,\, \neg\phi(t, \vec{c})\, ,\, t \mathrel{\mathring{\in}} d \land t = t$

$\models^\star t \mathrel{\mathring{\notin}} a\, ,\, \neg\phi(t, \vec{c})\, ,\, t \in d \quad (\forall t{\in}\mathcal{T}_{|a|})$

$\models^\star \forall x{\in}a(\phi(x, \vec{c}) \to x \in d)$

b) is an immediate consequence of (Ref)*.

c) 1. If ϕ is an instance of (Ext),(Found),(Pair),(Union),(Δ_0-Sep), then $\models^\star \phi^\lambda$ holds by a).

2. Suppose that ϕ is an axiom (Ad1) or (Ad3). Then $\phi \equiv \forall x(Ad(x) \to \chi(x))$ with $\chi(x) \in \Delta_0$, and by 2.5 f,g and 2.9 a,b we have $\models^\star_1 \chi(\mathsf{L}_\kappa)$ for all $\kappa \in \mathrm{R}$. Since $\forall a{\in}\mathcal{T}_\lambda(\mathrm{rk}(\chi(a)) < \omega\lambda = \lambda)$, by (Ad)* we get $\forall a{\in}\mathcal{T}_\lambda(\models^\star_\lambda Ad(a) \to \chi(a))$ and thus $\models^\star_\lambda \phi^\lambda$.

3. In the same way as under 2. we obtain $\models^{\star}_{\lambda} (\mathrm{Ad}\,2)^{\lambda}$.

4. Now we prove $\models^{\star} (\mathrm{Lim})^{\lambda}$. Let $a \in \mathcal{T}_{\lambda}$ and $\kappa := |a|^{R}$. Then $|a| < \kappa < \lambda$, $\kappa \in \mathrm{k}(\exists y{\in}\mathsf{L}_{\lambda}(Ad(y) \wedge a \in y))^{\star}$ and $\models^{\star} Ad(\mathsf{L}_{\kappa}) \wedge a \in \mathsf{L}_{\kappa}$ (by 2.5). From this we get $\models^{\star} \exists y{\in}\mathsf{L}_{\lambda}(Ad(y) \wedge a \in y)$ by $(\exists^{\lambda})$.

3 $\mathcal{H}$-controlled derivations

In this section we introduce the infinitary proof system RS^{∞} and the notion of an *$\mathcal{H}$-controlled* RS^{∞}-derivation. We then prove that every $\mathrm{RS}^{\star}$-derivation can be transformed into an $\mathcal{H}$-controlled RS^{∞}-derivation and that the class of $\mathcal{H}$-controlled RS^{∞}-derivations is closed under predicative cut-elimination.

Definition 3.1 (The infinitary system RS^{∞})
We define RS^{∞} as the collection of all derivations (i.e. wellfounded trees of pairs $\Gamma:\alpha$) generated by the following inference rules

$$(\bigwedge)\quad \frac{\ldots\Gamma, A_{\iota} : \alpha_{\iota} \ldots (\iota \in J)}{\Gamma, \bigwedge(A_{\iota})_{\iota\in J} : \alpha} \qquad (\alpha_{\iota} < \alpha)$$

$$(\bigvee)\quad \frac{\Gamma, A_{\iota_0} : \alpha_0}{\Gamma, \bigvee(A_{\iota})_{\iota\in J} : \alpha} \qquad (\alpha_0 < \alpha,\ \iota_0 \in J,\ |\iota_0| < \alpha)$$

$$(\mathrm{Cut})\quad \frac{\Gamma, \neg C : \alpha_0 \qquad \Gamma, C : \alpha_0}{\Gamma : \alpha} \qquad (\alpha_0 < \alpha)$$

$$(\mathrm{Ref})\quad \frac{\Gamma, A : \alpha_0}{\Gamma, \exists z{\in}\mathsf{L}_{\kappa} A^{(z,\kappa)} : \alpha} \qquad (\alpha_0 + 1 < \alpha,\ A \in \Sigma(\kappa))$$

In RS^{∞} we identify every RS-sequent $\Gamma = (A_1, \ldots, A_n)$ with its underlying set $\{A_1, \ldots, A_n\}$, so that for example $\frac{\Gamma, A\vee B, A:\alpha}{\Gamma, A\vee B:\alpha+1}$ is an instance of $(\bigvee)$.
The *cut-rank* of an RS^{∞}-derivation d is defined as the least ordinal ρ such that $\mathrm{rk}(C) < \rho$ for all cut-formulas C in d.
If $\Gamma:\alpha$ is the bottommost pair of $d \in \mathrm{RS}^{\infty}$ we call d a *derivation of* $\Gamma:\alpha$ or a *derivation of* Γ *with ordinal* α.
We write $\vdash^{\alpha}_{\rho} \Gamma$ to express that there exists an RS^{∞}-derivation of $\Gamma:\alpha$ with cut-rank $\leq \rho$.

According to Lemma 1.7 the rules $(\bigwedge), (\bigvee), (\mathrm{Cut})$ are correct with respect to our standard semantics of $\mathcal{L}_{RS}$. This gives us the following lemma.

Lemma 3.2 (Truth-Lemma)
$\kappa = \min(\mathrm{R})$ & $\mathrm{k}(\Gamma) \subseteq \kappa$ & $\vdash^{\alpha}_{\kappa} \Gamma \Longrightarrow \models \Gamma$

Note that — apart from the restrictions '$|\iota_0| < \alpha$' in ($\bigvee$) and '$\alpha_0 \underline{+1} < \alpha$' in (Ref) — the just defined notion of RS^∞-derivation is completely standard. Therefore, according to (Tait [20]), RS^∞ allows predicative cut-elimination, i.e. every derivation of $\Gamma : \beta$ with cut-rank $\leq \omega^\alpha$ can be transformed into a derivation of $\Gamma : \varphi\alpha\beta$ where all cut-formulas are of the form $\overset{\exists}{\forall} z \in \mathsf{L}_\kappa A^{(z,\kappa)}$ with $\kappa < \omega^\alpha$, $A \in \Sigma(\kappa)$. Moreover it is fairly obvious that every RS^*-derivation of Γ can be transformed into an RS^∞-derivation of $\Gamma : \|\Gamma\|$. But of course these facts are not sufficient to establish nontrivial upper bounds for the proof theoretic ordinals of KPi, KPℓ or similar theories. In order to get such bounds we introduce the concept of *$\mathcal{H}$-controlled* RS^∞-derivations. Compared to the already existing methods this concept has the great advantage of being entirely independent from any system of collapsing functions or ordinal notations. Collapsing functions are now localized very sharply just to that part of the story where they really show up in the formulation of the result(s), i.e. the Collapsing Theorem.

We continue with some preliminaries to the definition of $\mathcal{H}$-controlled RS^∞-derivations. Let SEQ be the class of all RS-sequents. We identify each RS^∞-derivation in the usual way with a function $d : \mathrm{dom}(d) \longrightarrow \mathrm{SEQ} \times \mathrm{On}$ where $\mathrm{dom}(d)$ is a subset of $\{\langle \iota_0, \ldots, \iota_{n-1} \rangle : n \in \omega \;\&\; \iota_0, \ldots, \iota_{n-1} \in \mathcal{T}^{0,1}\}$ closed under initial segments. The elements of $\mathrm{dom}(d)$ are called the *nodes* of d, and the empty sequence $\langle\,\rangle \in \mathrm{dom}(d)$ is called the *bottom node* or *root* of d. For $\mathsf{s} \in \mathrm{dom}(d)$ and $d(\mathsf{s}) = (\Gamma : \alpha)$ we call Γ (α, resp.) the sequent (ordinal, resp.) at node s, and set $\mathrm{k}(d(\mathsf{s})) := \mathrm{k}(\Gamma) \cup \{\alpha\}$.
(To avoid a possible misunderstanding we point out that the index of the premise Γ, A_{ι_0} of an ($\bigvee$)-inference is 0 and not at all ι_0. So, if the conclusion of an ($\bigvee$)-inference is at node s, then its premise is at node $\mathsf{s} * \langle 0 \rangle$.)

Definition 3.3 ($\mathcal{H}$-controlled RS^∞-derivations)
Functions $\mathcal{H} : \mathcal{P}(\mathrm{On}) \longrightarrow \mathcal{P}(\mathrm{On})$ are henceforth called *operators*.
Let $\mathcal{H}$ be an operator, and $d : \mathrm{dom}(d) \longrightarrow \mathrm{SEQ} \times \mathrm{On}$ an RS^∞-derivation.
We say that d is *$\mathcal{H}$-controlled* if, and only if

$$\mathrm{k}(d(\mathsf{s})) \subseteq \mathcal{H}(\mathrm{k}(\mathsf{s})) \quad \text{for all } \mathsf{s} \in \mathrm{dom}(d).$$

The intuitive idea behind this definition is that, for each node s of d, $\mathcal{H}$ tells us which ordinals are allowed (or available) at s.

Definition 3.4
Let $\mathcal{H}$ be an operator and Θ a finite sequence of RS-sentences and elements of $\mathcal{T}^{0,1}$. Then we define the operator $\mathcal{H}[\Theta] : \mathcal{P}(\mathrm{On}) \longrightarrow \mathcal{P}(\mathrm{On})$ by

$$\mathcal{H}[\Theta](X) := \mathcal{H}(\mathrm{k}(\Theta) \cup X).$$

Abbreviations
Let $\mathcal{H}$ be an operator and f some ordinal function.
$\alpha \in \mathcal{H} \;:\Leftrightarrow\; \alpha \in \mathcal{H}(\emptyset)$
$X \subseteq \mathcal{H} \;:\Leftrightarrow\; X \subseteq \mathcal{H}(\emptyset)$
$\mathcal{H} \subseteq X \;:\Leftrightarrow\; \mathcal{H}(\emptyset) \subseteq X$
$\mathcal{H}$ is *closed under* f $\;:\Leftrightarrow\; \forall X{\in}\mathcal{P}(\mathrm{On})[\, \mathcal{H}(X)$ is closed under $f\,]$

Remarks
1. Note that '$\alpha \in \mathcal{H}[\Theta]$' ('$X \subseteq \mathcal{H}[\Theta]$', resp.) is synonymous with '$\alpha \in \mathcal{H}(\mathrm{k}(\Theta))$' ('$X \subseteq \mathcal{H}(\mathrm{k}(\Theta))$', resp.).
2. We always have $\mathcal{H}[\Theta, \Theta'] = \mathcal{H}[\Theta][\Theta']$.

In order to come up with a smooth theory of $\mathcal{H}$-controlled derivations we will from now on restrict our considerations to operators $\mathcal{H}$ which satisfy certain minimal closure conditions. These operators will be called *nice*.

Definition 3.5 (Nice operators)

i) A set $X \subseteq \mathrm{On}$ is called *nice* iff
$0 \in X \;\&\; \forall n{\in}\omega \forall \alpha_0, \ldots, \alpha_n(\, \omega^{\alpha_0} \# \ldots \# \omega^{\alpha_n} \in X \Leftrightarrow \{\alpha_0, \ldots, \alpha_n\} \subseteq X\,)$

ii) An operator $\mathcal{H}$ is called *nice* iff the following holds for all $X, X' \in \mathcal{P}(\mathrm{On})$:
(H.1) $\mathcal{H}(X)$ is nice.
(H.2) $X \subseteq \mathcal{H}(X)$
(H.3) $X' \subseteq \mathcal{H}(X) \Longrightarrow \mathcal{H}(X') \subseteq \mathcal{H}(X)$

Lemma 3.6
If $\mathcal{H}$ is a nice operator then the following holds for all Θ.
a) $\mathcal{H}[\Theta]$ *is nice.*
b) $\mathrm{k}(\Theta) \subseteq \mathcal{H} \Longrightarrow \mathcal{H}[\Theta] = \mathcal{H}$
c) $\forall X, X'{\in}\mathcal{P}(\mathrm{On})[\, X' \subseteq X \Longrightarrow \mathcal{H}(X') \subseteq \mathcal{H}(X)\,]$
d) $\mathcal{H}$ *is closed under addition, multiplication and exponentiation to base* ω.
e) *If* $\mathcal{H}$ *is closed under* $\xi \mapsto \xi^{\mathrm{R}}$ *then* $X^\star \subseteq \mathcal{H}(X)$ *for all* $X \in \mathcal{P}(\mathrm{On})$.

Definition 3.7
$\mathcal{H}\vdash^{\alpha}_{\rho}\Gamma :\Longleftrightarrow \exists\,\mathcal{H}$-controlled RS^∞-derivation of $(\Gamma:\alpha)$ with cut-rank $\le\rho$

Abbreviation: $\mathcal{H}\vdash^{\alpha}_{\rho}\Gamma,(\neg)C :\Longleftrightarrow \mathcal{H}\vdash^{\alpha}_{\rho}\Gamma,\neg C \ \&\ \mathcal{H}\vdash^{\alpha}_{\rho}\Gamma,C$.

The following Theorem provides a characterization of $\mathcal{H}\vdash^{\alpha}_{\rho}\Gamma$ by transfinite recursion on α which as well could be taken as the definition of $\mathcal{H}\vdash^{\alpha}_{\rho}\Gamma$. Actually in what follows we are always working with this derivability relation and not with specific derivations.

Theorem 3.8
$\mathcal{H}\vdash^{\alpha}_{\rho}\Gamma$ if, and only if, $\{\alpha\}\cup\mathsf{k}(\Gamma)\subseteq\mathcal{H}$ and one of the following cases holds:

$(\bigwedge)$	$\bigwedge(A_\iota)_{\iota\in J}\in\Gamma$	$\&\ \mathcal{H}[\iota]\vdash^{\alpha_\iota}_{\rho}\Gamma,A_\iota$	$\&\ \alpha_\iota<\alpha$	$(\forall\iota\in J)$
$(\bigvee)$	$\bigvee(A_\iota)_{\iota\in J}\in\Gamma$	$\&\ \mathcal{H}\vdash^{\alpha_0}_{\rho}\Gamma,A_{\iota_0}$	$\&\ \alpha_0<\alpha$	$\&\ \iota_0\in J\vert\alpha$
(Cut)	$\mathrm{rk}(C)<\rho$	$\&\ \mathcal{H}\vdash^{\alpha_0}_{\rho}\Gamma,(\neg)C$	$\&\ \alpha_0<\alpha$	
(Ref)	$\exists z\in\mathsf{L}_\kappa A^{(z,\kappa)}\in\Gamma$	$\&\ \mathcal{H}\vdash^{\alpha_0}_{\rho}\Gamma,A$	$\&\ \alpha_0{+}1<\alpha$	$\&\ A\in\Sigma(\kappa)$

General Assumption
In the following $\mathcal{H}$ always denotes some **nice** *operator.*

Now we are going to prove the three main results of this section, i.e. the Embedding Theorem, the Predicative Cut-Elimination Theorem, and the Boundedness Lemma for $\mathcal{H}$-controlled RS^∞-derivations.

Lemma 3.9
a) $\mathcal{H}\vdash^{\alpha}_{\rho}\Gamma\ \&\ \alpha\le\alpha'\in\mathcal{H}\ \&\ \rho\le\rho'\ \&\ \mathsf{k}(\Gamma')\subseteq\mathcal{H}\Longrightarrow\mathcal{H}\vdash^{\alpha'}_{\rho'}\Gamma,\Gamma'$

b) $\mathcal{H}\vdash^{\alpha}_{\rho}\Gamma,A\vee B\Longrightarrow\mathcal{H}\vdash^{\alpha}_{\rho}\Gamma,A,B$

c) $\mathcal{H}\vdash^{\alpha}_{\rho}\Gamma,\forall x\in\mathsf{L}_\kappa A(x)\ \&\ \beta<\kappa\ \&\ \beta\in\mathcal{H}\Longrightarrow\mathcal{H}\vdash^{\alpha}_{\rho}\Gamma,\forall x\in\mathsf{L}_\beta A(x)$

Proof by induction on α.

Lemma 3.10
If $\mathcal{H}$ is closed under $\xi\mapsto\xi^{\mathrm{R}}$, then $\vdash^{\star}_{\rho}\Gamma$ implies $\mathcal{H}[\Gamma]\vdash^{\Vert\Gamma\Vert}_{\rho}\Gamma$.

Proof.
Abbreviation: $\mathcal{H}\vdash^{\star}_{\rho}\Gamma :\Leftrightarrow \mathcal{H}[\Gamma]\vdash^{\Vert\Gamma\Vert}_{\rho}\Gamma$.

We prove that $\mathcal{H}\vdash^{\star}_{\rho}$ is closed under the inference rules of $\mathsf{RS}^\star$.

1. Suppose that $\Gamma = \Gamma', A$ with $A \simeq \bigwedge(A_\iota)_{\iota\in J}$ and $\mathcal{H}|\frac{\star}{\rho}\ \Gamma', A_\iota$ for all $\iota \in J$. Let $\alpha := \|\Gamma\|$, $\alpha_\iota := \|\Gamma', A_\iota\|$. Then $\alpha_\iota < \alpha \in \mathcal{H}[\Gamma]$ and $\mathcal{H}[\Gamma', A_\iota]|\frac{\alpha_\iota}{\rho}\ \Gamma', A_\iota$ for all $\iota \in J$. Since $\mathrm{k}(\Gamma', A_\iota) \subseteq \mathrm{k}(\Gamma, \iota)$, the latter implies $\mathcal{H}[\Gamma][\iota]|\frac{\alpha_\iota}{\rho}\ \Gamma', A_\iota$ for all $\iota \in J$. Hence $\mathcal{H}[\Gamma]|\frac{\alpha}{\rho}\ \Gamma$ by ($\bigwedge$).

2. Suppose that $\Gamma = \Gamma', A$ with $A \simeq \bigvee(A_\iota)_{\iota\in J}$ and $\mathcal{H}|\frac{\star}{\rho}\ \Gamma', A_{\iota_0}, \ldots, A_{\iota_n}$ where $\iota_0, \ldots, \iota_n \in J$ and $\mathrm{k}(\iota_0, \ldots, \iota_n) \subseteq \mathrm{k}(\Gamma)^\star$. Let $\alpha := \|\Gamma\|$ and $\alpha_0 := \|\Gamma', A_{\iota_0}, \ldots, A_{\iota_n}\|$. Since $\mathrm{k}(\Gamma', A_{\iota_0}, \ldots, A_{\iota_n}) \subseteq \mathrm{k}(\Gamma, \iota_0, \ldots, \iota_n) \subseteq \mathrm{k}(\Gamma)^\star \subseteq \mathcal{H}[\Gamma]$, the assumption yields $\mathcal{H}[\Gamma]|\frac{\alpha_0}{\rho}\ \Gamma', A_{\iota_0}, \ldots, A_{\iota_n}$. From this and the fact that $\alpha_0 + \omega \leq \alpha \in \mathcal{H}[\Gamma]$ we obtain $\mathcal{H}[\Gamma]|\frac{\alpha}{\rho}\ \Gamma$ by n+1 applications of ($\bigvee$). (Note that $|\iota_i| < \|A\| \leq \|\Gamma\| = \alpha$.)

3. Suppose that $\Gamma = \Gamma', Ad(a) \rightarrow B(a)$ with $\mathrm{rk}(B(a)) < \rho$ and $\mathcal{H}|\frac{\star}{\rho}\ \Gamma', B(\mathsf{L}_\kappa)$ for all $\kappa \leq |a|$. Let $\alpha := \|\Gamma\|$, $\alpha_0 := \|\Gamma', \neg Ad(a), B(a), B(a)\|$. Then we have $\alpha_0, \alpha \in \mathcal{H}[\Gamma]$, $\forall\kappa \leq |a|(\|\Gamma', B(\mathsf{L}_\kappa)\| < \alpha_0)$ and $\mathcal{H}[\Gamma, \mathsf{L}_\kappa]|\frac{\alpha_0}{\rho}\ \Gamma', B(\mathsf{L}_\kappa)$ for all $\kappa \leq |a|$. By 2.7 we have $|\frac{\star}{}\ \mathsf{L}_\kappa \neq a, \neg B(\mathsf{L}_\kappa), B(a)$. By 1. and 2. above $\mathcal{H}|\frac{\star}{\rho}$ is closed under $(\bigwedge)^\star$ and $(\bigvee)^\star$. Hence $\mathcal{H}[\Gamma, \mathsf{L}_\kappa]|\frac{\alpha_0}{\rho}\ \mathsf{L}_\kappa \neq a, \neg B(\mathsf{L}_\kappa), B(a)$, for all $\kappa \leq |a|$, and by (Cut) we get $\mathcal{H}[\Gamma, \mathsf{L}_\kappa]|\frac{\alpha_0+1}{\rho}\ \Gamma', \mathsf{L}_\kappa \neq a, B(a)$, for all $\kappa \leq |a|$. This yields $\mathcal{H}[\Gamma]|\frac{\alpha_0+2}{\rho}\ \Gamma', \neg Ad(a), B(a)$ and then $\mathcal{H}[\Gamma]|\frac{\alpha}{\rho}\ \Gamma', Ad(a) \rightarrow B(a)$, since $\alpha_0 < \alpha \in \mathrm{Lim}$.

4. Let $A \in \Sigma(\kappa)$. By 2.4 we have $|\frac{\star}{}\ \neg A, A$ and therefore $\mathcal{H}[A]|\frac{\alpha_0}{\rho}\ \neg A, A$ with $\alpha_0 := \|\neg A, A\|$. From this by (Ref) and ($\bigvee$) we get $\mathcal{H}[C]|\frac{\|C\|}{\rho}\ C$ with $C :\equiv A \rightarrow \exists z{\in}\mathsf{L}_\kappa A^{(z,\kappa)}$.

5. Suppose that $\Gamma = \Gamma', C, \forall x{\in}\mathsf{L}_\alpha A(x)$ with $C \equiv \exists x{\in}\mathsf{L}_\alpha(\forall y{\in}x A(y) \wedge \neg A(x))$. Let $\gamma_t := \|C\| + \omega|t|$. By induction on $|a|$ we prove $\mathcal{H}[C, a]|\frac{\gamma_a}{\rho}\ C, \forall x{\in}a A(x)$ for all $a \in \mathcal{T}$ with $|a| \leq \alpha$. This yields $\mathcal{H}[\Gamma]|\frac{\|\Gamma\|}{\rho}\ \Gamma$, since $\mathrm{k}(C, \mathsf{L}_\alpha) \subseteq \mathrm{k}(\Gamma)$ and $\|C\| + \omega|\mathsf{L}_\alpha| \leq \|\Gamma\|$. So let $|a| \leq \alpha$. By I.H. we have (1) $\mathcal{H}[C, t]|\frac{\gamma_t}{\rho}\ C, \forall y{\in}t A(y)$ for all $t \in \mathcal{T}_{|a|}$. By 1. and 2. above we have (2) $\mathcal{H}[A(t)]|\frac{\alpha_t}{\rho}\ \neg A(t), A(t)$ with $\alpha_t := \|\neg A(t), A(t)\|$. Since $\mathrm{k}(A(t)) \subseteq \mathrm{k}(C, t)$ and $\alpha_t \leq \gamma_t$ for $t \in \mathcal{T}_\alpha$,

from (1) and (2) we obtain $\mathcal{H}[C,t]\vert\frac{\gamma_{t+2}}{\rho}\, C, t \mathring{\in} \mathsf{L}_\alpha \wedge \forall y{\in}t A(y) \wedge \neg A(t), A(t)$ for all $t \in \mathcal{T}_{|a|}$. By ($\bigvee$) we get $\mathcal{H}[C,t]\vert\frac{\gamma_{t+3}}{\rho}\, C, A(t)$ for all $t \in \mathcal{T}_{|a|}$. Hence $\mathcal{H}[C,a]\vert\frac{\gamma_a}{\rho}\, C, \forall x{\in}a A(x)$.

Lemma 3.11
Let $\lambda \in \mathcal{H}$. Then for every logically valid sequent $\Delta(\vec{x})$ of $\mathcal{L}_{Ad}$-formulas there is an $m < \omega$ such that $\mathcal{H}[\vec{a}]\vert\frac{\omega^{\omega\lambda+m}}{\omega\lambda}\, \Delta^\lambda(\vec{a})$ for all $\vec{a} \in \mathcal{T}_\lambda$.

Proof. Abbreviation: $\mathcal{H} \vdash \Delta(\vec{x}) \;:\Leftrightarrow\; \exists m < \omega\, \forall \vec{a} \in \mathcal{T}_\lambda[\, \mathcal{H}[\vec{a}]\vert\frac{\omega^{\omega\lambda+m}}{\omega\lambda}\, \Delta^\lambda(\vec{a})\,]$.
It suffices to prove that '$\mathcal{H} \vdash$' is closed under the rules of Tait's (cutfree) calculus for first order predicate logic.
1. By 2.4 and 3.10 for every atomic formula $\phi(\vec{x})$ and $\vec{a} \in \mathcal{T}_\lambda$ we have $\mathcal{H}[\vec{a}]\vert\frac{\omega^{\omega\lambda}}{0}\, \neg\phi^\lambda(\vec{a}), \phi^\lambda(\vec{a})$.

2. Suppose that $\forall y\phi(\vec{x},y) \in \Delta(\vec{x})$ and $\mathcal{H} \vdash \Delta(\vec{x}), \phi(\vec{x},y)$ with $y \notin \{\vec{x}\}$. Then for some $\alpha = \omega\lambda + m$ we have $\quad (*)\; \mathcal{H}[\vec{a},b]\vert\frac{\omega^\alpha}{\omega\lambda}\, \Delta^\lambda(\vec{a}), \phi^\lambda(\vec{a},b) \quad (\forall \vec{a}, b \in \mathcal{T}_\lambda)$.
Let $\vec{a} \in \mathcal{T}_\lambda$ be fixed.

2.1. Suppose that $\forall y$ is unrestricted. Then $(\forall y\phi(\vec{a},y))^\lambda \equiv \forall y{\in}\mathsf{L}_\lambda \phi^\lambda(\vec{a},y)$ and from $(*)$ we get $\mathcal{H}[\vec{a}]\vert\frac{\omega^{\alpha+1}}{\omega\lambda}\, \Delta^\lambda(\vec{a}), \forall y{\in}\mathsf{L}_\lambda\phi^\lambda(\vec{a},y)$.

2.2. Suppose that $\phi(\vec{x},y) \equiv y \in x_i \to \psi(\vec{x},y)$. In this case $(\forall y\phi(\vec{a},y))^\lambda \equiv \forall y{\in}a_i\phi^\lambda(\vec{a},y)$, and from $(*)$ we get $\mathcal{H}[\vec{a},b]\vert\frac{\omega^\alpha}{\omega\lambda}\, \Delta^\lambda(\vec{a}), b \notin a_i, \psi^\lambda(\vec{a},b)$ for all $b \in \mathcal{T}_\lambda$. By 2.5c and 3.10 we also have $\mathcal{H}[\vec{a},b]\vert\frac{\omega^\alpha}{\omega\lambda}\, b \in a_i, b \mathring{\notin} a_i$ for all $b \in \mathcal{T}_{|a_i|}$. By (Cut) we obtain $\mathcal{H}[\vec{a},b]\vert\frac{\omega^\alpha+1}{\omega\lambda}\, \Delta^\lambda(\vec{a}), b \mathring{\notin} a_i, \psi^\lambda(\vec{a},b) \quad (\forall b{\in}\mathcal{T}_{|a_i|})$. Now we apply ($\bigvee$) and ($\bigwedge$) and get $\mathcal{H}[\vec{a}]\vert\frac{\omega^{\alpha+1}}{\omega\lambda}\, \Delta^\lambda(\vec{a}), \forall y{\in}a_i\psi^\lambda(\vec{a},y)$.

3. The case of an $\exists$-inference is treated similarly to case 2.
4. The $\wedge$- and $\vee$-cases are easy.

From 2.9, 3.10 and 3.11 we get the following theorem.

Theorem 3.12 (Embedding)
Suppose that $\lambda \in \mathcal{H}$ with $\lambda \in \mathrm{R}$ & $\forall \alpha < \lambda \exists \kappa{\in}\mathrm{R}(\alpha < \kappa < \lambda)$, and that $\mathcal{H}$ is closed under $\zeta \mapsto \zeta^{\mathrm{R}}$. Then for each theorem ϕ of KPi there is an $m < \omega$ such that $\mathcal{H}\vert\frac{\omega^{\lambda+m}}{\lambda+m}\, \phi^\lambda$.

We now turn to the Predicative Cut-Elimination Theorem.

Lemma 3.13 (Inversion)
$\mathcal{H}|\frac{\alpha}{\rho}\,\Gamma, \bigwedge(A_\iota)_{\iota\in J}$ & $\iota_0 \in J \Longrightarrow \mathcal{H}[\iota_0]|\frac{\alpha}{\rho}\,\Gamma, A_{\iota_0}$
Proof by induction on α.

Lemma 3.14 (Reduction)
Suppose that $C \simeq \bigvee(C_\iota)_{\iota\in J}$ *and* $\mathrm{rk}(C) = \rho \notin \mathrm{R}$. *Then the following holds:*
$\mathcal{H}|\frac{\alpha}{\rho}\,\Gamma', \neg C$ & $\mathcal{H}|\frac{\beta}{\rho}\,\Gamma, C \Longrightarrow \mathcal{H}|\frac{\alpha+\beta}{\rho}\,\Gamma', \Gamma.$

Proof by induction on β.
We treat only the crucial case where Γ, C is the conclusion of an $(\bigvee)$-inference with principal part C. So assume that $\mathcal{H}|\frac{\beta_0}{\rho}\,\Gamma, C, C_{\iota_0}$ with $\iota_0 \in J|\beta$ and $\beta_0 < \beta \in \mathcal{H}$. Then by I.H. we have (1) $\mathcal{H}|\frac{\alpha+\beta_0}{\rho}\,\Gamma', \Gamma, C_{\iota_0}$.
We also have $\beta_0 \in \mathcal{H}$, $\neg C \simeq \bigwedge(\neg C_\iota)_{\iota\in J}$, $\mathrm{k}(\iota_0) \subseteq \mathrm{k}(C_{\iota_0}) \subseteq \mathcal{H}$. The latter yields $\mathcal{H}[\iota_0] = \mathcal{H}$. Therefore by 3.13 and 3.9a from $\mathcal{H}|\frac{\alpha}{\rho}\,\Gamma', \neg C$ we get (2) $\mathcal{H}|\frac{\alpha+\beta_0}{\rho}\,\Gamma', \Gamma, \neg C_{\iota_0}$. Now we apply (Cut) to (1),(2) and obtain $\mathcal{H}|\frac{\alpha+\beta}{\rho}\,\Gamma', \Gamma,$ since $\mathrm{rk}(C_{\iota_0}) < \mathrm{rk}(C) = \rho$ and $\alpha + \beta_0 < \alpha + \beta \in \mathcal{H}$.
Note that, since $\mathrm{rk}(C) \notin \mathrm{R}$, C cannot be the main part of a (Ref)-inference.

Definition 3.15 (The Veblen function φ)
$\varphi\alpha\beta := \varphi_\alpha(\beta)$, where φ_α is defined by transfinite recursion on α as the ordering function of the class $\{\omega^\beta : \beta \in \mathrm{On}$ & $\forall\xi{\in}\alpha(\,\varphi_\xi(\omega^\beta) = \omega^\beta\,)\}$

Corollary (Basic properties of φ)
(φ.1) $\varphi 0\beta = \omega^\beta$, $\varphi 1\beta = \varepsilon_\beta$
(φ.2) $\xi, \eta < \varphi\alpha\beta \Longrightarrow \xi + \eta < \varphi\alpha\beta$
(φ.3) $\beta_0 < \beta \Longrightarrow \varphi\alpha\beta_0 < \varphi\alpha\beta$
(φ.4) $\alpha_0 < \alpha \Longrightarrow \varphi\alpha_0(\varphi\alpha\beta) = \varphi\alpha\beta$

Theorem 3.16 (Predicative Cut-Elimination)
If $\mathcal{H}$ *is closed under the Veblen-function* φ *then the following holds:*
$\mathcal{H}|\frac{\beta}{\rho+\omega^\alpha}\,\Gamma$ & $[\rho, \rho+\omega^\alpha[\cap \mathrm{R} = \emptyset$ & $\alpha \in \mathcal{H} \Longrightarrow \mathcal{H}|\frac{\varphi\alpha\beta}{\rho}\,\Gamma.$

Proof by main induction on α and subsidiary induction on β.
Again we only treat the crucial case.

Assume $\mathcal{H}|\frac{\beta_0}{\rho+\omega^\alpha}(\neg)C,\Gamma$ & $\beta_0 < \beta \in \mathcal{H}$ & $\mathrm{rk}(C) < \rho + \omega^\alpha$.

Then by S.I.H. we have (1) $\mathcal{H}|\frac{\varphi\alpha\beta_0}{\rho}(\neg)C,\Gamma$.

From $\alpha,\beta \in \mathcal{H}$ we get (2) $\varphi\alpha\beta \in \mathcal{H}$.

CASE 1: $\mathrm{rk}(C) < \rho$. In this case we apply (Cut) to (1) and use the fact that $\varphi\alpha\beta_0 < \varphi\alpha\beta \in \mathcal{H}$. This gives us $\mathcal{H}|\frac{\varphi\alpha\beta}{\rho}\Gamma$.

CAES 2: $\mathrm{rk}(C) = \rho + \omega^{\alpha_1} + \ldots + \omega^{\alpha_n}$ with $n \geq 0$, $\alpha > \alpha_1 \geq \ldots \geq \alpha_n$.
From $\mathrm{k}(C) \subseteq \mathcal{H}$ it follows that $\mathrm{rk}(C) \in \mathcal{H}$ and thus $\alpha_1,\ldots,\alpha_n \in \mathcal{H}$.

The Reduction-Lemma applied to (1) yields (3) $\mathcal{H}|\frac{\varphi\alpha\beta_0+\varphi\alpha\beta_0}{\mathrm{rk}(C)}\Gamma$,

and from this we obtain (4) $\mathcal{H}|\frac{\varphi\alpha\beta}{\mathrm{rk}(C)}\Gamma$, since $\varphi\alpha\beta_0+\varphi\alpha\beta_0 < \varphi\alpha\beta \in \mathcal{H}$.
Now using $\alpha_1,\ldots,\alpha_n \in \mathcal{H}$, $\mathrm{rk}(C) = \rho + \omega^{\alpha_1} + \ldots + \omega^{\alpha_n}$ and $\varphi\alpha_i(\varphi\alpha\beta) = \varphi\alpha\beta$ $(i = 1,\ldots,n)$ by n applications of the main I.H. we get $\mathcal{H}|\frac{\varphi\alpha\beta}{\rho}\Gamma$.

Corollary

$\mathcal{H}|\frac{\beta}{\rho+1}\Gamma$ & $\rho \notin \mathrm{R} \implies \mathcal{H}|\frac{\omega^\beta}{\rho}\Gamma$

Lemma 3.17 (Boundedness)

$\mathcal{H}|\frac{\alpha}{\rho}\Gamma,C$ & $\alpha \leq \beta < \kappa$ & $C \in \Sigma(\kappa)$ & $\beta \in \mathcal{H} \Longrightarrow \mathcal{H}|\frac{\alpha}{\rho}\Gamma,C^{(\beta,\kappa)}$

Proof by induction on α.

1. Suppose that $C \simeq \bigwedge(C_\iota)_{\iota\in J}$ and $\mathcal{H}[\iota]|\frac{\alpha_\iota}{\rho}\Gamma,C,C_\iota$ with $\alpha_\iota < \alpha \in \mathcal{H}$, for all $\iota \in J$. Then, since $C \in \Sigma(\kappa)$, we have $C^{(\beta,\kappa)} \simeq \bigwedge(C_\iota^{(\beta,\kappa)})_{\iota\in J}$. By (two applications of) the I.H. we obtain $\mathcal{H}[\iota]|\frac{\alpha_\iota}{\rho}\Gamma,C^{(\beta,\kappa)},C_\iota^{(\beta,\kappa)}$ $(\forall\iota\in J)$ and from this $\mathcal{H}|\frac{\alpha}{\rho}\Gamma,C^{(\beta,\kappa)}$ by an application of $(\bigwedge)$.

2. Suppose that $C \simeq \bigvee(C_\iota)_{\iota\in J}$ and $\mathcal{H}|\frac{\alpha_0}{\rho}\Gamma,C,C_{\iota_0}$ with $\iota_0 \in J|\alpha$ and $\alpha_0 < \alpha \in \mathcal{H}$. Then $C^{(\beta,\kappa)} \simeq \bigvee(C_\iota^{(\beta,\kappa)})_{\iota\in J'}$ with $J' = J$ or $J' = J|\beta$. Since $\alpha \leq \beta$ and $\iota_0 \in J|\alpha$, we also have $\iota_0 \in J'|\alpha$. Therefore by I.H. and $(\bigvee)$ we obtain $\mathcal{H}|\frac{\alpha}{\rho}\Gamma,C^{(\beta,\kappa)}$ as in the first case.

3. Suppose that $C \equiv \exists z \in \mathsf{L}_\kappa A^{(z,\kappa)}$ and $\mathcal{H}|\frac{\alpha_0}{\rho}\Gamma,C,A$ with $A \in \Sigma(\kappa)$ and

$\alpha_0 + 1 < \alpha \in \mathcal{H}$. Then by two applications of the I.H. we obtain
(1) $\mathcal{H}\vert\frac{\alpha_0}{\rho}\,\Gamma, C^{(\beta,\kappa)}, A^{(\alpha_0,\kappa)}$. We also have (2) $\mathcal{H}\vert\frac{\alpha_0}{\rho}\,\Gamma, C^{(\beta,\kappa)}, \mathsf{L}_{\alpha_0} \notin \mathsf{L}_0$.
By ($\bigwedge$) from (1),(2) we get (3) $\mathcal{H}\vert\frac{\alpha_0+1}{\rho}\,\Gamma, C^{(\beta,\kappa)}, \mathsf{L}_{\alpha_0} \notin \mathsf{L}_0 \wedge A^{(\alpha_0,\kappa)}$.
Now observe that $C^{(\beta,\kappa)} \simeq \bigvee(\iota \notin \mathsf{L}_0 \wedge A^{(\iota,\kappa)})_{\iota \in T_\beta}$, and that for $\iota := \mathsf{L}_{\alpha_0}$ we have $\iota \in J|\alpha$ and $A^{(\iota,\kappa)} \equiv A^{(\alpha_0,\kappa)}$. Therefore by ($\bigvee$) from (3) we obtain $\mathcal{H}\vert\frac{\alpha}{\rho}\,\Gamma, C^{(\beta,\kappa)}$.

4. In all other cases the assertion follows immediately from the I.H. .

4 The Collapsing Theorem

In this section we can no longer do with the extremely weak assumption that R is just a class of ε-numbers, but we have to assume much stronger closure properties for the elements of R. The most natural approach would be to define R as the class of all admissible ordinals $> \omega$. But from the technical side it is much more convenient to assume that the elements of R are uncountable regular cardinals. Under this assumption one can prove much more easily that the functions ψ_κ ($\kappa \in$ R) defined below are indeed collapsing functions, i.e. that $\psi_\kappa\alpha < \kappa$ holds for all $\alpha \in$ On, $\kappa \in$ R. Moreover using regular cardinals instead of admissibles does not affect the size of the ordinal υ which we will obtain as an upper bound for the proof theoretic ordinal of KPi.

Definition 4.1

$\Omega_0 := 0\ ,\ \ \Omega_\sigma := \aleph_\sigma$ for $\sigma > 0$.

We assume the existence of a weakly inaccessible cardinal, i.e. a regular fixpoint of $\sigma \mapsto \Omega_\sigma$, and set

$$\mathrm{I} := \min\{\sigma : \sigma \text{ regular } \ \&\ \ \Omega_\sigma = \sigma\}$$

$$\mathrm{R} := \{\sigma : \omega < \sigma \leq \mathrm{I}\ \ \&\ \ \sigma \text{ regular}\} = \{\mathrm{I}\} \cup \{\Omega_{\sigma+1} : \sigma < \mathrm{I}\}$$

As before we use κ, π, τ to denote elements of R.

Definition 4.2 (The collapsing functions ψ_κ)
By transfinite recursion on α we define ordinals $\psi_\kappa\alpha$ and sets $C(\alpha,\beta) \subseteq \mathrm{On}$ as follows

$\psi_\kappa\alpha := \min\{\beta : \kappa \in C(\alpha,\beta) \ \& \ C(\alpha,\beta)\cap\kappa \subseteq \beta\}$

$$C(\alpha,\beta) := \begin{cases} \text{the closure of } \beta\cup\{0,\mathrm{I}\} \text{ under the functions} \\ +\,,\ \varphi\,,\ \sigma\mapsto\Omega_\sigma\,,\ (\xi,\pi)\mapsto\psi_\pi\xi\ (\xi<\alpha,\ \pi\in\mathrm{R}) \end{cases}$$

(Note that by I.H. $\psi_\pi\xi$ is already defined for all $\xi < \alpha$, $\pi \in \mathrm{R}$.)

We then set $\psi_\kappa : \mathrm{On} \longrightarrow \mathrm{On}$, $\psi_\kappa(\alpha) := \psi_\kappa\alpha$.

Definition 4.3 (The operators $\mathcal{H}_\gamma$)

$\mathcal{H}_\gamma(X) := \bigcap\{C(\alpha,\beta) : X \subseteq C(\alpha,\beta) \ \& \ \gamma < \alpha\}$

The remainder of this section is devoted to the proof of the following theorem, called *Collapsing Theorem* or *Impredicative Cut-Elimination Theorem*.

$\mathcal{H}_0 \vert\frac{\alpha}{\mathrm{I}+1}\, \Gamma \ \& \ \Gamma \subseteq \Sigma(\Omega_1) \implies \vert\frac{\beta}{\beta}\, \Gamma$ with $\beta := \psi_{\Omega_1}(\omega^{\mathrm{I}+1+\alpha})$

This theorem in combination with 3.12, 3.16, 3.17, 3.2, 1.5 then yields the final result that $|\mathrm{KPi}| \le \psi_{\Omega_1}\varepsilon_{\mathrm{I}+1}$.

The above defined functions ψ_κ ($\kappa \in \mathrm{R}$) constitute a subsystem of the system $(\Psi_\kappa : \kappa < \Lambda_0)$ introduced in (Jäger [7]) which on the other hand was obtained by extending our system $(\psi_\kappa : \kappa < \Omega_\omega)$ from (Buchholz [2]). Actually the above definition looks a little bit different from that in (Jäger [7]), but nevertheless, restricted to $\kappa \le \mathrm{I}$, both definitions are equivalent.

Before proving the Collapsing Theorem we have to prove some basic properties of the functions ψ_κ and the sets $C(\alpha,\beta)$.

Abbreviation: $C_\kappa(\alpha) := C(\alpha, \psi_\kappa\alpha)$.

Lemma 4.4
a) $\beta < \pi \implies \mathrm{cardinality}(C(\alpha,\beta)) < \pi$
b) $C(\alpha,\beta) = \bigcup_{\eta<\beta} C(\alpha,\eta)$, *for each limit ordinal* β
c) $\kappa \in C(\alpha,\kappa)$
d) $C_\kappa(\alpha) \cap \kappa = \psi_\kappa\alpha$

Proof. All statements are immediate consequences of definition 4.2.

Lemma 4.5

a) $\psi_\kappa\alpha < \kappa$ & $\psi_\kappa\alpha \notin C_\kappa(\alpha)$

b) $\alpha_0 < \alpha$ & $\alpha_0 \in C_\kappa(\alpha) \implies \psi_\kappa\alpha_0 < \psi_\kappa\alpha$

c) $\psi_\kappa\alpha \notin \{\Omega_\sigma : \sigma < \Omega_\sigma\} \cup \{0\}$ & $\forall\xi,\eta < \psi_\kappa\alpha(\ \varphi\xi\eta < \psi_\kappa\alpha\ )$

d) $\Omega_\sigma \in C(\alpha,\beta) \implies \sigma \in C(\alpha,\beta)$

e) $\omega^{\xi_0}\#\ldots\#\omega^{\xi_n} \in C(\alpha,\beta) \implies \{\xi_0,\ldots,\xi_n\} \subseteq C(\alpha,\beta)$

f) $\kappa = \Omega_{\sigma+1} \implies \Omega_\sigma < \psi_\kappa\alpha < \Omega_{\sigma+1}$

g) $\Omega_{\psi_I\alpha} = \psi_I\alpha$

h) $\Omega_\sigma \leq \gamma \leq \Omega_{\sigma+1}$ & $\gamma \in C(\alpha,\beta) \implies \sigma \in C(\alpha,\beta)$

i) $\alpha_0 \leq \alpha \implies \psi_\kappa\alpha_0 \leq \psi_\kappa\alpha$ & $C_\kappa(\alpha_0) \subseteq C_\kappa(\alpha)$

Proof.

a) Let $\beta_0 := \min\{\eta : \kappa \in C(\alpha,\eta)\}$, $\beta_{n+1} := \min\{\eta : C(\alpha,\beta_n) \cap \kappa \subseteq \eta\}$ and $\beta := \sup\{\beta_n : n \in \omega\}$. Using 4.4a) we obtain $\forall n\in\omega(\beta_n \leq \beta_{n+1} < \kappa)$. Hence $\beta < \kappa$, $\kappa \in C(\alpha,\beta)$ and $C(\alpha,\beta) \cap \kappa = \bigcup\{C(\alpha,\beta_n) \cap \kappa : n \in \omega\} \subseteq \bigcup\{\beta_{n+1} : n \in \omega\} = \beta$. By definition of $\psi_\kappa\alpha$ this yields $\psi_\kappa\alpha \leq \beta < \kappa$. From $C_\kappa(\alpha) \cap \kappa = \psi_\kappa\alpha < \kappa$ it follows that $\psi_\kappa\alpha \notin C_\kappa(\alpha)$.

b) $\alpha_0 < \alpha$ & $\alpha_0 \in C_\kappa(\alpha)$ together with $\kappa \in C_\kappa(\alpha)$ implies $\psi_\kappa\alpha_0 \in C_\kappa(\alpha)$. Using a) and 4.4d) we obtain $\psi_\kappa\alpha_0 \in C_\kappa(\alpha) \cap \kappa = \psi_\kappa\alpha$.

c) Let us assume that $\psi_\kappa\alpha = \Omega_\sigma$ with $\sigma = 0$ or $\sigma < \Omega_\sigma$. Then by definition of $C_\kappa(\alpha)$ we would have $\psi_\kappa\alpha \in C_\kappa(\alpha)$ which contradicts a). — The second part is an immediate consequence of $\psi_\kappa\alpha = C_\kappa(\alpha) \cap \kappa$ and the fact that κ and $C_\kappa(\alpha)$ both are closed under φ.

d) Let us assume that $\sigma < \Omega_\sigma$ and $\sigma \notin C(\alpha,\beta)$. Then $\Omega_\sigma \notin \beta \cup \{0,\mathrm{I}\}$ and, according to c), $\Omega_\sigma \neq \psi_\pi\xi$ $(\forall\xi,\pi)$. Moreover we have $\forall\xi,\eta(\ \Omega_\sigma \in \{\xi+\eta,\varphi\xi\eta\} \implies \Omega_\sigma \in \{\xi,\eta\}\ )$. Therefore the set $C(\alpha,\beta)\setminus\{\Omega_\sigma\}$ contains $\beta \cup \{0,\mathrm{I}\}$ and is closed under $+,\varphi,\zeta \mapsto \Omega_\zeta$, $(\xi,\pi) \mapsto \psi_\pi\xi$ $(\xi < \alpha, \pi \in \mathrm{R})$. By definition of $C(\alpha,\beta)$ this implies $C(\alpha,\beta) \subseteq C(\alpha,\beta)\setminus\{\Omega_\sigma\}$, i.e. $\Omega_\sigma \notin C(\alpha,\beta)$.

e) This is proved in the same way as d), now using the fact that the ordinals Ω_σ and $\psi_\pi\xi$ are closed under φ.

f) From $\Omega_{\sigma+1} = \kappa \in C_\kappa(\alpha)$ it follows by d) and e) that $\sigma \in C_\kappa(\alpha)$. Hence $\Omega_\sigma \in C_\kappa(\alpha) \cap \kappa = \psi_\kappa\alpha$.

g) Let $\Omega_\sigma \le \psi_I\alpha < \Omega_{\sigma+1}$. Then $\Omega_{\sigma+1} < I$ and therefore $\Omega_{\sigma+1} \notin C_I(\alpha)$, since $\Omega_{\sigma+1} \notin \psi_I\alpha = C_I(\alpha) \cap I$. It follows that $\sigma \notin C_I(\alpha)$ and thus $\psi_I\alpha \le \sigma \le \Omega_\sigma$.

h) We assume $\sigma \notin C(\alpha,\beta)$. Then also $\Omega_\sigma, \Omega_{\sigma+1} \notin C(\alpha,\beta)$. Obviously $\beta \cup \{0, I\} \subseteq Y := C(\alpha,\beta) \setminus [\Omega_\sigma, \Omega_{\sigma+1}]$ and Y is closed under $+, \varphi, \zeta \mapsto \Omega_\zeta$. By f) and g) it follows that Y is also closed under $(\xi,\pi) \mapsto \psi_\pi\xi$ $(\xi < \alpha, \pi \in R)$. Hence $C(\alpha,\beta) \subseteq C(\alpha,\beta) \setminus [\Omega_\sigma, \Omega_{\sigma+1}]$, i.e. $C(\alpha,\beta) \cap [\Omega_\sigma, \Omega_{\sigma+1}] = \emptyset$.

i) By f) it follows that $\kappa \in C(\alpha_0, \psi_\kappa\alpha)$. We also have $C(\alpha_0, \psi_\kappa\alpha) \cap \kappa \subseteq C(\alpha, \psi_\kappa\alpha) \cap \kappa = \psi_\kappa\alpha$. By the definition of $\psi_\kappa\alpha_0$ from $\kappa \in C(\alpha_0, \psi_\kappa\alpha)$ and $C(\alpha_0, \psi_\kappa\alpha) \cap \kappa \subseteq \psi_\kappa\alpha$ it follows that $\psi_\kappa\alpha_0 \le \psi_\kappa\alpha$.

As an immediate consequence of the above lemma we get the following which summarizes the basic closure properties of the operators $\mathcal{H}_\gamma$.

Lemma 4.6

a) $\mathcal{H}_\gamma$ *is a nice operator.*

b) $\mathcal{H}_\gamma$ *is closed under* φ.

c) $\xi \le \gamma \;\&\; \xi, \pi \in \mathcal{H}_\gamma(X) \implies \psi_\pi\xi \in \mathcal{H}_\gamma(X)$

d) $\Omega_\sigma \le \alpha \le \Omega_{\sigma+1} \;\&\; \alpha \in \mathcal{H}_\gamma(X) \implies \Omega_\sigma, \Omega_{\sigma+1} \in \mathcal{H}_\gamma(X)$

e) $\gamma < \delta \implies \mathcal{H}_\gamma(X) \subseteq \mathcal{H}_\delta(X)$

Abbreviations

$$\bar{\mathrm{K}} := \{\bar\Omega_\sigma : \sigma \le I\} \text{ with } \bar\Omega_\sigma := \begin{cases} \Omega_\sigma + 1 & \text{if } \Omega_\sigma \in R \\ \Omega_\sigma & \text{otherwise} \end{cases}$$

$$\mathcal{A}(\Theta; \gamma, \kappa, \mu) :\Leftrightarrow \mu \in \bar{\mathrm{K}} \;\&\; \gamma, \kappa, \mu \in \mathcal{H}_\gamma[\Theta] \;\&\; \mathrm{k}(\Theta) \subseteq \bigcap_{\tau \ge \kappa} C_\tau(\gamma + 1)$$

Lemma 4.7

Suppose $\mathcal{A}(\Theta; \gamma, \kappa, \mu)$. *Then the following holds:*

($\mathcal{A}$1) $\xi \in \mathcal{H}_\gamma[\Theta] \;\&\; \gamma' = \gamma + \omega^{\mu+\xi} \implies \gamma' \in \mathcal{H}_\gamma[\Theta] \;\&\; \psi_\kappa\gamma' \in \mathcal{H}_{\gamma'}[\Theta]$

($\mathcal{A}$2) $\xi \in \mathcal{H}_\gamma[\Theta] \;\&\; \gamma + \omega^{\mu+\xi} < \eta \implies \psi_\kappa(\gamma + \omega^{\mu+\xi}) < \psi_\kappa\eta$

($\mathcal{A}$3) $\kappa \le \tau \implies \mathcal{H}_\gamma[\Theta] \cap \tau \subseteq \psi_\tau(\gamma + 1)$

($\mathcal{A}$4) $\gamma' < \gamma + \omega^{\mu+\alpha} \;\&\; \mu' + \alpha' < \mu + \alpha \implies \gamma' + \omega^{\mu'+\alpha'} < \gamma + \omega^{\mu+\alpha}$

Proof.

1. From $\xi, \gamma, \mu \in \mathcal{H}_\gamma[\Theta]$ by 4.6a) it follows that $\gamma' \in \mathcal{H}_\gamma[\Theta]$. From $\gamma', \kappa \in \mathcal{H}_\gamma[\Theta] \;\&\; \gamma \le \gamma'$ we get $\psi_\kappa\gamma' \in \mathcal{H}_{\gamma'}[\Theta]$ by 4.6c),e).

2. Let $\gamma' := \gamma + \omega^{\mu+\xi}$. Then $\gamma' \in \mathcal{H}_\gamma[\Theta]$ (by ($\mathcal{A}1$)), and $\mathcal{H}_\gamma[\Theta] \subseteq C_\kappa(\gamma+1)$, since $\mathrm{k}(\Theta) \subseteq C_\kappa(\gamma+1)$. By 4.5b),i) from $\gamma' \in C_\kappa(\gamma+1)$ and $\gamma < \gamma' < \eta$ it follows that $\psi_\kappa\gamma' < \psi_\kappa\eta$.
3. $\mathcal{H}_\gamma[\Theta] \cap \tau \subseteq C_\tau(\gamma+1) \cap \tau = \psi_\tau(\gamma+1)$.
4. Obvious.

Remark
In ($\mathcal{A}2$) above the crucial interplay between $\mathcal{H}_\gamma$ and ψ_κ shows up most clearly. Assuming $\mathcal{A}(\Theta;\gamma,\kappa,\mu)$ the function $\xi \mapsto \psi_\kappa(\gamma+\omega^{\mu+\xi})$ provides an *order preserving* map from $\mathcal{H}_\gamma[\Theta]$ into κ.

Theorem 4.8 (Collapsing and impredicative cutelimination)
$\mathcal{A}(\Theta;\gamma,\kappa,\mu)$ & $\Gamma \subseteq \Sigma(\kappa)$ & $\mathcal{H}_\gamma[\Theta] \overset{\alpha}{\underset{\mu}{\vdash}} \Gamma \implies$

$$\implies \mathcal{H}_{\widehat{\alpha}}[\Theta] \overset{\psi_\kappa\widehat{\alpha}}{\underset{\psi_\kappa\widehat{\alpha}}{\vdash}} \Gamma \quad \textit{with} \quad \widehat{\alpha} := \gamma + \omega^{\mu+\alpha}.$$

Proof by main induction on μ and subsidiary induction on α.
Abbreviation: $\mathcal{H} \overset{\alpha}{\underset{\cdot}{\vdash}} \Gamma \;:\Leftrightarrow\; \mathcal{H} \overset{\alpha}{\underset{\alpha}{\vdash}} \Gamma$.

First note that from $\mathcal{A}(\Theta;\gamma,\kappa,\mu)$ and $\alpha \in \mathcal{H}_\gamma[\Theta]$ by ($\mathcal{A}1$), ($\mathcal{A}2$) we get:
(1) $\psi_\kappa\widehat{\alpha} \in \mathcal{H}_{\widehat{\alpha}}[\Theta]$
(2) $\mathcal{A}(\Theta';\gamma,\kappa,\mu)$ & $\alpha_0 \in \mathcal{H}_\gamma[\Theta']$ & $\alpha_0 < \alpha \implies \psi_\kappa\widehat{\alpha_0} < \psi_\kappa\widehat{\alpha}$.

Now we distinguish cases according to the last inference of $\mathcal{H}_\gamma[\Theta] \overset{\alpha}{\underset{\mu}{\vdash}} \Gamma$:

1. Suppose that $A \simeq \bigwedge(A_\iota)_{\iota\in J} \in \Gamma$ and $\mathcal{H}_\gamma[\Theta][\iota] \overset{\alpha_\iota}{\underset{\mu}{\vdash}} \Gamma, A_\iota$ with $\alpha_\iota < \alpha$ for all $\iota \in J$. Since $A \in \Gamma \subseteq \Sigma(\kappa)$, there is a $\beta \in \mathrm{k}(A) \cap \kappa$ such that $\forall\iota \in J(|\iota| \le \beta)$. Since $\mathrm{k}(A) \subseteq \mathcal{H}_\gamma[\Theta]$, by ($\mathcal{A}3$) it follows that $\forall\tau \ge \kappa(\beta < \psi_\tau(\gamma+1))$ and thus $\forall\iota \in J\forall\tau \ge \kappa(\mathrm{k}(\iota) \subseteq C_\tau(\gamma+1))$. Hence $\mathcal{A}(\Theta,\iota;\gamma,\kappa,\mu)$ and therefore (by S.I.H.) $\mathcal{H}_{\widehat{\alpha}}[\Theta][\iota] \overset{\psi_\kappa\widehat{\alpha_\iota}}{\underset{\cdot}{\vdash}} \Gamma, A_\iota$ for all $\iota \in J$. From this we obtain $\mathcal{H}_{\widehat{\alpha}}[\Theta] \overset{\psi_\kappa\widehat{\alpha}}{\underset{\cdot}{\vdash}} \Gamma$ by ($\bigwedge$) and (1),(2).

2. Suppose that $\bigvee(A_\iota)_{\iota\in J} \in \Gamma$ and $\mathcal{H}_\gamma[\Theta] \overset{\alpha_0}{\underset{\mu}{\vdash}} \Gamma, A_{\iota_0}$ with $\iota_0 \in J$ and $\alpha_0 < \alpha$.

By S.I.H. we obtain $\mathcal{H}_{\widehat{\alpha_0}}[\Theta] \overset{\psi_\kappa\widehat{\alpha_0}}{\underset{\cdot}{\vdash}} \Gamma, A_{\iota_0}$ and then $\mathcal{H}_{\widehat{\alpha}}[\Theta] \overset{\psi_\kappa\widehat{\alpha}}{\underset{\cdot}{\vdash}} \Gamma$ using ($\bigvee$), (1), (2) and $\mathrm{k}(\iota_0) \subseteq \mathrm{k}(A_{\iota_0}) \cap \kappa \subseteq \mathcal{H}_\gamma[\Theta] \cap \kappa \subseteq \psi_\kappa(\gamma+1) \subseteq \psi_\kappa\widehat{\alpha}$.

3. If the last inference was an instance of (Ref) then the assertion follows immediately from (1), (2). and the S.I.H. .

Before treating (Cut) we prove the following proposition.

($\square$) *Assume* $\gamma \leq \gamma' < \hat{\alpha}$ & $\gamma' \in \mathcal{H}_{\gamma'}[\Theta]$ & $\mathrm{rk}(C'), \beta < \pi \leq \mu$ *and*

$\mathcal{H}_{\gamma'}[\Theta] \overset{\beta}{\underset{\cdot}{\vdash}} \Gamma, (\neg)C'$. *Then* $\mathcal{H}_{\hat{\alpha}}[\Theta] \overset{\psi_\kappa \hat{\alpha}}{\underset{\cdot}{\vdash}} \Gamma$.

Proof. Let $\rho := \max\{\mathrm{rk}(C'), \beta\} + 1$ and $\sigma \in \mathrm{On}$ such that $\Omega_\sigma < \rho < \Omega_{\sigma+1}$. Then for $\mu' := \bar{\Omega}_\sigma$ we have $[\mu', \mu' + \omega^\rho] \cap \mathrm{R} = \emptyset$ and $\mu' \in \mathcal{H}_{\gamma'}[\Theta]$ (since $\rho \in \mathcal{H}_{\gamma'}[\Theta]$). By (Cut) we obtain $\mathcal{H}_{\gamma'}[\Theta] \overset{\beta+1}{\underset{\mu'+\omega^\rho}{\vdash}} \Gamma$, and then by the Predicative Cut-Elimination Theorem $\mathcal{H}_{\gamma'}[\Theta] \overset{\alpha'}{\underset{\mu'}{\vdash}} \Gamma$ with $\alpha' := \varphi\rho(\beta+1)$. From $\mu' \in \mathcal{H}_{\gamma'}[\Theta]$ together with $\gamma \leq \gamma' \in \mathcal{H}_{\gamma'}[\Theta]$ and $\mathcal{A}(\Theta; \gamma, \kappa, \mu)$ we obtain $\mathcal{A}(\Theta; \gamma', \kappa, \mu')$. Since $\mu' < \mu$, we can now apply the M.I.H. and obtain $\mathcal{H}_{\alpha^*}[\Theta] \overset{\psi_\kappa \alpha^*}{\underset{\cdot}{\vdash}} \Gamma$ with $\alpha^* := \gamma' + \omega^{\mu'+\alpha'}$. Since $\mu' + \alpha' < \pi \leq \mu$ & $\gamma' < \hat{\alpha}$, we have $\alpha^* < \hat{\alpha}$ and $\psi_\kappa \alpha^* \leq \psi_\kappa \hat{\alpha}$. Hence $\mathcal{H}_{\hat{\alpha}}[\Theta] \overset{\psi_\kappa \hat{\alpha}}{\underset{\cdot}{\vdash}} \Gamma$.

4. Suppose that $\mathcal{H}_\gamma[\Theta] \overset{\alpha_0}{\underset{\mu}{\vdash}} \Gamma, (\neg)C$ with $\alpha_0 < \alpha$ and $\mathrm{rk}(C) < \mu$.

4.1. $\mathrm{rk}(C) < \kappa$.
Since $\mathrm{k}(C) \subseteq \mathcal{H}_\gamma[\Theta]$, we then have $\mathrm{rk}(C) \in \mathcal{H}_\gamma[\Theta] \cap \kappa \subseteq \psi_\kappa(\gamma+1) \subseteq \psi_\kappa \hat{\alpha}$, and the assertion follows immediately from the S.I.H.

4.2. $\kappa \leq \mathrm{rk}(C) \notin \mathrm{R}$.
Let $\pi := \mathrm{rk}(C)^{\mathrm{R}}$. Then $\kappa \leq \mathrm{rk}(C) < \pi \leq \mu$ & $\pi \in \mathcal{H}_\gamma[\Theta]$. Hence $\mathcal{A}(\Theta; \gamma, \pi, \mu)$. Since $C, \neg C \in \Sigma(\pi)$, the S.I.H. yields $\mathcal{H}_{\widehat{\alpha_0}}[\Theta] \overset{\psi_\pi \widehat{\alpha_0}}{\underset{\cdot}{\vdash}} \Gamma, (\neg)C$. From $\gamma, \alpha_0, \mu \in \mathcal{H}_\gamma[\Theta]$ & $\gamma < \widehat{\alpha_0}$ we obtain $\widehat{\alpha_0} \in \mathcal{H}_{\widehat{\alpha_0}}[\Theta]$. Now the assertion follows by ($\square$).

4.3. $\kappa \leq \mathrm{rk}(C) = \pi$.
W.l.o.g. we have $C \equiv \exists x \in \mathrm{L}_\pi A(x) \in \Sigma(\pi)$. We also have $\kappa \leq \pi \in \mathcal{H}_\gamma[\Theta]$ and thus $\mathcal{A}(\Theta; \gamma, \pi, \mu)$. Now the S.I.H. gives us $\mathcal{H}_{\widehat{\alpha_0}}[\Theta] \overset{\beta}{\underset{\cdot}{\vdash}} \Gamma, C$ with $\beta := \psi_\pi \widehat{\alpha_0}$. By the Boundedness-Lemma from this we get

(3) $\mathcal{H}_{\widehat{\alpha_0}}[\Theta] \overset{\beta}{\underset{\cdot}{\vdash}} \Gamma, \exists x \in \mathrm{L}_\beta A(x)$.

Now we apply Lemma 3.9c) to the premise $\mathcal{H}_\gamma[\Theta] \overset{\alpha_0}{\underset{\mu}{\vdash}} \Gamma, \neg C$.
Since $\neg C \equiv \forall x \in \mathrm{L}_\pi \neg A(x)$ and $\beta \in \mathcal{H}_{\widehat{\alpha_0}}[\Theta] \cap \pi$, this gives us

(4) $\mathcal{H}_{\widehat{\alpha_0}}[\Theta] \overset{\alpha_0}{\underset{\mu}{\vdash}} \Gamma, \forall x \in \mathrm{L}_\beta \neg A(x)$.

From $\mathcal{A}(\Theta;\gamma,\pi,\mu)$ and $\gamma<\widehat{\alpha_0}\in\mathcal{H}_\gamma[\Theta]$ we get $\mathcal{A}(\Theta;\widehat{\alpha_0},\pi,\mu)$. Therefore we can apply the S.I.H. to (4) and obtain

(5) $\mathcal{H}_{\gamma'}[\Theta]\overset{\psi_\pi\gamma'}{\underset{\cdot}{\vdash}}\Gamma,\forall x{\in}\mathsf{L}_\beta\neg A(x)$ with $\gamma':=\widehat{\alpha_0}+\omega^{\mu+\alpha_0}$.

For $C':\equiv\exists x{\in}\mathsf{L}_\beta A(x)$ we now have

$\gamma\le\gamma'<\hat{\alpha}$ & $\gamma'\in\mathcal{H}_{\gamma'}[\Theta]$ & $\mathrm{rk}(C'),\psi_\pi\gamma'<\pi\le\mu$ & $\mathcal{H}_{\gamma'}[\Theta]\overset{\psi_\pi\gamma'}{\underset{\cdot}{\vdash}}\Gamma,(\neg)C'$.

Hence by ($\Box$) we obtain $\mathcal{H}_{\hat{\alpha}}[\Theta]\overset{\psi_\kappa\hat{\alpha}}{\underset{\cdot}{\vdash}}\Gamma$.

Corollary

$\mathcal{H}_0\overset{\alpha}{\underset{\mathrm{I}+1}{\vdash}}\Gamma$ & $\Gamma\subseteq\Sigma(\Omega_1)$ $\Longrightarrow$ $\overset{\beta}{\underset{\beta}{\vdash}}\Gamma$ with $\beta:=\psi_{\Omega_1}(\omega^{\mathrm{I}+1+\alpha})$.

Theorem 4.9 (MAIN THEOREM)

Let $\upsilon:=\psi_{\Omega_1}(\varepsilon_{\mathrm{I}+1})$. Then for each Σ_1-sentence ϕ of $\mathcal{L}$ we have:

$$\mathrm{KPi}\vdash\forall x(\,Ad(x)\rightarrow\phi^x\,)\Longrightarrow L_\upsilon\models\phi.$$

Proof.

Suppose that $\mathrm{KPi}\vdash\forall x(\,Ad(x)\rightarrow\phi^x\,)$. Then we get successively

(1) $\mathcal{H}_0\overset{\omega^{\mathrm{I}+m}}{\underset{\mathrm{I}+m}{\vdash}}\forall x{\in}\mathsf{L}_\mathrm{I}(\,Ad(x)\rightarrow\phi^x\,)$, for some $m\in\mathbb{N}$ [by 3.12, 4.6 a,d]

(2) $\mathcal{H}_0\overset{\omega^{\mathrm{I}+m}}{\underset{\mathrm{I}+m}{\vdash}}\mathsf{L}_{\Omega_1}\mathrel{\mathring{\notin}}\mathsf{L}_\mathrm{I},\neg Ad(\mathsf{L}_{\Omega_1}),\phi^{\Omega_1}$ [by 3.9b, 3.13, $\Omega_1\in\mathcal{H}_0$]

(3) $\mathcal{H}_0\overset{\omega^{\mathrm{I}+m}}{\underset{\mathrm{I}+m}{\vdash}}\neg Ad(\mathsf{L}_{\Omega_1}),\phi^{\Omega_1}$ [since $\mathsf{L}_{\Omega_1}\mathrel{\mathring{\notin}}\mathsf{L}_I\simeq\bigvee(A_\iota)_{\iota\in\emptyset}$]

(4) $\mathcal{H}_0\overset{\omega^{\mathrm{I}+m}+1}{\underset{\mathrm{I}+m}{\vdash}}\phi^{\Omega_1}$ [by 2.5h, 3.10, (Cut)]

(5) $\mathcal{H}_0\overset{\alpha}{\underset{\mathrm{I}+1}{\vdash}}\phi^{\Omega_1}$ with $\alpha<\varepsilon_{\mathrm{I}+1}$ [by 3.16 (Corollary)]

(6) $\overset{\beta}{\underset{\beta}{\vdash}}\phi^{\Omega_1}$ with $\beta:=\psi_{\Omega_1}(\omega^{\mathrm{I}+1+\alpha})$ [by 4.8 (Corollary)]

(7) $\overset{\beta}{\underset{\beta}{\vdash}}\phi^\beta$ [by 3.17]

(8) $L_\upsilon\models\phi$ [by 3.2, 1.5, 4.5i]

As shown in the introduction 4.9 together with [8](Th.4.6) yields

Corollary. $|\mathrm{KPi}|\le\psi_{\Omega_1}(\varepsilon_{\mathrm{I}+1})$.

References

[1] Arai,T.: *Proof theory for reflecting ordinals II: recursively Mahlo ordinals.* Handwritten notes (1989).

[2] Buchholz,W.: *A new system of proof-theoretic ordinal functions.* Annals of Pure and Applied Logic 32 (1986), 195-207.

[3] Buchholz,W.: *A note on the ordinal analysis of* KPM. In: J.Väänänen (ed.) Proceedings Logic Colloquium '90. To appear.

[4] Jäger,G.: *Die konstruktible Hierarchie als Hilfsmittel zur beweistheoretischen Untersuchung von Teilsystemen der Analysis.* Dissertation, München 1979.

[5] Jäger,G.: *Zur Beweistheorie der Kripke-Platek-Mengenlehre über den natürlichen Zahlen.* Arch. math. Logik 22 (1982), 121-139.

[6] Jäger,G.: *Iterating admissibility in proof theory.* In J.Stern (ed.): *Proceedings of the Herbrand Logic Colloquium '81.* North-Holland (1982), 137-146.

[7] Jäger,G.: *ρ-inaccessible ordinals, collapsing functions and a recursive notation system.* Arch. math. Logik 24 (1984), 49-62.

[8] Jäger,G.: *Theories for admissible sets: a unifying approach to proof theory.* Bibliopolis, Napoli 1986.

[9] Jäger,G. and Pohlers,W.: *Eine beweistheoretische Untersuchung von* (Δ^1_2-CA)+(BI) *und verwandter Systeme.* Sitzungsberichte der Bayer. Akademie der Wissenschaften, Mathematisch-Naturwissenschaftliche Klasse (1982).

[10] Pohlers,W.: *Cut elimination for impredicative infinitary systems, part I: Ordinal analysis of* ID_1. Arch. math. Logik 21 (1981), 69-87.

[11] Pohlers,W.: *Proof-theoretical analysis of* ID_ν *by the method of local predicativity.* In: W.Buchholz,S.Feferman,W.Pohlers,W.Sieg: *Iterated Inductive Definitions and Subsystems of Analysis: Recent Proof-Theoretical Studies.* Springer Lecture Notes in Mathematics 897 (1981)

[12] Pohlers,W.: *Cut elimination for impredicative infinitary systems,part II: Ordinal analysis for iterated inductive definitions.* Arch. math. Logik 22 (1982), 113-129.

[13] Pohlers,W.: *Contributions of the Schütte school in Munich to proof theory.* In: G.Takeuti: *Proof Theory* 2nd edition. North-Holland (1987)

[14] Pohlers,W.: *Ordinal functions and notations based on a hierarchy of inaccessible cardinals.* Annals of Pure and Applied Logic 33 (1987).

[15] Pohlers,W.: *Proof theory and ordinal analysis.* Arch. math. Logic 30 (1991), 311-376.

[16] Pohlers,W.: *A Short Course in Ordinal Analysis.* This Volume.

[17] Rathjen,M.: *Untersuchungen zu Teilsystemen der Zahlentheorie zweiter Stufe und der Mengenlehre mit einer zwischen* Δ^1_2-CA *und* Δ^1_2-CA+BI *liegenden Beweisstärke.* Dissertation Münster 1988.

[18] Rathjen,M.: *Ordinal Notations Based on a Weakly Mahlo cardinal.* Arch. math. Logic 29 (1990), 249-263.

[19] Rathjen,M.: *Proof-Theoretic Analysis of* KPM. Arch. math. Logic 30 (1991), 377-403.

[20] Tait,W.W.: *Normal derivability in classical logic.* In: J.Barwise (ed.) *The Syntax and Semantics of Infinitary Languages.* Springer Lecture Notes in Mathematics 72 (1968), 204-236

[21] Tait,W.W.: *Applications of the cut elimination theorem to some subsystems of classical analysis.* In: *Intuitionism and Proof Theory.* Proceedings of the summer conference at Buffalo, N.Y. 1968 A.Kino,J.Myhill, R.E.Vesley (eds.) North-Holland 1970, 475-488.

Mathematisches Institut der
Universität München
Theresienstr. 39
D-8000 München 2
Germany

A note on bootstrapping intuitionistic bounded arithmetic

S. BUSS

A Note on Bootstrapping Intuitionistic Bounded Arithmetic

SAMUEL R. BUSS*

Department of Mathematics
University of California, San Diego†

Abstract

This paper, firstly, discusses the relationship between Buss's definition and Cook and Urquhart's definition of BASIC axioms and of IS_2^1. The two definitions of BASIC axioms are not equivalent; however, each intuitionistically implies the law of the excluded middle for quantifier-free formulas. There is an elementary proof that the definitions of IS_2^1 are equivalent which is not based on realizability or functional interpretations.

Secondly, it is shown that any negated positive consequence of S_2^1 is also a theorem of IS_2^1. Some possible additional axioms for IS_2^1 are investigated.

1. Introduction and Definitions

In [1,2] we introduced a hierarchy of formal theories of arithmetic called collectively Bounded Arithmetic; these theories were shown to have a very close connection to the computational complexity of polynomial time, the levels of the polynomial hierarchy, polynomial space and exponential time. Of particular interest is theory called S_2^1 which has proof-theoretic strength closely linked to polynomial time computability. Later we introduced an intuitionistic version of this theory called IS_2^1 and proved a feasibility result for this theory based on a realizability interpretation using a notion of polynomial time functionals [3]. Recently, Cook and Urquhart [7,6] have given

*Supported in part by NSF Grants DMS-8701828 and DMS-8902480.
† E-mail address: sbuss@ucsd.edu.

an alternative definition of IS_2^1. They also gave an improved treatment of polynomial time functionals, introduced new powerful theories using lambda calculus, strengthened the feasibility results for IS_2^1, and reproved the 'main theorem' for S_2^1 as a corollary of their results for IS_2^1.

The work in the first part of this paper was motivated by an desire to clarify the relationship between these two definitions of IS_2^1; more precisely, while reading Cook and Urquhart's paper I tried to verify their assertion that the bootstrapping argument for S_2^1 could be followed to bootstrap their version of IS_2^1. As it turned out, there is a general reason why their assertion in true (Corollary 12) and it was not necessary to trace the bootstrapping argument step-by-step to formalize it in IS_2^1. We show below that the BASIC axioms of Cook and Urquhart are not equivalent to the BASIC axioms of Buss; however, we also give an elementary proof that the different definitions of IS_2^1 are equivalent (a fact already proved by Cook and Urquhart based on their Dialectica interpretation).

In the last part of this paper we show that S_2^1 is conservative over IS_2^1 in the following sense: If A is a positive formula and B is an $H\Sigma_1^b$ formula and if $S_2^1 \vdash A \supset B$ then IS_2^1 also proves $A \supset B$. This generalises the fact that S_2^1 and IS_2^1 have the same $H\Sigma_1^b$-definable functions. As a corollary, if A is a positive formula and $S_2^1 \vdash \neg A$ then $IS_2^1 \vdash \neg A$. An intuitionistic theory IS_2^{1+} which is apparently stronger that IS_2^1 is defined by allowing PIND on formulas of the form $A(b) \vee B$ where $A \in H\Sigma_1^b$ and B is an arbitrary formula in which the induction variable b does not appear. The theory IS_2^{1+} is shown in [5] is shown to be the intuitionistic theory which is valid in every S_2^1-normal Kripke model; we prove here a proof-theoretic theorem needed in [5].

We presume familiarity with the first part of chapter 2 of Buss [2], with the definitions of IS_2^1 in Buss [3] and in section 1 of Cook-Urquhart [7], and with the sequent calculus. The realizability and functional interpretations of IS_2^1 are not needed.

Buss [2] and Cook-Urquhart [7] use a finite set of BASIC axioms which form a base theory to which induction axioms are later added. However, the two definitions of BASIC are different; for reference, we list all 32 BASIC axioms of Buss and all 21 BASIC axioms of Cook and Urquhart in a table below.

We briefly review some definitions; see [2,3,7] for the full definitions. A *bounded* quantifier is one of the form $(Qx \le t)$ and it is *sharply bounded* if t is of the form $|s|$. A *(sharply) bounded formula* is one in which every quantifier is (sharply) bounded. The class $\Sigma_0^b = \Pi_0^b = \Delta_0^b$ is the set of sharply bounded formulas. The classes Σ_i^b and Π_i^b are sets of bounded formulas defined by counting alternations of bounded quantifiers, ignoring the sharply bounded quantifiers. The class $H\Sigma_1^b$ of *hereditarily* Σ_1^b formulas is the set of formulas A such that each subformula of A is Σ_1^b. A *positive* formula is one that contains no implication or negation signs. A formula is Σ_1^{b+} if and only if it is positive and is Σ_1^b. Clearly every Σ_1^{b+}-formula is $H\Sigma_1^b$.

We now define two variants of IS_2^1, denoted IS_2^1B and IS_2^1CU in this paper. We shall actually prove they are equivalent and hence the preferred name for either theory is just IS_2^1. IS_2^1B is the theory called IS_2^1 in [3] and called IS_2^1B by Cook-Urquhart [7], whereas IS_2^1CU is the theory called IS_2^1 in [7]. Both theories are formulated with PIND axioms which are (universal closures of) axioms of the form

$$A(0) \land (\forall x)(A(\lfloor \tfrac{1}{2}x \rfloor) \supset A(x)) \supset (\forall x)A(x).$$

Definition The theory IS_2^1B is the intuitionistic theory which has axioms

(a) All formulas of the form

$$B_1 \land B_2 \land \cdots \land B_k \supset B_{k+1}$$

with each B_i a $H\Sigma_1^b$-formula, which are consequences of the (classical) theory S_2^1,

(b) The PIND axioms for each $H\Sigma_1^b$ formula A.

Definition The theory IS_2^1CU is the intuitionistic theory which has axioms

(a) The BASIC axioms of Cook and Urquhart,

(b) The PIND axioms for each Σ_1^{b+} formula A.

Buss's BASIC axioms	Cook-Urquhart's BASIC axioms
(B-1) $y \leq x \supset y \leq Sx$	
(B-2) $\neg x = Sx$	(CU-1) $x = Sx \supset A$
(B-3) $0 \leq x$	(CU-2) $0 \leq x$
(B-4) $x \leq y \wedge \neg x = y \leftrightarrow Sx \leq y$	(CU-3) $x \leq y \supset (x = y \vee Sx \leq y)$
(B-5) $\neg x = 0 \supset \neg 2x = 0$	
(B-6) $y \leq x \vee x \leq y$	(CU-6) $y \leq x \vee x \leq y$
(B-7) $x \leq y \wedge y \leq x \supset x = y$	(CU-5) $x \leq y \wedge y \leq x \supset x = y$
(B-8) $x \leq y \wedge y \leq z \supset x \leq z$	(CU-4) $x \leq y \wedge y \leq z \supset x \leq z$
(B-9) $\|0\| = 0$	(CU-7) $\|0\| = 0$
(B-10) $\neg x = 0 \supset \|2x\| = S(\|x\|) \wedge$ $\|S(2x)\| = S(\|x\|)$	(CU-8) $1 \leq x \supset \|2x\| = S(\|x\|)$ (CU-9) $\|S(2x)\| = S(\|x\|)$
(B-11) $\|1\| = 1$	
(B-12) $x \leq y \supset \|x\| \leq \|y\|$	(CU-10) $x \leq y \supset \|x\| \leq \|y\|$
(B-13) $\|x\#y\| = S(\|x\| \cdot \|y\|)$	(CU-11) $\|x\#y\| = S(\|x\| \cdot \|y\|)$
(B-14) $0\#y = 1$	(CU-12) $1\#1 = 2$
(B-15) $\neg x = 0 \supset 1\#(2x) = 2(1\#x) \wedge$ $1\#(S(2x)) = 2(1\#x)$	
(B-16) $x\#y = y\#x$	(CU-13) $x\#y = y\#x$
(B-17) $\|x\| = \|y\| \supset x\#z = y\#z$	
(B-18) $\|x\| = \|u\| + \|v\| \supset$ $x\#y = (u\#y) \cdot (v\#y)$	(CU-14) $\|x\| = \|u\| + \|v\| \supset$ $x\#y = (u\#y) \cdot (v\#y)$
(B-19) $x \leq x + y$	
(B-20) $x \leq y \wedge \neg x = y \supset$ $S(2x) \leq 2y \wedge \neg S(2x) = 2y$	
(B-21) $x + y = y + x$	
(B-22) $x + 0 = x$	(CU-15) $x + 0 = x$
(B-23) $x + Sy = S(x + y)$	(CU-16) $x + Sy = S(x + y)$
(B-24) $(x + y) + z = x + (y + z)$	(CU-17) $(x + y) + z = x + (y + z)$
(B-25) $x + y \leq x + z \leftrightarrow y \leq z$	(CU-18) $x + y \leq x + z \leftrightarrow y \leq z$
(B-26) $x \cdot 0 = 0$	(CU-19) $x \cdot 1 = x$
(B-27) $x \cdot (Sy) = (x \cdot y) + x$	
(B-28) $x \cdot y = y \cdot x$	
(B-29) $x \cdot (y + z) = (x \cdot y) + (x \cdot z)$	(CU-20) $x \cdot (y + z) = (x \cdot y) + (x \cdot z)$
(B-30) $1 \leq x \supset (x \cdot y \leq x \cdot z \leftrightarrow y \leq z)$	
(B-31) $\neg x = 0 \supset \|x\| = S(\|\lfloor \frac{1}{2}x \rfloor\|)$	(CU-21) $x = (\lfloor \frac{1}{2}x \rfloor + \lfloor \frac{1}{2}x \rfloor) \vee$ $x = S(\lfloor \frac{1}{2}x \rfloor + \lfloor \frac{1}{2}x \rfloor)$
(B-32) $x = \lfloor \frac{1}{2}y \rfloor \leftrightarrow (2x = y \vee S(2x) = y)$	

Similar definitions can be formulated for intuitionistic theories IS_2^i; however, we shall only consider the case $i = 0$ since the complications in 'bootstrapping' apply mainly to BASIC and IS_2^1. V. Harnik [8] has generalized Cook and Urquhart's work to IS_2^i for $i > 1$.

I wish to thank Stephen Cook and Alasdair Urquhart for making their unpublished notes on bootstrapping IS_2^1CU available to me.

2. Consequences of the BASIC Axioms

We shall show that both formulations of the BASIC axioms imply the law of the excluded middle for atomic formulas. However, the two formulations are **not** equivalent: Buss's BASIC axioms imply Cook-Urquhart's BASIC axioms but not vice-versa. For the rest of this paper we let BBASIC denote the 32 BASIC axioms of Buss and CUBASIC denote the 21 BASIC axioms of Cook and Urquhart.

Proposition 1 *The following formulas are intuitionistic consequences of both BBASIC and CUBASIC:*

(a) $x \leq x$

(b) $x \leq Sx$

(c) $\neg Sx \leq x$

(d) $Sx \leq y \supset \neg y \leq x$

(e) $0 \neq Sx$

We are adopting the convention that a formula with free variables is a consequence of a theory iff its generalization (universal closure) is. So "$x = x$" means "$(\forall x)(x = x)$", etc.

Proof Formula (a) follows from (B-6) or (CU-6). Formula (b) follows from (a) and (B-1), while (B-1) follows from (CU-15), (CU-16), (CU-18) and (CU-2). Formula (c) follows from (b), (B-7) and (B-2) or, equivalently, from (b), (CU-5) and (CU-1). Formula (d) follows from (c) and either (B-8) or

(CU-4). Finally (e) follows from (a), (b), (B-8) or (CU-4), and (c). □

Theorem 2 *(Cook-Urquhart [7]) CUBASIC intuitionistically implies the law of the excluded middle for atomic formulas.*

Proof The axiom (CU-6) states that $x \le y \lor y \le x$; this plus (CU-3) intuitionistically implies $x = y \lor Sx \le y \lor Sy \le x$. Now formulas (d) and (a) imply $x = y \lor \neg x = y$. Also from (CU-6) and (CU-3) we get $y \le x \lor x = y \lor Sx \le y$; so by (d) and (a) and equality axioms, $y \le x \lor \neg y \le x$. □

The BBASIC axioms were originally formulated for a classical theory so no attempt was made to ensure that they were appropriate for intuitionistic theories; however, the next theorem shows that the BBASIC axioms do indeed imply the law of the excluded middle for atomic formulas.

Theorem 3 *BBASIC intuitionistically implies the law of the excluded middle for atomic formulas.*

Proof We prove a series of claims:

Claim (B-i): BBASIC intuitionistically implies $x \le y \leftrightarrow Sx \le Sy$ and $x = y \leftrightarrow Sx = Sy$.

Proof: Note that (B-22), (B-23) and (B-21) imply that $S0 + x = Sx$. Now $x \le y \leftrightarrow Sx \le Sy$ follows from (B-25). From this, (B-6) and (B-7) imply $x = y \leftrightarrow Sx = Sy$.

Claim (B-ii): BBASIC intuitionistically implies $x + x \le y + y \supset x \le y$.

Proof: It is easy to prove that $x + x = 2 \cdot x$ and $y + y = 2 \cdot y$ using (B-26)-(B-28). Now the claim follows from axiom (B-30) since by (b) of Proposition 1, $1 \le 2$.

Claim (B-iii): BBASIC intuitionistically implies $x + x \le y + y + 1 \supset x \le y$.

Proof: Now we need to show that $2 \cdot x \leq 2 \cdot y + 1 \supset x \leq y$. Let's argue informally intuitionistically from BBASIC. By (B-6) either $Sy \leq x$ or $x \leq Sy$ or both. If $Sy \leq x$ then $Sy + Sy \leq x + x \leq y + y + 1$ and hence $S(y + y + 1) \leq y + y + 1$ which contradicts formula (c) of Proposition 1. So $x \leq Sy$. (This a valid intuitionistic use of proof-by-contradiction.) Now $x \neq Sy$, else $x = Sy$ implies $Sy \leq x$ which we just showed implied $S(y + y + 1) \leq y + y + 1$. (Again, it is intuitionistically valid to prove $x \neq Sy$ by assuming $x = Sy$ and obtaining a contradiction; however, it would not be valid to prove $x = Sy$ by deriving a contradiction from $x \neq Sy$.) Thus $x \leq Sy \wedge x \neq Sy$ so $Sx \leq Sy$ by (B-4) and thus $x \leq y$ by (B-*i*).

Claim (B-iv): BBASIC intuitionistically implies

$$y \leq x \wedge x \leq Sy \supset x = y \vee x = Sy.$$

Proof: To prove this, note that axiom (B-32) implies that either $y = \lfloor \frac{1}{2}y \rfloor + \lfloor \frac{1}{2}y \rfloor$ or $y = S(\lfloor \frac{1}{2}y \rfloor + \lfloor \frac{1}{2}y \rfloor)$. Let's first assume that the first case holds. Another use of axiom (B-32) shows that $\lfloor \frac{1}{2}(Sy) \rfloor = \lfloor \frac{1}{2}y \rfloor$. Now we further split into two subcases depending on whether $x = \lfloor \frac{1}{2}x \rfloor + \lfloor \frac{1}{2}x \rfloor$ or $x = \lfloor \frac{1}{2}x \rfloor + \lfloor \frac{1}{2}x \rfloor + 1$; one of these subcases holds by yet another use of (B-32). In either subcase we can use Claim (B-*ii*) or (B-*iii*), respectively, to show that $\lfloor \frac{1}{2}y \rfloor \leq \lfloor \frac{1}{2}x \rfloor$. A similar argument shows that $\lfloor \frac{1}{2}x \rfloor \leq \lfloor \frac{1}{2}Sy \rfloor$. Hence $\lfloor \frac{1}{2}x \rfloor = \lfloor \frac{1}{2}y \rfloor$. Now by axiom (B-32) again, $x = y \vee x = Sy$.

For the second case, assume that $y = S(\lfloor \frac{1}{2}y \rfloor + \lfloor \frac{1}{2}y \rfloor)$. Then $Sy = S\lfloor \frac{1}{2}y \rfloor + S\lfloor \frac{1}{2}y \rfloor$ so $S\lfloor \frac{1}{2}y \rfloor = \lfloor \frac{1}{2}(Sy) \rfloor$. And $Sy \leq Sx \leq S(Sy)$. We can now use the first case to see that $Sx = Sy \vee Sx = S(Sy)$, thus by (B-*i*), $x = y \vee x = Sy$.

Claim (B-v): BBASIC intuitionistically implies $x \leq y \vee \neg x \leq y$.

Proof: By (B-6) twice, $x \leq y \vee Sy \leq x \vee (y \leq x \wedge x \leq Sy)$. By (B-*iv*), this implies $x \leq y \vee Sy \leq x \vee x = y \vee x = Sy$; so $x \leq y \vee \neg x \leq y$ by (a) and (d) of Proposition 1.

Claim (B-vi): BBASIC intuitionistically implies $x = y \vee x \neq y$.

Proof: By claim (B-*v*) twice, $(x \leq y \wedge y \leq x) \vee \neg x \leq y \vee \neg y \leq x$ and thus by axiom (B-7) and by (a) of Proposition 1, $x = y \vee x \neq y$.
Q.E.D. Theorem 3

Theorem 4 *BBASIC intuitionistically implies CUBASIC.*

Proof Because BBASIC and CUBASIC are (generalizations of) atomic formulas and because BBASIC intuitionistically implies the law of the excluded middle, it is actually sufficient to show that BBASIC classically implies CUBASIC. The only CUBASIC axioms that do not immediately follow from BBASIC are (CU-3) and (CU-12). (CU-3) is a classical consequence of (B-4) and thus follows by the law of the excluded middle for the formula $x = y$. (CU-12) is the axiom $1\#1 = 2$. To derive this, use (B-15) with $x = 1$ to show $1\#2 = 2 \cdot (1\#1)$ then use (B-18) with $x = 2$ and $u = v = y = 1$ to derive $2\#1 = (1\#1) \cdot (1\#1)$. Now by use of (B-16) and (B-28), $(1\#1)\#(1\#1) = (1\#1) \cdot 2$ and by using (B-30) twice, $1\#1 = 2$ is derived (note that $1\#1 \neq 0$ by (B-13), (B-11), and (B-12)). □

The converse to Theorem 4 does not hold; before we prove this we show that adding three additional axioms to CUBASIC is sufficient to make it equivalent to BBASIC.

Theorem 5 *Let* CUBASIC$^+$ *be the the axioms of CUBASIC plus the axioms (B-21), (B-28) and (B-30). Then* CUBASIC$^+$ *intuitionistically implies the BBASIC axioms.*

Proof (B-1) follows from formula (b) of Proposition 1 and (CU-4). (B-4) is an immediate consequence of (CU-3) and (b) and (c) of Proposition 1. To show CUBASIC$^+$ $\models$ (B-5), first note that $x \neq 0 \supset 1 \leq x$ by (CU-2) and (CU-3); hence $x \neq 0 \supset 0 \neq |2x|$ by (CU-8) and (e) of Proposition 1 and finally, by (CU-7), $x \neq 0 \supset 2x \neq 0$. Axiom (B-19) follows from (CU-15), (CU-18) and (CU-2). (B-10) and (B-11) are consequences of (CU-8) and (CU-9).

By (CU-11) and (e) of Proposition 1, $x\#y \neq 0$ is a consequence of

CUBASIC$^+$. By (CU-14) with $x = u = v = 0$, $0\#y = (0\#y) \cdot (0\#y)$ and by (CU-19) and (B-30), $0\#y = 1$, which is (B-14). It is straightforward to derive (B-15) from (B-10), (B-11), (CU-12) and (CU-14). Also, (B-17) is implied by (CU-14) and the fact that $|0| = 0$ and $0\#z = 1$.

To derive (B-20), first use (B-28) and (CU-19) and (CU-20) to show that $S(2x) = x + x + 1$. Now, if $x \leq y \wedge x \neq y$ then by (B-4), $Sx \leq y$. And by (B-28) and (B-30), $2(Sx) \leq 2y$. Thus $S(2x) < 2(Sx) \leq 2y$.

(B-26) follows readily from (CU-19) and (CU-20); (B-27) is an immediate consequence of (CU-20) with the aid of $x \cdot 1 = x$ and $Sy = y + 1$. Finally to derive (B-32) from (CU-21) it will suffice to show that $x + x = y + y \supset x = y$. Suppose that $x + x = y + y$ and $x \neq y$; then w.l.o.g. $Sx \leq y$ and so (B-20) yields a contradiction. And (B-31) follows from (B-32), (CU-8) and (CU-9). □

Theorem 6 *The CUBASIC axioms do not (classically) imply the BBASIC axioms.*

Proof We shall prove this by constructing a model of CUBASIC in which multiplication is not commutative, violating axiom (B-28). Let $\mathcal{M}$ be a model of S_2^1 in which exponentiation is not total and in which the function $x \mapsto 2^{|x|\#|x|}$ is total. Let M be the universe of $\mathcal{M}$. We shall say that $m \in M$ is *large* if and only if there is no $n \in M$ with $m = |n|$, i.e., m is large if and only if 2^m does not exist. An object is *small* if and only if it is not large. Note that the small elements are closed under $\#$ since $x \mapsto 2^{|x|\#|x|}$ is total. Let $\mathcal{N}$ be the substructure of $\mathcal{M}$ with universe N the set of objects that can be expressed as $a \cdot 2^b + c$ with b and c small and with 2^b large: Clearly $\mathcal{N}$ is well-defined as a substructure since N is closed under all the functions of CUBASIC. Since CUBASIC consists of universal formulas, $\mathcal{N} \models$ CUBASIC (since $\mathcal{M}$ is a model of CUBASIC).

Pick some fixed large $a_0 \in N$ which is not a power of two. Form a structure $\mathcal{N}^*$ from $\mathcal{N}$ with the same universe as $\mathcal{N}$ and with all functions and relations, other than multiplication, unchanged. For multiplication, any product of the form $a_0 \cdot (a \cdot 2^b + c)$ with c small and 2^b large is defined to be equal to $a_0 \cdot c$. Any other product $a \cdot b$ with $a \neq a_0$ is equal to its product in $\mathcal{N}$ (and in $\mathcal{M}$). It is easy to see that $\mathcal{N}^*$ still satisfies all the CUBASIC axioms: since a_0 is not small, (CU-11) still holds, and since a_0 is not a power of two, (CU-14) is unaffected. Obviously (CU-19) and (CU-20) hold in $\mathcal{N}^*$. But multiplication is not commutative in $\mathcal{N}^*$ so $\mathcal{N}$ is not a model of BBASIC. □

Another way that multiplication could have been defined in $\mathcal{N}^*$ would be to let $a_0 \cdot (a \cdot 2^b + c)$ be equal to $m \cdot a \cdot 2^b + a_0 \cdot c$ for some arbitrary m in M.

3. Equivalence of the Definitions of IS_2^1

Next we show that the two definitions IS_2^1CU and IS_2^1B of IS_2^1 are equivalent. There are three steps necessary for this: first, we must show that IS_2^1CU implies all the BBASIC axioms; second, that IS_2^1CU implies the $H\Sigma_1^b$-PIND axioms; and third, that IS_2^1CU implies all the axioms of IS_2^1B. All three of these steps are done by Cook and Urquhart in [7]; our new contribution here is to give a simple proof of the third step that does not depend on the realizability or functional interpretations of IS_2^1. Our simple proof for the third step allows one to reduce the bootstrapping of IS_2^1CU to the bootstrapping of S_2^1.

Theorem 7 *(Cook-Urquhart [7]) $IS_2^1CU \models BBASIC$. In fact, PIND on open formulas is sufficient to derive the BBASIC axioms from the CUBASIC axioms.*

Proof (Sketch) By Theorem 5 it will suffice to show that (B-21), (B-28) and (B-30) are consequences of IS_2^1. We sketch the steps in the proof, leaving the details to the reader: (This derivation is only slightly different from Cook and Urquhart's original unpublished proof.)

1. Prove $0 + x = x$ by PIND on x.

2. Prove $1 + x = x + 1$ by PIND on x.

3. Prove $x + y = y + x$ by PIND on x. This is (B-21).

4. Prove $x \cdot 0 = 0$. No PIND necessary, derive the equality $x + 0 = x + x \cdot 0$ and use (CU-18).

5. Prove $0 \cdot x = 0$ by PIND on x.

6. Prove $(y+y) \cdot x = y \cdot x + y \cdot x$ by PIND on x.

7. Prove $(y+y+1) \cdot x = y \cdot x + y \cdot x + x$ by PIND on x.

8. Prove $x \cdot y = y \cdot x$ by PIND on x. This is (B-28).

9. Prove $x + x \leq y + y \leftrightarrow x \leq y$ without use of induction. This follows from the fact that if $x < y$ then $x + x < x + y = y + x < y + y$ which can be derived from (CU-18).

10. Prove $1 \leq x \supset (x \cdot y \leq x \cdot z \leftrightarrow y \leq z)$ by PIND on x. This is (B-30).

□

The next theorem is relatively simple to prove; see Lemma 1.3 through Theorem 1.7 of [7].

Theorem 8 *(Cook-Urquhart [7])*

(1) *IS_2^1CU proves $A \vee \neg A$ for A a Σ_0^b-formula.*

(2) *IS_2^1CU proves that every $H\Sigma_1^b$-formula is equivalent to a Σ_1^{b+}-formula.*

(3) *IS_2^1CU implies the $H\Sigma_1^b$-PIND axioms.*

The next lemma will aid in the proof that IS_2^1CU proves all the axioms of IS_2^1B.

Lemma 9 *The following are intuitionistically valid:*

(a) $A \supset A \vee B$

(b) $(A \vee C) \wedge (B \vee C) \supset (A \wedge B) \vee C$

(c) $(B \supset A \vee C) \supset (\neg A \wedge B \supset C)$

(d) $(A \vee \neg A) \supset (A \wedge B \supset C) \supset (B \supset \neg A \vee C)$

(e) $(B \supset A \vee C) \wedge (A \wedge B \supset C) \supset (B \supset C)$

(f) $(B \vee \neg B) \supset (B \wedge C \supset A \vee D) \supset (C \supset (B \supset A) \vee D)$

(g) $(C \supset A \vee D) \wedge (C \wedge B \supset D) \supset (C \wedge (A \supset B) \supset D)$

(h) $A(s) \wedge s \leq t \supset (\exists x \leq t)A(x)$

The proof of Lemma 9 is straightforward.

Theorem 10 *(Cook-Urquhart [7]) All axioms of IS^1_2B are consequences of IS^1_2CU.*

A generalization of Theorem 10 is presented in section below.

Proof Recall that S^1_2 is a classical theory of Bounded Arithmetic with the BBASIC axioms and Σ^b_1-PIND rules. We shall show that any sequent of $H\Sigma^b_1$-formulas which is a theorem of S^1_2 is also a consequence of IS^1_2CU. More precisely, if $\Gamma \longrightarrow \Delta$ is a sequent containing only $H\Sigma^b_1$-formulas and is a theorem of S^1_2 then the formula $(\bigwedge \Gamma) \supset (\bigvee \Delta)$ is a consequence of IS^1_2CU. (Frequently intuitionistic logic is formulated in the sequent calculus by restricting succedents to have only one formula; however, it still makes sense to talk about a sequent with more than one succedent formula being a theorem of an intuitionistic system. The way to do this is to think of the formulas in the succedent as being disjoined into a single formula.) By classical prenex operations, any Σ^b_1-formula is equivalent to an $H\Sigma^b_1$-formula so S^1_2 may be equivalently formulated with the $H\Sigma^b_1$-PIND rule instead of Σ^b_1-PIND. Thus if S^1_2 proves a sequent $\Gamma \longrightarrow \Delta$ containing only $H\Sigma^b_1$-formulas, then there is an S^1_2-proof in which every induction formula is a $H\Sigma^b_1$-formula. Now, by free-cut elimination, there is an S^1_2 proof of $\Gamma \longrightarrow \Delta$ such that every formula in the proof is an $H\Sigma^b_1$-formula.

Given an S^1_2 proof of $\Gamma \longrightarrow \Delta$ in which every formula is a $H\Sigma^b_1$-formula, we prove that every sequent in the proof is a theorem of IS^1_2CU by beginning at the initial sequents (axioms) and proceeding inductively on the number of inferences needed to derive a sequent. The initial sequents are logical axioms, equality axioms or BBASIC formulas and are consequences of IS^1_2CU by

Theorem 7. For the induction step, suppose for example that a $\neg$*:right* inference

$$\frac{A, \Pi \longrightarrow \Lambda}{\Pi \longrightarrow \Lambda, \neg A}$$

has its upper sequent a theorem of IS_2^1CU; then since both A and $\neg A$ are $H\Sigma_1^b$-formulas, A is actually a Σ_0^b formula, and by Theorem 8(1) and Lemma 9(d), the lower sequent is also a theorem of IS_2^1. The fact that $\vee$*:right*, $\wedge$*:right*, $\neg$*:left*, *Cut*, $\supset$*:right*, $\supset$*:left*, and $\exists\leq$*:right* inferences preserve the property of being a theorem of IS_2^1 follows in a similar manner from Lemma 9(a)-(c),(e)-(h), respectively. The structural inferences and the other *left* inference rules are even easier to handle.

The $\forall\leq$*:right* and $H\Sigma_1^b$-PIND inference rules remain. Suppose that the upper sequent of

$$\frac{b \leq t, \Pi \longrightarrow A(b), \Lambda}{\Pi \longrightarrow (\forall x \leq t)A(x), \Lambda}$$

is a theorem of IS_2^1CU (recall b must not appear in the lower sequent). Since $(\forall x \leq t)A(x)$ is a $H\Sigma_1^b$-formula, the indicated quantifier must be sharply bounded and the term t must be of the form $t = |s|$. Then IS_2^1 also proves

$$b \leq t, \Pi, \left[(\forall x \leq |(\lfloor \tfrac{1}{2}b \rfloor)|)A(x) \vee \left(\bigvee \Lambda\right)\right] \longrightarrow \left[(\forall x \leq |b|)A(x) \vee \left(\bigvee \Lambda\right)\right]$$

and now it is easy to use $H\Sigma_1^b$-PIND on the formula in square brackets with respect to the variable b to show that the lower sequent of the $\forall\leq$*:right* inference is a theorem of IS_2^1CU.

Finally, suppose that the upper sequent of a $H\Sigma_1^b$-PIND inference

$$\frac{A(\lfloor \tfrac{1}{2}b \rfloor), \Pi \longrightarrow A(b), \Lambda}{A(0), \Pi \longrightarrow A(t), \Lambda}$$

is a theorem of IS_2^1CU. It follows that

$$\Pi, A(\lfloor \tfrac{1}{2}b \rfloor) \vee \left(\bigvee \Lambda\right) \longrightarrow A(b) \vee \left(\bigvee \Lambda\right)$$

is also a consequence of IS_2^1CU, from whence, by an intuitionistic use of $H\Sigma_1^b$-PIND,

$$\Pi, A(0) \vee \left(\bigvee \Lambda\right) \longrightarrow A(t) \vee \left(\bigvee \Lambda\right)$$

which intuitionistically implies the lower sequent of the inference.
Q.E.D. Theorem 10

Corollary 11 *(Cook-Urquhart [7]) The systems IS^1_2CU and IS^1_2B are equivalent.*

Corollary 12 *(Cook-Urquhart [7]) Any Σ^b_1-definable function of S^1_2 is Σ^{b+}_1-definable in IS^1_2CU.*

Corollary 13 *(Cook-Urquhart [7]) IS^1_2 is closed under Markov's Rule for $H\Sigma^b_1$-formulas. In other words, if A is an $H\Sigma^b_1$-formula and if $IS^1_2 \vdash \neg\neg A$ then $IS^1_2 \vdash A$.*

4. On the Choice of Axioms for IS^1_2

We have shown that although the BBASIC axioms and the CUBASIC axioms are not equivalent, the different definitions of IS^1_2 by Buss and by Cook and Urquhart are equivalent. It is worth asking what is the best or right definition of these systems. The original BASIC axioms (the BBASIC axioms) were defined to serve as a base theory for a number of theories of bounded arithmetic: we stated in [2] that any "sufficiently large" set of universal axioms would suffice as the BASIC axioms. Although the CUBASIC axioms are sufficient as a base theory for IS^1_2CU they may well not be strong anough for other (weaker) theories. Let us formulate five general criteria for the choice of BASIC axioms: (1) The BASIC axioms should be universal, true formulas. (2) The BASIC axioms should be strong enough to prove elementary facts about the non-logical symbols. (3) The BASIC axioms should not be too strong; for example, they should not state something equivalent to the consistency of Peano arithmetic. (4) Let I_m be a term with value equal to m and length linear in $|m|$. Then for any fixed term $t(\vec{x})$ there should be polynomial size BASIC proofs of $t(I_{\vec{n}}) = I_{t(\vec{n})}$ for all natural numbers $\vec{n}$. More generally, if $A(\vec{x})$ is a fixed Σ^b_1-formula then for all $\vec{n} \in \mathbb{N}$, if $A(\vec{n})$ is true there should be a free-cut free BASIC proof of $A(I_{\vec{n}})$. In addition, this statement should be formalizable in IS^1_2 or S^1_2 (this is Theorem 7.4 of [2]). (5) For every term $t(\vec{x})$, there should be a term $\sigma_t(\vec{x})$ such that the BASIC axioms imply (without induction) that

$$\forall\vec{x}\forall\vec{y}((\bigwedge_{i=1}^{k} x_i \le y_i) \supset t(\vec{x}) \le \sigma_t(\vec{y})).$$

This fifth condition states that BASIC is a "sufficient" theory in the terminology of [4]. Note that the remark at the very end of section 2 can be used to show that the CUBASIC axioms are not sufficient. It is important that a theory be sufficient in order to be able to introduce new function symbols and use them freely in terms bounding quantifiers and it seems expedient that the BASIC axioms themselves be sufficient (without any induction). In addition, Theorem 4.10 of [2] seems to depend crucially on the fact that that BASIC axioms are sufficient.

Thus we prefer the BBASIC axioms, or equivalently and slightly more elegantly, the CUBASIC axioms plus (B-21), (B-28) and (B-30), over just the CUBASIC axioms.

Finally let's consider consider the axiomatizations of IS^1_2CU and IS^1_2B. Since IS^1_2CU proves that any $H\Sigma^b_1$-formula is equivalent to a Σ^{b+}_1-formula, the choice of $H\Sigma^b_1$-PIND versus Σ^{b+}_1-PIND is unimportant‡. Of more significance is the choice of non-induction axioms. The theory IS^1_2B is defined with a set of consequences of S^1_2 as its non-induction axioms, whereas, IS^1_2CU has just the CUBASIC axioms as non-induction axioms. In the former case, Buss thus required the "main theorem" for S^1_2 to prove that every definable function of IS^1_2B is polynomial time computable; but in the latter case, Cook and Urquhart are able to obtain the main theorem for S^1_2 as a corollary to their Dialectica interpretation of the intuitionistic systems. By using our simplified proof of Theorem 11 above, the main theorem for S^1_2 follows already from the corresponding theorem for IS^1_2B or IS^1_2CU without requiring the Dialectica interpretation. Thus Cook and Urquhart's use of BASIC axioms as a base theory is a nice improvement over using the sequents of $H\Sigma^b_1$-formulas which are consequences of S^1_2.

‡ Cook and Urquhart use Σ^{b+}_1-formulas to simplify the bootstrapping.

5. Conservation Results for S_2^1 over Intuitionistic Theories

In this section, an extension of IS_2^1 called IS_2^{1+} is defined; actually, it is open whether IS_2^1 and IS_2^{1+} are distinct. We are interested in IS_2^{1+} because it allows a rather general extension of Theorem 10 and because IS_2^{1+} arises naturally in the study of Kripke models for intuitionistic Bounded Arithmetic. First we state a generalization of Theorem 10 that still applies if IS_2^1.

Theorem 14

(a) *If A is a positive formula and $S_2^1 \vdash \neg A$ then $IS_2^1 \vdash \neg A$.*

(b) *If A is a positive formula and B is an $H\Sigma_1^b$-formula, then if $S_2^1 \vdash A \supset B$ then $IS_2^1 \vdash A \supset B$.*

Corollary 15 *A positive sentence is classically consistent with S_2^1 if and only if it is intuitionistically consistent with IS_2^1.*

Proof The proof of Theorem 14 is almost exactly like the proof the Theorem 10. First note that (b) implies (a) by taking B to be $0 = 1$, so it suffices to prove (b). By using free-cut elimination and by restricting induction in the S_2^1-proof to PIND on $H\Sigma_1^b$-formulas, there is an S_2^1-proof P of the sequent $A \longrightarrow B$ such that every formula in the antecedent of a sequent in P is either positive or an $H\Sigma_1^b$-formula and such that every formula in the succedent of a sequent in P is an $H\Sigma_1^b$-formula. Now the rest of the proof of Theorem 10 applies word-for-word. □

Definition An *$H\Sigma_1^{b*}$-formula with distinguished variable* b is a formula of the form $A(b, \vec{c}) \vee B(\vec{c})$ where A is an $H\Sigma_1^b$-formula, B is an arbitrary formula and b does not occur in $B(\vec{c})$. The variables $\vec{c}$ will act as parameters.

Definition IS_2^{1+} is the intutionistic theory axiomatized as IS_2^1 plus the PIND axioms for $H\Sigma_2^{b*}$-formulas with respect to their distinguished variables.

Note that S_2^1 implies (classically) all the axioms of IS_2^{1+} since it can classically consider the two cases $B(\vec{c})$ and $\neg B(\vec{c})$. However, we don't know if IS_2^1 implies IS_2^{1+}. The main reason for our interest in IS_2^{1+} is that it is the intuitionistic theory which is valid in Kripke models in which every world is a classical model of S_2^1. This fact is proved in Buss [5] and depends crucially on the next theorem.

Definition Let A be a positive formula and let B be an arbitrary formula. The formula A^B is obtained from A by replacing every atomic subformula C of A by $(C \vee B)$. (We are using the conventions of Gentzen's sequent calculus: there are distinct free and bound variables and hence free variables in B can not become bound in A^B.)

Theorem 16 *Let A be a positive formula and suppose $S_2^1 \vdash \neg A$. Then, for any formula B, $IS_2^{1+} \vdash A^B \supset B$.*

Proof As argued above, if $S_2^1 \vdash \neg A$ then there is a tree-like, free-cut free S_2^1-proof P of the sequent $A \longrightarrow$ in which every formula is either (a) in an antecedent, positive and an ancestor of the formula A in the endsequent, or (b) is an $H\Sigma_1^b$-formula which is an ancestor of a cut formula. Form another "proof" P^* by replacing every formula C in P of type (a) by the formula C^B, and, for any sequent in which such a replacement is made, adding the formula B to the succedent. P^* ends with the sequent $A^B \longrightarrow B$; although P^* is not quite a valid IS_2^{1+}-proof, we claim that all the "inferences" in P are sound for IS_2^{1+}.

To prove this claim, consider the ways that P^* may fail to be an IS_2^{1+}-proof. Initial sequents in P contain only atomic formulas, so in P^* each initial sequent is either (a) unchanged from P or (b) has at least one formula, say D, in the antecedent replaced by $D \vee B$ and has B added as an additional formula in the succedent. In either case, the initial sequent of P^* is a consequence of IS_2^{1+} (and of IS_2^1). Just as in the proof of Theorem 10, any $\neg$*:right*, $\vee$*:right*, $\wedge$*:right*, $\neg$*:left*, *Cut*, $\supset$*:right*, $\supset$*:left*, $\exists\leq$*:left*, $\vee$*:left*, $\wedge$*:left* and structural inferences in P become IS_2^{1+} sound "inferences" in P^*. It remains to consider the cases of $\forall\leq$*:right* and PIND. These latter two cases are handled similarly to the corresponding cases in the proof of Theorem 10. Suppose, for instance, that P contains the inference

$$\frac{b \leq t, \Pi \longrightarrow A(b), \Lambda}{\Pi \longrightarrow (\forall x \leq t) A(x), \Lambda}$$

where b is the eigenvariable and does not occur in the lower sequent. Since $(\forall x \le |t|)A(x)$ is an $H\Sigma_1^b$-formula, the indicated quantifier must be sharply bounded and $t = |s|$ for some term s. In P^*, this inference is either unchanged or becomes

$$\frac{b \le t, \Pi^* \longrightarrow A(b), \Lambda, B}{\Pi^* \longrightarrow (\forall x \le t)A(x), \Lambda, B}$$

where Π^* represents Π with one or more formulas C replaced by $C \vee B$. We claim that if the upper sequent of this latter "inference" is IS_2^{1+}-provable, then so is the lower inference. This is because if the upper sequent is provable, then IS_2^{1+} proves

$$b \le t, \Pi^*, \left[(\forall x \le |(\lfloor \tfrac{1}{2}b \rfloor)|)A(x) \vee (\bigvee \Lambda) \vee B\right] \longrightarrow$$
$$\longrightarrow [(\forall x \le |b|)A(x) \vee (\bigvee \Lambda) \vee B].$$

The formula in square brackets is an $H\Sigma_1^{b*}$-formula since every formula in Λ is in $H\Sigma_1^b$-formula. Hence IS_2^{1+} can use its PIND axioms on this formula to prove the lower sequent.

Similarly, any induction inference in P corresponds to an IS_2^{1+}-sound inference in P^*; this is shown as in the proof of Theorem 10, except again the $(\bigvee \Lambda)$ may become $(\bigvee \Lambda) \vee B$.
Q.E.D. Theorem 16

There are several open problems regarding axiomatizations of IS_2^1. As noted above, we don't know if IS_2^{1+} is equivalent to IS_2^1. Also, S. Cook asked whether Π_1^{b+}-PIND is a consequence of IS_2^1. Current techniques (feasible realizability or functional interpretations) can not be used to show that Π_1^{b+}-PIND is *not* a consequence of IS_2^1 since the Π_1^{b+}-PIND axioms are polynomial-time realizable. Likewise, it is open whether the Σ_1^b-PIND axioms are consequences of IS_2^1. Again, the Σ_1^b-PIND axioms are polynomial-time realizable.

One final observation: if S_2^1 can prove that $P = NP$ then any bounded formula is IS_2^1-provably equivalent to a Σ_1^{b+}-formula and IS_2^1 would have

PIND and the law of the excluded middle for all bounded formulas. By S_2^1 proving P = NP we mean that there is a Δ_1^b-definable, polynomial-time predicate which, provably in S_2^1, is equivalent to some NP-complete problem (such as SAT). Hence it is expected to be difficult to show that, say Π_1^{b+}-PIND is not a consequence of IS_2^1 since this would require proving that S_2^1 does not prove P = NP. Similarly, it is expected to be difficult to show that IS_2^1 is not equal to IS_2^2 or, more generally, to show that the hierarchy of intuitionistic theories of Bounded Arithmetic is proper.

References

[1] S. R. BUSS, *The polynomial hierarchy and fragments of bounded arithmetic*, in Proceedings of the 17-th Annual ACM Symposium on Theory of Computing, 1985, pp. 285–290.

[2] ——, *Bounded Arithmetic*, Bibliopolis, 1986. Revision of 1985 Princeton University Ph.D. thesis.

[3] ——, *The polynomial hierarchy and intuitionistic bounded arithmetic*, in Structure in Complexity, Lecture Notes in Computer Science #223, Springer Verlag, 1986, pp. 77–103.

[4] ——, *A conservation result concerning bounded theories and the collection axiom*, Proceedings of the American Mathematical Society, 100 (1987), pp. 709–716.

[5] ——, *On model theory for intuitionistic bounded arithmetic with applications to independence results*, in Feasible Mathematics: A Mathematical Sciences Institute Workshop held in Ithaca, New York, June 1989, Birkhäuser, 1990, pp. 27–47.

[6] S. A. COOK AND A. URQUHART, *Functional interpretations of feasibly constructive arithmetic (extended abstract)*, in Proceedings of the 21-st Annual ACM Symposium on Theory of Computing, 1989, pp. 107–112. Synopsis of [7].

[7] ——, *Functional interpretations of feasibly constructive arithmetic*, Tech. Rep. 256/91, Department of Computer Science, University of Toronto, September 1991.

[8] V. HARNIK, *Provably total functions of intuitionistic bounded arithmetic.* Typewritten manuscript, 1989.

Termination orderings and complexity characterisations

E. CICHON

Termination Orderings and Complexity Characterisations

E.A.CICHON[1]

Royal Holloway and Bedford New College

1 INTRODUCTION

This paper discusses proof theoretic characterisations of termination orderings for rewrite systems and compares them with the proof theoretic characterisations of fragments of first order arithmetic.

Rewrite systems arise naturally from systems of equations by orienting the equations into rules of replacement. In particular, when a number theoretic function is introduced by a set of defining equations, as is the case in first order systems of arithmetic, this set of equations can be viewed as a rewrite system which *computes* the function.

A termination ordering is a well-founded ordering on terms and is used to prove termination of a term rewriting system by showing that the rewrite relation is a subset of the ordering and hence is also well founded thus guaranteeing the termination of any sequence of rewrites.

The successful use of a specific termination ordering in proving termination of a given rewrite system, R, is necessarily a restriction on the form of the rules in R, and, as we show here in specific cases, translates into a restriction on the proof theoretical complexity of the function computed by R. We shall mainly discuss two termination orderings. The first, the so-called *recursive path ordering* (recently re-christened as the *multiset path ordering*) of [Der79], is widely known and has been implemented in various theorem provers. The second ordering is a derivative of another well known ordering, the *lexicographic path ordering* of [KL80]. This derivative we call the *ramified lexicographic path ordering*. We shall show that the recursive path ordering and the ramified lexicographic path ordering prove termination of different algorithms yet characterise the same class of number-theoretic functions, namely the *primitive recursive functions*. In [DO88], Dershowitz and Okada characterise various termination orderings according to their *order types*. In [Cic90], we showed, in specific cases, how to exploit the embedding of a termination ordering into the ordinals to obtain complexity bounds for lengths of deriva-

[1]The author's research was supported by 'Logic for IT' Fellowship B/ITF/218

tions of its terminating rewrite systems. In this paper we shall show that both the recursive path ordering and the ramified lexicographic path ordering are of order type up to the same ordinal and that termination proofs for rewrite systems via the recursive path ordering or the ramified lexicographic path ordering imply primitive recursive bounds on derivation lengths. In particular this means that if the rewrite systems compute number theoretic functions, then those functions are primitive recursive.

It is traditional to characterise a formal theory by the class of (recursive) functions that can be proved total in it—the so-called *provably recursive functions* of the theory. It is well known that extending the scheme of primitive recursion to admit recursion with substitution for parameters allows no new functions to be defined, but obviously gives rise to new algorithms. The recursive path ordering cannot prove the termination of algorithms defined in this way. On the other hand, the ramified lexicographic path ordering is able to prove terminating a function defined by primitive recursion with substitution for parameters. The situation is similar for the fragments Σ_1^0-IR and Π_2^0-IR of Peano arithmetic (where induction is restricted to Σ_1^0 and Π_2^0 formulae respectively). These are known to have exactly the same provably recursive functions, namely the primitive recursive ones, but differ in which schemes of definition they allow for these functions. In this respect we shall give examples which suggest that termination of rewrite systems via the recursive path ordering is connected to provability of termination in Σ_1^0-IR, and termination of rewrite systems via the ramified lexicographic path ordering is connected to provability of termination in Π_2^0-IR. A similar connection, based on our results in [Cic90], is shown between the lexicographic path ordering and Σ_2^0-IR.

In the next section we give some basic definitions of term rewriting theory. In sections 3 and 4 we define the recursive path ordering, ramified lexicographic path ordering and the lexicographic path ordering, and we give examples of rewrite systems which contrast their power for termination proofs. Sections 5 and 6 introduce the system $\mathbf{OT^0}$ of ordinal terms and describe their fundamental sequences. In section 7 we discuss some aspects of the slow-growing hierarchy. Our bounding results are obtained using functions from this hierarchy. Section 8 is devoted to the proof of a general bounding theorem. In section 9 we apply the bounding theorem to obtain the complexity characterisations, theorems 9.10 and 9.22.

2 TERM REWRITING SYSTEMS

Here we give a concise description of those aspects of term rewriting theory which are relevant to the discussion in this paper.

2.1 Definition
A set T(F,X) of terms over a finite set F of function symbols and a countable set X of variables is defined by

1. constants (i.e. 0-ary function symbols) and variables are terms.
2. If $t_1, \ldots, t_n$ are terms and f is an n-ary function symbol then $f(t_1, \ldots, t_n)$ is a term.

We write T(F) for the set of terms in T(F,X) which contain no variables. The elements of T(F) are called *ground* or *closed* terms.

2.2 Definition
A Term Rewriting System, $\mathcal{R}$, over a set of terms, T(F,X), is a set of rewrite rules

$$\{l_i \rightarrow r_i\},$$

where l_i and r_i are terms belonging to T(F,X) and such that r_i contains only variables already contained in l_i.

A rule $l_i \rightarrow r_i$ applies to a term t in T(F,X) if t or some subterm s of t matches l_i after substituting terms of T(F,X) for the variables in l_i. The rule is applied by replacing s by r_i after substitution of the same terms for variables as in l_i.

From an equational calculus i.e. a theory where terms are introduced by defining equations, a rewrite system can be obtained by suitably orienting the equations, and replacing "=" by "→". Then a proof of $t_1 = t_2$ is obtained by showing that t_1 and t_2 rewrite to the same term.

We write

$$t \underset{\mathcal{R}}{\Rightarrow} s$$

to mean that the term t reduces to the term s by application of a rule in $\mathcal{R}$. A sequence $t \underset{\mathcal{R}}{\Rightarrow} t_1 \underset{\mathcal{R}}{\Rightarrow} t_2 \underset{\mathcal{R}}{\Rightarrow} \ldots$ is often referred to as a *derivation*. We also write

$$t \overset{n}{\underset{\mathcal{R}}{\Rightarrow}} s$$

to mean that t reduces to s after n applications of rules in $\mathcal{R}$. So $t \overset{1}{\underset{\mathcal{R}}{\Rightarrow}} s$ and $t \underset{\mathcal{R}}{\Rightarrow} s$ are the same. A term rewriting system $\mathcal{R}$ is said to be *terminating* if the rewrite relation on terms is well founded. All rewrite systems considered here will be finite.

2.3 Definition
We define the *rank*, |t|, of a term t in T(F,X) as follows:

$$|t| = \begin{cases} 0 & \text{when t is a constant,} \\ 0 & \text{when t is a variable,} \\ \max_{i\in 1..n}\{k, n, |t_i|\} + 1 & \text{when } t = f_k(t_1, \ldots, t_n). \end{cases}$$

3 RECURSIVE PATH ORDERING (rpo)

The definition of the recursive path ordering makes use of an ordering on finite multisets of terms. A *multiset* is a collection of objects in which elements may occur more than once. The number of times an element occurs in a multiset is called its *multiplicity*. For multisets A, B we write $A \cap B$ and $A \setminus B$ to denote the sets formed so that if x occurs m times in A and n times in B then it occurs min(m,n) times in $A \cap B$ and $m \dot{-} n$ times in $A \setminus B$, where $x \dot{-} y = x - y$ if $x > y$, $= 0$ otherwise.

3.1 Definition
Suppose that S is a set ordered by <. The induced ordering, $\ll$, on finite multisets of elements of S is defined as follows :
If A and B are finite multisets (of elements of S) then $A \ll B$ if $A \neq B$ and

1. $A = \emptyset$ or
2. $A \cap B \neq \emptyset$ and $A \setminus (A \cap B) \ll B \setminus (A \cap B)$ or
3. $A \cap B = \emptyset$ and for all $a \in A$ there exists $b \in B$ such that $a < b$.

3.2 Definition
We write $f \equiv g$ to mean that f and g belong to the same equivalence class with respect to some quasi-ordered set of function symbols. *Permutative congruence* between terms, $\approx$, is defined:

$$f(s_1, \ldots, s_n) \approx g(t_1, \ldots, t_n) \text{ iff } f \equiv g \text{ and } s_i \approx t_{\pi(i)}$$

for some permutation π of {1,...,n}.

3.3 Definition [Der79]
Suppose that < is a total quasi-ordering on F. The *recursive path ordering*, $<_{rpo}$, is induced on T(F) by

$$s = f(s_0, \ldots, s_{m-1}) <_{rpo} g(t_0, \ldots, t_{n-1}) = t$$

if one of the following holds:

1. $s \leq_{rpo} t_i$ for some i = 0,...,n-1,

2. $f < g$ and $s_i <_{rpo} t$ for all i = 0,...,m-1,

3. $f \equiv g$ and $\{s_0, \ldots, s_{m-1}\} \ll_{rpo} \{t_0, \ldots, t_{n-1}\}$.

where $\ll_{rpo}$ is the multiset ordering induced by $<_{rpo}$.

The usual definition of the recursive path ordering assumes that $<$ is a quasi-ordering on F. For our purposes we have assumed that this quasi-ordering is total.

3.4 Theorem
If $<$ is well-founded on F, then $<_{rpo}$ is well-founded on T(F).

4 RAMIFIED LEXICOGRAPHIC PATH ORDERING (rlpo)

4.1 Definition
If $<$ is an order on the set F of function symbols and $f \in F$, we define

$$F\lceil f := \{g \in F \ : \ g < f\}$$

4.2 Definition
Suppose, that $<$ is a total quasi-order on the set F of function symbols. The *ramified lexicographic path ordering*, $<_{rlpo}$, is induced on T(F) as follows :

$$s = f(s_1, \ldots, s_m) <_{rlpo} g(t_1, \ldots, t_n) = t \text{ if}$$

1. $s \leq_{rlpo} t_i$ for some i = 1,...,n,
   or

2. $f < g$ and $s_i <_{rlpo} t$ for all i = 1,...,m,
   or

3. $f \equiv g$ and $(t_1, \ldots, t_n)$ extends $(s_1, \ldots, s_m)$, or, for some $i \leq \min\{m, n\}$, $s_1 \approx t_1, \ldots, s_{i-1} \approx t_{i-1}$, $s_i <_{rlpo} t_i$, and $\{s_{i+1}, \ldots, s_m\} \subseteq T(F\lceil f)$.

The definition of the *lexicographic path ordering* (lpo) of [KL80] is the same as above except for part 3. To obtain the lexicographic path ordering one has only to replace part 3 by

3'. $f \equiv g$ and $(t_1, \ldots, t_n)$ extends $(s_1, \ldots, s_m)$, or, for some $i \leq \min\{m, n\}$, $s_1 \approx t_1, \ldots, s_{i-1} \approx t_{i-1}$, $s_i <_{lpo} t_i$, and $s_{i+1} <_{lpo} t, \ldots, s_n <_{lpo} t$.

Our definition of rlpo induces an ordering on terms which is not total. This is not a cause for concern but it does indicate the limited practical use of the ordering. It is not difficult to see that a rewrite system which has a termination proof using rlpo will also have a termination proof using lpo. The converse is false, however. We shall see later that our modification results in rlpo being considerably weaker for termination proofs than lpo.

4.3 Theorem

If F is well-founded by $<$, then T(F) is well-founded by $<_{rlpo}$.

4.4 Examples

1. The nth level of the Ackermann Hierarchy is given by the system:

$$A_1(m) \rightarrow s(m)$$

and, for k = 1..n-1,

$$\begin{aligned} A_{k+1}(0) &\rightarrow A_k(s(0)) \\ A_{k+1}(s(m)) &\rightarrow A_k(A_{k+1}(m)) \end{aligned}$$

The termination of this system can be proved using any of rpo, rlpo, lpo where the precedence is $A_n > \ldots > A_1 > s > 0$.

2. Simultaneous Primitive Recursion.

$$\begin{aligned} f_1(0, x_1, \ldots, x_n) &\rightarrow g_1(x_1, \ldots, x_n) \\ &\vdots \\ f_m(0, x_1, \ldots, x_n) &\rightarrow g_m(x_1, \ldots, x_n) \\ f_1(s(y), x_1, \ldots, x_n) &\rightarrow h_1(x_1, \ldots, x_n, y, f_1(y, x_1, \ldots, x_n), ..., f_m(y, x_1, \ldots, x_n)) \\ &\vdots \\ f_m(s(y), x_1, \ldots, x_n) &\rightarrow h_m(x_1, \ldots, x_n, y, f_1(y, x_1, \ldots, x_n), ..., f_m(y, x_1, \ldots, x_n)) \end{aligned}$$

Any function defined according to these schemes has a termination proof via rpo, rlpo or lpo where the precedence contains $f_1 \equiv \ldots f_m$, $f_1 > g_1, \ldots, g_m$, $f_1 > h_1, \ldots, h_m$.

3. Primitive Recursion with Substitution for Parameters.

$$\begin{aligned} f(0, x_1, ..., x_n) &\rightarrow g(x_1, ..., x_n) \\ f(s(y), x_1, ..., x_n) &\rightarrow h(x_1, ..., x_n, y, f(y, p_1(x_1, ..., x_{m_1}), \ldots, p_n(x_1, ..., x_{m_n}))) \\ & \quad \text{where } m_i \preceq n, \text{ for } i \in 1..n. \end{aligned}$$

With precedence $f > g$, $f > h$, $f > p$, termination is provable using rlpo or lpo. rpo fails to prove termination.

4. Unnested Multiple Recursion

$$\begin{aligned} f(x,0) &\rightarrow g(x,0) \\ f(0,y) &\rightarrow g(0,y) \\ f(s(x),s(y)) &\rightarrow h(x,y,f(x,p(x,y)),f(s(x),y)) \end{aligned}$$

As in example 3, only rpo fails to prove termination.

5. Neither rpo nor rlpo provides a proof of termination of the rewrite system for computing the Ackermann function :

$$\begin{array}{rcl} A(0,m) & \rightarrow & m \\ A(s(n),0) & \rightarrow & A(n,s(0)) \\ A(s(n),s(m)) & \rightarrow & A(n,A(s(n),m)). \end{array}$$

Rule (iii) is not reducing with respect to rpo and rlpo. This system is, however, provably terminating using lpo.

A traditional way of characterising a formal theory is by its class of *provably recursive functions*. These are the functions that can be proved total in the theory.

The fragments Σ_1^0-IR and Π_2^0-IR of Peano arithmetic (where induction is restricted to Σ_1^0 and Π_2^0 formulae respectively) are known to have exactly the same provably recursive functions, namely the primitive recursive ones. However, Σ_1^0-IR does not prove termination of a function defined by primitive recursion with substitution for parameters, whereas Π_2^0-IR does. Neither Σ_1^0-IR nor Π_2^0-IR prove termination of the Ackermann function as the Ackermann function is not primitive recursive.

The following table gives equivalences between formal theories and termination orderings in terms of their respective classes of provably recursive functions. The connection given here for Σ_2^0-IR and the lexicographic path ordering was worked out in [Cic90].

FORMAL THEORY		TERMINATION ORDERING
Σ_1^0–IR	$\sim$	rpo
Π_2^0–IR	$\sim$	rlpo
Σ_2^0–IR	$\sim$	lpo

5 THE SET OT^0 OF ORDINAL TERMS

In [DO88], Dershowitz and Okada describe the *Ackermann* system of notations for ordinals and demonstrate embeddings of various termination orderings, including the recursive path ordering, into the Ackermann system. This gives a characterisation of these termination orderings according to their *order types*.

In [Cic90], we showed how knowledge of the order type of a termination ordering can be used to obtain complexity bounds for lengths of derivations of

its terminating rewrite systems. This was done for the recursive path ordering and the lexicographic path ordering. We showed that
if $\mathcal{R}$ is a finite rewrite system whose rules are reducing under the recursive path ordering then there is a primitive recursive function f and a constant c (which depend on the rewrite system) such that

$$\textit{length of longest derivation starting from term } t < \mathrm{f}(|\mathrm{t}| + \mathrm{c}).$$

For the lexicographic path ordering the corresponding result is :
if $\mathcal{R}$ is a finite rewrite system whose rules are reducing under the lexicographic path ordering then there is a multiply recursive function f (in the sense of Péter in [Pét67]) and a constant c such that

$$\textit{length of longest derivation starting from term } t < \mathrm{f}(2.|\mathrm{t}| + \mathrm{c}).$$

In this paper we shall show that both the recursive path ordering and the ramified lexicographic path ordering are of order type up to the same ordinal and that termination proofs for rewrite systems via the recursive path ordering or the ramified lexicographic path ordering imply primitive recursive bounds on derivation lengths. In particular this means that if the rewrite systems compute number theoretic functions, then those functions are primitive recursive.

We introduce here the set $\mathbf{OT^0}$ of ordinal terms. In [Cic90] we described a system $\mathbf{OT}$ of ordinal terms. The present system $\mathbf{OT^0}$ is a subsystem of $\mathbf{OT}$, providing notations for a smaller initial segment of the ordinals. Both systems are subsystems of larger systems, details of which can be found in [Buc75] or [Schü80]. Ordinal terms of $\mathbf{OT^0}$ will be used to measure the order types of recursive path orderings and ramified lexicographic path orderings.

5.1 Definition
The set $\mathbf{OT^0}$ of ordinal terms and the ordering $\prec$ on $\mathbf{OT^0}$ are defined simultaneously by the schemes:

1. (a) $0 \in \mathbf{OT^0}$.
   (b) If $\alpha, \beta \in \mathbf{OT^0}$ then $\theta_\alpha\beta \in \mathbf{OT^0}$.
   (c) If $\alpha_1, \ldots, \alpha_n \in \mathbf{OT^0}$ ($\mathrm{n} \in \mathbf{N}$) and $\alpha_1 \succeq \ldots \succeq \alpha_n \succ 0$ where each α_i is of the form $\theta_{\xi_i}\eta_i$, then $\alpha_1 + \cdots + \alpha_n \in \mathbf{OT^0}$.

2. By $\alpha = \beta$, we mean that α, β are identical as terms.
   (a) $0 \preceq \alpha$.
   (b) $\theta_{\alpha_1}\beta_1 \prec \theta_{\alpha_2}\beta_2$ iff one of the following three conditions holds:
      i. $\alpha_1 \prec \alpha_2$ and $\max\{\alpha_1, \beta_1\} \prec \theta_{\alpha_2}\beta_2$
      ii. $\alpha_1 = \alpha_2$ and $\beta_1 \prec \beta_2$

iii. $\alpha_1 \succ \alpha_2$ and $\theta_{\alpha_1}\beta_1 \preceq \max\{\alpha_2, \beta_2\}$

3. $\alpha_1 + \cdots + \alpha_n \prec \beta_1 + \cdots + \beta_m$ if, for some $i \leq \min\{m, n\}$,
$\alpha_1 = \beta_1, \ldots, \alpha_{i-1} = \beta_{i-1}, \alpha_i \prec \beta_i$
or
$n < m$ and $\alpha_1 = \beta_1, \ldots, \alpha_n = \beta_n$.

5.2 Definition
The *natural sum*, $\alpha \# \beta$, of terms $\alpha, \beta \in \mathbf{OT^0}$.

1. $\alpha \# 0 = 0 \# \alpha := \alpha$

2. If $\alpha = \xi_1 + \cdots + \xi_m$ and $\beta = \xi_{m+1} + \cdots + \xi_{m+n}$ then

$$\alpha \# \beta := \xi_{\pi(1)} + \cdots + \xi_{\pi(m+n)}$$

where π is a permutation of 1, ..., m+n such that $\xi_{\pi(1)} \succeq \ldots \succeq \xi_{\pi(m+n)}$.

5.3 Remark The function # is commutative and associative. Its main use here will be to enable us to define the embedding of terms ordered by $\prec_{rpo}$ into $\mathbf{OT^0}$.

We are not able here to give an exhaustive account of the properties of $\mathbf{OT^0}$ but mention only those that suffice for the purposes of this work. Most of the properties of $\mathbf{OT^0}$ follow from work of Buchholz in [Buc75]. In particular, $\mathbf{OT^0}$ is well-ordered by $\prec$. A useful technical result is that

$$\max\{\alpha, \beta\} \prec \theta_\alpha\beta.$$

The term $\theta_0 0$ is the immediate successor of 0 in $\mathbf{OT^0}$ and so, where there is no confusion, we write 1 for $\theta_0 0$. A *successor* term is a term of the form $\alpha \# 1$. $\alpha \# 1$ is the immediate successor of α in $\mathbf{OT^0}$. A *limit* term is a term which is not zero and not a successor term. A limit term has no immediate predecessors and satisfies the property that if $\alpha \prec \lambda$ where λ is a limit term, then $\alpha \# 1 \prec \lambda$. An *additive principle term* is a term λ with the property that if $\alpha, \beta \prec \lambda$ then $\alpha \# \beta \prec \lambda$. In $\mathbf{OT^0}$ all terms of the form $\theta_\xi\eta$ are additive principal terms. Note that if each α_i and β_j ($i \in 1..n$, $j \in 1..m$) is an additive principal term, then $\alpha_1 \# \cdots \# \alpha_n \prec \beta_1 \# \cdots \# \beta_m$ if and only if $\{\alpha_1, \ldots, \alpha_n\} \ll \{\beta_1, \ldots, \beta_m\}$, where $\ll$ is the multiset ordering induced by $\prec$.

Some of the key ordinal correspondences in $\mathbf{OT^0}$ are:

$$\begin{aligned} \theta_0 1 &= \omega \\ &= \text{the first limit ordinal.} \end{aligned}$$

$$\begin{aligned} \theta_1 0 &= \varepsilon_0. \\ &= \text{the first non-zero fixed point of ordinal exponentiation.} \end{aligned}$$

The ordinal term $\theta_\omega 0$ plays a key role in this paper. We shall show that it provides the least upper bound for the possible order types of $(\mathrm{T(F)}, \prec_{\mathrm{rpo}})$ and $(\mathrm{T(F)}, \prec_{\mathrm{rlpo}})$. The precise order types of these orderings depend essentially on the size of the set F.

6 FUNDAMENTAL SEQUENCES IN $\mathbf{OT^0}$

The standard method for defining a number-theoretic hierarchy over the ordinals overcomes the problem of what to do at limit stages by the use of *fundamental sequences* to limit ordinals.

Each limit ordinal α is equipped with its own fundamental sequence, that is, a sequence of ordinals, indexed by integers, which converges to α. The xth member of of the fundamental sequence is written $\{\alpha\}(\mathrm{x})$. Thus $\{\alpha\}$ is a function : $\mathbf{N} \mapsto \alpha$ such that, for each x, $\{\alpha\}(\mathrm{x}) \prec \{\alpha\}(\mathrm{x}+1)$ and $\sup\{\{\alpha\}(\mathrm{x}) : \mathrm{x} \in \mathbf{N}\} = \alpha$.

Now, in a hierarchy of functions $\{\mathrm{f}_\gamma\}$ indexed by ordinals, when α is a limit ordinal the function f_α can be defined as follows :

$$\mathrm{f}_\alpha(\mathrm{x}) = \textit{term in } \mathrm{f}_{\alpha(\mathrm{x})} \textit{ and } \mathrm{x}.$$

The purpose of this section is to give a definition of fundamental sequences to limit terms on $\mathbf{OT^0}$ and to indicate some of consequences of these definitions.

6.1 Definition

The *rank*, $|\alpha|$, of a term $\alpha \in \mathbf{OT^0}$ is defined

1. $|0| := 0$.
2. $|\theta_\xi \eta| = \max\{|\xi|, |\eta|\} + 1$.
3. $|\alpha_1 + \cdots + \alpha_n| := \max\{|\alpha_i|, \mathrm{n}\}$.

6.2 Definition

$$\mathbf{OT^0_n}(\alpha) := \{\gamma \in \mathbf{OT^0} : \gamma \prec \alpha \text{ and } |\gamma| \leq \mathrm{n}\}$$

6.3 Lemma

The sets $\mathbf{OT^0_n}(\alpha)$ are finite.

This definition of the sets $\mathbf{OT^0_n}(\alpha)$ is a preliminary step to defining fundamental sequences to limit ordinals $\alpha \in \mathbf{OT^0}$.

6.4 Definition
For $x \in \mathbf{N}$ and $\alpha \in \mathbf{OT^0}$, $\{\alpha\}$: $\mathbf{N} \mapsto \mathbf{OT^0}(\alpha)$ is defined by

$$\{\alpha\}(x) := \max \mathbf{OT}^{\mathbf{0}}_{|\alpha|+x}$$
$$(= \max\{\beta : \beta \prec \alpha \text{ and } |\beta| \leq |\alpha| + x\}).$$

6.5 Lemma

$$\{\alpha + 1\}(x) = \alpha, \text{ for all } x \in \mathbf{N}.$$

6.6 Theorem
Suppose $x, y \in \mathbf{N}$ and α is a limit ordinal. Then

1. $x < y \Rightarrow \{\alpha\}(x) \prec \{\alpha\}(y)$
2. $\alpha = \sup\{\{\alpha\}(x) : x \in \mathbf{N}\}$

6.7 Lemma
If α is a limit ordinal, then, for all $x \in \mathbf{N}$,

$$|\{\alpha\}(x)| = |\alpha| + x.$$

6.8 Definition
For $x \in \mathbf{N}$, the *pointwise-at-x ordering*, $\prec_x$, on $\mathbf{OT^0}$ is defined as follows :

$\beta \prec_x \alpha$ if and only if
there is a finite sequence $\gamma_0, \ldots, \gamma_m$ of terms of $\mathbf{OT^0}$ such that
$$\gamma_0 = \alpha, \; \gamma_m = \beta,$$
and, for each i = 0, ..., m-1, $\gamma_{i+1} = \{\gamma_i\}(x)$.

6.9 Lemma
If $\alpha, \beta \in \mathbf{OT^0}$ and $\beta \prec \alpha$, then $\beta \prec_{|\beta| \dot{-} |\alpha|} \alpha$.

6.10 Corollary
If $x, y \in \mathbf{N}$ and α, δ are limit ordinals then

1. If $\{\alpha\}(x) \prec \delta \preceq \{\alpha + 1\}(x)$ then $\{\alpha\}(x) \prec \{\delta\}(0)$.
2. $\{\alpha\}(x) + 1 \preceq_y \{\alpha\}(y)$.

6.11 Remark
Part 1 of corollary 6.10 tells us that, with respect to our definition of fundamental sequences, $\mathbf{OT^0}$ possesses the *Bachmann Property.* Part 2 tells us that the terms in $\mathbf{OT^0}$ provide a set of notations for an initial segment of the *structured tree ordinals* of [D-J,W83].

7 THE SLOW GROWING HIERARCHY

The following defines a version of the *Slow Growing hierarchy* indexed by ordinal terms from $\mathbf{OT^0}$:

7.1 Definition

$$\begin{aligned} G_0(x) &= 0, \\ G_\gamma(x) &= G_{\{\gamma\}(x)}(x) + 1, \text{ when } \gamma \neq 0. \end{aligned}$$

The following lemma is immediate from the definition of the Slow Growing hierarchy:

7.2 Lemma

$$G_\alpha(x) = \textit{cardinality of } \{\gamma : \gamma \prec_x \alpha\}.$$

We shall also need the following technical results:

7.3 Lemma

1. if $\beta \prec_x \alpha$ then $\{\gamma : \gamma \prec_x \beta\} \subset \{\gamma : \gamma \prec_x \alpha\}$, and hence, $G_\beta(x) < G_\alpha(x)$.
2. if $x < y$ then $\{\gamma : \gamma \prec_x \alpha\} \subseteq \{\gamma : \gamma \prec_y \alpha\}$, and hence, $G_\alpha(x) \leq G_\alpha(y)$. Equality occurs only when α is finite.

The Slow Growing hierarchy is important to us because we shall show that functions from the hierarchy can be used to give bounds on the lengths of derivations for rewrite systems. Our results will then depend crucially on the complexity of these functions. We arrive at these complexity characterisations by appealing to the Hierarchy Comparison Theorem which relates the rates of growth of functions in the Slow Growing hierarchy with rates of growth of functions representing the well known Grzegorczyk, or Fast Growing, hierarchy. The Hierarchy Comparison Theorem was first proved by Girard in 1975 and appears in [Gir81]. Other proofs have been given in [Acz80], [Buc80], [CW83], [Jer79], [Sch80] and [Wai89].

The main results of the Hierarchy Comparison Theorem which we use here are with reference to the following version of the Fast Growing hierarchy:

$$\begin{aligned} f_0(x) &= x+1, \\ f_\gamma(x) &= f^{(x+1)}_{\{\gamma\}(x)}(x), \text{ when } \gamma \neq 0. \end{aligned}$$

where the superscript denotes iterated composition.

These results are:

1. For $n \in \mathbf{N}$, f_{2+n} and $G_{\theta_n 0}$ are elementarily equivalent, and hence $G_{\theta_n 0}$ is primitive recursive.
2. f_ω and $G_{\theta_\omega 0}$ are elementarily equivalent, and so $G_{\theta_\omega 0}$ is a version of the Ackermann function.

8 THE BOUNDING THEOREM

8.1 Theorem

Suppose that $\mathcal{R}$ is a finite set of rewrite rules over a set T(F,X) of terms and that there is an embedding $\pi : T(F) \mapsto \mathbf{OT}^0$ such that the rules in $\mathcal{R}$ are reducing under π. Suppose further that there is a constant $C \in \mathbf{N}$ such that $|\pi(t_2)| \dot{-} |\pi(t_1)| \leq C$, whenever $t_1 \overset{1}{\underset{\mathcal{R}}{\Rightarrow}} t_2$. Let $\Lambda = \sup\{\pi(t) : t \in T(F)\}$. We have

$$\text{if } t \overset{n}{\underset{\mathcal{R}}{\Rightarrow}} s \text{ then } n \leq G_\Lambda(|\pi(t)| + C)$$

where G_Λ is a function in the slow-growing hierarchy.

Proof We note that s does not appear in the bound for n, thus the bound is for any derivation which starts from t.

$t \overset{n}{\underset{\mathcal{R}}{\Rightarrow}} s$ means that there is a sequence $t_0, \ldots, t_n$ of terms in T(F) such that

$$t = t_0 \overset{1}{\underset{\mathcal{R}}{\Rightarrow}} t_1 \overset{1}{\underset{\mathcal{R}}{\Rightarrow}} \cdots \overset{1}{\underset{\mathcal{R}}{\Rightarrow}} t_n = s.$$

By the supposition, for each i = 0, ..., n-1,

$$|\pi(t_{i+1})| \dot{-} |\pi(t_i)| \leq C.$$

By lemma 6.9,

$$\pi(t_{i+1}) \prec_{|\pi(t_{i+1})| \dot{-} |\pi(t_i)|} \pi(t_i),$$

so that, for each i = 0, ..., n-1, using lemma 7.3.2,

$$\pi(t_{i+1}) \prec_C \pi(t_i).$$

Hence, again using lemma 7.3.2,

$$\{\pi(t_1), \ldots, \pi(t_n)\} \subseteq \{\beta : \beta \prec_C \pi(t)\} \subseteq \{\beta : \beta \prec_{|\pi(t)|+C} \pi(t)\}.$$

By lemma 6.9, since $\pi(t) \prec \Lambda$,

$$\pi(t) \prec_{|\pi(t)| \dot{-} |\Lambda|} \Lambda,$$

hence

$$\pi(t) \prec_{|\pi(t)|} \Lambda,$$

and hence

$$\pi(t) \prec_{|\pi(t)|+C} \Lambda.$$

hence

$$\{\pi(t_1), \ldots, \pi(t_n)\} \subseteq \{\beta : \beta \prec_{|\pi(t)|+C} \Lambda\}.$$

That is, if $t \overset{n}{\underset{\mathcal{R}}{\Rightarrow}} s$ then

$$n \leq \text{cardinality of } \{\beta : \beta \prec_{|\pi(t)|+C} \Lambda\}$$

and hence, by lemma 7.2,

$$n \leq G_\Lambda(|\pi(t)| + C).$$

9 COMPLEXITY CHARACTERISATIONS

In this section we show that theorem 8.1 can be applied to rpo and rlpo and obtain the complexity characterisations. We write $l_i(x_1, \ldots, x_n)$ to indicate the left hand term in the ith rule of a rewrite system $\mathcal{R}$ where $x_1, \ldots, x_n$ are all its variables. $r_i(x_1, \ldots, x_n)$ denotes the corresponding right hand term in the ith rule and its variables are *contained* in $x_1, \ldots, x_n$.

9.1 Definition

The embedding π_1: $T(F) \mapsto \mathbf{OT^0}$, where $F = \{f_0, \ldots, f_p\}$, is given by:

$\pi_1(0) = 0$;

$\pi_1(f_k(t_1, \ldots, t_n)) = \theta_k(\pi_1(t_1) \# \ldots \# \pi_1(t_n))$

9.2 Theorem

$$\text{If } t \prec_{rpo} s \text{ then } \pi_1(t) \prec \pi_1(s).$$

Proof The proof is relatively straightforward and so is omitted.

9.3 Lemma

$$\text{If } t \in T(F) \text{ then } |t| = |\pi_1(t)|$$

Proof The definitions of $|t|$ for $t \in T(F,X)$ and of $|\tau|$ for $\tau \in \mathbf{OT^0}$ were adjusted to produce this result.

9.4 Lemma

For any substitution $d_1, \ldots, d_n$ for $x_1, \ldots, x_n$,

$$|t(d_1, \ldots, d_n)| \leq |t(x_1, \ldots, x_n)| + \max_{i \in 1..n}\{|d_i|\}.$$

Proof The proof is by induction on the term tree for $t(x_1, \ldots, x_n)$. When t is a constant or a variable, the result is trivial.

If $t(x_1, \ldots, x_n) = f_k(t_1(x_1, \ldots, x_n), \ldots, t_m(x_1, \ldots, x_n))$ then

$$\begin{aligned} |t(d_1, \ldots, d_n)| &= \max_{j \in 1..m}\{k, m, |t_j(d_1, \ldots, d_n)|\} \\ &\leq \max_{j \in 1..m}\{k, m, |t_j(x_1, \ldots, x_n)| + \max_{i \in 1..n}\{|d_i|\}\} \\ &\qquad \text{(by induction hypothesis)} \\ &\leq \max_{j \in 1..m}\{k, m, |t_j(x_1, \ldots, x_n)|\} + \max_{i \in 1..n}\{|d_i|\} \\ &= |t(x_1, \ldots, x_n)| + \max_{i \in 1..n}\{|d_i|\}. \end{aligned}$$

9.5 Lemma

There is a $K_R \in \mathbf{N}$ such that $|r_i(x_1, \ldots, x_n)| \leq K_R$

Proof This is obvious since $\mathcal{R}$ contains only finitely many rules.

9.6 Lemma
For any substitution $d_1, \ldots, d_n$ for $x_1, \ldots, x_n$,

$$|r_i(d_1, \ldots, d_n)| \leq |l_i(d_1, \ldots, d_n)| + K_R$$

Proof By lemma 9.4,

$$\begin{aligned} |r_i(d_1, \ldots, d_n)| &\leq |r_i(x_1, \ldots, x_n)| + \max_{i \in 1..n}\{| d_i |\} \\ &\leq K_R + \max_{i \in 1..n}\{| d_i |\}, \text{ by lemma 9.5}, \\ &\leq K_R + |l_i(d_1, \ldots, d_n)|. \end{aligned}$$

The next lemma generalises lemma 9.6 to the case where a one step rewrite occurs by applying a rule in $\mathcal{R}$ to a proper subterm of a term t. We shall use the notation t[u] to denote a term t with u as a proper subterm.

9.7 Lemma
For any substitution $d_1, \ldots, d_n$ for $x_1, \ldots, x_n$,

$$|t[r_i(d_1, \ldots, d_n)]| \dot{-} |t[l_i(d_1, \ldots, d_n)]| \leq K_R.$$

Proof This is now a straightforward induction over the term tree for t.

9.8 Corollary

$$\text{If } t \overset{1}{\underset{\mathcal{R}}{\Rightarrow}} s \text{ then } |s| \dot{-} |t| \leq K_R.$$

9.9 Lemma

$$\text{If } t \in T(\{f_0, \ldots, f_{p-1}\}) \text{ where } f_0 < \ldots < f_{p-1} \text{ then } \pi_1(t) \prec \theta_p 0.$$

Proof The proof is by induction over the term tree for t and uses the property that if $\beta \prec \theta_p 0$ and $k < p$ then $\theta_k \beta \prec \theta_p 0$.

9.10 Theorem
If $\mathcal{R}$ is a rewrite system over $T(\{f_1, \ldots, f_p\}, X)$ which admits a termination proof using the recursive path ordering then

$$t \overset{n}{\underset{\mathcal{R}}{\Rightarrow}} s \text{ implies } n \leq G_{\theta_p 0}(|t| + K_R)$$

Proof The theorem follows from corollary 9.8, lemma 9.9, bounding theorem 8.1 and lemma 9.3.

We now analyse the ramified lexicographic path ordering in a similar way.

9.11 Definition
The definition of $\pi_2 : T(F) \mapsto \mathbf{OT^0}$, where $F = \{f_0, \ldots, f_{p-1}\}$. Let $M = 1 +$ (maximum of the arities of the function symbols in F).

$$\begin{aligned}\pi_2(0) &= 0\\ \pi_2(f_k(t_1,\ldots,t_n)) &= \#_{i=1}^{n}\theta_k^{M-i+1}\pi_2(t_i) \text{ for } 0 \le k \le p-1.\end{aligned}$$

9.12 Lemma

$$\text{If } t \in T(\{f_0,\ldots,f_{k-1}\})_{0\le k\le p-1} \text{ where } f_0 < \ldots < f_{p-1}$$
$$\text{then } \pi_2(t) \prec \theta_k 0.$$

Proof The proof is similar to that of lemma 9.9.

9.13 Theorem

$$\text{If } t \prec_{rlpo} s \text{ then } \pi_2(t) \prec \pi_2(s).$$

The proof of theorem 9.13 uses the following lemma:

9.14 Lemma

$$\pi_2(t_i) \prec_{rlpo} \pi_2(f_k(t_1,\ldots,t_n)) \text{ for all } i = 1, \ldots, n.$$

Proof The proof is straightforward as each $\pi_2(t_i)$ is a subterm of $\pi_2(f_k(t_1,\ldots,t_n))$.

9.15 Proof of Theorem 9.13
There are three cases to consider. Using lemma 9.14, the first two cases are straightforward. We give the details in the case $s = g(s_1,\ldots,s_m) \prec_{rlpo} f(t_1,\ldots,t_n) = t$, where $f = f_k \approx g$ and $s_1 \approx t_1$, ..., $s_{i-1} \approx t_{i-1}$, $s_i \prec_{rlpo} t_i$, $s_{i+1},\ldots,s_m \in T(F\lceil f_k)$. Then

$$\pi_2(s) = \sigma = \#_{j=1}^{m}\theta_k^{M-j+1}\pi_2(s_j) \text{ and } \pi_2(t) = \tau = \#_{j=1}^{n}\theta_k^{M-j+1}\pi_2(t_j).$$

From the assumption that $s_1 \approx t_1$, ..., $s_{i-1} \approx t_{i-1}$, we obtain

$$\#_{j=1}^{i-1}\theta_k^{M-j+1}\pi_2(s_j) = \#_{j=1}^{i-1}\theta_k^{M-j+1}\pi_2(t_j).$$

From the assumption that $s_i \prec_{rlpo} t_i$ we obtain by the induction hypothesis

$$\pi_2(s_i) \prec \pi_2(t_i)$$

and hence

$$\theta_k^{M-i+1}\pi_2(s_i) \prec \theta_k^{M-i+1}\pi_2(t_i).$$

Now, by lemma 9.12, $\pi_2(s_{i+1}) \prec \theta_k 0, \ldots, \pi_2(s_m) \prec \theta_k 0$. Hence

$$\begin{aligned} \#_{j=i+1}^{m}\ \theta_k^{M-j+1}\pi_2(s_j) &\prec \#_{j=i+1}^{n}\ \theta_k^{M-j+1}\theta_k 0 \\ &= \#_{j=i}^{n-1}\ \theta_k^{M-j+1}0. \end{aligned}$$

Since $0 \preceq \pi_2(s_i) \prec \pi_2(t_i)$, and since $\theta_k^{M-i+1}\pi_2(t_i)$ is an additive principal term,

$$\theta_k^{M-i+1}\pi_2(s_i) \# \#_{j=i}^{n-1}\theta_k^{M-j+1}0 \prec \theta_k^{M-i+1}\pi_2(t_i).$$

It follows that $\pi_2(s) \prec \pi_2(t)$.

9.16 Lemma

$$|\pi_2(t)| \leq M.|t|$$

Proof. The proof is by induction on the term tree for t. Note that

$$\begin{aligned} |\theta_k^{M-j+1}\pi_2(t_j)| &= \max\{k, |\pi_2(t_j)|\} + M - j + 1 \\ &= \max\{k + M - j + 1, |\pi_2(t_j)| + M - j + 1\} \qquad (*) \end{aligned}$$

and therefore we have

$$\begin{aligned} &|\pi_2(f_k(t_1, \ldots, t_n))| \\ &= |\#_{j=1}^{n}\theta_k^{M-j+1}\pi_2(t_j)| \\ &= \max_{j\in 1..n}\{n, |\theta_k^{M-j+1}\pi_2(t_j)|\} \\ &= \max_{j\in 1..n}\{n, \max\{k + M - j + 1, |\pi_2(t_j)| + M - j + 1\}\} \\ &\qquad \text{by } (*) \text{ above} \\ &= \max_{j\in 1..n}\{n, k + M, |\pi_2(t_j)| + M - j + 1\} \\ &= \max_{j\in 1..n}\{k + M, |\pi_2(t_j)| + M - j + 1\} \qquad (**) \\ &\qquad \text{since } M > n \\ &\leq \max_{j\in 1..n}\{k + M, |\pi_2(t_j)| + M\} \\ &= \max_{j\in 1..n}\{k, |\pi_2(t_j)|\} + M \\ &\leq \max_{j\in 1..n}\{n, k, |\pi_2(t_j)|\} + M \end{aligned}$$

By the induction hypothesis, for each $j = 1,\ldots,n$, $|\pi_2(t_j)| \leq M.|t_j|$ and so

$$\begin{aligned}|\pi_2(f_k(t_1,\ldots,t_n))| &\leq \max_{j\in 1..n}\{n,k,M.|t_j|\} + M \\ &\leq M.\max_{j\in 1..n}\{n,k,|t_j|\} + M \\ &= M.|f_k(t_1,\ldots,t_n)|\end{aligned}$$

9.17 Lemma

There is a constant $C_R \in \mathbf{N}$ such that, for each rule $l_i \to r_i \in \mathcal{R}$,

$$|\pi_2(r_i(0,\ldots,0))| \leq C_R.$$

where $r_i(0,\ldots,0)$ denotes the replacement of all variables in r_i by 0.

Proof. This is clear since there are finitely many terms in $\mathcal{R}$.

9.18 Lemma

For any substitution $d_1,\ldots,d_n$ for $x_1,\ldots,x_n$,

$$|\pi_2(t(d_1,\ldots,d_n))| \leq |\pi_2(t(0,\ldots,0))| + \max_{i\in 1..n}\{|\pi_2(d_i)|\}$$

Proof. The proof is by induction on the term tree for t. The result is true when $t = 0$. When $t = x$, $|\pi_2(t(d))| = |\pi_2(d)|$, and the result follows easily. When $t(d_1,\ldots,d_n) = f_k(t_1(d_1,\ldots,d_n), \ldots, t_m(d_1,\ldots,d_n))$,

$$|\pi_2(t(d_1,\ldots,d_n))|$$

$$= \max_{j\in 1..n}\{k+M, |\pi_2(t_j(d_1,\ldots,d_n))| + M - j + 1\}$$

from (**) in the proof of lemma 9.16

$$\leq \max_{j\in 1..m}\{k+M, |\pi_2(t_j(0,\ldots,0))| + \max_{i\in 1..n}\{|\pi_2(d_i)|\} + M - j + 1\}$$

(by induction hypothesis)

$$\leq \max_{j\in 1..m}\{k+M, |\pi_2(t_j(0,\ldots,0))| + M - j + 1\} + \max_{i\in 1..n}\{|\pi_2(d_i)|\}$$

$$= |\pi_2(t(0,\ldots,0))| + \max_{i\in 1..n}\{|\pi_2(d_i)|\} \text{ as required.}$$

9.19 Lemma

For any substitution $d_1,\ldots,d_n$ for $x_1,\ldots,x_n$,

$$|\pi_2(r_i(d_1,\ldots,d_n))| \mathbin{\dot-} |\pi_2(l_i(d_1,\ldots,d_n))| \leq C_R$$

Proof. By lemma 9.18,

$$|\pi_2(r_i(d_1,\ldots,d_n))| \leq |\pi_2(r_i(0,\ldots,0))| \;+\; \max_{i\in 1..n}\{|\pi_2(d_i)|\}.$$

So, by lemma 9.17,

$$|\pi_2(r_i(d_1,\ldots,d_n))| \leq C_R \;+\; \max_{i\in 1..n}\{|\pi_2(d_i)|\}.$$

Therefore, since $|\pi_2(l_i(d_1,\ldots,d_n))| \geq \max_{i\in 1..n}\{|\pi_2(d_i)|\}$,

$$|\pi_2(r_i(d_1,\ldots,d_n))| \leq C_R \;+\; |\pi_2(l_i(d_1,\ldots,d_n))|$$

and the result follows.

9.20 Lemma
For any substitution $d_1,\ldots,d_n$ for $x_1,\ldots,x_n$,

$$|\pi_2(t[r_i(d_1,\ldots,d_n)])| \dot{-} |\pi_2(t[l_i(d_1,\ldots,d_n)])| \leq C_R.$$

Proof. If $t[x]$ is the variable x, the result is lemma 9.19.
If $t[x] = f_k(t_1,\ldots,t_{n-1}, t_n[x])$, then

$|\pi_2(t[r_i(d_1,\ldots,d_n)])|$

$= \max_{j\in 1..m-1}\{k+M, |\pi_2(t_j)|+M-j+1, |\pi_2(t_n[r_i(d_1,\ldots,d_n)])|+M-n+1\}$

from (**) in the proof of lemma 9.16

$\leq \max_{j\in 1..m-1}\{k+M, |\pi_2(t_i)|+M-j+1, |\pi_2(t_n[l_i(d_1,\ldots,d_n)])|+C_R+M-n+1\}$

by induction hypothesis,

$\leq \max_{i\in 1..m-1}\{k+M, |\pi_2(t_i)|, |t_n[l_i(s_1,\ldots,s_n)]|\}+C_R$

$= |\pi_2(t[l_i(d_1,\ldots,d_n)])|+C_R,$

and hence the result.

9.21 Corollary

$$\text{If } t \overset{1}{\underset{\mathcal{R}}{\Rightarrow}} s \text{ then } |\pi_2(s)| \dot{-} |\pi_2(t)| \leq C_R.$$

9.22 Theorem
If $\mathcal{R}$ is a rewrite system over $T(\{f_1,\ldots,f_p\},X)$ which admits a termination proof using the ramified lexicographic path ordering then

$$t \overset{n}{\underset{\mathcal{R}}{\Rightarrow}} s \text{ implies } n \leq G_{\theta_p 0}(M.|t|+C_R)$$

Proof The theorem follows from bounding theorem 8.1, lemma 9.13, lemma 9.16 and corollary 9.21.

When a function f is computed by a rewrite system $\mathcal{R}$, and $\mathcal{R}$ can be proved terminating using the recursive path ordering (or the ramified lexicographic path ordering), then theorem 9.10 (or theorem 9.22) can be used to show that f is primitive recursive.

References

[Acz80] P. Aczel. Another elementary treatment of Girard's result connecting the slow and fast growing hierarchies of number-theoretic functions. Manuscript, 1980.

[Buc75] W. Buchholz. Normalfunktionen und konstruktive Systeme von Ordinalzahlen. In *Proof Theory Symposium, Kiel*, pages 4–25. Springer lecture Notes in Math., **500**., 1975.

[Buc80] W. Buchholz. Three contributions to the conference on recent advances in proof theory. Manuscript, 1980.

[Cic90] E.A. Cichon. Bounds on derivation lengths from termination proofs. Report CSD-TR-622. June 1990. Royal Holloway and Bedford New College, University of London.

[CW83] E.A. Cichon and S.S. Wainer. The slow-growing and the Grzegorczyk hierarchies. *Journal of Symbolic Logic*, (48):399–408, 1983.

[Der79] N. Dershowitz. A note on simplification orderings. *Inf. Proc. Lett.*, 9, 1979.

[DO88] N. Dershowitz and M. Okada. Proof theoretic techniques for term rewriting theory. In *Proceedings of the Third Annual Symposium on Logic in Computer Science*, Edinburgh, July 1988.

[D-J,W83] E. Dennis-Jones and S.S. Wainer. Subrecursive hierarchies via direct limits. In Richter, Borger, Oberschelp, Schinzel, and Thomas, editors, *Logic Colloquium 83*, pages 117–128. Springer Lecture Notes **1104**., 1983.

[Gir81] Jean-Yves Girard. Π^1_2-Logic, part 1. *Ann. Math. Logic*, (21):75–219, 1981.

[Jer79] H.R. Jervell. Homogeneous Trees. Lecture Notes at the University of Munich, 1979.

[KL80] S. Kamin and J-J. Levy. Two generalisations of the recursive path ordering. Department of Computer Science, University of Illinois, Urbana, IL, 1980.

[Pét67] R. Péter. Recursive functions. Academic Press, 1967.

[Schü80] K. Schütte. Proof Theory Springer, 1977.

[Sch80] H. Schwichtenberg. Homogeneous trees and subrecursive hierarchies. Lecture, 1980.

[Wai89] S.S. Wainer. Slow-growing v fast-growing. *Journal of Symbolic Logic*, 54(2):608–614, 1989.

Logics for termination and correctness of functional programs, II. Logics of strength PRA

S. FEFERMAN

Logics for Termination and Correctness of Functional Programs, II. Logics of Strength PRA *

Solomon Feferman

Stanford University

1. INTRODUCTION

This continues the work of Feferman [1991], which will be referred to in the following as [LTC.I]. More specifically, we take up the logics of strength PRA introduced in [LTC.I]§19, but in a modified form, more suitable to practice. While the present paper is designed to be read independently, the reader is recommended to look at [LTC.I] (and its predecessor, Feferman [1990]) for motivational discussions.

For simplicity in the following, only logics for implicit polymorphism ('λ' logics) are considered, *not* explicit polymorphism ('Λ' logics) as in Feferman [1990] and [LTC.I]§18. Also (again for simplicity), we do not include the relation $\dot{\epsilon}$ for the representation of types by objects. In place of the logics $QL_0(\lambda)$, $PL_0(\lambda)$ we introduce here new systems QL(F_0-IR), PL(F_0–IR), also shown to be of strength PRA. The main modification is in the replacement of the Induction Axiom for N, IA_N, by a Function-Induction Rule for N, $F_0\text{-}IR_N$. From this we shall also derive a rule $F_0\text{-}IR_T$ for recursively generated types T.

2. SYNTAX OF QL(F_0–IR)

As in [LTC.I], 'QL' is used to denote a two-sorted quantificational logic, one sort for individuals and the second for types (or classes). Type constructions (as given by the type terms) are of three kinds: general (G), user (U) and function (F_0), where the F_0-terms represent certain function spaces between U-types.

2.1 Individual terms ($s, t, ...$). These are just those of one of the following forms:

$x, y, z, ...,$

$0,$

$st, \lambda x.t,$

$p(t_1, t_2), p_1(t), p_2(t),$

$sc(t), pd(t), eq_N(s, t),$

$cond(s, t_1, t_2),$

$rec(t)$

* Research supported in part by NSF grant CCR-8917606.

2.2 General (G-)type terms and formulas

These are given by a simultaneous inductive definition.

The G-type terms $(\rho, \sigma, \tau...)$ are just those of one of the following forms:

$X, Y, Z, ...,$

$N,$

$\{x \mid \phi\}$ (where ϕ is a general formula).

The general formulas $(\phi, \psi, \theta...)$ are just those of one of the following forms:

$t\downarrow, t_1 = t_2, t_1 \leq t_2, t \in \tau$ (where τ is a G-term)

$\neg\, \phi, \phi \wedge \psi, \phi \vee \psi, \phi \Rightarrow \psi,$

$\forall x \phi, \exists x \phi, \forall X \phi, \exists X \phi$

2.3 User (U-)type terms and Σ_1^+ - formulas. These are given by a simultaneous inductive definition.

The U-*type terms* $(R, S, T, ...)$ are just those of one of the following forms:

$X, Y, Z, ...,$

$N,$

$\{x \mid A\}$ (where A is a Σ_1^+-formula).

The Σ_1^+*-formulas* $(A, B, C, ...)$ are just those of one of the following forms:

$t\downarrow, t_1 = t_2, t_1 \leq t_2, t \in T$ (where T is a U-term),

$A \vee B, A \wedge B,$

$\exists x A, (\forall y \leq x) A$

2.4 Function (F_0-) type terms. Define $(\sigma \to \tau) = \{x \mid \forall y(y \in \sigma \Rightarrow xy \in \tau)\}$. Then the F_0-type terms $(\mathbf{S}, \mathbf{T}, ...)$ are just those of one of the following forms:

$$\left.\begin{array}{c} S \\ S \to \mathbf{T} \end{array}\right\} \text{ where } S \text{ is a U-term.}$$

Note that every F_0-term $\mathbf{T}$ has the form $S_1 \to ... \to S_n \to S$ where $S_1, ..., S_n, S$ are all U-terms, $n \geq 0$, and association is to the right.

2.5 Syntactic notation and abbreviations. Substitution of terms for variables is assumed to be carried out under the usual restrictions to avoid collisions of free and bound variables. When substituting s for x at all free occurrences of x in t, we write $t[x]$ for t and $t[s]$ for $t[s/x]$; similarly for $\phi[x]$ and $\phi[s]$, $\phi[X]$ and $\phi[S]$, etc.

We shall use the following abbreviations:

$(s \simeq t) = [(s\downarrow) \vee (t\downarrow) \Rightarrow s = t],$

$(s, t) = p(s, t),$

$(s_1, ..., s_{n+1}) = ((s_1, ..., s_n), s_{n+1}),$

$t' = sc(t),$

$1 = 0',$

$(t-1) = pd(t)$,
$(S \subseteq T) = \forall x[x \in S \Rightarrow x \in T]$,
$(S = T) = [S \subseteq T \wedge T \subseteq S]$.

We write $t : T$ and $t \in T$ interchangeably. When a class R is dealt with as a binary relation we write $R(s,t)$ for $(s,t) \in R$; similarly for n-ary R and $R(s_1, ..., s_n)$.

2.6 Informal interpretation (cf. [LTC.I] §5). The individual variables $x, y, z, ...$ are conceived of as ranging over a universe V of computationally amenable objects. V is closed under a pairing operation p for which p_1, p_2 are the inverse operations. The class N of natural numbers is assumed to be a subclass of V; $0, sc, pd$ and $\leq$ have their usual meaning on N, while eq_N is the test for equality on N. We identify the Boolean values **t**, **f** with $1, 0$ resp.; *cond* is interpreted as the *if...then...else* operation. Certain elements s of V may be considered to represent programs; then st is the value of s at input t if the program terminates there, i.e. if $(st)\downarrow$; $\lambda x.t$ or $\lambda x.t[x]$ represents the program whose value at each input x is given by $t[x]$ when defined. In general, we write $t\downarrow$ for a (compound) individual term t to express that t denotes a value in V. The operator *rec* associates with each program t a solution $y = rec(t)$ of the recursion equation $yx \simeq tyx$ (all x).

The type terms denote subclasses of V, but the type variables $X, Y, Z, ...$ are intended to range *only* over the classes denoted by U-type terms. The latter correspond to a basic collection of recursively generated types. Then with the usual (classical) interpretation of the logical connectives and quantifiers, each formula ϕ in the language of QL determines a subclass (G-type) $\{x \mid \phi[x]\}$ of V; this is in general *not* in the range of the class variables, i.e. the G-types are much more comprehensive than the U-types. If τ is a G-type, $t : \tau$ tells us something about the "global" behaviour of t relative to all U-types, e.g. $t : \{x \mid \forall X(\phi[X] \Rightarrow x \in X)\}$ tells us that $t : S$ for each U-type S satisfying $\phi[S]$.

Note the following differences from [LTC.I] §4:

(i) We here use different kinds of letters to range over U-types and G-types.

(ii) The *eq* operation is here assumed only for equality on N, not on V as before.

(iii) The relation $x \dot{\in} y$ is not included in the syntax.

3. THE LOGIC OF QL(F_0- IR)

3.1 The logic of partial terms (LPT) and equality axioms.

The axioms of LPT are as in [LCT.I]§7(1), without the axiom for $\in$; namely:

(i) $x \downarrow$

(ii) $0 \downarrow$

(iii) $F(s_1, ..., s_n) \downarrow \Leftrightarrow (s_1 \downarrow) \wedge ... \wedge (s_n \downarrow)$ for $F = p, p_1, p_2, sc, pd, eq_N, cond$ and rec and $n =$ arity of F.

(iv) $(st) \downarrow \Rightarrow (s \downarrow) \wedge (t \downarrow)$

(v) $(\lambda x.t) \downarrow$

(vi) $(s = t) \Rightarrow (s \downarrow) \wedge (t \downarrow)$

(vii) $(s \in \tau) \Rightarrow (s \downarrow)$

The equality axioms are as usual. Note that extensionality is not assumed for operations.

3.2 Propositional part of the logic.

This may be classical or intuitionistic; the main proof-theoretic results below do not depend on which is chosen. In semantical discussions our models verify classical logic. Restriction to intuitionistic logic may be useful when one wishes to apply realizability interpretations in order to obtain constructive closure conditions.

3.3 Quantificational logic for individuals

The basic axioms and rules are

(i) $\forall x \phi[x] \wedge (t \downarrow) \Rightarrow \phi[t]$,

(ii) $\dfrac{\psi \Rightarrow \phi[x]}{\psi \Rightarrow \forall x \phi[x]}$, for '$x$' not free in ψ,

as well as the duals of (i), (ii) for $\exists$.

3.4 Quantificational logic for types.

The basic axioms and rules are:

(i) $\forall X \phi[X] \Rightarrow \phi[T]$, for T a U-type

(ii) $\dfrac{\psi \Rightarrow \phi[X]}{\psi \Rightarrow \forall X \phi[X]}$, for '$X$' not free in ψ,

as well as the duals of (i) (ii) for $\exists$.

Note that (i) was derived in [LTC.I] using the axioms for the representation relation $\dot{\in}$, but must be assumed directly here. Note also that we do *not* in general have $\forall X \phi[X] \Rightarrow \phi[\tau]$, for τ a G-type or even an F_0-type.

4. AXIOMS OF QL(F_0-IR) AND THE RULE F_0-IR$_N$.

The Axioms I-IV are the same as those for $QL_1(\lambda)$ and $QL_0(\lambda)$ in [LTC.I]§8, except that eq_N is restricted to N. The induction axiom there for N is here replaced by the rule (F_0-IR$_N$).

I. Abstraction-reduction

$(\lambda x.t[x])y \simeq t[y]$

II. Pairing, projections; successor, predecessor

(i) $p_1(x, y) = x \wedge p_2(x, y) = y$

(ii) $x' \neq 0 \wedge (x' - 1) = x$

III. Equality on N; conditional definition

(i) $x \in N \wedge y \in N \Rightarrow [eq_N(x, y) = 0 \vee eq_N(x, y) = 1] \wedge [eq_N(x, y) = 1 \Leftrightarrow x = y]$

(ii) $cond(1, y, z) = y \wedge cond(0, y, z) = z$

IV. Recursion

$y = rec(z) \Rightarrow yx \simeq zyx$

V. Natural numbers

(i) $0 \in N \wedge (x \in N \Rightarrow x' \in N)$

(ii) $[y \leq 0 \Leftrightarrow y = 0] \wedge [y \leq x' \Leftrightarrow y \leq x \vee y = x']$

VI. G-type comprehension

$y \in \{x \mid \phi[x]\} \Leftrightarrow \phi[y]$

for any general formula ϕ.

Function-Induction Rule on N

$$(\mathrm{F}_0\text{-IR}_N) \qquad \frac{t0 : \mathbf{T}\,, [x \in N \wedge tx : \mathbf{T} \Rightarrow tx' : \mathbf{T}]}{t : N \to \mathbf{T}}\,, \text{ for each } \mathrm{F}_0\text{-type } \mathbf{T}\,.$$

The system QL(F_0-IR$_N$) is now determined by the logical axioms and rules of §3, the axioms I-VI and the induction rule (F_0-IR$_N$). Note that even though we cannot instantiate type variables by G-terms, we can still reason about the latter via the G-type comprehension axiom VI.

5. SEMANTICS OF QL($\mathbf{F}_0$-IR$_N$).

We here direct the reader, first of all, to the description in [LTC.I]§9 of a great variety of models for $QL_1(\lambda)$, all of which are automatically models of QL(F_0 IR). Among these one should distinguish particularly the *standard recursion-theoretic model*, in which $V = N = \omega$ and $xy \simeq \{x\}(y)$. It may be seen (from §6 below) that the Σ_1^+ formulas without type variables in this interpretation define exactly the same subsets of ω as the Σ_1^0 formulas, namely the r.e. (recursively enumerable) sets, and that the least interpretation for the U-types is then just the collection of r.e. sets.

Another model deserving special attention is NT, the *normal term model*, which is made possible here by restriction of the equality operator to N. Namely, consider the reduction relation $\geq$ between individual terms, generated by the following immediate reductions:

(i) $(\lambda x.t[x])s \geq t[s]$
(ii) $p_i(t_1, t_2) \geq t_i$ $(i = 1, 2)$
(iii) $pd(sc(t)) \geq t$
(iv) $eq_N(\bar{n}, \bar{m}) \geq$ (1 if $n = m$, else 0)
(v) $\text{cond}(\bar{n}, t_1, t_2) \geq$ (t_1 if $n = 1$, else t_2)
(vi) $rec(t)s \geq t(rec(t))s$,
where $\bar{0}$ is the symbol 0, and $\overline{n+1} = \bar{n}' = sc(\bar{n})$. As rec is definable in the λ-calculus by means of the Y-combinator to satisfy (vi), it follows from known results (e.g. in Barendregt [1981]) that $\geq$ satisfies the Church-Rosser theorem. Hence if $t \geq t^*$ where t^* is irreducible, then t^* is unique and is the normal form of t, $NF(t)$. Then the universe V for the model NT is taken to consist of all terms in normal form, with $st \simeq NF(st)$ (if it exists). This provides a model of LPT as shown by Beeson [1985], pp. 119-120, where in general, for any t, we have $t\downarrow$ if and only if $NF(t)$ exists. In this model N consists of the numerals $\bar{n}(n \in \omega)$, which is again standard, and the application relation restricted to N again yields all (and only) the partial recursive functions. The model NT may be considered as providing an operational semantics for the applicative part of QL(F_0–IR), with computations carried out by reduction in parallel.

6. FIRST STEPS IN QL(F_0–IR).

The following are some quick useful consequences of our system QL(F_0-IR). We work informally within it.

6.1 Tupling. Recall that we defined k-tuples $(x_1, ..., x_k)$ by

(1) $$(x_1) = x_1 \text{ and, for } k \geq 2, (x_1, ..., x_k) = ((x_1, ..., x_{k-1}), x_k)$$

Then define $p_i^k(x)$ for $1 \leq i \leq k$ by

(2) $$\begin{aligned}(i)\,& p_1^1(x) = x \text{ and, for } k \geq 2,\\ (ii)\,& p_i^k(x) = p_i^{k-1}(p_1(x)) \text{ if } i \leq k-1, \text{ and}\\ (iii)\,& p_k^k(x) = p_2(x).\end{aligned}$$

This has the property

(3) $$p_i^k(x_1, ..., x_k) = x_i \text{ for } 1 \leq i \leq k.$$

Next define

(4) $$\begin{aligned} S_1 \times \cdots \times S_k &= \{(x_1, ..., x_k) \mid x_1 \in S_1 \wedge \cdots \wedge x_k \in S_k\} \\ &= \{x \mid x = (p_1^k(x), ..., p_k^k(x)) \wedge p_1^k(x) \in S_1 \wedge \cdots \wedge p_k^k(x) \in S_k\}. \end{aligned}$$

This is a U-type for each S_i a U-type. When $S_1 = \cdots = S_k = S$, we write S^k for $S_1 \times \cdots \times S_k$. We need to distinguish $S^k \to T$ from $S^{(k)} \to T$, where the latter is defined by

$$(5) \qquad (S^{(k)} \to T) = \underbrace{S \to \cdots \to S}_{k} \to T\,,$$

$$\text{i.e. } (S^{(1)} \to T) = (S \to T) \text{ and } (S^{(k+1)} \to T) = S \to (S^{(k)} \to T)\,.$$

As usual, we have a biunique correspondence (up to extensional equality) between $S^k \to T$ and $S^{(k)} \to T$. Given $z : S^k \to T$ we associate $\tilde{z} : S^{(k)} \to T$ by $\tilde{z} = \lambda x_1 \cdots \lambda x_k . z(x_1, ..., x_k)$, so that

$$(6) \qquad \tilde{z}x_1 \cdots x_k = z(x_1, ..., x_k) \text{ for } x_1, ..., x_k \in S\,.$$

Conversely, given $\tilde{z} : S^{(k)} \to T$ we associate $z : S^k \to T$ satisfying (6) by taking $z = \lambda x . \tilde{z}(p_1^k(x))...(p_k^k(x))$. This obviously generalizes to a biunique correspondence between $S_1 \times \cdots \times S_k \to T$ and $S_1 \to \cdots \to S_k \to T$.

6.2 Strong definition by cases.

Lemma: We have a closed term d_s such that

(i) $a, b \in N \wedge a = b \Rightarrow d_s(a, b, f, g, x) \simeq fx$, and

(ii) $a, b \in N \wedge a \neq b \Rightarrow d_s(a, b, f, g, x) \simeq gx$.

Thus $t = \lambda x \cdot d_s(a, b, f, g, x)$ satisfies

$$tx \simeq \begin{cases} fx \text{ if } a = b \\ gx \text{ if } a \neq b \end{cases}, \text{ for } a, b \in N$$

Proof. (Beeson [1985] p. 103). Note that $d_s = \lambda a, b, f, g, x . cond(eq_N(a, b), fx, gx)$ doesn't work for this since the inner term is defined only when all its subterms (including fx, gx) are defined. Instead, take

(1) $d_s = \lambda a, b, f, g, x . cond(eq_N(a, b), \lambda y . fy, \lambda y . gy) x$

Then $a, b \in N$ implies $cond(eq_N(a, b), \lambda y . fy, \lambda y . gy)$ is defined, since abstracts are always defined; moreover, if $a = b$ this equals $\lambda y . fy$ and if $a \neq b$ it equals $\lambda y . gy$. Hence d_s satisfies the required conditions.

Corollary. Given terms t_1, and $t_2[x]$ with x not free in t_1, we can find a term t whose free variables are those of t_1 and t_2 other than x, with

$$tx \simeq \begin{cases} t_1 \text{ if } x = 0 \\ t_2[x] \text{ if } x \in N \wedge x \neq 0\,. \end{cases}$$

Proof. Apply the lemma to $f = \lambda y . t_1$ and $g = \lambda y . t_2[y]$ where y is a fresh variable.

6.3 The Π_2-Induction Rule.
By a Π_2-*formula* $\phi[x]$ we mean one of the form

$$\psi[x] = \forall y(A[y] \Rightarrow B[x,y])$$

where $A[y]$ and $B[x,y]$ are Σ_1^+-formulas. By the Π_2-*Induction Rule* for N we mean

$$(\Pi_2 - \mathrm{IR}_N) \qquad \frac{\psi[0]\ ,\ x \in N \wedge \psi[x] \Rightarrow \psi[x']}{(\forall x \in N)\psi[x]}\ , \text{ for } \psi \text{ a } \Pi_2\text{-formula}\ .$$

Theorem. QL(F_0-IR) is closed under (Π_2-IR_N).
Proof. Let ψ be as above, and then take $S = \{y \mid A[y]\}$ and $T = \{(x,y) \mid B[x,y]\} = \{z \mid z = (p_1(z), p_2(z)) \wedge B[p_1(z), p_2(z)]\}$. Let $t = \lambda x \lambda y.(x,y)$. Then

(1) $\qquad$ (i) $(tx : S \to T) \Leftrightarrow \psi[x]$, and
$\qquad$ (ii)$t : N \to (S \to T) \Leftrightarrow (\forall x \in N)\psi[x]$.

For, $\quad (tx : S \to T) \Leftrightarrow \forall y(y \in S \Rightarrow txy \in T) \Leftrightarrow \forall y(A[y] \Rightarrow B[x,y])$
and $t : N \to (S \to T) \Leftrightarrow (\forall x \in N)(tx : S \to T) \Leftrightarrow (\forall x \in N)\psi[x]$.
Since S, T are U-Types, $(S \to T)$ is an F_0-type, and the (Π_2-IR_N) is recast by (1) in the form

$$(2) \qquad \frac{t0 : (S \to T),\ x \in N \wedge tx : (S \to T) \Rightarrow tx' : (S \to T)}{t : N \to (S \to T)}$$

which is just an instance of the rule (F_0-IR_N).

7. PROOF-THEORETICAL STRENGTH OF QL(F_0-IR_N).

7.1 Overview. PRA is used to denote Skolem's system of Primitive Recursive Arithmetic, which is a quantifier-free logic with a symbol together with defining equations for each primitive recursive function, plus a quantifier-free rule of induction. It is known from Parsons [1970] that certain subsystems of PA(Peano Arithmetic) in the language of first-order (quantificational) logic are conservative extensions of PRA, in particular the systems (Σ_1^0-IA) and (Π_2^0-IR) based on the Σ_1^0-Induction Axiom and the Π_2^0- Induction Rule, resp. [1)] The main result of this § is that the systems QL(F_0-IR) and PRA have the same proof-theoretical strength. The reader who is only interested in how the system QL(F_0-IR) may be used as a

[1)] However, one should be careful to note Parsons' result (op.cit.) that the *combined* system (Σ_1^0-IA) + (Π_2^0-IR) is *stronger* than PRA.

logic of computation should simply look at the statements of results that lead up to this, before turning to §8.

It will first be shown in §7.2 that every primitive recursive function is provably defined in QL(F_0-IR). This will be used in §7.3 to establish a translation of the system (Π^0_2-IR) into QL(F_0-IR). The proof of the main theorem will be concluded in §7.4 with a reduction of QL(F_0-IR) to the system PRA in a manner preserving the provably recursive functions. It follows that those are exactly the primitive recursive functions.

7.2 Provable definability of the primitive recursive functions in QL(F_0-IR).

A function $F : \omega^k \to \omega$ is said to be *provably defined* by a closed term t in our system if:

(D) (i) QL(F_0-IR) $\vdash (t : N^k \to N)$, and

(ii) QL(F_0-IR) $\vdash t(\bar{n}_1, ..., \bar{n}_k) = \overline{F(n_1, \cdots, n_k)}$ for each $n_1, \cdots, n_k \in \omega$.

If just D(ii) holds, then we say that t *numeralwise defines* F in our system. [2] F is said to be *provably recursive* in QL(F_0-IR) if we can find t satisfying D(i)(ii).

We regard each primitive recursive function F as introduced by a specific sequence of defining equations obtained from the initial functions (zero, successor and projections) by the schemes of composition and primitive recursion.

Lemma. With each sequence E of defining equations for a prim.rec.F is associated a closed term t_F which provably (in QL(F_0-IR)) satisfies the same equations when we replace '=' throughout E by '$\simeq$'.

Proof. For the initial functions F we take the terms $\lambda x.0$, sc and $\lambda x.p^k_i(x)$ $(1 \leq i \leq k)$, resp. If the system of equations E ends with a composition, say of the form

(1) $$F(x) = G(H_1(x) , H_2(x))$$

we take

(2) $$t_F = \lambda x.t_G(t_{H_1}(x), t_{H_2}(x)), \text{ so that}$$
$$t_F(x) \simeq t_G(t_{H_1}(x), t_{H_2}(x)) .$$

[2] This implies that for each $n_1, \cdots, n_k \in \omega$, $t(\bar{n}_1, \cdots, \bar{n}_k)$ denotes $F(n_1, \cdots, n_k)$ in the standard recursion- theoretic model of §5 and that $t(\bar{n}_1, \cdots, \bar{n}_k) \geq \overline{F(n_1, \cdots, n_k)}$ in the normal term model NT described there.

Finally, in the case that E ends with definition by prim. recursion, say in the form

$$(3) \qquad \text{(i) } F(0,y) = G(y)$$
$$\text{(ii) } F(x',y) = H(x,y,F(x,y)) \, ,$$

we apply strong definition by cases (6.2 Corollary) to find a term $t[x,y,z]$ such that

$$(4) \qquad t[x,y,z] \simeq \begin{cases} t_G(y) \text{ if } x = 0 \\ t_H(pd(x), y, z(pd(x), y)) \text{ if } x \in N \wedge x \neq 0 \end{cases}$$

Thus

$$(5) \qquad \text{(i) } t[0,y,z] \simeq t_G(y)$$
$$\text{(ii) } t[x',y,z] \simeq t_H(x,y,z(x,y)) \text{ for } x \in N$$

Now take

$$(6) \qquad t_F = \text{ rec } (\lambda z.\lambda u.t[p_1(u), p_2(u), z]) \, ,$$

so that

$$(7) \qquad t_F(x,y) \simeq t[x,y,t_F] \, ,$$

and hence

$$(8) \qquad \text{(i) } t_F(0,y) \simeq t_G(y)$$
$$\text{(ii) } t_F(x',y) \simeq t_H(x,y,t_F(x,y)) \text{ for } x \in N \, ,$$

as required to match (4). This completes the proof.

Theorem. For each sequence E of defining equations for a prim. rec. F, and associated closed term t_F satisfying the same equations (in the sense of the preceding lemma) we have that t_F provably defines F in QL(F_0-IR).

Proof. This is proved by meta-induction on E. The only case requiring special consideration is that of definition by primitive recursion, as illustrated by (3), (8) of the preceding proof. Suppose that t_G and t_H provably define G and H resp. in our system. Then it follows from (8) of the preceding that

$$(1) \qquad \text{(i) } t_F(\bar{0}, \bar{m}) = \overline{G(m)}$$
$$\text{(ii) } t_F(\bar{n}, \bar{m}) = \bar{k} \Rightarrow t_F(\overline{n+1}, \bar{m}) = \overline{H(n,m,k)} \, .$$

are provable. Hence we have by (a subsidiary) induction on $n \in w$ that

(2) $$t_F(\bar{n}, \bar{m}) = \overline{F(n,m)}$$

is provable. It only remains to show

(3) $$t_F : N^2 \to N, \text{ assuming } t_G : N \to N \text{ and } t_H : N^3 \to N\ .$$

We shall here use the F_0-Induction Rule, and for that purpose pass to $\tilde{t}_F$ given (as in 6.1) by:

(4) $$\tilde{t}_F xy \simeq t_F(x,y)\ ,$$

so that

(5) $$\text{(i) } \tilde{t}_F 0y \simeq t_G(y), \text{ and}$$
$$\text{(ii) } \tilde{t}_F x'y \simeq t_H(x, y, \tilde{t}_F xy) \text{ for } x \in N$$

Then we claim that

(6) $$\text{(i) } \tilde{t}_F 0 : (N \to N) \text{ and}$$
$$\text{(ii) } x \in N \wedge (\tilde{t}_F x : N \to N) \Rightarrow (\tilde{t}_F x' : N \to N)$$

These are immediate from (5) and the assumptions $t_G : N \to N$, $t_H : N^3 \to N$. Hence by (F_0-IR_N) we have

(7) $$\tilde{t}_F : N \to N \to N, \text{ and so } t_F : N^2 \to N\ ,$$

as required.

In the following we shall identify each prim. rec. F with the associated t_F in our system.

7.3. Translation of the system (Π^0_2-IR) into QL(F_0- IR).
We assume here that (Π^0_2-IR) is given as a subsystem of PA with a symbol and defining equation for each primitive recursive function. By the identification just mentioned, each atomic formula $t_1 = t_2$ of $\mathcal{L}$(PA) translates directly into an equation $(t_1 = t_2)^{(N)}$ of the language of QL(F_0-IR). Then the translation $(\cdot)^{(N)}$ is defined inductively to preserve all propositional operations, with $(\forall x\phi)^{(N)} = (\forall x \in N)\phi^{(N)}$ and $(\exists x\phi)^{(N)} = (\exists x \in N)\phi^{(N)}$. By definition, the Π^0_2-formulas of the arithmetical language are those $\psi[x]$ of the form $\forall y \exists z R(x,y,z)$ where R is a prim. rec. relation, thus one given as $R(x,y,z) \Leftrightarrow F(x,y,z) = 0$ for F prim. rec. Hence $\psi[x]$ is of the form $\forall y \exists z(F(x,y,z) = 0)$ and then $(\psi[x])^{(N)}$ is of the form $(\forall y \in N)(\exists z \in$

$N)(F(x,y,z)=0)$ in the QL language. Let $A[y]$ be $(y \in N)$ and $B[x,y]$ be $(\exists z)[z \in N \wedge F(x,y,z)=0]$. Thus A and B are Σ_1^+ formulas and

$$(1) \qquad \psi[x]^{(N)} \Leftrightarrow \forall y(A[y] \Rightarrow B[x,y])\,,$$

i.e. $\psi[x]^{(N)}$ is (equivalent to) a Π_2-formula in the sense of §6.3. By the result of that section we have closure of the system QL (F_0-IR) under the rule

$$(2) \qquad \frac{\psi[0]^{(N)}\ ,\ x \in N \wedge \psi[x]^{(N)} \Rightarrow \psi[x']^{(N)}}{(\forall x \in N)\psi[x]^{(N)}}$$

But this is just the translation of the rule of induction of the system (Π_2^0-IR). Of course, all the basic axioms for 0,′ hold under the translation, and the defining equations of all the prim. rec. functions translate into provable statements of our system by §7.2 when the free variables are restricted to N. We thus have:

Main Theorem (Part 1).

If (Π_2^0-IR) $\vdash \phi[x_1,\ldots,x_n]$ then QL(F_0-IR) $\vdash x_1,\ldots,x_n \in N \Rightarrow \phi[x_1,\ldots,x_n]^{(N)}$.

7.4 Reduction of QL(F_0-IR) to PRA.

Here it is convenient to replace the rule (F_0-IR_N) by the rule (Π_2-IR) of §6.3. We showed closure of our system under the latter rule (loc. cit.); we now note that in the system QL(Π_2-IR) obtained by replacing the first rule by the second, we have closure under (F_0-IR_N). For if $T = (S_1 \to \cdots S_n \to S)$ is an F_0-type, the formula $tx : T$ is equivalent to $\forall y_1 \cdots \forall y_n(y_1 \in S_1 \wedge \ldots \wedge y_n \in S_n \Rightarrow txy_1 \cdots y_n \in S)$ which, using tupling and Cartesian product, is equivalent to a formula $\psi[x]$ of the form $\forall y(y \in S_1^* \Rightarrow t^*xy \in S)$; this is a Π_2-formula since S_1^*, S are U-types. Thus the systems QL(F_0-IR) and QL(Π_2-IR) have the same theorems.

Let $\mathcal{L}_1$ be the second-order language in which we have been working and $\mathcal{L}_0$ be its first-order part, i.e. without class variables or type terms $\{x|\phi\}$, though retaining the constant N and the atomic formulas $t \in N$. The notions of Σ_1^+ and Π_2-formulas still make sense for $\mathcal{L}_0$, as does the rule (Π_2-IR). We denote by QL^0(Π_2-IR) the system obtained by restricting the language to $\mathcal{L}_0$ and dropping Axiom VI, the G-type comprehension axiom (G-CA).

Lemma 1. QL(Π_2-IR) is a conservative extension of QL^0(Π_2-IR).

Proof. The proof breaks into two parts. The first step is to eliminate G-types in favor of U-types. This is easily done by the following translation:

$(t \in \{x|\phi[x]\})' = \phi'[t]$, and $(\cdot)'$ preserves all other atomic formulas and all the logical operations in $\mathcal{L}_2$. Then (G-CA) reduces to a tautology under the translation. On the other hand, wherever a formula contains an occurrence $(t \in S)$ with a U-type $S = \{x|A[x]\}$, this occurrence is replaced under the translation by $A[t]$. To restore each such formula to its original form, we simply restore the CA-axiom for U-types:

$$\text{(U-CA)} \qquad y \in \{x|A[x]\} \Leftrightarrow A[y] \quad , \quad \text{for each } \Sigma_1^+\text{-formula } A\,.$$

The result is a subsystem $\mathrm{QL}^{(\mathrm{U})}(\Pi_2\text{-IR})$ which looks just like our original system except that the only type terms are now U-types S, the only atomic formulas involving these are now of the form $t \in S$, and the axiom (G-CA) is replaced by (U-CA).

Part 2. it now suffices to prove that $\mathrm{QL}^{(\mathrm{U})}(\Pi_2\text{-IR})$is conservative over $\mathrm{QL}^0(\Pi_2\text{-IR})$. First associate (uniformly) with any $\mathcal{L}_0$ structure $\mathcal{M}$ the $\mathcal{L}_1$ structure $\mathcal{M}^*$ obtained by taking as the range of the second order (type) variables, all Σ_1^+-definable subsets of $V^{\mathcal{M}}$.

Sublemma. If $\mathrm{QL}^{(\mathrm{U})}(\Pi_2\text{-IR})$proves $\phi(x_1, \ldots, x_n, Y_1, \ldots, Y_m)$ then for any closed U-terms $S_1, \ldots, S_m$ and any model $\mathcal{M}$ of $\mathrm{QL}^0(\Pi_2\text{-IR})$, we have $\mathcal{M}^* \models \phi(x_1, \ldots, x_n, S_1, \ldots, S_m)$ for all $x_1, \ldots, x_n \in V^{\mathcal{M}}$.

Proof. By induction on the axioms and rules of $\mathrm{QL}^{(\mathrm{U})}(\Pi_2\text{-IR})$. All the first-order axioms and rules are automatically satisfied. The quantificational axioms and rules for type variables and terms are easily checked; so is (*U-CA*), which now takes the place of (*G-CA*). Thus we need only verify that the statement of the sublemma is preserved under an application of the rule (Π_2-IR_N). Suppose, for simplicity, that ψ is a Π_2-formula with the free variables x, y and Y, and that S is any closed U-term. Then $\psi[x, y, S]$ is equivalent to a Π_2-formula $\psi_0[x, y]$ of $\mathcal{L}_0$; note that this equivalence uses only (*U-CA*), which holds in $\mathcal{M}^*$. Thus if the hypothesis for (Π_2-IR_N) is valid in $\mathcal{M}^*$ under the substitution of S for Y, we have for any $y \in V^{\mathcal{M}}$:

$$(1) \qquad \psi_0[0, y] \wedge (\forall x \in N)(\psi_0[x, y] \Rightarrow \psi_0[x', y])\,,$$

where N is given its (possibly non-standard interpretation) in $\mathcal{M}$. Since (1) is an $\mathcal{L}_0$ formula, it is valid in $\mathcal{M}$. But this holds for any $\mathcal{M}$ which is a model of $\mathrm{QL}^0(\Pi_2\text{-IR})$; hence (1) is provable in that system by Gödel's completeness theorem. It follows that $\mathrm{QL}^0(\Pi_2\text{-IR})$proves $(\forall x \in N)\psi_0[x, y]$, which is thus valid in any model $\mathcal{M}$ of $\mathrm{QL}^0(\Pi_2\text{-IR})$. Returning to $\mathcal{M}^*$ and using the above equivalence once more, it follows that the conclusion $(\forall x \in N)\psi[x, y, S]$ of this instance of (Π_2-IR_N) is also valid in $\mathcal{M}^*$.

Corollary. $\mathrm{QL}^{(\mathrm{U})}(\Pi_2\text{-IR})$is a conservative extension of $\mathrm{QL}^0(\Pi_2\text{-IR})$.

Proof. Apply the completeness theorem once more.

Note. A finitary proof-theoretical demonstration can also be given for this corollary, using an Herbrand-style argument to eliminate $(U\text{-}CA)$, but the details are more complicated.

Lemma 1 now follows from Part 1 and the Corollary.

Now to reduce our system $\mathrm{QL}^0(\Pi_2\text{-IR})$ to PRA, we need only translate it into an arithmetical system known to be conservative over PRA. For this purpose we make a slight extension of the system $(\Pi^0_2\text{-IR})$ by the *finite axiom of choice*

(FAC) $\quad \forall x \leq a \exists y R(x,y) \Rightarrow \exists z(seq(z) \wedge \forall x \leq a\ R(x,(z)_x))$, for R prim. rec.

which implies the *boundedness principle*

$$\text{(BP)} \qquad \forall x \leq a \exists y R(x,y) \Rightarrow \exists b \forall x \leq a \exists y \leq b R(x,y)\,.$$

It was proved in Parsons [1970] that the system $(\Pi^0_2\text{-IR}) + (\mathrm{FAC})$ is also a conservative extension of PRA (cf. also Sieg [1985]). One use of (BP) is to show that every essentially Σ^0_1 formula is equivalent to a (strict) Σ^0_1-formula, i.e. one of the form $\exists y R_1(x,y)$ with R_1 prim. rec. (A formula is essentially Σ^0_1 if in prenex form it has a quantifier prefix consisting of existential and bounded universal quantifiers, which may be intermixed.)

Lemma 2. $\mathrm{QL}^0(\Pi_2\text{-IR})$ is translated into $(\Pi^0_2\text{-IR}) + (\mathrm{FAC})$ in a way preserving all number-theoretical statements.

Proof. The translation $(\cdot)^r$ is obtained by formalizing the standard recursion-theoretic model of our system described in §5, i.e. we translate application xy as $\{x\}(y)$. Standard recursion-theoretic arguments serve to specify an interpretation of the λ-terms and the recursor *rec*, so that all the applicative axioms are satisfied. Beyond this $(\cdot)^r$ is defined to preserve all logical operations and the quantifiers $(\forall x)$ and $(\exists x)$. Of course, 0, *sc* and *pd* are given their standard meaning, and $x \in N$ is translated as $x = x$. Thus under $(\cdot)^r$, every Σ^0_1-formula translates into an essentially Σ^0_1-formula. But then by (BP), its translation is equivalent to a (strict) Σ^0_1-formula. It follows that every Π_2 formula of $\mathcal{L}_0$ translates into a Π^0_2 number-theoretic formula. Hence the rule $(\Pi_2\text{-IR})$ simply translates under $(\cdot)^r$ into $(\Pi^0_2\text{-IR})$. Now if we start with a closed formula ϕ of arithmetic, its translation $\phi^{(N)}$ into $\mathcal{L}_0$ replaces each quantifier $\forall x$ (resp. $\exists x$) by $(\forall x \in N)$ (resp. $(\exists x \in N)$). Then $(\phi^{(N)})^{(r)}$ is directly equivalent to ϕ. It is in this sense that all number-theoretical statements are preserved under $(\cdot)^r$.

We now have as a corollary to Lemmas 1 and 2 and Parsons [1970]:

Main Theorem (Part 2). QL(Π_2-IR) ($\equiv$ QL(F_0-IR)) is a conservative extension of PRA, and its provably recursive functions are exactly the primitive recursive functions.

8. APPLICATIONS OF F_0-IR_N.

We show here by means of our rule of induction that the provably recursive functions of QL(F_0-IR) are closed under various schemes which were established by special arguments for the primitive recursive functions in the literature (cf. e.g. the books Péter [1951], Rose [1984]). It is convenient for some of these, to first derive a variant of the rule of induction, corresponding to complete induction and course-of-values recursion.

8.1 The rule of complete function-induction.

$$\overline{(F_0\text{-}IR_N)} \qquad \frac{x \in N \wedge (\forall i < x)(ti : \mathbf{T}) \Rightarrow tx : \mathbf{T}}{t : N \to \mathbf{T}} \quad \text{for each } F_0\text{-type } \mathbf{T}\,.$$

To prove closure under ($\overline{F_0\text{-}IR_N}$), assume its hypothesis, and write

$$\mathbf{T} = S_1 \to \cdots \to S_n \to S \tag{1}$$

where $S_1, \ldots, S_n, S$ are all U-types. Then define

$$S^* = \{(x, y_1, \ldots, y_n) | \forall i < x(ti\, y_1 \ldots y_n \in S)\}\,, \tag{2}$$

so that also S^* is a U-type, and

$$\mathbf{T}^* = S_1 \to \cdots \to S_n \to S^* \tag{3}$$

is an F_0-type. Finally take

$$t^* = \lambda x \lambda y_1 \cdots \lambda y_n.(x, y_1, \ldots, y_n)\,. \tag{4}$$

We claim that (for $x \in N$):

(5) $\qquad t^*x : \mathbf{T}^* \Leftrightarrow (\forall i < x)(ti : \mathbf{T})$

For, $\qquad t^* : \mathbf{T}^* \Leftrightarrow (\forall y_1 \in S_1) \cdots (\forall y_n \in S_n)[t^*xy_1 \cdots y_n \in S^*]$

$$\begin{aligned}
&\Leftrightarrow (\forall y_1 \in S_1) \cdots (\forall y_n \in S_n)[(x, y_1, \cdots, y_n) \in S^*] \\
&\Leftrightarrow (\forall y_1 \in S_1) \cdots (\forall y_n \in S_n)(\forall i < x)[tiy_1 \cdots y_n \in S] \\
&\Leftrightarrow (\forall i < x)(\forall y_1 \in S_1) \cdots (\forall y_n \in S_n)[tiy_1 \cdots y_n \in S] \\
&\Leftrightarrow (\forall i < x)[ti : S_1 \to \cdots \to S_n \to S] \\
&\Leftrightarrow (\forall i < x)(ti : \mathbf{T})\,.
\end{aligned}$$

Also we have

$$\text{(6)} \qquad \begin{array}{l}\text{(i) } t^*0 : \mathbf{T}^* \text{ , and} \\ \text{(ii) } x \in N \wedge t^*x : \mathbf{T}^* \Rightarrow t^*(x') : \mathbf{T}^*\end{array}$$

(i) is trivial by (5). For (ii), if $x \in N \wedge t^*x : \mathbf{T}^*$ then $\forall i < x(ti : \mathbf{T})$ by (5), so $tx : \mathbf{T}$ by hypothesis of $\overline{(\mathrm{F}_0\text{-IR}_N)}$. Hence $\forall i \leq x(ti : \mathbf{T})$, i.e. $\forall i < x'(ti : T)$ so $t^*x' : \mathbf{T}^*$. Then by $(\mathrm{F}_0\text{-IR}_N)$, we conclude from (6) that

$$\text{(7)} \qquad t^* : N \to \mathbf{T}^* \, .$$

Hence $(\forall x \in N)(t^*x : \mathbf{T}^*)$, i.e.

$$\text{(8)} \qquad (\forall x \subset N)(\forall i < x)(ti : \mathbf{T}) \, .$$

Now given any $i \in N$, let $x = i'$; then $ti : \mathbf{T}$. In other words

$$\text{(9)} \qquad t : N \to \mathbf{T} \, ,$$

which is the desired conclusion of $\overline{(\mathrm{F}_0\text{-IR}_N)}$. More formally, we have shown that whenever $\mathrm{QL}(\mathrm{F}_0\text{-IR}_N)$ proves the hypothesis of $\overline{(\mathrm{F}_0\text{-IR}_N)}$ (for given t, T) then it proves the conclusion.

8.2 Primitive recursion with varying parameters. To show that if G, H_1, H_2 are primitive recursive, then so also is F, defined from them by the recursion

$$\text{(1)} \qquad \begin{array}{l}\text{(i) } F(0, y) = G(y) \\ \text{(ii) } F(x', y) = H_1(x, y, F(x, H_2(x, y)))\, ,\end{array}$$

we assume given t_G, t_{H_1}, t_{H_2} which provably define G, H in $\mathrm{QL}(\mathrm{F}_0\text{-IR}_N)$ in the sense of §7. Then we define $\tilde{t}$ by *rec* and *cond* so that

$$\text{(2)} \qquad \begin{array}{l}\text{(i) } \tilde{t}0y \simeq t_G(y) \\ \text{(ii) } \tilde{t}x'y \simeq t_{H_1}(x, y, \tilde{t}x(t_{H_2}(x, y)))\end{array}$$

We claim

$$\text{(3)} \qquad \begin{array}{l}\text{(i) } \tilde{t}0 : N \to N \\ \text{(ii) } x \in N \wedge (\tilde{t}x : N \to N) \Rightarrow (\tilde{t}x' : N \to N)\, .\end{array}$$

Each of these follows from the corresponding equation in (2) and the fact that $t_G : N \to N$, $t_{H_1} : N^3 \to N$ and $t_{H_2} : N^2 \to N$. Thus by $(\mathrm{F}_0\text{-IR}_N)$ we have

$$\text{(4)} \qquad \tilde{t} : N \to N \to N \, .$$

Hence we may provably define F in our system by t_F where

(5) $$t_F(x,y) \simeq \tilde{t}xy \ .$$

The argument is similar for definition of $F(x, y_1, \cdots, y_n)$ by recursion on x with each of the parameters y_i varied by a prior primitive recursive function. (A similar remark applies to the further examples in 8.3–8.5.)

8.3 Nested recursion on <.
Let

(1) $$z|_x = (z \text{ if } z < x, \text{ else } 0)$$

Consider a function F defined from given $G, H_1, \ldots, H_m$ (H_i k_i-ary) by a recursion of the following form:

(2) $$\text{(i) } F(0,y) = G(x,y)$$
$$\text{(ii) } x > 0 \Rightarrow F(x,y) = t[x, y; H_1, \ldots, H_m, F]$$

where

(3) each subterm s of t is either of the form
(i) $0, x$, or y, or (ii) $s = s_1'$, or (iii) $s = H_i(s_1, \ldots, s_{k_i})$,
or (iv) $s = F(s_1 \, |_x, s_2)$.

Then if $G, H_1, \ldots, H_m$ are primitive recursive, so also is F. The idea of the proof is, again, to replace G by t_G and each H_i by t_{H_i} which provably defines it, and $F(u,v)$ by $\tilde{t}uv$ in the scheme (2), to arrive at

(4) $$\text{(i) } \tilde{t}0y \simeq t_G(x,y)$$
$$\text{(ii) } x > 0 \Rightarrow \tilde{t}xy \simeq t[x, y; t_{H_1}, \ldots t_{H_m}, \tilde{t}] \ .$$

Then it is shown that

(5) $$x \in N \wedge (\forall i < x)(\tilde{t}i : N \to N) \Rightarrow (\tilde{t}x : N \to N) \ .$$

Assume the hypothesis of (5). If $x = 0$ then $\tilde{t}x : N \to N$ by (i) and the fact that $t_G : N^2 \to N$. If $x > 0$, then we prove by induction on the length of subterms s of t (finite in number) that $s \in N$. This uses (3); the main case to consider is (3)(iv) (after the replacement leading to (4)): here $s = \tilde{t} \, (s_1|_x)s_2$, and we know $s_1 \in N, s_2 \in N$. (If $(s_1 \, |_x) = 0$ apply (4)(i); otherwise $(s_1|_x) = i < x$, so we can apply the hypothesis of (5) to conclude that $s \in N$.) Now by the rule $\overline{(F_0\text{- IR}_N)}$ we can infer from (5) that

$$\tilde{t} : N \to N \to N \,. \tag{6}$$

Hence we may take $t_F(x, y) = \tilde{t}xy$ to provably define F in our system. (Similarly for any number of parameters $y_1, \ldots, y_n$.)

8.4 Nested recursion with respect to a "rank" function.
This is a generalization of 8.3. Suppose given a "rank" or "length" function

$$L : N \to N, \text{ with } L(x_0) = 0 \text{ for some specified } x \,. \tag{1}$$

Define

$$z|^L_x = (z \text{ if } L(z) < L(x), \text{ else } x_0) \,. \tag{2}$$

Consider a function F defined from $L, G, H_1, \ldots, H_m (H_i k_i\text{-ary})$ in the form

$$\text{(3)} \qquad \begin{aligned} &\text{(i) } L(x) = 0 \Rightarrow F(x,y) = G(x,y) \\ &\text{(ii) } L(x) > 0 \Rightarrow F(x,y) = t[x, y; H_1, \ldots, H_m, F] \end{aligned}$$

where

(4) each subterm s of t is either of the form
(i) $s = 0, x$ or y, or (ii) $s = s_1'$, or (iii) $s = H_i(s_1, \ldots, s_{k_i})$,
or (iv) $s = F(s_1 |^L_x, s_2)$.

Then if $L, G, H_1, \ldots, H_m$ are primitive recursive so also is F.

Here the method of proof is to first define an auxiliary function $F^*(u, x, y)$ which is to satisfy

$$F^*(u, x, y) = (F(x, y) \text{ if } L(x) < u, \text{ else } G(x, y)) \,. \tag{5}$$

with this as motivation, consider the recursion

$$\text{(6)} \qquad \begin{aligned} &\text{(i) } F^*(0, x, y) = G(x, y) \\ &\text{(ii) } F^*(u', x, y) = t^*[u, x, y; H_1, \ldots, H_m, F^*], \end{aligned}$$

where

(7) each subterm s of t^* is either of the form
(i) $s = 0, u, x$ or y, or (ii) $s = s_1'$, or (iii) $s = H_i(s_1, \ldots, s_{k_i})$,
or (iv) $s = F^*(u, s_1|^L_x, s_2)$.

(This recursion combines features of 8.2 and 8.3.) To show that if $L, G, H_1, \ldots, H_m$ are prim. rec., so also is F, we introduce a term $\tilde{t}_{F^*}$ by recursion to satisfy:

(8) (i) $\tilde{t}_{F^*} 0xy \simeq G(x,y)$

(ii) $\tilde{t}_{F^*} u'xy \simeq t^*[u,x,y; H_1, \ldots, H_m, \tilde{t}_{F^*}]$,

where each occurrence $F^*(u, s_1|^L_x, s_2)$ in t^* is replaced by $\tilde{t}_{F^*} u(s_1|^L_x)s_2$. Then it is shown that

(9) $\tilde{t}_{F^*} 0 : N^{(2)} \to N$ and $u \in N \wedge (\tilde{t}_{F^*} u : N^{(2)} \to N) \Rightarrow (\tilde{t}_{F^*} u' : N^{(2)} \to N)$,

the implication being carried out from (8)(ii) by induction on subterms of t^*. It follows by the rule (F_0-IR_N) that

(10) $\tilde{t}_{F^*} : N^{(3)} \to N$.

Hence, if we set $F^*(u,x,y) = \tilde{t}_{F^*} uxy$, F^* is provably recursive in our system, and satisfies the recursion equations (6) for $u, x, y \in N$. Then it is proved by induction on u that

(11) $\forall u, v, x, y \in N[L(x) < u \le v \Rightarrow F^*(u,x,y) = F^*(v,x,y)]$;

this makes use of the (Π_2-IR) (§6.3). Hence, finally, if we define

(12) $F(x,y) - F^*(L(x)+1, x, y)$

it follows from (6) and (11) that F satisfies the initial recursion equations (8). Since these subsume the scheme of nested recursion in §8.3 by taking $L(x) = x$, the argument for this section provides an alternative to that of the preceding section. (Again, the results extend to any number of parameters $y_1, \ldots, y_n$.)

8.5 Unnested multiple recursion

Consider, as an illustration, a recursion of the form

(1) (i) $F(x,y) = G(x,y)$ if $x = 0$ or $y = 0$

(ii) $F(x',y') = H(x,y,F(x,K(x,y)),F(x',y))$.

This may be regarded as justified by recursion on the ordinal ω^2, by assignment of the ordinal $\omega \cdot x + y$ to (x,y). Ackermann's non-primitive recursive function may also be defined by recursion on ω^2, but with nesting in the definition. Thus to show that (1) can be reduced to primitive recursion, a special argument is necessary, dependent on the fact that we have no nesting there. For this, we examine directly the predecessor relation $\prec$ induced by:

(2) $$(x, K(x,y)) \prec (x', y') \text{ and } (x', y) \prec (x', y') ,$$

i.e.

(3) $$(x_1, y_1) \prec (x_2, y_2) \Leftrightarrow (\exists x, y \in N)[x_2 = x' \wedge y_2 = y' \wedge (x_1 = x \wedge y_1 = K(x,y) \vee x_1 = x' \wedge y_1 = y)] .$$

Let $\prec^*$= the transitive closure of $\prec$. Under the assignment of ordinals above, the $\prec^*$ relation is well-founded, and therefore the set of $\prec^*$-predecessors of any (x, y) is finite by the (so-called) Weak König Lemma. Hence we can assign to each (x, y) a finite rank $L(x, y)$ by:

(4) $$\text{(i) } L(x,y) = 0 \text{ if } x = 0 \text{ or } y = 0$$
$$\text{(ii) } L(x', y') = \max(L(x, K(x,y)), L(x', y)) + 1 .$$

However, this has not advanced our work since the recursive definition (4) is just a special case of the form (1). Instead, we show that a *bound* $L^*(x, y)$ to $L(x, y)$ can be assigned which maps the $\prec$ relation into the $<$ relation. First define

(5) $$K^*(x,y) = \sum_{i \leq y} K(x,i) ,$$

and then

(6) $$\text{(i) } L^*(0,y) = 0$$
$$\text{(ii) } L^*(x',y) = L^*(x, K^*(x,y)) + y$$

Then L^* is provably total by 8.2: this is just primitive recursion with a parameter varied. Now it may be proved by induction on x that

(7)
$$\forall x, y, z[y \leq z \Rightarrow L^*(x,y) \leq L^*(x,z)] , \quad \text{so } \forall x, y, z[y < z \Rightarrow L^*(x',y) < L^*(x',z)] ,$$

and from this it is easily checked that

(8) $$(x_1, y_1) \prec (x_2, y_2) \Rightarrow L^*(x_1, y_1) < L^*(x_2, y_2) .$$

Hence F can be defined by recursion on the rank function L^*. It thus follows from 8.4 that if G, H, K are primitive recursive, so also is F.

8.6 Remark concerning an example of Colson.
In Colson [1989] it is proved that the primitive recursive function $F(x, y) = \min(x, y)$ can't be computed in $O(\min(x, y))$ time by an algorithm expressed in a programming language based directly on the schemata for primitive recursive functions. In our system (which has only the primitive recursive functions as its provably recursive functions), F is given by the recursion

$$(1) \qquad F(x, y) = \begin{cases} 0 \text{ if } y = 0 \\ F(x-1, y-1) + 1 \text{ otherwise} \end{cases}$$

which *does* compute $\min(x, y)$ in $O(\min(x, y))$ steps. Equivalently to (1),

$$(2) \qquad \begin{aligned} &\text{(i) } F(0, y) = 0 \\ &\text{(ii) } F(x', y) = \begin{cases} 0 \text{ if } y = 0 \\ F(x, y-1) \text{ if } y > 0 \,. \end{cases} \end{aligned}$$

This definition of F falls directly under the scheme of 8.3 for primitive recursion with parameter varied, and is thus verified to be prim. rec. by the main theorem of §7.

Colson pointed out (op.cit. p. 204) that if F is considered as being given by functional primitive recursion in the sense of Gödel [1958], i.e. for $F(x) = \lambda y.F(x, y)$,

$$(3) \qquad F(0) = \lambda y.0, \ F(x') = G(F(x))$$

for suitable $G(f)$, then $F(x, y)$ can be computed in $O(\min(x, y))$ steps using evaluation by call-by-name. He concluded that "functionality is useful for efficient programming." That comes out of our approach too, but by a different and somewhat more general means. Since our λ-terms are not typed, we cannot read off their loci of termination from their syntactic form, as one can with typed terms in Gödel's T or similar calculi. Instead, we must put our rules ($\mathrm{F_0}$-IR_N) or $\overline{(\mathrm{F_0}\text{-}\mathrm{IR}_N)}$ to work for that. These are, in general, rules for termination of a *functional* on N (when $\mathbf{T} = S_1 \to \cdots \to S_n \to S$ with $n > 0$). On the other hand, use of untyped λ-terms and *rec* provides for greater efficiency straight off (though improvement in efficiency may require a closer investigation in each case as to the order of evaluation of subterms).

9. Type constructions in QL($\mathrm{F_0}$-IR).

9.1 U-type constructions. The U-types (and more generally the G-types) are easily seen to be closed under the following constructions:

$$\text{(i)} \qquad V(= \{x | x = x\}) \,,\ B\,(= \{0, 1\})$$

(ii) $S \cap T$, $S \cup T$

(iii) $S \times T$, $S + T \; (= S \times \{0\} \cup T \times \{1\})$

(iv) $\{x : S | t_1[x] = t_2[x] : T\}$

(v) $\sum_{x:S} T[x] \; (= \{(x,y) | x \in S \wedge y \in T[x]\}$

They are further closed under

(vi) $I_m(S, R)$ for $m \geq 1$,

where $I_m(S, R)$ is the least X satisfying the closure conditions

$$(I_m) \qquad \text{(i)} \quad S \subseteq X \text{ and (ii)} \quad \frac{y_1, \cdots, y_m \in X}{x \in X} \quad R(x, y_1, \cdots, y_m)$$

For $m = 2$ this was defined in Σ_1^+ form in [LTC.I], §11, by:

$$I_2(S,R) = \{x | \exists n, z \, [n \in N \wedge n > 0 \wedge (\forall i < n)(zi \downarrow \wedge [zi \in S \vee (\exists j < i)(\exists k < i) R(zi, zj, zk)]) \wedge x = z(n-1)]\} \; .$$

The Σ_1^+ definition of $I_m(S, R)$ is similar.[4)]

9.2 U-type constructions which generate Σ_1^+. The following result may be considered as a mathematically more natural way of introducing the U-types.

Theorem. For every Σ_1^+ formula A, the type $\{x | A\}$ may be generated from V and B by means of a combination of the following operations:

(i) $\{x : S | t_1[x] = t_2[x] : T\}$

(ii) $S + T$

(iii) $S \times T$

(iv) $I_m(S, T) \quad (m \geq 1)$.

Proof (idea). The atomic formulas come from (i). One then shows how each logical operation which is used to build Σ_1^+ formulas is mirrored by a combination of (i)–(iv). The essential steps are to define $\{x | \exists y (x, y) \in S\}$ and $\{x | x \in N \wedge \forall y < x (x, y) \in S\}$. Both of these can be carried out by I_m constructions, for which see Feferman [1989] p. 214 and Feferman [1982] p. 108, resp. Note then that

4) Actually, it was shown in Feferman [1982,1989] how to define all the I_m operations from I_2.

disjunction, or $S \cup T$, comes from (ii) by existential quantification, while conjunction comes from $S \cap T = \{x : S|x = x : T\}$.

9.3 Some G-type constructions in QL(F_0-IR). Here we have the same freedom as for the more general type constructions in $QL_1(\lambda)$ of [LTC.I]§11,§12. Among these, the G-types are closed under:

(i) $\sigma \to \tau \; (= \{x | \forall y (y \in \sigma \Rightarrow xy \in \tau)\})$

(ii) $\sigma \to_p \tau \; (= \{x | \forall y (y \in \sigma \wedge (xy \downarrow) \Rightarrow xy \in \tau)\})$

(iii) $\prod_{x:\sigma} \tau[x] \; (= \{z | \forall x (x \in \sigma \Rightarrow zx \in \tau[x])\})$

(iv) $\bigcap_X \tau[X] \; (= \{x | \forall X (x \in \tau[X])\})$

This last provides for *implicit polymorphism* in our system just as in [LTC.I] §12. (See there for the examples of such.)

10. Consequences of the $I_m(S, R)$ constructions. The types $I_m(S, R)$ are said to be *inductively generated by finitary rules of inference* (f.i.g.) or also *recursively generated.* They are sometimes called *recursive types* in the literature, but that is misleading, since these types are not in general decidable (i.e. they do not have a characteristic function).

10.1 Function-induction rules on finitary inductively generated types. For each m, S, R and $I = I_m(S, R)$ we can formulate a rule (F_0-IR_I) analogous to (F_0-IR_N), which we illustrate as follows for $m = 2$:

$$(F_0\text{-}IR_I) \qquad \frac{t : S \to \mathbf{T},\ [ty_1 : \mathbf{T} \wedge ty_2 : \mathbf{T} \wedge R(x, y_1, y_2) \Rightarrow tx : \mathbf{T}]}{t : I \to \mathbf{T}} \quad \text{for } I = I_2(S, R)$$

and each F_0-type $\mathbf{T}$.

Theorem. QL(F_0-IR) is closed under the (F_0-IR_I) rules.

Proof (idea, for $m = 2$ as above). If S is empty, then I is empty and the result is trivial. Otherwise, fix $x_0 \in S$ and let

(1)
$$D = \{(n, z) | n > 0 \wedge n \in N \wedge z : N \to V \wedge (\forall i < n)[zi \in S \wedge (\exists j < i)(\exists k < i) R(zi, zj, zk)]\} .$$

Then D is a U-type and $(n, z) \in D$ represents a derivation of length n of an element x of I, in the sense that

(2) $$x \in I \Leftrightarrow \exists n, z[(n, z) \in D \wedge x = z(n-1)] .$$

Define t_1 in such a way that

$$(3) \qquad t_1 k(n,z) \simeq \begin{cases} tx_0 \text{ if } k = 0 \vee k < n \\ t(z(n-1)) \text{ if } 0 < n \leq k\,. \end{cases}$$

We claim that

$$(4) \qquad t_1 : N \to D \to \mathbf{T}\,.$$

This is proved by (F_0-IR_N), using

$$(5) \qquad \text{(i) } t_1 0 : D \to \mathbf{T} \text{ and, (ii) } k \in N \wedge (t_1 k : D \to \mathbf{T}) \Rightarrow (t_1 k' : D \to \mathbf{T})\,.$$

To show that $t : I \to \mathbf{T}$, consider any $x \in I$, and pick $(n,z) \in D$ for which $x = z(n-1)$; then $tx = t_1 n(n,z)$.

Remark. It should also be noted that QL(F_0-IR) is closed under an induction rule

$$(\Pi_2\text{-IR}_I) \qquad \frac{\forall x(x \in S \Rightarrow \psi[x])\,,\ \forall x, y_1, y_2(\psi[y_1] \wedge \psi[y_2] \wedge R(x,y_1,y_2) \Rightarrow \psi[x])}{\forall x(x \in I \Rightarrow \psi[x])\,,}$$

for Π_2 formulas ψ, by an argument just like that in §6.3.

10.2 Recursion on finitary inductively generated types. In practice it is only special $I_m(S,R)$ which give rise in a natural way to t satisfying the hypotheses of an (F_0-IR_I) rule. These are the *deterministic f.i.g.'s with associated predecessor functions* (cf. Feferman [1989] p. 209). For $m = 2$ and $I = I_2(S,R)$ this means we have closed terms q_1, q_2 such that:

$$(1) \qquad R(x, y_1, y_2) \Rightarrow y_1 = q_1 x \wedge y_2 = q_2 x\,.$$

We suppose also given a "case" function (or closed term) c with:

$$(2) \qquad \begin{array}{l} \text{(i) } x \in S \Rightarrow cx = 0 \\ \text{(ii) } R(x, y_1, y_2) \Rightarrow cx = 1 \end{array}$$

Then given $G : S \to T$, $H : I \times T^2 \to T$, we can justify recursion on I of the form

$$(3) \qquad F(x) = \begin{cases} G(x) \text{ if } cx = 0 \\ H(x, F(q_1 x), F(q_2 x)) \text{ if } cx = 1 \end{cases},$$

by taking

$$(4) \qquad tx \simeq \begin{cases} G(x) \text{ if } cx = 0 \\ H(x, t(q_1 x), t(q_2 x)) \text{ if } cx = 1 \end{cases}$$

and proving that $t : I \to T$ by the rule (F_0-IR_I).

10.3 Sequences, Lists, Trees, and All That. Up to now finite sequences from S have been treated as pairs (n, z) with $n \in N \wedge z : [0, n) \to S$. To carry out effective operations on sequences, we define them alternatively by inductive generation in such a way that 0 represents the empty sequence and if x represents $< x_0, \ldots, x_{n-1} >$ then the pair (x, y) represents $< x_0, \ldots, x_{n-1}, y >$ (just as in tupling, but with n variable). For this we must assume in addition to our axioms that

(1) $$(x, y) \neq 0 \text{ all } x, y\ .$$

Then for any S take

(2) $$\begin{aligned} S^* &= \text{least } x \text{ with } \{0\} \subseteq X \text{ and } \frac{x \in X}{(x, y) \in X}\ y \in S \\ &= I_1(\{0\}, R) \text{ for suitable } R\ . \end{aligned}$$

This is a deterministic f.i.g. with (single) predecessor function q_1 and case function $c = \lambda x.eq_N(x, 0)$. Then using §10.2 we can produce closed terms provably defining the following functions:

(3) $$Lh : S^* \to N,\ Val : S^* \times N \to S \cup \{e\},\ ConCat : S^* \times S^* \to S^*\ ,$$

where for x representing $< x_0, \ldots, x_{n-1} >$, $Lh(x) = n$ and $Val(x, i) = x_i$ for $0 \leq i < n$ and $Val(x, i) = e$ (an exception value) otherwise, and finally for $y \in S^*$, $ConCat(x, y) = x^\frown y$ (cf. Feferman [1989] §11).

Similarly we can introduced finitely branching labelled trees by a deterministic f.i.g. with predecessor functions, and carry out definition by recursion on such trees and other usual operations (cf. Feferman [1989] §14). Then one can go on to deal in our system with records, arrays and other finitary data types met in practice, with all the usual associated operations represented by closed terms.

But we can also deal with (potentially) infinitary data types such as S-streams, by treating them as maps $x : N \to S$, and S-"lazy lists", by treating them as partial maps $x : N \underset{p}{\to} S$.

Exercise. Show that all the termination and correctness results of (for example) Manna and Waldinger [1990], Part I, can be carried out in QL(F_0-IR_N) using the methods and results of §8 and §10 above.

11. Free Variable Logics of Strength PRA.

11.1 Why free variable logics? In these logics we consider propositional combinations only, of free variable (i.e. quantifier-free) statements $t_1 = t_2$ and $t : T$;

we may dispense with $t \downarrow$ in favor of $t : V$. Free variable logics bring program expressions t to the fore, together with their evaluation by the rules and their loci of termination (domain and range types). In [LTC.I] we set up several free-variable logics for deriving sequents of the form $A_1, \ldots, A_n \vdash B$ where the A_i's and B are atomic, similar in style to type-assignment (or type "reconstruction") logics in the literature. In particular, a minimal logic $\mathrm{PL}_0(\lambda)$ of strength PRA was described in [LTC.I]§19, whose only types are the N^k, with an induction rule, leading to provably recursive functions in the form $x_i : N, \ldots, x_k : N \vdash t[x_1, \ldots, x_k] : N$. This was enriched there to a logic $\mathrm{PL}_0^+(\lambda)$, still of strength PRA, more useful for practice.

Here, we consider instead more flexible Hilbert-style free variable logics which are contained directly in the quantifier-free fragment of QL(F_0-IR). Two such, PL(F_0-IR) and PL^+(F_0-IR), will be described very quickly in the following.

11.2 The system PL($\mathbf{F}_0$-IR).

11.2(a) Syntax of PL($\mathbf{F}_0$-IR). The *individual terms* are the same as in QL(F_0-IR). The U-*type terms* are just those generated as described in the Theorem of §9.3 above. The F_0-*type terms* are those of the form $\mathbf{T} = (S_1 \to \cdots \to S_n \to S_{n+1})$ for U-types S_i. The *formulas* are generated from atomic formulas $t_1 = t_2$, and $t : \mathbf{T}$ by $\vee, \wedge$ and $\Rightarrow$.

Define $t \downarrow$ as $t : V$ and $\phi \Leftrightarrow \psi$ as $(\phi \Rightarrow \psi) \wedge (\psi \Rightarrow \phi)$.

11.2(b) Logic of PL($\mathbf{F}_0$-IR).

Logic of partial terms (LPT) *and equality axioms* as in §3.1 above.

Propositional logic as in §3.2.

Instantiation rules $\phi[x]/(t \downarrow \Rightarrow \phi[t])$.

11.2(c) Axioms and Rules of PL($\mathbf{F}_0$-IR).

Applicative Axioms I-IV. Just as in §4.

V. *Universal type*

$$x : V$$

VI. *Boolean type*

$$x : B \Leftrightarrow x = 0 \vee x = 1$$

VII. *Direct sums*

$$x : S + T \Leftrightarrow x = (p_1 x, p_2 x) \wedge [(p_2 x = 0 \wedge p_1 x \in S) \vee (p_2 x = 1) \wedge (p_1 x \in T)]$$

VIII. *Cartesian products*

$$x : S \times T \Leftrightarrow x = (p_1 x, p_2 x) \wedge p_1 x : S \wedge p_2 x : T$$

IX. *Equality types*

$$x : \{y : S | t_1[y] = t_2[y] : T\} \Leftrightarrow x : S \wedge t_1[x] = t_2[x] \wedge t_1[x] : T$$

X. *Inductive generation types*

(i) (*Basis*) $x : S \Rightarrow x : I_m(S, R)$

(ii) (*Closure*) $y_1, \cdots, y_m : I_m(S,R) \wedge (x, y_1, \ldots, y_m) : R \Rightarrow x : I_m(S,R)$

XI. *Function types*

$$x : S \to \mathbf{T} \wedge y : S \Rightarrow xy : T$$

Rules

$$(\to \text{Rule}) \quad \frac{\phi \wedge y : S \Rightarrow xy : \mathbf{T}}{\phi \Rightarrow (x : S \to \mathbf{T})} \quad , \text{`}y\text{' fresh}$$

$$(\text{F}_0\text{-IR}_I) \quad \frac{x : S \Rightarrow tx : \mathbf{T}\ ,\ [ty_1, \ldots, ty_m : \mathbf{T} \wedge (x, y_1, \ldots, y_m) : R \Rightarrow tx : \mathbf{T}]}{t : I_m(S,R) \to \mathbf{T}}$$

11.2(d) Translation of PRA into PL(F$_0$-IR). Define $N = I_1(\{0\}, R)$ where $\{0\} = \{x : V | x = 0 : V\}$ and $R = \{z : V \times V | p_1 z = sc(p_2 z) : V\}$. Then N satisfies the usual closure conditions for $0,'$, and the (F$_0$-IR$_N$) rule. Translation of PRA into PL(F$_0$-IR) proceeds just as in §7.2 above.

11.3 The system PL$^+$(F$_0$-IR). This adds to the type constructions the following: type variables $X, Y, Z, \ldots, \sum_{x:S} T[x], \prod_{x:S} T[x]$ and $\bigcap X.T[X]$. The further axioms and rules are, as expected:

$(\sum)$ $$z : \sum_{x:S} T[x] \Leftrightarrow z = (p_1 z, p_2 z) \wedge p_1 z : S \wedge p_2 z : T[p_1 z]$$

$(\prod)$ $$z : \prod_{x:S} T[x] \wedge x : S \Rightarrow zx : T[x]$$

$$\frac{\phi \wedge x : S \Rightarrow zx : T[x]}{\phi \Rightarrow z : \prod_{x:S} T[x]} \quad \text{`}x\text{' not in } \phi, S\ .$$

$(\bigcap)$ $$z : \bigcap X.T[X] \Rightarrow z : T[Y]$$

$$\frac{\phi \Rightarrow z : T[X]}{\phi \Rightarrow z : \bigcap X.T[X]} \quad \text{`}X\text{' not in } \phi$$

(Instantiation) $\phi[X]/\phi(T)$ $\qquad$ T any U-type .

11.4 Theorem. PL(F$_0$-IR) and PL$^+$(F$_0$-IR) have the same proof theoretical strength as PRA, and the same provably recursive functions.

Proof. By 11.2(d), PRA is translated into PL(F$_0$-IR), and that is $\subseteq$ PL$^+$(F$_0$-IR) $\subseteq$ QL(F$_0$-IR), which is reduced to PRA by §7.4. [5)]

Questions.

(1) What stronger conservation results than in the Main Theorem of §7 or the preceding Theorem can be obtained? (Cf. Question (1) in [LTC.I] §22).

[5)] A more direct reduction of PL$^+$(F$_0$-IR) to PRA should be possible, since the system is quantifier- free.

(2) In partial answer to question (2) of [LTC.I] §22, S. Buss and J. Remmel have formulated (in unpublished notes) a quantificational logic whose provably computable functions are just the polynomial-time computable functions. What is an appropriate free-variable logic for the same?

Incidentally, contrary to the conjecture of [LTC.I] loc. cit., no restriction on the λ-calculus is involved in this Buss-Remmel system, but the logic of partial terms is replaced by Scott's logic of existence; the reason is that the predicate $t\downarrow$ implicitly introduces an unbounded existential quantifier. The strength of their system using LPT instead, is apparently open.

Corrections to Feferman [1990] and [LTC.I].

(i) [LTC.I] §11(a)(v). Delete '$z \in S$'

(ii) [LTC.I] §19.V(v). Replace by: $y \in N \Rightarrow (x \leq y' \Leftrightarrow x \leq y \vee x = y')$.

(ii) Feferman [1990] §6.2, and [LTCI]§18 Theorem 6. M. Felleisen noticed a bug in the $(\cdot)^*$ translation of the partial explicitly typed polymorphic lambda calculus into the partial untyped lambda calculus, due to the fact that $(\Lambda X.t)\downarrow$ even when its translate t^* may diverge. This can be fixed (also following his suggestion) by taking $(\Lambda X.t)^* = \lambda u.t^*$ where 'u' does not appear in t, and $(t \cdot S)^* = t^*0$.

References.

H. Barendregt [1981], **The lambda calculus, its syntax and semantics**, 2nd edition (North-Holland) .

M. Beeson [1985], **Foundations of constructive mathematics** (Springer-Verlag).

L. Colson [1989], *About primitive recursive algorithms*, in **Proc. ICALP '89**, Lecture Notes in Computer Science 372, 194–206.

S. Feferman [1968], *Lectures on proof theory*, Lecture Notes in Mathematics 70, 1–107.

S. Feferman [1982], *Inductively presented systems and the formalization of metamathematics*, in **Logic Colloquium '80** (North- Holland), 95–128.

S. Feferman [1989], *Finitary inductively presented logics*, in **Logic Colloquium '88** (North-Holland), 191–220.

S. Feferman [1990], *Polymorphic typed lambda-calculi in a type-free axiomatic framework*, in **Logic and Computation**, Contemporary Mathematics 104, (A.M.S.) , 101–136.

S. Feferman [1991] (= LTC.I), *Logics for termination and correctness of functional programs*, to appear in Proc. of the conference "Logic from computer science," MSRI, Berkeley, Nov. 1989.

K. Gödel [1958], *Über eine bisher noch nicht benützte Erweiterung des finiten Standpunktes*, Dialectica 12, 280–287 (Reproduced, with English translation, in K. Gödel, **Collected Works**, Vol. II, (Oxford Press, 1990)).

Z. Manna and R. Waldinger [1990], **The logical basis for computer programming, Vol. 2: Deductive systems**. (Addison-Wesley).

Parsons [1970], *On a number-theoretic choice schema and its relation to induction*, in **Intuitionism and proof theory** (North- Holland), 459–473.

R. Péter [1951], **Rekursive Funktionen** (Akad. Kiadó, English translation Academic Press 1967).

H. Rose [1984] **Subrecursion. Functions and hierarchies** (Oxford Press).

W. Sieg [1985], *Fragments of arithmetic*, J. of Pure and Applied Logic 28, 33–72.

Reflecting the semantics of reflected proof

D. HOWE

Reflecting the Semantics of Reflected Proof

DOUGLAS J. HOWE

Department of Computer Science, Cornell University

1 INTRODUCTION

One of the most widely used approaches to automating reasoning in interactive proof systems is to allow users to write their own proof-building programs, and to provide some mechanism that rules out unsound applications of these programs. The first system to take this approach was LCF [12], a system in which users can write programs called *tactics* that attempt to prove an input *goal* in a top-down, or goal-directed, fashion, either failing in the attempt, or producing a list of *subgoals* whose provability implies provability of the goal. There are now a number of systems that incorporate a tactic mechanism; these include Cambridge LCF [21], HOL [11] and Nuprl [8].

Among these systems Nuprl is unique in that proof objects are explicitly constructed and can contain references to tactics. A proof step may be an application of a primitive inference rule, as in

$$\frac{\vdash A \quad \vdash B}{\vdash A \,\&\, B}\ \textit{\&-intro}$$

where the step has attached to it the name *&-intro* of the rule used, or an application of the *tactic rule.* An example of the latter is

$$\frac{\vdash A_1 \quad \ldots \quad \vdash A_n}{\vdash A_1 \,\&\, \ldots \,\&\, A_n}\ \textit{\&-intro*}$$

where *&-intro** is the text of a program, written in the language ML, which, when given the conclusion of the above step as input goal produces as output subgoals the n premises. In addition, the program must produce a derivation of the conclusion from the premises; this could be, for example, a sequence of $n-1$ applications of the *&-intro* rule.

In order to use ML in this way we need data structures in ML for representing syntactic objects such as terms, formulas and goals. If x is such an object, denote its representation in ML by $\ulcorner x \urcorner$. The general form of a tactic step in a proof is

$$\frac{\sigma_1 \quad \ldots \quad \sigma_n}{\sigma} \; t$$

where t is a program in ML such that $t(\ulcorner\sigma\urcorner)$ evaluates to a data structure representing a proof with conclusion σ and assumptions $\sigma_1 \ldots \sigma_n$. The type system of ML is employed in such a way as to guarantee that the evaluation of $t(\ulcorner\sigma\urcorner)$, if it successfully completes, must result in a correct proof. One need not rely on a type system, though, since the resulting object could be directly checked for correctness.

All tactic proof systems rely for their soundness on the fact that tactics, when executed, must produce, explicitly or not, a proof that justifies any inference made. While this is the source of the flexibility of the tactic paradigm, it can also be a major drawback. Suppose we have an efficient decision procedure d for a fragment of our logic. We cannot apply d directly in theorem proving, but instead must use a tactic which, for the cases where d would answer that a goal is provable, computes a proof of the goal. The problem of how to use d directly yet be guaranteed soundness has an obvious solution: require a formal proof of correctness of d. This leads us to a new form of tactic rule where a tactic is split into two components u and t. The function u simply generates subgoals, and t is a tactic in the old sense of a function producing a proof. However, t is not executed; instead, we *prove* that if it were executed then it would produce a proof whose assumptions are the subgoals produced by u.

A possible form for this new rule is

$$\frac{\rho \quad \sigma_1 \quad \ldots \quad \sigma_n}{\sigma} \; u, t$$

where $u(\ulcorner\sigma\urcorner)$ evaluates to the list $[\sigma_1, \ldots, \sigma_n]$ and where ρ is

$$\vdash t(\ulcorner\sigma\urcorner) \in \mathit{Proof} \;\&\; \mathit{concl}(t(\ulcorner\sigma\urcorner)) = \ulcorner\sigma\urcorner \;\&\; \mathit{assums}(t(\ulcorner\sigma\urcorner)) = u(\ulcorner\sigma\urcorner)$$

The first premise could be proven in a separate logic that formalizes the metatheory of the original logic. In order to avoid an infinite "tower" of formalized metatheories, as in [19,18,23], it is desirable to use a single logic and *reflect* the logic in itself. We therefore call the above rule a *reflection rule.* The rule will need to be slightly modified to avoid paradox [5] (a form of stratification is necessary).

The reflection of proof can be thought of as supporting *applied proof theory,* in the sense that a user's knowledge of proofs and proof construction can be brought directly to bear on the practical problems of interactive proof development. This can be done via the reflection rule, and also by formal reasoning about proof transformation (see [4] for more on this).

In addition to reflected proofs, the first premise of the reflection rule also refers to programs in the tactic language. Thus the logic we use should contain a programming language of sufficient power to serve as a replacement for ML. In [3] and [4] we demonstrated that type theories in the lineage of Martin-Löf's polymorphic type theory [20], and in particular the type theory of the Nuprl proof development system [8], were suitable theories for this kind of reflection.

Here we present a modified type theory which is more convenient for reflection and within which a particularly direct formal account of its own semantics can be developed. We use this theory to give a somewhat simpler account of the reflected proof system developed in [4]. We then show how the internalized semantics can be used to *derive* the reflection rule of the proof system, thus showing that reflected proof is subsumed by reflected truth. Eliminating the reflection rule considerably simplifies the proof system. Also, there is evidence to suggest that the form of reflected truth we give here has practical advantages; see, for example, [13,14].

Martin-Löf's polymorphic type theory [20] and its descendants have similar "standard" models. In [2], Allen shows how to make precise the partial specification of a semantics Martin-Löf gives in [20]. Ignoring the issue of equality, the main idea is to start with an untyped functional programming language L, which includes terms for naming types, and then to inductively generate an association between terms and sets of terms. A term which ends up being associated with a set of terms is called a *type*, and the elements of the associated set are the *members* of the type. Membership in a type is a property of *values*, in the sense that a term is a member of a type if and only if it evaluates to a member of the type. The actual semantics builds-in equality by associating with each type an equivalence relation on its members. These equalities must be respected; for example, a function type $A \to B$ contains only operations which map equal members of A to equal members of B.

This semantics has much in common with the semantics of Feferman's T_0 [9]. The main thrust of the modifications we make to type theory are to incorporate some of the useful features of T_0 while retaining as much of the spirit of the theory as possible, in particular the coding of logic in the type system via propositions-as-types. The main changes are to eliminate the equalities associated with types in favor of a single global equality, and to add types that represent membership propositions. The first of these changes considerably simplifies the part of the semantics that needs to be formalized and does not seem to be a practical loss. The second is clearly useful in reflecting the semantics since the semantics concerns membership in types.

The fact that the type theory is built from an untyped programming language is used to advantage in the reflection of truth. We anticipate the reflection by including in the language an operator $\downarrow$ which maps type-theoretic representations to the objects they represent. For example, if $\ulcorner T \urcorner$ is a value that will represent a type expression, then $\downarrow(\ulcorner T \urcorner)$ is an expression which will be equivalent in the theory to the type T. Because the language is untyped, in order to introduce this operator we only need to explain how to evaluate it.

In Section 2 we give a semantic account of our type theory. In Section 3 we reconstruct the reflected proof system of [4]. In the last section we show how to reflect truth and how to use this reflection to derive the reflection rule. We ignore issues related to extracting programs from proofs in type theory; see [4] for a discussion of ways to deal with extraction.

2 A TYPE THEORY

Our semantic account of a simple type theory begins with a programming language consisting of a set of terms together with an evaluation relation. From this we inductively generate a *type system* which designates some of the terms as *types* and associates to each of them a set of terms. We need the set of terms of the programming language to be closed under certain specific constructors for data values and for expressions that will name types. However, the construction of the type system is "open-ended" in the sense that it applies to any programming language that contains at least the required constructors and that satisfies certain global conditions. We will therefore not define a particular programming language, but instead will state our requirements for the language and will introduce new features as needed during the subsequent development of the reflective apparatus.

2.1 Terms

We assume we are given a set *op* of *operators* that contains at least the operators to be introduced below. Assume that each operator is designated either *canonical* or *noncanonical*. Informally, the canonical operators construct data values, and the noncanonical operators are language constructs like function application that build programs. The letter θ will always stand for a canonical operator. Assume fixed some denumerable set *var* of variables.

Terms are inductively defined as follows. A variable is a term. If τ is an operator then $\hat{\tau}$ is a term, called a *degenerate operator.* If $t_1, \ldots, t_n$ are terms and if $x_1, \ldots, x_n$ are lists of variables, then $\tau(\overline{x}_1.\ t_1; \ldots ; \overline{x}_n.\ t_n)$ is a term, called a *complex term*, where in each of the operands $\overline{x_i}.\ t_i$, the variables $\overline{x_i}$ *bind* in t_i. This term is also called an *instance* of the operator τ. When no confusion can result we write the term $\tau()$ as simply τ.

The usual notions of α-equivalence, substitution, and so on, apply in the obvious way to terms. In a simultaneous substitution $t[\overline{a}/\overline{x}]$, if a particular variable appears more than once in the list $\overline{x}$, only the first occurrence is significant. As usual, we will identify terms which are the same up to renaming of bound variables. A term $\tau(\overline{x}_1.\, t_1; \ldots ; \overline{x}_n.\, t_n)$ is (non-) canonical just if τ is. A *fully canonical* term is a degenerate operator or a canonical term $\theta(u_1; \ldots ; u_n)$ where $u_1, \ldots, u_n$ are fully canonical terms.

Some of the canonical operators we will need are r, λ, *pair*, *cons*, *nil*, $\underline{n}$ for each natural number $n \in N$, and $\underline{id}$ for each $id \in var$ (not to be confused with variable terms). We will use common notations for terms built from these operators: $\lambda x.\, b$ for $\lambda(x.\ b)$, $\langle a, b\rangle$ for $pair(a; b)$, $a :: l$ for $cons(a; l)$, $[]$ for *nil*, and $[a_1, \ldots, a_n]$ for $a_1 :: a_2 :: \ldots :: a_n :: nil$. When no confusion can result, we will write n for $\underline{n}$ and id for $\underline{id}$. We will also need canonical operators for building type expressions. These include N, *Eq*, *Set*, M, *Op*, *Var*, *Sum*, Σ, Π and $Type_i$ for each $i \geq 0$. Notations for instances of these operators are introduced in a later section.

Reflection will use terms to represent the syntactic objects of our theory, objects such as proofs, sequents, and terms themselves. These objects have a simple structure, and can be thought of as being built using mathematical notions such as pairing, sequences, and numbers. These notions correspond directly to canonical operators of our term language. We make this correspondence precise by defining when a fully canonical term is a "standard" representative of a mathematical object. Nonstandard representatives will be terms which are computationally equivalent to a standard representative.

Inductively define $[\![t]\!]$, for fully canonical terms t, as follows. $[\![\underline{n}]\!] = n$. $[\![\underline{id}]\!]$ is the variable *id*. $[\![\hat{\tau}]\!]$ is the operator τ. $[\![\langle a, b\rangle]\!]$ is the pair $([\![a]\!], [\![b]\!])$. $[\![nil]\!]$ is the empty sequence. $[\![a :: l]\!]$ is the sequence with first element $[\![a]\!]$ and remainder $[\![l]\!]$, if $[\![l]\!]$ is a sequence. $[\![inl(a)]\!]$ is the left injection of $[\![a]\!]$ into a disjoint union. $[\![inr(a)]\!]$ is the right injection of $[\![a]\!]$ into a disjoint union.

t is the *standard representative* of the object x if $[\![t]\!]$ is defined and is x. The standard representative of an object x will be denoted by $\ulcorner x \urcorner$.

As an example we consider the standard representation of terms. The form of representation depends on exactly how the definition of terms is formalized. Assume that pairing and sequences are used to form complex terms, and that the distinction between variables, degenerate operators and complex terms is accomplished using disjoint union (associated to the right, say). We have

$$\begin{aligned}
\ulcorner id \urcorner &= inl(\underline{id}) \\
\ulcorner \hat{\tau} \urcorner &= inr(inl(\hat{\tau})) \\
\ulcorner \tau(\overline{x}_1.t_1;\ldots;\overline{x}_n.t_n) \urcorner &= inr(inr(\langle \hat{\tau}, [\langle \ulcorner \overline{x_1} \urcorner, \ulcorner t_1 \urcorner \rangle, \ldots, \langle \ulcorner \overline{x_n} \urcorner, \ulcorner t_n \urcorner \rangle] \rangle))
\end{aligned}$$

where for $\overline{y}$ a sequence of variables $y_1, \ldots, y_k$, $\ulcorner \overline{y} \urcorner$ is $[\underline{y_1}, \ldots, \underline{y_k}]$.

2.2 Evaluation

Evaluation is a binary relation $\cdot \Downarrow \cdot$ on closed terms. Since we are not completely specifying the term language, we cannot give a complete definition of the evaluation relation. In fact, we will only define evaluation for two specific noncanonical operators. It is completely straightforward to include noncanonical operators for almost all of the usual constructs from functional programming languages. In particular, we could include the operators of Martin-Löf's polymorphic type theory [20]. These are sufficient for encoding the programs which are written below using a somewhat informal style. To simplify the presentation, in the following treatment of evaluation we will regard degenerate operators as canonical terms with no subterms.

The type theory we construct requires that evaluation satisfy certain properties, most of which are related to a particular form of program equivalence which will be the global equality of the theory. Three of the properties are easy to state.

- If $a \Downarrow b$ then b is a canonical term.
- If b is canonical then $b \Downarrow b$.
- If $a \Downarrow b$ and $a \Downarrow b'$ then $b = b'$.

The remaining properties (to be stated shortly) and the first two properties above are satisfied if the evaluation relation is presented using a particular form of structural operational semantics (of the general kind developed by Plotkin [22] and Kahn [17]). The idea is to use inference rules to inductively define the relation. The axioms include all formulas of the form $c \Downarrow c$ where

c is a canonical term. The rules must satisfy certain natural syntactic conditions which are given in [16]. Most functional programming language constructs can be naturally specified in this formalism. For example, call-by-name function application is specified by the rule

$$\frac{F \Downarrow \lambda x.\, B[x] \quad B[a] \Downarrow C}{F(A) \Downarrow C}$$

Here we have written $f(a)$ for the instance $ap(f; a)$ of the noncanonical operator ap and have used capital letters for syntactic variables. In the expression $B[x]$, B ranges over terms with a single free variable for which x is substituted. The third condition listed above, that evaluation be determinate, must be checked in an *ad hoc* manner, but this is typically trivial.

The key to reflecting truth is the noncanonical operator $\downarrow$ which can be thought of as a simple kind of metacircular interpreter. Informally, $\downarrow$ takes three arguments: a representative t of a term, a list of variable representatives and a list of terms. The last two arguments can be thought of as forming an environment that binds terms to variables. Informally, the result of applying $\downarrow$ is the term represented by t where the environment is used to give values for free variables. To give a precise definition of the evaluation of $\downarrow$, it is convenient to use a notational device where $A \Downarrow\!* \; u$, for u a fully canonical term, stands for a sequence of formulas containing syntactic variables. In particular, let $A \Downarrow\!* \; \theta(u_1; \ldots; u_n)$ stand for $A \Downarrow \theta(U_1; \ldots; U_n)$ followed by the concatenation of $U_i \Downarrow\!* \; u_i$ for $1 \leq i \leq n$, where syntactic variables are chosen to be all distinct. For example, $A \Downarrow\!* \; \langle 1, 3\rangle$ stands for

$$A \Downarrow \langle U_1, U_2\rangle \quad U_1 \Downarrow 1 \quad U_2 \Downarrow 3$$

We now give the rules defining the evaluation of instances of $\downarrow$. For each term t and sequence of variables $x_1, \ldots, x_n$ that contains the free variables of t, add a rule

$$\frac{T \Downarrow\!* \ulcorner t \urcorner \quad X \Downarrow\!* [\underline{x_1}, \ldots, \underline{x_n}] \quad t[sel(A, \underline{1}), \ldots, sel(A, \underline{n})/\overline{x}] \Downarrow C}{\downarrow(T; X; A) \Downarrow C}$$

where $sel(l, i)$ is a program that selects the ith member of the list l. Write $\downarrow s$ for $\downarrow(s; []; [])$.

For technical reasons we will also need functions giving a bijection between the natural numbers and the terms Type_i, $0 \leq i$. In particular, assume that there are noncanonical operators *Type* and *Typelevel* with evaluation rules, for each $n \geq 0$, as follows.

$$\frac{N \Downarrow \underline{n}}{\mathit{Type}(N) \Downarrow \mathit{Type}_n} \qquad \frac{A \Downarrow \mathit{Type}_n}{\mathit{Typelevel}(A) \Downarrow \underline{n}}$$

2.3 Equality

The global equality of our type theory is a natural computational equivalence which has proved to be valuable in our experience with Nuprl. We develop the theory of this equivalence in [15,16]. Here we will just define it, give some examples, and state a few of its properties.

The preorder $\leq$ is defined as the largest relation on closed terms such that $a \leq a'$ if and only if $a \Downarrow \theta(\overline{x}_1.t_1;\ldots;\overline{x}_n.t_n)$ implies there are terms $t_1',\ldots,t_n'$ such that $a' \Downarrow \theta(\overline{x}_1.t'_1;\ldots;\overline{x}_n.t'_n)$ and such that for each i, $1 \leq i \leq n$, and every sequence of closed terms $\overline{a}$ of the appropriate length, $t_i[\overline{a}/\overline{x}] \leq t_i'[\overline{a}/\overline{x}]$. Define $a \leq b$, for a and b open terms, if $\sigma(a) \leq \sigma(b)$ for every substitution σ such that $\sigma(a)$ and $\sigma(b)$ are closed. Finally, define $a \sim b$ if $a \leq b$ and $b \leq a$.

Two important properties of $\sim$ are, first, that it is a congruence, so in particular if $a \sim a'$ and $b \sim b'$ then $b[a/x] \sim b'[a'/x]$, and, second, it contains the usual redex-contractum relationship, so that, for example, $(\lambda x.\, b)(a) \sim b[a/x]$. These properties hold because of the form of presentation of evaluation described above. Another important property of $\sim$ relates to the type system to be defined below.

Following are some examples.

- $\langle 2+2, 3\rangle \sim \langle 4, 3\rangle$.
- $\lambda x.\, x+2 \sim \lambda x.\, 2+x$.
- For the pure untyped λ-calculus, the following are equivalent for closed terms a and a'.
    1. $a \sim a'$.
    2. For all $n \geq 0$ and closed $b_1,\ldots,b_n$, $ab_1\ldots b_n$ has a value if and only if $a'b_1\ldots b_n$ does.
    3. For every context (*i.e.* term with a hole) $C[\cdot]$, $C[a]$ has a value if and only if $C[a']$ does.
- If b is fully canonical then $a \Downarrow^* b$ if and only if $a \sim b$.
- $\downarrow(\ulcorner\tau(x_1,\ldots x_k.\, t;\ldots)\urcorner) \sim \tau(x_1,\ldots x_k.\downarrow(t;\ulcorner x_1,\ldots,x_k\urcorner;[x_1,\ldots,x_k]);\ldots)$

We can now give a more complete definition of representation. A term t *represents* an object x if $\ulcorner x \urcorner$ is defined and $t \sim \ulcorner x \urcorner$.

2.4 The Type System

Let $\mathcal{T}$ be the set of closed terms. A *type system* is a partial function $\tau : \mathcal{T} \to P(\mathcal{T})$, where $P(\mathcal{T})$ is the set of all subsets of $\mathcal{T}$. We construct the desired type system in two stages. First we give a parameterized construction which closes a type system under all of the basic type constructors. We then iterate this to obtain a cumulative hierarchy of universes of types.

Let $\sigma \subseteq \mathcal{T} \times P(\mathcal{T})$. Inductively define $\sigma' = \mathcal{F}(\sigma) \subseteq \mathcal{T} \times P(\mathcal{T})$ as follows. If $u \in \sigma$ then $u \in \sigma'$. If $(T, x) \in \sigma'$ and $T' \Downarrow T$ then $(T', x) \in \sigma'$. For S a set of closed terms, define the set S^E to be all terms t such that there exists $t' \in S$ with $t \Downarrow t'$. The following are in σ'.

$$\begin{array}{ll}
(N, \{\underline{n} \mid n \geq 0\}^E) & \\
(Op, \{\hat{\tau} \mid \tau \in op\}^E) & \\
(Var, \{\underline{id} \mid id \in var\}^E) & \\
(Eq(a; b), \{r\}^E) & \textit{if } a, b \textit{ are closed and } a \sim b \\
(Eq(a; b), \emptyset) & \textit{if } a, b \textit{ are closed and } a \not\sim b.
\end{array}$$

If for every closed term t there is a set X_t such that $(P[t/x], X_t) \in \sigma'$, then

$$(Set(x.P), \{t \mid X_t \neq \emptyset\}) \in \sigma'.$$

If $(T, X) \in \sigma'$ then for all closed t, $(M(t; T), Y) \in \sigma'$ where $Y = \{r\}^E$ if $t \in X$ and $Y = \emptyset$ otherwise. If $(A, X), (B, Y) \in \sigma'$ then

$$(Sum(A; B), \{inl(a) \mid a \in X\}^E \cup \{inr(b) \mid b \in Y\}^E) \in \sigma'.$$

If $(A, X) \in \sigma'$ and for each $a \in X$ there exists Y_a such that $(B[x/a], Y_a) \in \sigma'$, then

$$(\Pi\, x{:}\, A \,.\, B, \{\lambda x.\, b \mid a \in X \Rightarrow b[a/x] \in Y_a\}^E) \in \sigma'$$

and

$$(\Sigma\, x{:}\, A \,.\, B, \{\langle a, b\rangle \mid a \in X \;\&\; b \in Y_a\}^E) \in \sigma'.$$

Now define $\sigma_0 = \mathcal{F}(\emptyset)$ and for $n \geq 0$ define

$$\sigma_{n+1} = \mathcal{F}(\sigma_n \cup \{(Type_n, \{T \mid \exists X.\, (T, X) \in \sigma_n\})\}$$

Let $\sigma_\omega = \bigcup_{n \geq 0} \sigma_n$. It is straightforward to show that σ_ω is a type system. A term T is a *type* if $\sigma_\omega(T)$ is defined. If T is a type and t is a closed term, define $t \in T$ if $t \in \sigma_\omega(T)$.

When no confusion can result we use the notation $a \sim b$ for $Eq(a; b)$, $A+B$ for $Sum(A; B)$, $\{x \mid P\}$ for $Set(x.P)$, and $t \in T$ for $M(t, T)$. When x is not free in B we write $A \rightarrow B$ for $\Pi\, x{:}\, A\,.\, B$ and $A \times B$ for $\Sigma\, x{:}\, A\,.\, B$. Write $\{x, y \mid P\}$ for $\{x \mid \{y \mid P\}\}$ and $\{x : A \mid P\}$ for

$$\{x \mid x \in A \,\&\, P\}.$$

We call the type $Type_i$ the *universe* at *level* i. We will often identify a type with its set of members. In particular, when we write $T = T'$ for types T and T' we mean that they have the same members.

To appreciate the significance of the above definitions of M, *Set* and *Eq* types it must be understood that we intend to employ the propositions-as-types correspondence to encode logic in the type system. In the usual correspondence (see the book [10], for example) there is a direct structural translation between formulas and types, with Σ, Π, $\times$, $\rightarrow$, $+$ corresponding to $\exists$, $\forall$, $\&$, $\Rightarrow$ and $\vee$ respectively. Under this correspondence, a proposition is intuitionistically true if and only if the corresponding type has a member. (This is not quite true here — see [1] for a discussion of some of the subtleties.) To complete this correspondence, we define an empty type $\emptyset = Eq(1; 2)$ to correspond to falsity. The M and Eq types are designed precisely to represent atomic propositions of membership and equality. A type $M(t; T)$ has a member (which evaluates to the constant r) exactly if $t \in T$, and a type $Eq(a; b)$ has a member if and only if $a \sim b$. The *Set* types add unbounded comprehension: a type $Set(x.P)$ has as members all t such that the proposition represented by $P[t/x]$ is true.

Classical logic can also be encoded in this type system. One way to do this is to change the translation of disjunction and existential quantification. Define the "squash" $sq(A)$ of a type A as $\{x \mid x \in Eq(1;1) \,\&\, A\}$. $sq(A)$ has r as its unique canonical member if A is non-empty, otherwise $sq(A)$ is empty. To obtain classical logic, we take $P \vee Q$ to be $sq(P+Q)$ and $\exists\, x{:}\, A.P$ to be $sq(\Sigma\, x{:}\, A\,.\, P)$.

In the rest of this paper we use the *classical* correspondence. For any type T which represents a proposition via this correspondence we can find, by analyzing the structure of T, a term t such that $t \in T$ if and only if T has a member. For example, the type

$$\forall x{:}\, N\,.\, x \in N \,\&\, \exists\, y{:}\, N\,.\, y \sim x+1$$

has a member if and only if $\lambda x.\,\langle r, r\rangle$ is a member. This fact will allow us to ignore members of certain types.

An important fact concerning the type system we just defined is that it respects the equality $\sim$. In particular, if T is a type and $T \sim T'$ then T' is a type with $T = T'$. Also, if T is a type such that $t \in T$ and $t \sim t'$, then $t' \in T$.

What is missing from our type system is a way to introduce inductively defined types. Including a form such as the recursive type constructor of Nuprl would have complicated the semantics and is not necessary here. Common forms of recursive data types can already be defined via unbounded comprehension and primitive recursion over N. For example, consider the type A *list* of lists over A; this is the least type T satisfying

$$T = \{\, t \mid t \sim [\,] \,\} \cup \{\, t \mid \exists\, a\colon A.\ \exists\, l\colon T.\ t \sim a::l.\,\}$$

Write the right hand side of this equation as $F[T]$, and define

$$f(n) = \textit{if } n{=}0 \textit{ then } \emptyset \textit{ else } F[f(n-1)]$$

We can define T as $\{\, x \mid \exists\, n\colon N.\ x \in f(n)\,\}$.

2.5 Representing Sets and Other Objects

We can use types to collect together all the terms representing objects in some set. We will say that a type T represents a set S if for every $t \in T$, t represents a member of S, and if for every $s \in S$, $\ulcorner s \urcorner \in T$. Thus the type *Term* defined by

$$\textit{Term} = \textit{Id} + \textit{Op} + \textit{Op} \times ((\textit{Var list} \times \textit{Term})\ \textit{list})$$

represents the set of terms.

Functions and predicates can be represented in type theory in a natural way. Suppose that sets S and S' are represented by types T and T', that $f : S \to S'$ is a function, and that t is a term of type $T \to T'$. Then t represents f if for every $s \in S$, the term $t(\ulcorner s \urcorner)$ represents $f(s)$. A predicate P on S is represented by a term t of type $T \to \textit{Type}_i$ if for every $s \in S$, $t(\ulcorner s \urcorner)$ has a member if and only if $P(s)$ is true. Extend these definitions to functions and predicates of several arguments in the obvious way.

Since the definition of proof refers to the representation of proofs, and since we want to give an internal definition of proofs, we need to represent the notion of representation itself. The operator $\downarrow$ can be used for this. For example,

$$\lambda x.\,{\downarrow}x\ \in\ \{\, t\colon \textit{Term} \mid {\downarrow}t \in \textit{Term}\,\} \to \textit{Term}$$

represents the function mapping a member of *Term* to the term it represents. We will also need to represent an inverse of this. It is clear that we can write a program t of type $Term \to Term$ representing the function $u \mapsto \ulcorner u \urcorner$ that maps terms to members of *Term*. We will also need to represent the standard representation function for other syntactic classes such as sequents (defined in the next section). We will denote all of these programs by $\uparrow$.

3 PROOFS

We now simultaneously develop a proof system for our type theory and a reflection of it within the type theory. We want to retain some of the features of the proof system for the Nuprl type theory that have proved to be useful in practice. In particular, we use a sequent logic with "refinement style" inference rules, and incorporate tactics in the proof structure.

In what follows we want to define mathematical sets such as the set of sequents and the set of proofs, and also to define types representing these sets. Since we have a formalism for defining types and a uniform notion of representation, we will sometimes not give an explicit definition of a mathematical class and instead leave it implicitly defined as the set of objects represented by an explicitly given type.

3.1 Sequents

Sequents are represented by the type

$$Sequent = (Var \times Term \times N)\ list \times (Term \times Term \times N).$$

We will write a sequent as

$$x_1{:}\, {A_1}^{i_1}, \ldots, x_n{:}\, {A_n}^{i_n} \vdash t \in T^j$$

Informally, this sequent means that if $x_1, \ldots, x_n$ are such that for each i, $1 \le i \le n$, A_i is a member of $Type_i$ and $x_i \in A_i$, then $T \in Type_j$ and $t \in T$. We will call the numbers $i_1, \ldots, i_n, j$ *level tags*. The *level* of a sequent is the maximum of its level tags. The *hypotheses* of the sequent are the terms $A_1, \ldots, A_n$, and the *conclusion* is $t \in T$.

We will omit level tags when they are of no interest. We will also omit the term t from a conclusion $t \in T$ when an appropriate term is obvious from the structure of T. As discussed in Section 2.4, this will apply when T is a type that expresses a proposition via the classical propositions-as-types correspondence.

Nuprl does not use level tags, although [6] proposes their use. We include them for two reasons. First, it is useful to know what universe a hypothetical type is a member of (in our semantics, every type is a member of some universe). Second, they are needed for a "complete" reflection of truth of sequents.

The precise definition of the truth of a sequent is given by induction on the length of the hypothesis list. The sequent $\vdash t \in T^j$ is true if $T \in \mathit{Type}_j$ and $t \in T$. Suppose that $A_1 \in \mathit{Type}_{i_1}$, and for every term a such that $a \in A$, the sequent

$$x_2\colon A_2[a/x_1]^{i_2}, \ldots, x_n\colon A_n[a/x_1]^{i_n} \vdash t[a/x_1] \in T[a/x_1]^j$$

is true. Then

$$x_1\colon {A_1}^{i_1}, \ldots, x_n\colon {A_n}^{i_n} \vdash t \in T^j$$

is true (assuming $x_1, \ldots, x_n$ are distinct).

3.2 Primitive Rules

The proof rules for our type theory fall into 2 classes. One class concerns the representation of proofs within type theory and consists of the *tactic* and *reflection* rules to be discussed below. The other class consists of the *primitive rules.* These are rules directly related to the semantics of the theory, and include the rules for reasoning about membership in the various kinds of types and for reasoning about the computational properties of the specific non-canonical operators of the theory. A full set of primitive rules would be too large to deal with here. A fairly minor modification of Nuprl's set of rules would form a reasonable set. The operator $\downarrow$ requires an additional rule which will be specified in Section 4.2.

We assume that we have a set of names for primitive rules, and that this set is represented by a type *PrimRule.* The inference rules are given by a refinement function which maps a rule name and a sequent to a list of sequents. The output list of sequents and the input sequent form the premises and conclusion, respectively, of the named inference rule. In a practical implementation we would like refinement to be a partial function that *fails* when the named rule is inapplicable. To avoid the slight complications that partiality would cause, refinement, instead of failing, will return the singleton list containing its input. We assume that the refinement function is represented by a term *primrefine* of type

$$\mathit{PrimRule} \rightarrow \mathit{Sequent} \rightarrow (\mathit{Sequent\ list}).$$

3.3 Preproofs and Parameterized Proofs

There are two circularities in the naive view of proofs which must be broken. First, a proof can contain a *tactic rule*, the specification of which refers to the representation of proofs. This circularity is easily removed since it suffices to refer to the representation of objects in a larger set of *preproofs*. A preproof can be thought of as a tree-structured proof where there is no necessary connection between the rule names and sequents appearing in it. The second circularity is in the reflection rule, where one of the premises refers to the type of all proofs. We break this circularity by first parameterizing the set of proofs with respect to the term used to name the type of proofs, and then taking a fixed-point inside the type theory, at the level of representations, in much the same way as in the diagonalization argument used to prove Gödel's first incompleteness theorem (see, for example, [5]).

Rules are represented by the type

$$Rule = Unit + PrimRule + Term + (Term \times Term \times N).$$

The four disjuncts correspond to four kinds of rules. *Unit* is a fixed one-element type, and a member of it is taken to represent a bogus rule, called the *empty rule*, that indicates the absence of a rule. When such a "rule" is associated with a sequent in a proof, then the sequent is not the conclusion of any inference step of the proof and so is called an *assumption* of the proof. The third disjunct represents *tactic rules*, and the fourth represents reflection rules. The term associated with a tactic rule is called a *tactic* and will eventually be restricted to produce the representation of a proof. The first term associated with a reflection rule is called the *subgoal generator*, the second is called the *tactic* and plays a role similar to the tactic in the tactic rule, and the number is the *level* of the rule.

Preproofs are represented by the type recursively defined (see Section 2.4) by

$$Preproof = Sequent \times Rule \times (Preproof\ list).$$

Proofs are be obtained as a subtype of *Preproof* by restricting the rule so that "refining" the sequent by the rule produces a list of sequents matching the roots of the trees in the preproof list. Before we can do this, we need to define some auxiliary functions. In particular, we can write programs

$$\begin{aligned} roots &\in Preproof\ list \to Sequent\ list \\ assums &\in Preproof \to Sequent\ list \\ subst &\in Var\ list \to Term\ list \to Term, \end{aligned}$$

where *roots* represents the function returning the list of roots of a list of preproof trees, where *assums* represents the function that returns the list of assumptions, in left-to-right order, of a preproof tree, and where *subst* represents the simultaneous substitution operation on terms.

The reflection rule requires a notion of *level* of a proof. The level is the largest number used in a reflection rule or as a level tag. We need to take the maximum not just over the rules and sequents appearing in the given tree, but also over those appearing in proofs produced by tactics. Since, in a preproof, tactic terms may not necessarily represent anything, not all preproofs will have a level. Nevertheless, we can write the program that computes levels when they exist. Let *tlevel* represent the function that returns the largest level tag of a sequent.

$$\begin{aligned}
&\mathit{level}(p) = \mathit{let}\ s,r,pl = p\ \mathit{in}\\
&\quad \mathit{max}(\mathit{tlevel}(s),\\
&\qquad \mathit{max}(\mathit{map}(\mathit{level},pl)),\\
&\qquad \mathit{case}\ r\ \mathit{of}\ \mathit{empty}(\cdot) \Rightarrow 0\\
&\qquad\qquad \mathit{primrule}(x) \Rightarrow 0\\
&\qquad\qquad \mathit{tactic}(t) \Rightarrow \mathit{level}(\downarrow(t(\uparrow s)))\\
&\qquad\qquad \mathit{refl}(u,t,i) \Rightarrow i
\end{aligned}$$

This program uses suggestive notation for several common features of functional programming languages. The *let* construct decomposes the tuple *p* into components *s*, *r* and *pl*. The *case* construct performs a case analysis on what disjunct the rule *r* comes from, in each case returning a value that possibly depends on the value(s) in the disjunct. *map* maps a function over a list, and *max* takes the maximum of a list or tuple of numbers.

We can now define the type of parameterized proofs. We do this by defining a predicate

$$wf \in N \to \mathit{Term} \to \mathit{Preproof} \to \mathit{Type}_0$$

by induction on the first argument.

$$\begin{aligned}
&wf(0,t,p) = \mathit{false}\\
&wf(n{+}1,q,p) =\\
&\quad \mathit{let}\ s,r,pl = p\ \mathit{in}\\
&\quad \mathit{let}\ l = \mathit{roots}(pl)\ \mathit{in}\\
&\quad \textstyle\bigwedge \mathit{map}(wf(n,q),pl)\ \&\\
&\quad \mathit{case}\ r\ \mathit{of}\ \mathit{empty}(\cdot) \Rightarrow pl \sim []\\
&\qquad \mathit{primrule}(x) \Rightarrow \mathit{primrefine}(x,s) \sim l\\
&\qquad \mathit{tactic}(t) \Rightarrow\ \downarrow(t(\uparrow s)) \in \mathit{Preproof}\ \&\\
&\qquad\qquad \mathit{root}(\downarrow(t(\uparrow s))) \sim s\ \&\\
&\qquad\qquad \mathit{assums}(\downarrow(t(\uparrow s))) \sim l\ \&\ wf(n,q,\downarrow(t(\uparrow s)))\\
&\qquad \mathit{refl}(u,t,i) \Rightarrow \mathit{length}(l) \geq 1\ \&\ \mathit{tail}(l) \sim\ \downarrow(u(\uparrow s))\ \&\\
&\qquad\qquad \mathit{head}(l) \sim \langle [], \langle \ulcorner a \urcorner, A, i\rangle\rangle
\end{aligned}$$

where A is

$$\begin{aligned}
subst(\ & \ulcorner x_u, x_t, x_q, x_{\uparrow s}, x_{\uparrow i} \urcorner, \\
& [u, t, q, \uparrow s, \uparrow i], \\
& \ulcorner x_t(x_{\uparrow s}) \in x_q \ \ \&\ \ root(x_t(x_{\uparrow s})) \sim x_{\uparrow s} \ \ \&\ \ assums(x_t(x_{\uparrow s})) \sim x_u(x_{\uparrow s}) \\
& \quad \&\ \ level(x_t(x_{\uparrow s})) < x_{\uparrow i} \urcorner),
\end{aligned}$$

where $\bigwedge z$ is the conjunction of the members of the list z of propositions, and where a is the appropriate term. Finally, define

$$PProof \in Term \rightarrow Type_0$$

by

$$PProof(q) = \{\, p : Preproof \mid \exists\, n{:}\, N.\ wf(n, q, p) \,\}.$$

This is the type of "parameterized proofs".

3.4 Proofs

It is now a simple matter to define the type representing the set of proofs. Let d be the term

$$\lambda x.\, PProof(ap\,(\uparrow x, x))$$

where ap represents the function that takes two terms t and t' and returns the term which is their application $t(t')$. Define the term *Proof* to be $d(\ulcorner d \urcorner)$. Note that

$$\begin{aligned}
Proof &= d(\ulcorner d \urcorner) \\
&\sim PProof(ap\,(\uparrow(\ulcorner d \urcorner), \ulcorner d \urcorner)) \\
&\sim PProof(\ulcorner Proof \urcorner)
\end{aligned}$$

A proof is *valid* if the truth of its assumptions implies the truth of its root. Assume that all primitive rules are true, in the sense that if s is a sequent and if $primrefine(\ulcorner s \urcorner)$ represents a list of true sequents, then s is true.

Theorem. All proofs are valid.

Proof. The argument is by induction on the level n of a proof. For each n, we use induction on the structure of proofs. Suppose that $p = (s, r, (p_1, \ldots, p_n))$ is a proof whose assumptions are true. The root of each p_i is inductively true. We consider the cases for r.

If r is the empty rule then σ is an assumption hence true. If r is a primitive rule then σ is true by our assumption of the truth of primitive rules. If

r is a tactic rule with tactic t then $t(\ulcorner\sigma\urcorner)$ represents a proof p' which is inductively valid. The assumptions of p' are the roots of $p_1, \ldots, p_n$, so they are true, hence the root of p' is true, and this is σ. Finally, if r is a reflection rule with level i, subgoal generator u and tactic t, then the root of p_1,

$$\vdash\ t(\ulcorner\sigma\urcorner) \in \mathit{Proof}\ \&\ \mathit{root}(t(\ulcorner\sigma\urcorner)) \sim \ulcorner\sigma\urcorner\ \&\ \mathit{assums}(t(\ulcorner\sigma\urcorner)) \sim u(\ulcorner\sigma\urcorner)$$
$$\&\ \mathit{level}(t(\ulcorner\sigma\urcorner)) < \underline{i},$$

is true, so t represents a proof p' which is of level less than i and which is therefore valid. The assumptions of p' are the roots of $p_2, \ldots, p_n$, which are true, so the root of p' must then be true, and this is σ. □

4 REFLECTING TRUTH

We now define a reflection of truth and use it to show that the reflection rule is derivable in terms of the other rules. We define a predicate *true* on the type *Sequent* such that $\mathit{true}(s)$ has a member if and only if s represents a true sequent. For each sequent σ the equivalence of σ and $\mathit{true}(\ulcorner\sigma\urcorner)$ is derivable in our proof system. This fact, together with the fact that the argument that proofs are valid can be internalized, is sufficient to derive the reflection rule.

The main consequence of this derivability is that the reflection rule can be eliminated. We can modify the definitions in Section 3 to remove all references to the reflection rule. This involves removing a disjunct from the type *Rule* and removing the reflection rule cases from the functions *level* and *wf*. The results below are easily simplified to show that the reflection rule can be derived in the resulting proof system.

4.1 Reflecting the Semantics of Sequents

The semantics of sequents can be translated into type theory directly. We define the function *true* on sequents by primitive recursion over lists.

$$\begin{aligned}
\mathit{true}(\langle[], \langle t, T, j\rangle\rangle) &= \downarrow T \in \mathit{Type}(j)\ \&\ \downarrow t \in \downarrow T \\
\mathit{true}(\langle\langle x, A, i\rangle :: \mathcal{H}\rangle, \mathcal{C}) &= \downarrow A \in \mathit{Type}(i) \Rightarrow \forall a\colon \mathit{Term}. \\
&\qquad \downarrow a \in \downarrow A \Rightarrow \mathit{true}(\langle \mathit{subst}([x], [a], \langle\mathcal{H}, \mathcal{C}\rangle)\rangle)
\end{aligned}$$

where $\mathit{subst}([x], [a], \langle\mathcal{H}, \mathcal{C}\rangle)$ is the obvious extension of *subst* to sequents. The function *true* cannot be given a single type since it may return a universe of arbitrarily high level. Instead, we can give it a stratified set of types. In particular, for each $n \geq 0$, the sequent

$$\vdash \mathit{true}\ \in \{\, s\colon \mathit{Sequent} \mid \mathit{tlevel}(s) < n \,\} \rightarrow \mathit{Type}_n$$

is provable.

4.2 Reflecting the Proof of Validity

Since the internal notion of truth is stratified with respect to universe levels, we must also stratify the internal statement of the validity of proofs. Define

$$Proof_n = \{\, p\colon Proof \mid level(p) \leq n \,\}$$

and

$$valid(p) = (true(assums(p)) \Rightarrow true(root(p)))$$

where *true* is extended to lists of sequents in the obvious way. For each $n \geq 1$, the sequent expressing validity of proofs of level at most n is

$$\vdash (\forall p\colon Proof_n .\ valid(p))^{n+1}.$$

We claim that this sequent is in fact provable with a "reasonable" set of primitive inference rules, as discussed in Section 3.2. In addition to the rules dealing with the basic type constructors and non-canonical forms, we require two primitive rules related to reflection. The first relates *subst* and $\downarrow$:

$$\vdash \forall a, b\colon Term.\ \forall x\colon Var.\ \downarrow(subst([x],[a],b); xs; as) \sim \downarrow(b; x :: xs; \downarrow(a) :: as).$$

The second asserts that the type *Term* completely reflects the set of terms.

$$\vdash \forall t\colon \{\, t \mid 0 \sim 0 \,\}.\ \exists t'\colon Term.\ \downarrow t' \sim t$$

A verification of provability would be too lengthy to include here. Instead, we describe the structure of the proof, consider some examples of primitive rules, and discuss how to deal with tactic and reflection rules. The structure of the formalized proof is similar to that of the proof given in Section 3.4. Fix k. We prove

$$\vdash [\forall n, i\colon N.\ \forall p\colon Proof_k .\ level(p) < n \ \&\ wf(i, \ulcorner Proof \urcorner, p) \Rightarrow valid(p)]^{k+1}$$

by induction on n and then, for each n, by induction on i, performing a case analysis on the kind of rule used at the root of the given proof tree.

For the primitive rule case we must prove

$$\vdash \forall r\colon Rule.\ \forall s\colon Sequent.\ true(primrefine(r, s)) \Rightarrow true(s).$$

There will be a subproof for every member of *PrimRule*. Some rules are trivial to check. If the rule is a simple axiom of the form $\vdash t \in T^j$, then we must prove

$$\vdash \mathit{true}(\ulcorner \vdash t \in T^j \urcorner).$$

Reasoning about the computational properties of $\downarrow$, this can be reduced to

$$\vdash T \in \mathit{Type}_j \;\&\; t \in T$$

which can be derived from the axiom $\vdash t \in T^j$. As an example of a more typical inference rule, consider the rule for *function elimination:*

$$\frac{\mathcal{H} \vdash f \in \Pi\, x{:}\, A\,.\, B \qquad \mathcal{H} \vdash a \in A}{\mathcal{H} \vdash f(a) \in B[a/x]}$$

This can be proved by induction on the length of the list $\mathcal{H}$. The interesting case is the base case. For this it suffices to prove the following (and also an analogous statement involving membership in a universe).

$$\begin{aligned}\vdash\;& \forall a, f, A, B{:}\; \mathit{Term}.\; \forall x{:}\; \mathit{Var}.\\ &\quad {\downarrow} a \in {\downarrow} A \;\&\; {\downarrow} f \in \Pi\, y{:}\, {\downarrow} A\,.\, {\downarrow}(B; [x]; [y])\\ &\quad \Rightarrow {\downarrow} f({\downarrow} a) \in {\downarrow}(\mathit{subst}(x, a, B))\end{aligned}$$

By our rule relating $\downarrow$ and *subst*, we get that ${\downarrow}(\mathit{subst}(x, a, B))$ is equivalent to ${\downarrow}(B; [x]; [{\downarrow} a])$ and so we can apply the function elimination rule itself to finish this case.

Checking the case for tactic rules is a simple matter of applying the induction hypothesis. The key part of the reflection rule case is to make use of the truth of the first premise of the reflection rule. Using the computational properties of $\downarrow$, this part amounts to proving

$$\begin{aligned}\mathcal{H} \vdash\;& \forall t{:}\; \mathit{Term}.\\ &\quad [{\downarrow} t \in \mathit{Proof} \;\&\; \mathit{level}({\downarrow} t) < i \;\&\; \mathit{true}(\mathit{assums}({\downarrow} t))] \Rightarrow \mathit{true}(\mathit{root}({\downarrow} t))\end{aligned}$$

where $\mathcal{H}$ contains the induction hypotheses, and this is easily accomplished.

4.3 A Derived Reflection Rule for Reflected Truth

It is straightforward to derive an analog of the reflection rule for reflected truth. Let σ be a sequent of level n. We want to show that there is a proof with assumption σ and conclusion $\vdash \mathit{true}(\ulcorner \sigma \urcorner)^{n+1}$, and a proof with assumption $\vdash \mathit{true}(\ulcorner \sigma \urcorner)^{n+1}$ and conclusion σ. Both proofs are similar, except that the latter uses the rule, given in Section 4.2, expressing the completeness of the reflection of terms. Both use the fact that every sequent is provably equivalent to a closed formula. Specifically, define

$$\begin{aligned}\overline{\vdash t \in T^j} &= M(T, Type_j) \,\&\, M(t, T)\\ \overline{x{:}\, A^i, \mathcal{H} \vdash C} &= M(A, Type_i) \Rightarrow \forall x{:}\, A.\ \overline{\mathcal{H} \vdash C}.\end{aligned}$$

It is straightforward to show that σ can be derived from $\vdash \overline{\sigma}$ and *vice versa.*

These proofs can be easily computed, and so we can a write tactics *lift* which on a sequent σ generates the single subgoal $\vdash \mathit{true}(\ulcorner\sigma\urcorner)$ (with the appropriate level tag), and a tactic *drop* which on a sequent of the form $\vdash \mathit{true}(\ulcorner\sigma\urcorner)$ generates the single subgoal σ.

4.4 Deriving the Reflection Rule

Showing that the reflection rule is redundant is now straightforward. We informally describe the actions a tactic could be programmed to take to emulate the reflection rule.

Suppose that we want to apply to a sequent σ the reflection rule at level i with tactic t and subgoal generator u. Using the tactic *lift* we can reduce σ to $\vdash \mathit{true}(\ulcorner\sigma\urcorner)$. Let R be the formula

$$\begin{aligned}&t(\ulcorner\sigma\urcorner) \in \mathit{Proof} \,\&\, \mathit{root}(t(\ulcorner\sigma\urcorner)) \sim \ulcorner\sigma\urcorner \,\&\, \mathit{assums}(t(\ulcorner\sigma\urcorner)) \sim u(\ulcorner\sigma\urcorner)\\ &\&\, \mathit{level}(t(\ulcorner\sigma\urcorner)) < \underline{i}.\end{aligned}$$

Find the list $\sigma_1, \ldots, \sigma_n$ of sequents that $u(\ulcorner\sigma\urcorner)$ represents (if this list does not exist then i, u, t, and σ could not be part of an instance of the reflection rule). Using the cut rule $n+1$ times with the formulas R and $\mathit{true}(\ulcorner\sigma_i\urcorner)$, $1 \leq i \leq n$, we get $n+2$ subgoals. The first is $\vdash R$ which is the first subgoal of the reflection rule. The next n are the sequents $\vdash \mathit{true}(\ulcorner\sigma_i\urcorner)$, and these can be reduced to the remaining subgoals of the reflection rule by using the tactic *drop.* The remaining subgoal is

$$\mathcal{H} \vdash \mathit{true}(\ulcorner\sigma\urcorner)$$

where $\mathcal{H}$ contains the $n+1$ cut formulas. Because proofs are valid internally, this sequent is provable.

ACKNOWLEDGMENTS

We wish to thank Bill Aitken for his careful reading of the technical portions of this paper. This work was supported, in part, by the Office of Naval Research under contract N00014-88-K-0409.

REFERENCES

[1] S. F. Allen. *A Non-Type-Theoretic Semantics for Type-Theoretic Language.* PhD thesis, Cornell University, 1987.

[2] S. F. Allen. A non-type theoretic definition of Martin-Löf's types. In *Proceedings of the Second Annual Symposium on Logic in Computer Science*, pages 215–221. IEEE, 1987.

[3] S. F. Allen, R. L. Constable, and D. J. Howe. Reflecting the open-ended computation system of constructive type theory. In *Working Material, International Summer School on Logic, Algebra and Computation*, Marktoberdorf, West Germany, 1989.

[4] S. F. Allen, R. L. Constable, D. J. Howe, and W. E. Aitken. The semantics of reflected proof. In *Proceedings of the Fifth Annual IEEE Symposium on Logic and Computer Science*, pages 95–107. IEEE Computer Society, June 1990.

[5] G. S. Boolos and R. C. Jeffrey. *Computability and Logic.* Cambridge University Press, Cambridge, third edition, 1989.

[6] R. Constable and J. Bates. The Nearly Ultimate Pearl. Technical Report TR 83-551, Cornell University, Ithaca, NY, January 1983.

[7] R. Constable and D. Howe. Implementing metamathematics as an approach to automatic theorem proving. In R. Banerji, editor, *Formal Techniques in Artificial Intelligence: A Source Book.* Elsevier Science Publishers (North-Holland), 1990.

[8] R. L. Constable, et al. *Implementing Mathematics with the Nuprl Proof Development System.* Prentice-Hall, Englewood Cliffs, New Jersey, 1980.

[9] S. Feferman. A language and axioms for explicit mathematics. In Dold, A. and B. Eckmann, editor, *Algebra and Logic*, volume 450 of *Lecture Notes in Mathematics*, pages 87–139. Springer-Verlag, 1975.

[10] J. Y. Girard, P. Taylor, and Y. Lafont. *Proofs and Types*, volume 7 of *Cambridge Tracts in Computer Science.* Cambridge University Press, 1989.

[11] M. Gordon. A proof generating system for higher-order logic. In *Proceedings of the Hardware Verification Workshop*, 1989.

[12] M. J. Gordon, R. Milner, and C. P. Wadsworth. *Edinburgh LCF: A Mechanized Logic of Computation*, volume 78 of *Lecture Notes in Computer Science.* Springer-Verlag, 1979.

[13] D. J. Howe. *Automating Reasoning in an Implementation of Constructive Type Theory.* PhD thesis, Cornell University, 1988.

[14] D. J. Howe. Computational metatheory in Nuprl. In E. Lusk and R. Overbeek, editors, *9th International Conference on Automated Deduction*, pages 238–257, New York, 1988. Springer-Verlag.

[15] D. J. Howe. Equality in lazy computation systems. In *Proceedings of the Fourth Annual Symposium on Logic in Computer Science*, pages 198–203. IEEE Computer Society, June 1989.

[16] D. J. Howe. On computational open-endedness in Martin-Löf's type theory. In *Proceedings of the Sixth Annual Symposium on Logic in Computer Science.* IEEE Computer Society, 1991.

[17] G. Kahn. Natural semantics. In *Proceedings of the Symposium on Theoretical Aspects of Computer Software*, pages 22–39. Springer-Verlag LNCS, 1987. Vol. 247.

[18] T. B. Knoblock. *Metamathematical Extensibility in Type Theory.* PhD thesis, Cornell University, 1987.

[19] T. B. Knoblock and R. L. Constable. Formalized metareasoning in type theory. In *Proceedings of the First Annual Symposium on Logic in Computer Science.* IEEE, 1986.

[20] P. Martin-Löf. Constructive mathematics and computer programming. In *Sixth International Congress for Logic, Methodology, and Philosophy of Science*, pages 153–175, Amsterdam, 1982. North Holland.

[21] L. C. Paulson. *Logic and Computation: Interactive Proof with Cambridge LCF.* Cambridge University Press, Cambridge, 1987.

[22] G. Plotkin. A structural approach to operational semantics. Technical report, Computer Science Department, Aarhus University, 1981.

[23] A. S. Troelstra, editor. *Metamathematical Investigation of Intuitionistic Arithmetic and Analysis*, volume 344 of *Lecture Notes in Mathematics.* Springer-Verlag, 1973.

Fragments of Kripke-Platek set theory with infinity

M. RATHJEN

Fragments of Kripke–Platek Set Theory with Infinity

MICHAEL RATHJEN*

Institut für Mathematische Logik der Universität Münster

1 Introduction

Kripke-Platek set theory plus Infinity (hereinafter called KPω) is a truly remarkable subsystem of ZF. Though considerably weaker than ZF, a great deal of set theory requires only the axioms of this subsystem (cf.[Ba]). KPω consists of the axioms Extensionality, Pair, Union, (Set)Foundation, Infinity, along with the schemas of Δ_0–Collection, Δ_0–Separation, and Foundation for Definable Classes. So KPω arises from ZF by completely omitting Power Set and restricting Separation and Collection to Δ_0–formulas. These alterations are suggested by the informal notion of "predicative". KPω is an impredicative theory, notwithstanding. It is known from [Ho1], [Ho2] and [J] that KPω proves the same arithmetical sentences as Feferman's system ID_1 of positive inductive definitions (cf.[Fe]). Its proof–theoretic ordinal is the Howard ordinal $\theta\varepsilon_{\Omega+1}0$.

This article deals with fragments resulting from KPω by restricting the amount of foundation. The *Foundation Schema* is considered in the form

$$\forall x[(\forall y \in x)A(y) \rightarrow A(x)] \rightarrow \forall x A(x).$$

For a class of set–theoretic formulas $\mathcal{H}$, we denote by *$\mathcal{H}$–Foundation* this schema with $A(x)$ belonging to $\mathcal{H}$.

KPω^- is KPω without the Foundation Schema.
As usual, L_α denotes the α–th level of the constructible hierarchy.

A set–theoretic formula is said to be Π_k (respectively Σ_k) if it consists of a string of k alternating quantifiers beginning with an universal (respectively existential) one, followed by a Δ_0–formula. A Δ_0*–formula* is a set–theoretic formula in which all quantifiers appear restricted.
The division of Foundation into Σ_k– and Π_k–Foundation is reminiscent of

*This work was supported in part by the Deutsche Forschungsgemeinschaft the commonly used hierarchy of subsystems of PA (= Peano Arithmetic). However, while Σ^0_n–Induction and Π^0_n–Induction are equivalent over PA without Induction, neither Π_n–Foundation nor Σ_n–Foundation needs to imply the other over $\mathrm{KP}\omega^-$ (according to R. Lubarsky; personal communication).

1.1 Definition. Let T be a subtheory of ZFC. For a collection of set theoretic sentences $\mathcal{H}$, we call L_α an *$\mathcal{H}$–model of T* if $\mathsf{L}_\alpha \models A$ holds for all theorems A of T with A from $\mathcal{H}$. By $|T|_{\mathcal{H}}$ we denote the least ordinal $\alpha > 0$ such that L_α is an $\mathcal{H}$ model of T.

$\alpha = |T|_{\Pi_2}$ will serve as a measure of strength for T. This is because for theories T (entailing $\mathrm{KP}\omega^- + \Sigma_1$–Foundation), L_α is the least (non empty) transitive set closed under functions Σ_1–*definable in T*. Here a function $f : V \longrightarrow V$ ($V :=$ universe of sets) is called Σ_1–definable in T if there is a Σ_1–formula $A(x, y)$ such that $V \models \forall x A(x, f(x))$ and $T \vdash \forall x\, \exists! y A(x, y)$. Another justification for viewing $|T|_{\Pi_2}$ as a good measure of strength is that this ordinal equals the proof-theoretic ordinal $|T|$ of T (defined in [P]) provided that T is an impredicative theory.

In terms of Feferman-Aczel functions θ_α (cf. [Schü IX]), the main result of this paper reads as follows (with $\Omega := \Omega_1$):

1.2 Theorem. *Let $\delta_1 = \Omega^\omega$, $\delta_{k+1} = \Omega^{\delta_k}$. Then*

$$|\mathrm{KP}\omega^- + \Pi_{n+1}\text{–Foundation}| = |\mathrm{KP}\omega^- + \Pi_{n+1}\text{–Foundation}|_{\Pi_2} = \theta\delta_n 0$$

holds for $n \geq 1$.

Let *$\mathcal{H}$–Induction* denote the schema

$$F(0) \wedge (\forall x \in \omega)[F(x) \rightarrow F(x+1)] \rightarrow (\forall x \in \omega) F(x)$$

where $F(x)$ is an $\mathcal{H}$–formula and ω stands for the first limit ordinal.
By *IND* we denote $\mathcal{H}$–Induction with $\mathcal{H}$ the collection of all set theoretic formulas.

By employing an infinitary calculus with ω–rule, the methods used for establishing 1.2 can also be utilized to show the following result:

1.2* **Theorem.** *For $n \geq 1$, we have*

$$|\mathrm{KP}\omega^- + \Pi_{n+1}\text{–Foundation} + \mathit{IND}|_{\Pi_2} = \theta\eta_n 0$$

where $\eta_1 = \Omega^{\varepsilon_0}$ *and* $\eta_{k+1} = \Omega^{\eta_k}$.

There are some results known from the literature which we want to go into. They require some notations.

1.3 Definition. For ordinals α, we define a function φ_α from ordinals to ordinals by the following recursion: $\varphi_0(\xi)$ is ω^ξ; for $\alpha > 0$, $\varphi_\alpha(\xi)$ is the ξth simultaneous fixed point of all functions φ_β with $\beta < \alpha$.
We write ε_α for $\varphi_1(\alpha)$ and $\varphi\alpha\beta$ for $\varphi_\alpha(\beta)$. The least α such that $\varphi\alpha 0 = \alpha$ is usually denoted by Γ_0. For further background information on these functions cf.[Schü] and [P].

Cantini ([Ca2]) proves $\mid \mathrm{KP}\omega^- + \Sigma_1\text{–Foundation} \mid_\Sigma = \varphi\omega 0$ and $\mid \mathrm{KP}\omega^- + \Sigma_1 - \text{Foundation} + \mathit{IND} \mid_\Sigma = \varphi\varepsilon_0 0$. Furthermore, it is known from Cantini [Ca1] that $\mid \mathrm{KP}\omega^- + \Pi_1 - \text{Foundation} + \mathit{IND} \mid_\Sigma = \varepsilon_0$. Here Σ means the smallest collection of formulas containing the Δ_0–formulas closed under $\wedge, \vee, (\exists x \in a), (\forall x \in a)$, and $\exists x$ (cf.[Ba]). The methods of [Ca1] can be easily adapted to yield $\mid \mathrm{KP}\omega^- + \Pi_1\text{–Foundation} + \Sigma_1\text{–Induction} \mid_{\Pi_2} = \omega^\omega$. However, Π_1–Foundation is not Foundation enough to yield an interesting fragment of KPω. KPω^- + Π_1–Foundation + *IND* is even too weak to prove totality of the ordinal function $\alpha \mapsto \alpha + \alpha$.

We commence with a brief description of the content of this paper. In Section 2 we set up sequent calculus versions of KPω^- and KPω^-+ω–rule, the benefit of which is to admit partial cut–elimination. This technique will be exploited in Section 3. We also show that $\mid T \mid_{\Sigma_1}$ and $\mid T \mid_{\Pi_2}$ coincide for reasonable theories T. Section 3 is devoted to establishing upper bounds for $\mid \mathrm{KP}\omega^- + \Pi_n\text{–Foundation} \mid_{\Pi_2}$ where $n \geq 2$. This requires elaborated techniques from impredicative proof theory. In part we shall build on Pohlers [P] (this volume). Finally, we show in Section 4 that the upper bounds obtained in Section 3 are best possible. Unfortunately, it is by no means clear how to adapt the techniques used for Π_n–Foundation to Σ_n–Foundation.

2 Partial models, partial cut–elimination

The usual proof of the Σ Reflection Principle goes through in KPω^- (cf.[Ba I.4.3]). In particular, every Σ–formula is equivalent to a Σ_1–formula in KPω^-. Therefore, KPω^-+Σ_1–Foundation implies Σ-Foundation. Moreover, if T comprises KPω^-, every Σ_1–model of T needs to be a Σ–model of T. By the next theorem we can even go further. Hereinafter, we use the following notations: If B is a formula then B^a results from B by replacing each unrestricted quantifier $\forall y(\cdots)$ and $\exists y(\cdots)$ by $(\forall y \in a)(\cdots)$ and $(\exists y \in a)(\cdots)$, respectively (cf.[Ba I.4]).

2.1 Theorem. *Let* $\mathrm{KP}\omega^- \subseteq T$. *Furthermore, suppose that* $T \vdash B$ *implies* $T \vdash \exists\alpha\exists x(x = L_\alpha \wedge B^x)$ *for all* Σ_1*-sentences* B. *If* T *has a* Σ_1*-model then* T *has a* Π_2*-model and*

$$|T|_{\Sigma_1} = |T|_{\Pi_2} .$$

Proof. Let L_σ be the minimal Σ_1-model of T. Assume $T \vdash \forall u \exists w H(u,w)$ with $H(u,w)$ being Δ_0. Let $a \in \mathsf{L}_\sigma$. We have to verify that $\mathsf{L}_\sigma \models \exists w H(a,w)$. σ is a limit, so there is $\xi < \sigma$ such that $a \in \mathsf{L}_\xi$. Since L_ξ is not a Σ_1 model of T, we have $T \vdash B$ and $\mathsf{L}_\xi \models \neg B$ for some Σ_1 sentence B. By assumption, we also get $T \vdash \exists\alpha\exists x(x = \mathsf{L}_\alpha \wedge B^x)$. Then, using Δ_0–Collection, we obtain

$$T \vdash \exists z \exists\alpha\exists x[x = \mathsf{L}_\alpha \wedge B^x \wedge (\forall u \in x)(\exists w \in z) H(u,w)]$$

Since this formula is equivalent to a Σ_1–formula in $\mathrm{KP}\omega^-$, we get $\mathsf{L}_\sigma \models \exists\alpha\exists x[x = \mathsf{L}_\alpha \wedge B^x \wedge (\forall u \in x)\exists w H(u,w)]$. As σ is a limit $> \omega$, the formula "$x = \mathsf{L}_\alpha$" doesn't shift its meaning when we move from L_σ to the universe (see [D II.2.12]). Hence there exists $\alpha < \sigma$ such that $\mathsf{L}_\alpha \models B$ and $(\forall u \in \mathsf{L}_\alpha)(\exists w \in \mathsf{L}_\sigma) H(u,w)$. By the choice of B, this implies $\xi < \alpha$, hence $a \in \mathsf{L}_\alpha$, thus $\mathsf{L}_\sigma \models \exists w H(a,w)$. □

2.2 Remark. The construction of the constructible hierarchy can be carried out in $\mathrm{KP}\omega^- + \Sigma_1$–Foundation, and it can be shown that for every theorem A of $\mathrm{KP}\omega^-$, we have $\mathrm{KP}\omega^- + \Sigma_1$–Foundation $\vdash A^{\mathsf{L}}$ (cf.[Ba]). Hence the theorem above applies to such theories as $\mathrm{KP}\omega^- + \Pi_k$–Foundation $+ \Pi_r$–*IND* and $\mathrm{KP}\omega^- + \Sigma_n$–Foundation $+ \Pi_r$–*IND*, where $k \geq 2$ and $n, r \geq 1$.

When using $|T|_{\Pi_2}$ as a measure of strength, one is naturally led to ask for the relation of this ordinal to the proof–theoretic ordinal $|T|$ of T (cf.[P]). As a rule of thumb we have for $\alpha = \omega^\alpha$ and $\mathrm{KP}\omega^- \subseteq T \subseteq \mathrm{KP}\omega$

$$|T|_{\Pi_2} = \alpha \Rightarrow |T| = \varphi\alpha 0.$$

Why? Usually, the proof of $|T|_{\Pi_2} \geq \alpha$ lends itself to an interpretation of the system $RA_{<\alpha}$ of ramified analysis in T (cf.[FS] and [Schü]). Schütte established that $|RA_{<\alpha}| = \varphi\alpha 0$. Since for the theories T we have in mind here, the determination of $|T|_{\Pi_2}$ also yields an embedding of T into a system $RS_{<\alpha}$ of ramified set theory, we also get $|T| \leq \varphi\alpha 0$ by the methods of [P Theorem 25].

For technical reasons we shall diverge from the usual presentation of $\mathrm{KP}\omega$. As our basic system underlying the various theories we choose a Tait–style

sequent calculus version of $KP\omega^-$ in which finite sets of formulas can be derived. In addition, formulas have to be in negation normal form (cf.[Schw]).
The language consists of: free variables $a_0, a_1, \cdots$, bound variables $x_0, x_1, \cdots$; the predicate symbol $\in$; the logical symbols $\neg, \vee, \wedge, \forall, \exists$.
We will use $a, b, c, \cdots,\ x, y, z, \cdots,\ A, B, C, \cdots$ as metavariables whose domains are the domain of the free variables, bound variables, formulas, respectively.
The *atomic formulas* are those of the form $(s \in t), \neg(s \in t)$.
The *formulas* are defined inductively as follows:
(i) Atomic formulas are formulas.
(ii) If A and B are formulas, then so are $(A \wedge B)$ and $(A \vee B)$.
(iii) If $A(b)$ is a formula in which x does not occur, then $\forall x A(x), \exists x A(x)$, $(\forall x \in a)A(x), (\exists x \in a)A(x)$ are formulas.
The quantifiers $\exists x, \forall x$ will be called *unrestricted.* A Δ_0*–formula* is a formula which contains no unrestricted quantifiers.
The *negation* $\neg A$ of a formula A is defined to be the formula obtained from A by (i) putting $\neg$ in front of any atomic formula, (ii) replacing $\wedge, \vee, \forall x, \exists x, (\forall x \in a), (\exists x \in a)$ by $\vee, \wedge, \exists x, \forall x, (\exists x \in a), (\forall x \in a)$, respectively, and (iii) dropping double negations.
$\vec{a}, \vec{b}, \vec{c}, \cdots$ and $\vec{x}, \vec{y}, \vec{z}, \cdots$ will be used to denote finite sequences of free and bound variables, respectively.
We use $F[a_1, \cdots, a_n]$ (by contrast with $F(a_1, \cdots, a_n)$) to denote a formula the free variables of which are among $a_1, \cdots, a_n$. We will write
$a = \{x \in b : G(x)\}$ for $(\forall x \in a)[x \in b \wedge G(x)] \wedge (\forall x \in b)[G(x) \rightarrow x \in a]$.
By $\mathsf{Tran}(a)$, $\mathsf{Ord}(a)$, $\mathsf{Lim}(a)$ we abbreviate the Δ_0–formulas expressing that a is transitive, a is an ordinal, a is a limit ordinal, respectively.
$a = b$ stands for $(\forall x \in a)(x \in b) \wedge (\forall x \in b)(x \in a)$.

2.3 Definition. (The theory T_n) T_n derives finite sets of formulas denoted by $\Gamma, \Lambda, \Theta, \Xi, \cdots$. The intended meaning of Γ is the disjunction of all formulas of Γ. We use the notation Γ, A for $\Gamma \cup \{A\}$, Γ, Ξ for $\Gamma \cup \Xi$.

The *axioms of* T_n are:

Logical axioms:	$\Gamma, A, \neg A$ for every Δ_0–formula A.
Extensionality:	$\Gamma, a{=}b \wedge B(a) \rightarrow B(b)$ for every Δ_0-formula $B(a)$.
Pair:	$\Gamma, \exists x[a \in x \wedge b \in x]$
Union:	$\Gamma, \exists x(\forall y \in a)(\forall z \in y)(z \in x)$
Δ_0 *–Separation:*	$\Gamma, \exists y(y = \{x \in a : G(x)\})$ for every Δ_0–formula $G(b)$.
Foundation Axiom:	$\Gamma, (\exists x \in a)(x \in a) \rightarrow (\exists y \in a)(\forall z \in y)\neg(z \in a)$
Infinity:	$\Gamma, \exists x\, \mathsf{Lim}(x)$.

The *logical rules of inferences* are:

$(\wedge)$	$\vdash \Gamma, A$ and $\vdash \Gamma, B$	$\Rightarrow$	$\vdash \Gamma, A \wedge B$
$(\vee)$	$\vdash \Gamma, A_i$ for $i \in \{0,1\}$	$\Rightarrow$	$\vdash \Gamma, A_0 \vee A_1$
$(b\forall)$	$\vdash \Gamma, a \in b \rightarrow F(a)$	$\Rightarrow$	$\vdash \Gamma, (\forall x \in b) F(x)$
$(\forall)$	$\vdash \Gamma, F(a)$	$\Rightarrow$	$\vdash \Gamma, \forall x F(x)$
$(b\exists)$	$\vdash \Gamma, a \in b \wedge F(a)$	$\Rightarrow$	$\vdash \Gamma, (\exists x \in b) F(x)$
$(\exists)$	$\vdash \Gamma, F(a)$	$\Rightarrow$	$\vdash \Gamma, \exists x F(x)$
(Cut)	$\vdash \Gamma, A$ and $\vdash \Gamma, \neg A$	$\Rightarrow$	$\vdash \Gamma$.

Of course, it is demanded that in $(b\forall)$ and $(\forall)$ the free variable a is not to occur in the conclusion; a is called the *eigenvariable* of that inference.

The *non-logical rules of inferences* are:

$(\Delta_0$–COLLR) $\vdash \Gamma, (\forall x \in a) \exists y H(x,y) \quad \Rightarrow \quad \vdash \Gamma, \exists z (\forall x \in a)(\exists y \in z) H(x,y)$

for every Δ_0–formula $H(b,c)$.

$(\Pi_n$–FR) $\vdash \Gamma, \exists x \exists y \neg Q\vec{z}\,[x \in a \rightarrow H(x,y,\vec{z})],\ Q\vec{z} H(a,b,\vec{z}) \quad \Rightarrow$
$\vdash \Gamma, Q\vec{z} H(c,d,\vec{z})$,

where $Q\vec{z}$ stands for a string of n–1 alternating quantifiers beginning with an existential one, and $H(a,b,\vec{e})$ is a Δ_0–formula. In addition, it is demanded that a and b are different free variables neither appearing in formulas of Γ nor in $\forall x \forall y Q\vec{z} H(x,y,\vec{z})$.

We shall conceive of axioms as inferences with an empty set of premisses. The *minor formulas* (m.f.) of an inference are those formulas which are rendered prominently in its premises. The *principal formulas* (p.f.) of an inference are the formulas rendered prominently in its conclusion. (Cut) has no p.f. So any inference has the form

$$(*) \quad \text{For all } i < k \ \vdash \Gamma, \Xi_i \quad \Rightarrow \quad \vdash \Gamma, \Xi$$

$(0 \le k \le 2)$, where Ξ consists of the p.f. and Ξ_i is the set of m.f. in the i–th premise. The formulas in Γ are called *side formulas* (s.f.) of $(*)$. *Derivations* of T_n are defined inductively, as usual. $\mathcal{D}$,$\mathcal{D}$',$\mathcal{D}_0, \cdots$ range as syntactic variables over T_n derivations. All this is completely standard, and we refer to [Schw] for notions like "*length of a derivation* $\mathcal{D}$" (abbreviated by $|\mathcal{D}|$), "*last inference of* $\mathcal{D}$", "*direct subderivation of* $\mathcal{D}$". We write $\mathcal{D} \vdash \Gamma$ if $\mathcal{D}$ is a derivation of Γ.

We are not going to prove Theorem 1.2*. In order to get this result, one has to adapt the techniques of this article to an infinitary system $\mathrm{KP}\omega_{\infty}^{-}$.

In addition to the language of $\mathrm{KP}\omega^-$, the language of $\mathrm{KP}\omega_\infty^-$ has constants $\underline{\omega}$ and $\underline{n}$ for every $n \in \mathbb{N}$. Additional axioms of $\mathrm{KP}\omega_\infty^-$ are

$$\Gamma, \mathsf{Lim}(\underline{\omega}) \wedge (\forall x \in \underline{\omega})\neg\mathsf{Lim}(x),$$

$$\Gamma, \underline{n} \in \underline{\omega},$$

$$\Gamma, \underline{n} \in \underline{m},$$

$$\Gamma, \underline{n'} \notin \underline{m'}$$

if $n < m$ and $n' \not< m'$.
Of course, the axioms and rules of inferences of $\mathrm{KP}\omega^-$ have to be adapted to the enriched language. Furthermore, we have in $\mathrm{KP}\omega_\infty^-$ the infinitary *ω–rule.*

$$\vdash \Gamma, F(\underline{n}) \text{ for every } n \in \mathbb{N} \Rightarrow \vdash \Gamma, (\forall x \in \underline{\omega})F(x).$$

$\mathrm{KP}\omega_\infty^-$ derivations may be infinite. The ω-rule allows one to derive all instances of *IND*.

The most fundamental property of sequent calculi is cut–elimination. Our sequent calculus T_n admits cut–elimination as far as it concerns cuts the cut formula of which is neither a principal formula of a non–logical rule of inference nor a principal formula of an axiom. This is a general phenomenon which will be exploited next. In order to state this fact in more precise terms, let us introduce a measure of complexity $cp(A)$ for formulas A:

Let $cp(A) = 0$ if A is Δ_0. If A is not Δ_0, then $cp(A)$ is inductively defined as follows: $cp(A) = \sup(cp(B), cp(C)) + 1$ if $A \in \{B \wedge C, B \vee C\}$; $cp(A) = cp(F(a)) + 2$ if $A \in \{(\forall x \in b)F(x), (\exists x \in b)F(x)\}$; $cp(A) = cp(F(a)) + 1$ if $A \in \{\forall x F(x), \exists x F(x)\}$.

The *cut–rank* $\rho(\mathcal{D})$ of a derivation $\mathcal{D}$ is also defined by induction:
Let $\mathcal{D}_i$, $i < k$, be the direct subderivations of $\mathcal{D}$. If the last inference of $\mathcal{D}$ is (Cut) with m.f. A and $\neg A$, let $\rho(\mathcal{D}) = \sup(cp(A) + 1, \sup\{\rho(\mathcal{D}_i) : i < k\}$. Otherwise, let $\rho(\mathcal{D}) = \sup\{\rho(\mathcal{D}_i) : i < k\}$. By $T_n \overset{k}{\underset{m}{\vdash}} \Gamma$ we mean that there is a derivation $\mathcal{D} \vdash \Gamma$ such that $|\mathcal{D}| \leq k$ and $\rho(\mathcal{D}) \leq m$.

2.4 Theorem. (Cut–elimination) *Let* $2_0^k := k$ *and* $2_{m+1}^k := 2^l$ *where* $l := 2_m^k$. *If* $n \geq 2$ *and* $T_n \overset{k}{\underset{n+m}{\vdash}} \Gamma$, *then* $T_n \overset{p}{\underset{n}{\vdash}} \Gamma$ *where* $p := 2_m^k$.

Proof. Observe that $cp(A) < n$ holds for every p.f. A of an axiom or a non logical rule of inference. So the result can be gotten by the same proof as in [Schw]. □

One readily verifies that T_n proves every theorem of $\mathrm{KP}\omega^-$. Thus it remains to verify:

2.5 Proposition. $T_n \vdash \Pi_n$–Foundation.

Proof. Let $Q\vec{z}H(a,b,\vec{z})$ be Σ_{n-1} with $H(a,b,e)$ Δ_0, $a \not\equiv b$ fresh. Then

$$T_n \vdash (\forall x \in a)\forall y Q\vec{z}H(x,y,\vec{z}), \exists x \exists y \neg Q\vec{z}[x \in a \to H(x,y,\vec{z})]$$

and

$$T_n \vdash \exists y \neg Q\vec{z}H(a,y,\vec{z}), Q\vec{z}H(a,b,\vec{z})$$

yield

$$T_n \vdash B(a), \exists x \exists y \neg Q\vec{z}[x \in a \to H(x,y,\vec{z})],\ Q\vec{z}H(a,b,\vec{z})$$

with $B(a) \equiv (\forall x \in a)\forall y Q\vec{z}H(x,y,\vec{z}) \wedge \exists y \neg Q\vec{z}H(a,y,\vec{z})$.
By $(\exists)$ we get

$$T_n \vdash \exists u B(u), \exists x \exists y \neg Q\vec{z}[x \in a \to H(x,y,\vec{z})], Q\vec{z}H(a,b,\vec{z}).$$

Using $(\Pi_n\text{–FR})$ we obtain $T_n \vdash \exists u B(u), Q\vec{z}H(a,b,\vec{z})$, thus, by $(\forall)$,

$$T_n \vdash \exists u B(u), \forall u \forall y Q\vec{z}H(u,y,\vec{z}).$$

Now apply $(\vee)$ twice to obtain $T_n \vdash \exists u B(u) \vee \forall u \forall y Q\vec{z}H(u,y,\vec{z})$. □

In the next section we shall embed T_n into an infinitary calculus $RS(\Omega)$. To handle this with optimal ordinal bounds, we have to resort to very well behaved derivations.

2.6 Definition. A T_n derivation $\mathcal{D} \vdash \Gamma$ is said to be *n–nice* if $\rho(\mathcal{D}) \leq n$ and every Σ_n–formula which is a side formula of an inference of $\mathcal{D}$ belongs to Γ. In other words, if A is Σ_n and $A \notin \Gamma$ then A can only appear in $\mathcal{D}$ as a m.f. or p.f. of an inference of $\mathcal{D}$.

Let $\exists\Sigma_n$ be the collection of formulas of the shape $\exists x \exists y A(x,y)$ with $A(a,b) \in \Pi_{n-1}$.
Let

$$\Sigma_n^* := \exists\Sigma_n \cup \bigcup_{i \leq n} \Sigma_i \cup \bigcup_{j<n} \Pi_j \cup \Sigma.$$

2.7 Lemma. *Let* $\Gamma \subseteq \Sigma_n^*$, $\Xi = \{\exists z_1 B_1(b_1,z_1), \cdots, \exists z_r B_r(b_r,z_r)\} \subseteq \Sigma_n$, $\Theta = \{\exists y_1 \exists z_1 B_1(y_1,z_1), \cdots, \exists y_r \exists z_r B_r(b_r,z_r)\}$.

(i) *If* $\mathcal{D} \vdash \Gamma, \Xi$, *then we can find an n–nice* $\mathcal{D}^\star \vdash \Gamma, \Theta$.

(ii) *If $\mathcal{D}_0 \vdash \Gamma$, then there is an n–nice $\mathcal{D}_0^\star \vdash \Gamma$.*

Proof. (i) By 2.4 we may assume $\rho(\mathcal{D}) \leq n$. We proceed by induction on $|\mathcal{D}|$. If Γ, Ξ is an axiom, then so is Γ; hence Γ, Θ is an axiom. The derivation consisting of this axiom is n–nice. Now suppose $0 < |\mathcal{D}|$. If neither a m.f. nor a p.f. of the last inference (l.i.) of $\mathcal{D}$ is Σ_n, then the assertion follows immediately by induction hypothesis.
Now assume that a formula $\exists z A(b, z) \in \Sigma_n$ is a m.f. of the l.i. of $\mathcal{D}$. Then this must be an instance of $(\exists)$ because $\rho(\mathcal{D}) \leq n$ and $\Gamma, \Xi \subseteq \Sigma_n^\star$. So we have a p.f. $\exists y \exists z A(y, z) \in \Gamma$ and the direct subderivation $\mathcal{D}_0$ takes the form $\mathcal{D}_0 \vdash \Lambda, \Xi'$ with $\Lambda \subseteq \Gamma$ and $\Xi' = \Xi, \exists z A(b, z)$. Now apply the induction hypothesis to this situation to get an n–nice derivation $\mathcal{D}^\star \vdash \Lambda, \Theta, \exists y \exists z A(y, z)$. As $\Lambda, \Theta, \exists y \exists z A(y, z) = \Gamma$, this gives the assertion.
Finally, suppose that $\exists z B(z) \in \Sigma_n$ is the p.f. of the l.i. of $\mathcal{D}$. This must be an instance of $(\exists)$. So there is a derivation $\mathcal{D}_0 \vdash \Gamma, \Xi, B(b)$ such that $\rho(\mathcal{D}_0) \leq n$ and $|\mathcal{D}_0| < |\mathcal{D}|$. Inductively we find an n–nice derivation $\mathcal{D}_0^\star \vdash \Gamma, \Theta, B(b)$. By use of $(\exists)$, we can continue $\mathcal{D}_0^\star$ to an n–nice derivation of $\Gamma, \Theta, \exists z B(z)$. If $\exists z B(z) \in \Gamma$, we are done. Otherwise, $\exists z B(z) \in \Xi$, thus another application of $(\exists)$ gives us an n–nice derivation $\mathcal{D}^\star \vdash \Gamma, \Theta$, since then $\exists z B(z)$ does not appear as a s.f. in $\mathcal{D}_0^\star$.
(ii) follows from (i) with $\Xi = \emptyset$. □

3 Upper Bounds

The reader would be advised to acquaint himself with [P Part II]. In this Section we adopt the calculus $RS(\Omega)$ and the terminology of [P].
The derivability relation $RS(\Omega) \mathrel{|\!\!\frac{\alpha}{\rho}} \Gamma$ embodies the notion of $RS(\Omega)$–derivation. We shall write $\mathcal{D}_\Omega \mathrel{|\!\!\frac{\alpha}{\rho}} \Gamma$ if $\mathcal{D}_\Omega$ is a proof tree witnessing $RS(\Omega) \mathrel{|\!\!\frac{\alpha}{\rho}} \Gamma$. We shall use $\mathcal{D}_\Omega, \mathcal{D}_\Omega^n, \cdots$ as syntactic variables for $RS(\Omega)$ derivations.
An $\mathcal{L}_{RS}$–formula is $\Sigma_n(\mathsf{L}_\alpha)$ $(\Pi_n(\mathsf{L}_n))$ if it is of the form $A(s_1, \cdots, s_n)^{\mathsf{L}_\alpha}$ for a Σ_n–formula (Π_n–formula) $A(a_1, \cdots, a_n)$ and RS–terms $s_1, \cdots, s_n$ being members of RS_α. Likewise, an $\mathcal{L}_{RS}$–formula is $\Sigma_n^*(\mathsf{L}_\alpha)$ if it is of the form $A(s_1, \cdots, s_n)^{\mathsf{L}_\alpha}$ with $A(a_1, \cdots, a_n)$ being Σ_n^* and $s_1, \cdots, s_n$ being members of RS_α.
Analogous with T_n, we say that a $RS(\Omega)$ derivation $\mathcal{D}_\Omega \mathrel{|\!\!\frac{\alpha}{\rho}} \Gamma$ is *n–nice* if $\rho < \Omega + n$ and every $\Sigma_n(\mathsf{L}_\Omega)$–formula appearing as a side formula of an inference of $\mathcal{D}_\Omega$ belongs to Γ.
If Γ is a set of $\mathcal{L}_{RS}$–formulas, we mean by $\Gamma \ll \alpha$ that $A \ll \alpha$ holds for every member A of Γ, where $A \ll \alpha$ means that, for every RS–term L_η occuring

in A, we have $\eta \ll \alpha$. $\alpha\#\beta$ stands for the natural sum of α and β (cf. [P Lemma 23]).

The nice thing about n–nice derivation is that they allow us to improve on the Reduction Lemma ([P Lemma 38]). But beforehand, we have to consider two simple transformations which lead from n–nice $RS(\Omega)$ derivations to n–nice $RS(\Omega)$ derivations.

3.1 Lemma. (Inversion and Weakening) *Let* $E \equiv (\forall y \in \mathsf{L}_\Omega)G(y)$. *Let* $s \in RS_\Omega$.

(i) If $\mathcal{D}_\Omega \mid\!\frac{\beta}{\rho}\ \Lambda, E$ *is an n–nice $RS(\Omega)$ derivation and* $|s| \ll \gamma$, *then there is an n–nice derivation* $\mathcal{D}_\Omega^\square$ *satisfying*

$$\mathcal{D}_\Omega^\square \mid\!\frac{\gamma\#\beta}{\rho}\ \Lambda, G(s)\,.$$

(ii) If $\mathcal{D}_\Omega \mid\!\frac{\beta}{\rho}\ \Gamma$ *is n–nice, then we can find an n–nice*

$$\mathcal{D}_\Omega^\diamond \mid\!\frac{\beta}{\rho}\ \Gamma, \Lambda\,.$$

Proof. Both of the assertions are to be proved by induction on β. (ii) is a triviality. As to (i), note that $E \notin \Sigma_n(\mathsf{L}_\Omega)$; thus cancelling E in a derivation does not affect its n–niceness. The additional parameter γ comes in when the last inference of $\mathcal{D}$ was an instance of $(\bigwedge)$ with principal formula E. In this situation we have a function f with $dom(f) = \mathcal{O}(E)$, $f \ll \beta$ and n–nice derivations $\mathcal{D}_\Omega^{G(t)} \mid\!\frac{f(G(t))}{\rho}\ \Lambda, E, G(t)$ for $t \in RS_\Omega$. Inductively we obtain an n–nice

$$\mathcal{D}_\Omega^\triangle \mid\!\frac{\gamma\#f(G(s))}{\rho}\ \Lambda, G(s)\,.$$

Now make use of $f \ll \beta$ and $|s| \ll \gamma$ to compute that $\gamma\#f(G(s)) \ll \gamma\#\beta$. Hence we get the desired derivation. □

3.2 Refined Reduction Lemma. *We identify* 0 *with* L_0. *Let* $B \equiv (\exists y \in \mathsf{L}_\Omega)(\exists z \in \mathsf{L}_\Omega)A(y,z)$ *where* $A(0,0)$ *is* $\Pi_{n-1}(\mathsf{L}_\Omega)$. *Let* $\rho = \Omega + (n-1)$. *Let* $\mathcal{D}_\Omega \mid\!\frac{\alpha}{\rho}\ \Gamma, B$ *as well as* $\mathcal{D}'_\Omega \mid\!\frac{\beta}{\rho}\ \Lambda, \neg B$ *be n–nice $RS(\Omega)$ derivations such that* $\Gamma, \Lambda \subseteq \Sigma_n^*(\mathsf{L}_\Omega)$. *Then we can find an n–nice derivation*

$$\mathcal{D}_\Omega^\star \mid\!\frac{\alpha\#\beta}{\rho}\ \Gamma, \Lambda\,.$$

Proof. By induction on α we construct a derivation $\mathcal{D}_\Omega^\star \mid\!\frac{\alpha\#\beta}{\rho}\ \Gamma, \Lambda$ such that every $\Sigma_n(\mathsf{L}_\Omega)$–formula appearing as a side formula in $\mathcal{D}_\Omega^\star$ also appears as a side formula in $\mathcal{D}_\Omega$ or $\mathcal{D}'_\Omega$. Hence, $\mathcal{D}_\Omega^\star$ will be automatically n–nice. We may assume that B is the *p.f.* of the *l.i.* of $\mathcal{D}_\Omega$ for otherwise the assertion follows immediately by induction hypothesis (*i.h.*). So the direct subderivation (*d.s.*) of $\mathcal{D}_\Omega$ has the form $\mathcal{D}^0_\Omega \stackrel{\alpha_0}{\vdash_\rho} \Gamma_0, C$ where $C \equiv (\exists z \in \mathsf{L}_\Omega)A(s,z)$, $\Gamma_0 \subseteq \Gamma, B$, $C \ll \alpha$, and $\alpha_0 \ll \alpha$. If $C \in \Gamma$, then the *i.h.* gives us an n–nice derivation

$$\mathcal{D}^+_\Omega \stackrel{\alpha_0\#\beta}{\vdash_\rho} \Gamma_0 \setminus \{B\}, \Lambda, C,$$

so we get a derivation $\mathcal{D}^\star_\Omega \stackrel{\alpha\#\beta}{\vdash_\rho} \Gamma, \Lambda$ by Weakening. If $C \notin \Gamma$, then n–niceness of $\mathcal{D}_\Omega$ implies that the l.i. of $\mathcal{D}^0_\Omega$ is $(\bigvee)$ with p.f. C, and the d.s. $\mathcal{D}^1_\Omega$ of $\mathcal{D}^0_\Omega$ has the form $\mathcal{D}^1_\Omega \stackrel{\alpha_1}{\vdash_\rho} \Gamma_1, A(s,t)$ where $\Gamma_1 \subseteq \Gamma_0$ and $A(s,t), \alpha_1 \ll \alpha_0$ Using the i.h. and $\alpha_1\#\beta \ll \alpha_0\#\beta$ we find a derivation

$$\mathcal{D}^2_\Omega \stackrel{\alpha_0\#\beta}{\vdash_\rho} \Gamma_1 \setminus \{B\}, \Lambda, A(s,t)$$

with all the required properties. From $A(s,t) \ll \alpha_0$ it follows $|s|, |t| \ll \alpha_0$, provided that both of s and t occur in $A(s,t)$. But if, for instance, s would not occur in $A(s,t)$, then $A(s,t) \equiv A(0,t)$, so we would be able to replace s by 0. Therefore we may assume $|s|, |t| \ll \alpha_0$. Consequently, by the use of Inversion and Weakening (3.1), $\mathcal{D}'_\Omega$ yields an n–nice derivation

$$\mathcal{D}^3_\Omega \stackrel{\alpha_0\#\beta}{\vdash_\rho} \Lambda, \neg A(s,t).$$

Now continue $\mathcal{D}^2_\Omega$ and $\mathcal{D}^3_\Omega$ via (*cut*) to get a derivation $\mathcal{D}^\star_\Omega \stackrel{\alpha\#\beta}{\vdash_\rho} \Gamma, \Lambda$ such that every $\Sigma_n(\mathsf{L}_\Omega)$ *s.f.* of $\mathcal{D}^\star_\Omega$ is among the side formulas of $\mathcal{D}_\Omega$ or $\mathcal{D}'_\Omega$. To ensure this, note that $A(s,t) \ll \alpha_0 \ll \alpha\#\beta$. □

3.3 Theorem. (T_n Embedding Theorem) *Let $\vec{e}$ denote the string $e_1, \cdots, e_j$. Let $\Gamma[\vec{e}] = \{A_1[\vec{e}]\}, \cdots, A_l[\vec{e}]\}$ be a set of Σ^*_n–formulas. Suppose $T_n \vdash \Gamma[\vec{e}]$. Then we can find an integer $k > 0$ such that for all $RS(\Omega)$ terms $s_1, \cdots, s_j$ with stages $< \Omega$, there exists an n–nice $RS(\Omega)$ derivation*

$$\mathcal{D}_\Omega \stackrel{\alpha}{\vdash_\rho} \Gamma[\vec{s}]^{\mathsf{L}_\Omega}$$

where $\alpha = \Omega^k \# |s_1| \# \cdots \# |s_j|$ and $\rho = \Omega + (n-1)$.

Proof. By 2.7 there is an n–nice T_n derivation $\mathcal{D} \vdash \Gamma[\vec{e}]$. We proceed by induction on $|\mathcal{D}|$. If the l.i. of $\mathcal{D}$ is (Cut) with cut formula $A[\vec{e}]$ then $\mathrm{cp}(A[\vec{e}]) < n$. This implies $\mathrm{rk}(A[\vec{s}]^{\mathsf{L}_\Omega}) < \rho$. So the assertion follows from the i.h. via (*cut*).
Here we would like to refer to [P] for an embedding of KPω^- into $RS(\Omega)$ which takes account of the various axioms of KPω^- with precise ordinal bounds. Unfortunately, [P] does not supply the necessary information. Fortunately, there is another article in this volume that does. For most of the

embedding we shall rely on [Bu].

We now restrict our attention to the situation in which (Π_n–FR) is the last inference of $\mathcal{D}$. Then the d.s. of $\mathcal{D}$ has the form

$$\mathcal{D}^0 \vdash \Lambda[\vec{e}], \exists x \exists y \neg Q\vec{z}(x \in a \rightarrow H[x,y,\vec{z},\vec{e}]), Q\vec{z}H[a,b,\vec{z},\vec{e}]$$

with $\Lambda[\vec{e}], Q\vec{z}H[a,b,\vec{z},\vec{e}] \subseteq \Gamma[\vec{e}]$. Inductively there exists an integer $k_0 > 0$ such that for all $RS(\Omega)$ terms $\vec{s}, r, t$ with stages $< \Omega$, there is an n–nice $RS(\Omega)$–derivation.

$$(1) \qquad \mathcal{D}^1_\Omega \overset{\beta}{\underset{\rho}{\vdash}} X, D(r), E(r,t)$$

where $\beta = \Omega^{k_0} \# |\vec{s}| \# |r| \# |t|$, $X = \Lambda[\vec{s}]^{L_\Omega}$,

$$D(r) \equiv (\exists x \exists y \neg Q\vec{z}(x \in r \rightarrow H[x,y,\vec{z},\vec{s}]))^{L_\Omega},$$

and

$$E(r,t) \equiv (Q\vec{z}H[r,t,\vec{z},\vec{s}])^{L_\Omega}.$$

Letting $f(r,t) := (\Omega^{k_0} \cdot \omega^{|r|+1}) \# |\vec{s}| \# |t|$ we want to show that there exists an n–nice derivation

$$(\star) \qquad \mathcal{D}^{r,t}_\Omega \overset{f(r,t)}{\underset{\rho}{\vdash}} X, E(r,t).$$

To verify $(\star)$ we induct on $|r|$. By assumption, for all r', q satisfying $|r'| < |r|$, there exists an n–nice derivation

$$\mathcal{D}^{r',q}_\Omega \overset{f(r',q)}{\underset{\rho}{\vdash}} X, E(r',q).$$

For every p there is an n–nice (cf. [Bu Lemma 2.7])

$$\mathcal{D}^p_\Omega \overset{\eta}{\underset{0}{\vdash}} p \neq r', \neg E(r',q), E(p,q)$$

with $\eta = f(r',q) \# |p|$.
Using (*cut*) we obtain for every $|r'| < |r|$ an n–nice

$$\mathcal{D}^\star_\Omega \overset{\eta+1}{\underset{\rho}{\vdash}} p \neq r', E(p,q), X$$

since $\mathsf{rk}(E(r',q)) < \rho$. By applying ($\bigwedge$), we get an n–nice

$$\mathcal{D}^+_\Omega \overset{\gamma}{\underset{\rho}{\vdash}} p \notin r, E(p,q), X$$

with $\gamma := (\Omega^{k_0} \cdot \omega^{|r|}) \# |\vec{s}| \# |q| \# |p|$.
Letting

$$B(p,q,r) \equiv (Q\vec{z}(p \in r \rightarrow H[p,q,\vec{z},\vec{s}]))^{L_\Omega},$$

there are n–nice derivations

$$\mathcal{D}^{\diamond}_{\Omega} \overset{\gamma}{\underset{0}{\vdash}} p\in r, B(p,q,r) \text{ and } \mathcal{D}^{\heartsuit}_{\Omega} \overset{\gamma}{\underset{0}{\vdash}} \neg E(p,q), B(p,q,r).$$

So using cuts we arrive at an n–nice derivation $\mathcal{D}^{\triangle}_{\Omega} \overset{\gamma+3}{\underset{\rho}{\vdash}} B(p,q,r), X$. Applying two $(\bigwedge)$–inferences gives us an nice

$$(2) \qquad \mathcal{D}^{2}_{\Omega} \overset{\delta}{\underset{\rho}{\vdash}} X, \neg D(r)$$

where $\delta := (\Omega^{k_0} \cdot \omega^{|r|}) \# \, |\vec{s}| \, \# \Omega \# \Omega$. Now 3.2 applied to $\mathcal{D}^{1}_{\Omega}$ and $\mathcal{D}^{2}_{\Omega}$ ((1),(2)) yields the desired n–nice

$$\mathcal{D}^{r,t}_{\Omega} \overset{f(r,t)}{\underset{\rho}{\vdash}} X, E(r,t).$$

This finishes the proof of $(\star)$. From $(\star)$ the assertion follows with $k := k_0 + 1$. □

3.4 Theorem. *Set $\Omega^{\alpha}(0) := \alpha$ and $\Omega^{\alpha}(k+1) := \Omega^{\Omega^{\alpha}(k)}$. Let A be a Σ_1 sentence. Put $B \equiv A^{\mathsf{L}_{\Omega}}$. If $n \geq 2$ and* KPω^{-} + Π_n–Foundation $\vdash A$, *then $RS(\Omega) \overset{\beta}{\underset{\beta}{\vdash}} B$ holds for some $\beta < \vartheta_{\Omega^{\omega}(n-1)}(0)$.*

Proof. The assumption implies $T_n \vdash A$ by 2.5. So we can employ 3.3 to get for some k, $RS(\Omega) \overset{\Omega^k}{\underset{\rho}{\vdash}} B$ with $\rho = \Omega + (n-1)$. Then cut elimination ([P Theorem 3.9]) yields $RS(\Omega) \overset{\delta}{\underset{\Omega+1}{\vdash}} B$ where $\delta = \Omega^{\Omega^k(n-2)} = \Omega^k(n-1)$. By the use of the Collapsing Lemma [P Corollary 42] this becomes $RS(\Omega) \overset{\vartheta_\delta(0)}{\underset{\vartheta_\delta(0)}{\vdash}} B$. As $\vartheta_\delta(0) < \vartheta_{\Omega^{\omega}(n-1)}(0)$, this proves our theorem. □

3.4 will provide an upper bound for the minimal Σ_1–model of KPω^{-} + Π_n–Foundation if we can show that such derivations are sound with respect to the constructible hierarchy.

Let $\mathcal{T}$ be the collection of terms of $RS(\Omega)$ with stages $< \Omega$. In order to state the next result, we need to differentiate between the RS-term $\check{\mathsf{L}}_\alpha$ and the α–th level of the constructible hierarchy, L_α. For $t \in \mathcal{T}$ we define $l(t)$ as follows:

$$l(t) = \mathsf{L}_\alpha \text{ if } t \equiv \check{\mathsf{L}}_\alpha,$$

$$l(t) = \{x \in \mathsf{L}_\alpha : \mathsf{L}_\alpha \models F[x, l(t_1), \cdots, l(t_k)]\}$$

$$\text{if } t \equiv \{u \in \check{\mathsf{L}}_\alpha : F[u, t_1, \cdots, t_k]^{\check{\mathsf{L}}_\alpha}\}.$$

3.5 Soundness Theorem. *Let* $\Gamma[a_1, \cdots, a_n]$ *be a set of* Σ*–formulas; let* $t_1, \cdots, t_k \in \mathcal{T}$ *with stages* $< \beta$. *If* $RS(\Omega) \overset{\beta}{\underset{\Omega}{\vdash}} \Gamma[t_1, \cdots, t_k]^{L_\Omega}$ *and* $\beta < \Omega$, *then* $L_\beta \models \Gamma[l(t_1), \cdots, l(t_k)]$, *where the last formula denotes the disjunction of the formulas* $\Gamma[l(t_1), \cdots l(t_k)]$.

Proof by induction on β. Note that no inference (Cl_Ω) appears. As to the inferences $(\bigwedge)$, one needs to verify that $l(t) \subseteq \{l(s) : s \in \mathcal{T}, |s| < |t|\}$. Since $l(t) \subseteq \mathsf{L}_{|t|}$, it suffices to show

$$\mathsf{L}_{|t|} = \{l(s) : s \in \mathcal{T}, |s| < |t|\}.$$

This is easily done by induction on $|t|$. □

3.6 Theorem. *For* $n \geq 2$ *we have*

$$|\mathrm{KP}\omega^- + \Pi_n\text{–Foundation}|_{\Pi_2} \leq \vartheta_{\Omega^{\omega}(n-1)}(0).$$

Proof. By 3.4, 3.5, 2.1. □

4 Lower Bounds

We are left with the task to show that the upper bounds for minimal Π_2 models established in the previous section are best possible. To this end, we shall first define a relation $\lhd$ which is Δ_1–definable in $KP^- + \Sigma_1$–Foundation. In order to illuminate the meaning of $\lhd$, let ω_1^{CK} be the least admissible ordinal above ω, and let $\mathcal{A}$ be $\mathsf{L}_{\omega_1^{CK}}$, i.e. the least admissible set containing ω (cf.[Ba II]). Then $\mathcal{A}$ is a model of KP. Finally, let δ be the least ordinal so that $(\omega_1^{CK})^\delta = \delta$. If $\lhd_\mathcal{A}$ denotes the relation on $\mathcal{A}$ induced by $\lhd$, then $\lhd_\mathcal{A}$ can be easily visualized if one considers it to be obtained by projecting (cf.[Ba V.5]) the order relation of the ordinals below δ into $\mathcal{A}$. Observe also that $\delta = \varepsilon_{\omega_1^{CK}+1}$, where $\varepsilon_{\omega_1^{CK}+1}$ stands for the first ordinal $\beta > \omega_1^{CK}$ satisfying $\omega^\beta = \beta$. This is because $(\omega_1^{CK})^\alpha = \omega^{\omega_1^{CK} \cdot \alpha}$ for all α.

We define, as usual, the ordered pair $\langle x, y\rangle$ of x, y by $\langle x, y\rangle = \{\{x\}, \{x, y\}\}$ and prove that $\langle x, y\rangle = \langle z, w\rangle$ iff $x = z$ and $y = w$. This gives rise to define ordered n–tuples for $n > 2$, as follows, by induction on n:

$$\langle x_1, \cdots, x_n\rangle = \langle x_1, \langle x_2, \cdots, x_n\rangle\rangle.$$

4.1 Definition. (KP$^-$+Σ_1–Foundation) We simultaneously define a class of ordinal representations OR along with a binary relation $\lhd$ on OR as follows:

(1) $0 \in \mathrm{OR}$.

(2) If $1 \leq n, \alpha_1, \cdots, \alpha_n \in \mathrm{Ord}\backslash\{0\}, s_1, \cdots, s_n \in \mathrm{OR}$ and $s_1 \rhd \cdots \rhd s_n$, then

$$\hat{\Omega}^{s_1}\alpha_1 \oplus \cdots \oplus \hat{\Omega}^{s_n}\alpha_n := \langle n, \langle s_1, \alpha_1\rangle, \cdots, \langle s_n, \alpha_n\rangle\rangle \ \in \mathrm{OR}.$$

(3) If $s \in \mathrm{OR}\backslash\{0\}$, then $0 \lhd s$.

(4) If $s = \hat{\Omega}^{s_n}\alpha_1 \oplus \cdots \oplus \hat{\Omega}^{s_n}\alpha_n \in \mathrm{OR}$ and $t = \hat{\Omega}^{t_1}\beta_1 \oplus \cdots \oplus \hat{\Omega}^{t_k}\beta_k \in \mathrm{OR}$, then
$s \lhd t$ if one of the following holds:
(i) $n < k$ and $s_i = t_i$ as well as $\alpha_i = \beta_i$ for $1 \leq i \leq n$.
(ii) There exists $m \leq n, k$ such that
 (a) $s_i = t_i$ and $\alpha_i = \beta_i$ for $1 \leq i < m$,
 (b) Either $s_m \lhd t_m$ or $s_m = t_m$ and $\alpha_m < \beta_m$.

OR as well as $\lhd$ are defined by a Σ_+ inductive definition with closure ordinal ω (cf.[Ba VI]). We are obliged to show that these definitions can be given within $\mathrm{KP}^- + \Sigma_1$–Foundation. Let $\chi_{OR}(s) = 1$ if $s \in \mathrm{OR}$, 0 otherwise. Let $\chi_\lhd(\langle s,t\rangle) = 1$ if $s \lhd t$, 0 otherwise. Then both functions can be defined by a recursion on a certain well–founded relation. To see this, define for $a \in \mathsf{L}$, $\mathsf{rank}_\mathsf{L}(a) = \mathsf{min}\{\alpha : a \in \mathsf{L}_\alpha\}$, and define for sets $x, y, u, v \in \mathsf{L}$,

$$\langle x, y\rangle \prec \langle u, v\rangle \quad \text{iff} \quad \mathsf{rank}_\mathsf{L}(x)\#\mathsf{rank}_\mathsf{L}(y) < \mathsf{rank}_\mathsf{L}(u)\#\mathsf{rank}_\mathsf{L}(v).$$

Then $\prec$ is easily seen to be a well–founded relation. If we now put,

$$G(\langle u, v\rangle) = \langle \chi_{OR}(u), \chi_\lhd(\langle u, v\rangle)\rangle,$$

then for some class function H, being Σ_1–definable in $\mathrm{KP}^-+\Sigma_1$–Foundation,

$$G(\langle u, v\rangle) = H(\langle u, v, G|\{\langle x, y\rangle : \langle x, y\rangle \prec \langle u, v\rangle\}\rangle).$$

This is a form of recursion which does not lead outside $\mathrm{KP}^-+\Sigma_1$–Foundation as $\{b : b \prec x\}$ is always a set and induction along $\prec$ with regard to Σ_1–formulas is implied by Σ_1–Foundation. Thus χ_{OR} and $\chi_\lhd$ are Σ_1–definable in the latter theory, hence OR and $\lhd$ are Δ_1–definable in this theory.

4.2 Definition. (i) Let $\hat{1} := \hat{\Omega}^0 1, \hat{\Omega} := \hat{\Omega}^{\hat{1}} 1$.

(ii) We define $s + b$ for $s, t \in \mathrm{OR}$ by the following recursion:
1. $s + 0 := s$ and $0 + s := s$.
2. Let $s = \hat{\Omega}^{s_1}\alpha_1 \oplus \cdots \oplus \hat{\Omega}^{s_k}\alpha_k$ and $t = \hat{\Omega}^{t_1}\beta_1 \oplus \cdots \oplus \hat{\Omega}^{t_m}\beta_m$ $(1 \leq k, m)$. If

$s_1 \lhd t_1$ put, $s + t := t$. Otherwise, look for the largest index n $(1 \le n \le k)$ such that $t_1 \unlhd s_n$, and set:
2.1 $s + t := \hat{\Omega}^{s_1}\alpha_1 \oplus \cdots \oplus \hat{\Omega}^{s_{n-1}}\alpha_{n-1} \oplus \hat{\Omega}^{t_1}(\alpha_n + \beta_1) \oplus \hat{\Omega}^{t_2}\beta_2 \oplus \cdots \oplus \hat{\Omega}^{t_m}\beta_m$
if $s_n = t_1$;
2.2 $s + t := \hat{\Omega}^{s_1}\alpha_1 \oplus \cdots \oplus \hat{\Omega}^{s_n}\alpha_n \oplus \hat{\Omega}^{t_1}\beta_1 \oplus \cdots \oplus \hat{\Omega}^{t_m}\beta_m$
if $t_1 \lhd s_n$.

(iii) Let $\hat{\Omega}^s 0 := 0$. The mapping $\alpha \mapsto \hat{\alpha} := \hat{\Omega}^0\alpha$ constitutes a bijection between the ordinals and $\{s \in \mathrm{OR} \mid s \lhd \hat{\Omega}\}$ which also preserves the respective orderings; i.e. $\alpha < \beta$ implies $\hat{\alpha} \lhd \hat{\beta}$.

In the sequel we use the following abbreviations: $\hat{\Omega}^s := \hat{\Omega}^s 1$, $\hat{\Omega}^\alpha := \hat{\Omega}^{\hat{\alpha}}$, $s + \alpha := s + \hat{\alpha}$, where $s \in \mathrm{OR}$ and $\alpha \in Ord$.
p, q, r, s, t are supposed to range over elements of OR.

4.3 Definition. For a formula $A(x)$ let

$$Prog(\lhd, A) := \forall s[(\forall t \lhd s)A(t) \rightarrow A(s)].$$

For a collection $\mathcal{H}$ of set-theoretic formulas we mean by $TI(s, \mathcal{H})$ the schema:

$$Prog(\lhd, A) \rightarrow (\forall t \lhd s)A(t)$$

for all $\mathcal{H}$–formulas $A(x)$.

4.4 Lemma. (i) $\mathrm{KP}^- + \Sigma_1$–Foundation $\vdash \lhd$ *is a linear ordering.*
(ii)*Let* $n \ge 2$. *Suppose* $A(x)$ *is* Π_n. *Let* A_k *be the formula*
$\forall s[(\forall t \lhd sA(t)) \rightarrow (\forall t \lhd s + \hat{\Omega}^k)A(t)]$. *Then*

$$\mathrm{KP}^- + \Pi_n\text{–Foundation} \vdash Prog(\lhd, A) \rightarrow A_k.$$

Proof. (i) follows from the definition of $\lhd$.
(ii) We proceed by outer induction on k. Assume $Prog(\lhd, A)$ and $(\forall t \lhd s)A(t)$. Then also $(\forall t \unlhd s)A(t)$. For $k = 0$ this gives the assertion, since $t \lhd s + \hat{\Omega}^0$ implies $t \unlhd s$. Now let $k = m + 1$. So we get A_m by the inductive assumption. Let $B(\alpha)$ be the formula $(\forall t \lhd s + \hat{\Omega}^m\alpha)A(t)$. Then $B(\alpha)$ is provably equivalent (in $\mathrm{KP}^- + \Sigma_1$–Foundation) to a Π_n–formula. Suppose $(\forall \beta < \alpha)B(\beta)$. Clearly, $B(0)$ holds. If α is a limit, then for $t \lhd s + \hat{\Omega}^m\alpha$ there exists $\beta < \alpha$ such that $t \lhd s + \hat{\Omega}^m\beta$ (this follows from the definition of $\lhd$), hence $B(\alpha)$ holds. Now let α be a successor $\gamma + 1$. Then $(\forall t \lhd s + \hat{\Omega}^m\gamma)A(t)$. Using A_m, this implies $(\forall t \lhd s + \hat{\Omega}^m\gamma + \hat{\Omega}^m)A(t)$, thus $(\forall t \lhd s + \hat{\Omega}^m\alpha)A(t)$, hence $B(\alpha)$. By the above considerations, we have $\forall\alpha[(\forall\beta < \alpha)B(\beta) \rightarrow B(\alpha)]$, hence $\forall\alpha B(\alpha)$ via Π_n–Foundation. In view of

the definition of $\triangleleft$, it becomes clear that for every $t \triangleleft s + \hat{\Omega}^k$ there is a δ such that $t \triangleleft s + \hat{\Omega}^m\delta$. Therefore $(\forall t \triangleleft s + \hat{\Omega}^k)A(t)$ follows from $\forall\alpha B(\alpha)$. □

4.5 Lemma. *Let* OT *be the smallest subset of* OR *containing* 0 *and* $\hat{1}$ *closed under the rule:*
If $s = \hat{\Omega}^{s_1}\alpha_1 \oplus \cdots \oplus \hat{\Omega}^{s_k}\alpha_k$ *and* $s_1, \cdots, s_k, \hat{\alpha}_1, \cdots \hat{\alpha}_k \in \mathrm{OT}$, *then* $s \in \mathrm{OT}$. *Every* $p \in \mathrm{OT}$ *is* Δ_1*-definable in* $\mathrm{KP}^- + \Sigma_1$–Foundation, *and so we may assume that the language of this theory contains a constant for every* $p \in \mathrm{OT}$.
Let $K_n := \mathrm{KP}^- + \Pi_n$–Foundation. For all $n \geq 2$ *and* $p \in \mathrm{OT}$

$$K_n + TI(p, \Pi_{n+1}) \vdash TI(\hat{\Omega}^p, \Pi_n).$$

Proof. Suppose $A(t) \in \Pi_n$ and let

$$B(s) := \forall r[(\forall t \triangleleft r)A(t) \rightarrow (\forall t \triangleleft r + \hat{\Omega}^s)A(t)].$$

Note that $B(s)$ is equivalent to a Π_{n+1}–formula. We will show

Claim $\quad K_n \vdash Prog(\triangleleft, A) \rightarrow Prog(\triangleleft, B).$

To see that the Claim implies the lemma, note that from the claim we can conclude

$$K_n + TI(p, \Pi_{n+1}) \vdash Prog(\triangleleft, A) \rightarrow (\forall t \triangleleft p)B(t).$$

Hence, $K_n + TI(p, \Pi_{n+1}) \vdash Prog(\triangleleft, A) \rightarrow B(p)$. Setting $r = 0$ in $B(p)$, we get

$$K_n + TI(p, \Pi_{n+1}) \vdash Prog(\triangleleft, A) \rightarrow (\forall t \triangleleft \hat{\Omega}^p)A(t),$$

which is what we needed for the lemma; hence we only need to prove the Claim.
We will work in K_n. Assume $Prog(\triangleleft, A)$ and $(\forall s' \triangleleft s)B(s')$; we want to conclude $B(s)$. By cases we have:

Case 1: $s = 0$. $B(0) \equiv \forall r[(\forall t \triangleleft r)A(t) \rightarrow (\forall t \triangleleft r + 1)A(t)]$, which is immediate from $Prog(\triangleleft, A)$.

Case 2: $s = s' + 1$. Suppose $(\forall t \triangleleft r)A(t)$. We want to show $(\forall t \triangleleft r + \hat{\Omega}^s)A(t)$. Let $C(\alpha) := (\forall t \triangleleft r + \hat{\Omega}^{s'}\alpha)A(t)$. Then $C(0)$. By the use of $B(s'), C(\beta)$ implies $C(\beta + 1)$. If α is a limit and $t' \triangleleft r + \hat{\Omega}^{s'}\alpha$, then there is a $\beta < \alpha$ such that $t' \triangleleft r + \hat{\Omega}^{s'}\beta$. This shows $(\forall \beta < \alpha)C(\beta) \rightarrow C(\alpha)$. And hence, using Π_n–Foundation, $\forall\alpha C(\alpha)$. Since for $t \triangleleft r + \hat{\Omega}^s$ there is an ordinal α such that $t \triangleleft r + \hat{\Omega}^{s'}\alpha$, we obtain $(\forall t \triangleleft r + \hat{\Omega}^s)A(t)$.

Case 3: s is of the shape $\hat{\Omega}^{s_1}\alpha_1 + \cdots + \hat{\Omega}^{s_j}\alpha_j$ where $s_j \neq 0$ or α_j is a limit. For $t \triangleleft r + \hat{\Omega}^s$, we then find a $s' \triangleleft s$ such that $t \triangleleft r + \hat{\Omega}^{s'}$. Therefore $B(s)$

is implied by $(\forall s' \lhd s)B(s')$. This completes the proof of Case 3, and hence the proof of the Claim. □

4.6 Proposition. *Let* $\hat{\Omega}^k(0) := k$, $\hat{\Omega}^k(m+1) := \hat{\Omega}^{\hat{\Omega}^k(m)}$. *Then for every* $n \geq 2$ *and* k

$$\mathrm{KP}^- + \Pi_n\text{–Foundation} \vdash TI(\hat{\Omega}^k(n-1), \Pi_2).$$

Proof. 4.4(ii) yields (setting $s = 0$)

$$\mathrm{KP}^- + \Pi_n\text{–Foundation} \vdash TI(\hat{\Omega}^k(1), \Pi_n).$$

Hence, using 4.5, $\mathrm{KP}^- + \Pi_n$–Foundation $\vdash TI(\hat{\Omega}^k(n-1), \Pi_2)$. □

The reason for the invention of $\lhd$ is that we want to mimic for certain $\alpha > \Omega$ the definition of ϑ_α within fragments of KPω. How far this is possible is foreshadowed by 4.6.

4.7 Definition. Let k and $n \geq 2$ be fixed. We intend to simultaneously define sets $\bar{C}(s,\beta) \subseteq \mathrm{OR}$ and functions $\bar{\vartheta}_s : Ord \to Ord$ for all $s \lhd \hat{\Omega}^k(n)$ and all ordinals β by recursion on s (with respect to $\lhd$). Thereby 4.6 will be employed to guarantee that this type of recursion is actually available in $\mathrm{KP}\omega^- + \Pi_n$ –Foundation.
It should also be recognized that the relations $t \in \bar{C}(s,\beta)$ and $\bar{\vartheta}_s(\alpha) = \beta$ are Σ_1–definable in the above theory.
Suppose that $\bar{C}(t,\gamma)$ and $\bar{\vartheta}_t(\gamma)$ are defined for all $t \lhd s$ and all $\gamma \in Ord$.
By Σ_1–Recursion on $i < \omega$, we then define sets $\bar{C}_i(s,\gamma)$ as follows:
$\bar{C}_0(s,\gamma) = \{0, \hat{1}\} \cup \{\hat{\alpha} \mid \alpha < \gamma\}$,
$\bar{C}_{i+1}(s,\gamma) = \bar{C}_i(s,\gamma) \cup \{t + t' \mid t, t \in \bar{C}_i(s,\gamma)\} \cup \{\hat{\Omega}^t \beta \mid t, \hat{\beta} \in \bar{C}_i(s,\gamma)\}$
$\cup \{\bar{\vartheta}_t(\beta) \mid t \lhd s \wedge t, \hat{\beta} \in \bar{C}_i(s,\gamma)\}$.
Let $\bar{C}(s,\gamma) := \bigcup_{i<\omega} \bar{C}_i(s,\gamma)$.
Then $\bar{C}_i(s,\gamma)$ is a set by Σ–Collection and Infinity; thus $\bar{C}(s,\gamma)$ is a set. So $\bar{C}(s,\gamma)$ is defined for every ordinal γ.
Before we can give a definition of $\bar{\vartheta}_s$, we have to observe two facts:

Fact 1: For every $t \unlhd s$ one can find an ordinal δ such that $t \in \bar{C}(t,\delta)$.

Fact 2: For every ξ there exists $\eta > \xi$ so that $\hat{\eta} \notin \bar{C}(s,\eta)$.

Fact 1 can be easily shown by induction on TC(t). For Fact 2, let
$\xi_0 = \sup\{\alpha + 1 \mid \hat{\alpha} \in \bar{C}(s, \xi + 1)\}$, $\xi_{j+1} = \sup\{\alpha + 1 \mid \hat{\alpha} \in \bar{C}(s, \xi_j + 1)\}$. Put

$\eta := \sup_{j<\omega} \xi_j$. Then $\xi_j < \eta$ for all $j < \omega$. Using induction on $i < \omega$, one shows $\bar{C}_i(s,\eta) \subseteq \bigcup_{j<\omega} \bar{C}(s,\xi_j)$. Consequently, $\hat{\eta} \notin \bar{C}(s,\eta)$, for otherwise we could find a $j < \omega$ such that $\hat{\eta} \in \bar{C}(s,\xi_j)$, which would yield the contradiction $\eta < \xi_{j+1}$. By virtue of Fact 1 and Fact 2, we define $\bar{\vartheta}_s(\xi)$ by recursion on ξ as follows

$$\bar{\vartheta}_s(\xi) = \text{ least } \eta \text{ such that: } [\hat{\eta} \notin \bar{C}(s,\eta) \wedge s \in \bar{C}(s,\eta) \wedge (\forall \varsigma < \xi)(\bar{\vartheta}_s(\varsigma) < \eta)].$$

4.8 Proposition. *For fixed k and $n \geq 2$, $\mathrm{KP}\omega^- + \Pi_n$–Foundation proves the assertion:*

For all $s \lhd \hat{\Omega}^k(n-1)$, the function $\bar{\vartheta}_s$ is totally defined on the ordinals.

Proof. By the above, if one assumes the totality of all the functions $\bar{\vartheta}_t$ for $t \lhd s$, then the totality of $\bar{\vartheta}_s$ only needs tools from $\mathrm{KP}\omega^- + \Sigma_1$–Foundation. Now, the totality of $\bar{\vartheta}_s$ can be expressed by a Π_2–formula. Therefore the assertion follows by $TI(\hat{\Omega}^k(n-1), \Pi_2)$. If we were to give a more rigorous proof, we would have to invoke the Second Recursion Theorem for KP (cf.[Ba V.2]). By glancing over the proof of [Ba V.2.3] it turns out that the Second Recursion Theorem is already provable in $\mathrm{KP}^- + \Sigma_1$–Foundation. The Second Recursion Theorem gives us a Σ–formula A such that

$$A(s,\xi,\eta) \quad \text{iff} \quad s \in \mathrm{OR} \wedge \xi, \eta \in \mathrm{Ord} \wedge$$

$$\exists f \, \exists g \, \Big[\mathrm{fun}(f) \wedge \mathrm{fun}(g) \wedge \mathrm{dom}(g) = (\eta+1) \times \omega \wedge$$

$$\mathrm{dom}(f) = (\{t \in \bigcup \mathrm{rng}(g) \mid t \lhd s\} \times \{\beta \mid \hat{\beta} \in \bigcup \mathrm{rng}(g)\}) \cup (\{s\} \times \{\varsigma \mid \varsigma < \eta\}) \wedge$$

$$(\forall \delta \leq \eta)\, (g_\delta(0) = \{0, \hat{1}\} \cup \{\hat{\alpha} \mid \alpha < \delta\} \wedge$$

$$(\forall i < \omega)[g_\delta(i+1) = g_\delta(i) \cup \{t + t' \mid t, t' \in g_\delta(i)\} \cup \{\hat{\Omega}^t \beta \mid t, \hat{\beta} \in g_\delta(i)\} \cup$$

$$\{\hat{\alpha} \mid \exists t \, \exists \hat{\beta}\, (t, \hat{\beta} \in g_\delta(i) \wedge t \lhd s \wedge \alpha = f_t(\beta))\}]) \wedge$$

$$\hat{\eta} \notin \mathrm{rng}(g_\eta) \wedge s \in \mathrm{rng}(g_\eta) \wedge (\forall \varsigma < \xi)(f_s(\varsigma) < \eta) \wedge$$

$$(\forall \delta < \eta)[\hat{\delta} \in \mathrm{rng}(g_\delta) \vee s \notin \mathrm{rng}(g_\delta) \vee (\exists \varsigma < \xi)(\delta \leq f_s(\varsigma))] \wedge$$

$$\forall t \, \forall \beta \, (\langle t, \beta \rangle \in \mathrm{dom}(f) \rightarrow A(t, \beta, f_t(\beta)))\Big].$$

In the formulation of $A(s,\xi,\eta)$, $f_s(\beta)$ abbreviates $f(\langle s,\beta\rangle)$; $\mathrm{fun}(f)$ means that f is a function, and $\mathrm{dom}(g)$ and $\mathrm{rng}(g)$ denote the domain of g and the range of g, respectively.
Setting $B(s) := \forall \xi \exists \eta A(s,\xi,\eta)$, we can apply (by 4.6) $TI(\hat{\Omega}^k(n), \Pi_2)$ on s to get (along with what we have been reflecting on in 4.7) $(\forall s \lhd \hat{\Omega}^k(n))B(s)$. By induction on s one also verifies in the outer world

$$\forall \xi \forall n (A(s,\xi,\eta) \longleftrightarrow \bar{\vartheta}_s(\xi) = \eta).$$

□

Let $\varepsilon_{\Omega+1}$ denote $\vartheta_0(\Omega+1)$ and let $C_{\varepsilon_{\Omega+1}}(0)$ be the set defined in [P Definition 26]. Note that $\Omega^\alpha = \omega^{\Omega\cdot\alpha}$.
The mapping

$$e : C_{\varepsilon_{\Omega+1}}(0) \to \mathrm{OR}$$

is defined to be $e(\alpha) = \hat{\alpha}$ for $\alpha < \Omega$,

$$e(\Omega^{\beta_1}\cdot\alpha_1 + \cdots + \Omega^{\beta_k}\cdot\alpha_k) = \hat{\Omega}^{e(\beta_1)}\alpha_1 \oplus \cdots \oplus \hat{\Omega}^{e(\beta_k)}\alpha_k$$

if $\beta_1 > 0$, $\beta_1 > \cdots > \beta_k$, and $0 < \alpha_i < \Omega$ $(1 \le i \le k)$. Here we have used the fact that any ordinal $\Omega \le \beta < \varepsilon_{\Omega+1}$ can uniquely be represented in such a way.
e is order preserving with respect to $<$ and $\triangleleft$: By induction on $\beta \in C_{\varepsilon_{\Omega+1}}(0)$ one establishes

$$(+) \qquad (\forall\alpha < \Omega)[\vartheta_\beta(\alpha) = \bar{\vartheta}_{e(\beta)}(\alpha)].$$

The inductive assumption then implies that ϑ_β and $\bar{\vartheta}_{e(\beta)}$ obey the same recursive definition, and thus they are equal.

4.9 Theorem *Let $n \ge 2$. Let ϱ_n be $\vartheta_{\Omega^\omega(n-1)}(0)$. L_{ϱ_n} is the minimal Σ_1 and Π_2 model of* $\mathrm{KP}\omega^- + \Pi_n$–Foundation.

Proof. Note that $\sup_{k<\omega} \Omega^k(n-1) = \Omega^\omega(n-1)$ and thus

$$\sup_{k<\omega} \vartheta_{\Omega^k(n-1)}(0) = \vartheta_{\Omega^\omega}(n-1)(0) = \varrho_n.$$

Hence, the assertion follows from 2.1, 3.6, 4.8 and the last (+). □

For proving Theorem 1.2 from 4.9 we need to verify that $\vartheta_{\Omega^\omega(m)}(0) = \theta_{\Omega^\omega(m)}(0)$. Here we have to invoke [Schü,IX]. From [Schü,IX.24] it follows that $\bar{\theta}_{\Omega^\omega(m)}$ is the fixed point free version of $\vartheta_{\Omega^\omega(m)}$; thus $\vartheta_{\Omega^\omega(m)}(0) = \bar{\theta}_{\Omega^\omega(m)}(0)$. As $\mu(\Omega^\omega(m)) = 0$ (cf.[Schü,IX.24]), this gives us $\vartheta_{\Omega^\omega(m)}(0) = \theta_{\Omega^\omega(m)}(0)$.

References

[Ba] J. BARWISE, *Admissible sets and structures,* Springer, 1975.

[Bu] W. BUCHHOLZ, *A simplified version of local predicativity,* this volume.

[Ca1] A. CANTINI, *Non-extensional theories of predicative classes over PA,* Rend.Sem.Mat. Torino 40, (1982), 47-49.

[Ca2] A. CANTINI, *A note on a theory of admissible sets with ϵ–induction restricted to formulas with one quantifier and related systems,*Boll. Unione.Mat.Ital., VISer, B, (1983), 721-737.

[D] K. DEVLIN, *Constructibility,*Springer, Berlin, 1984.

[Fe] S. FEFERMAN, *Formal theories for transfinite iterations of generalized inductive definitions and some subsystems of analysis.* In: Intuitionism and Proof Theory, ed. by J. Myhill, A. Kino, and R.E. Vesley, North-Holland, 1970.

[FS] S. FEFERMAN and W. SIEG, *Iterated inductive definitions and subsystems of analysis.* In: W. Buchholz, S. Feferman, W. Pohlers and W. Sieg, Iterated inductive definitons and subsystems of analysis: recent proof–theoretical studies, Lecture Notes in Mathematics, vol. 897, Springer, Berlin and New York, 1981, 16-77.

[Ho1] W.A. HOWARD, *Functional interpretation of bar induction by bar recursion,* Comp. Math. 20 (1968), 107-124.

[Ho2] W.A. HOWARD,*Ordinal analysis of bar recursion of type zero,* Comp. Math. 42 (1981), 105-119.

[J] G. JÄGER, *Zur Beweistheorie der Kripke-Platek-Mengenlehre über den natürlichen Zahlen,* Archiv für Mathematische Logik und Grundlagenforschung 23 (1983) 65-77.

[P] W. POHLERS, *A short course in ordinal analysis,* this volume

[Schü] K. SCHÜTTE, *Proof Theory.* Springer, Berlin, 1977.

[Schw] H. SCHWICHTENBERG, *Some applications of cut elimination.* In: Handbook of Mathematical Logic, ed. by J. Barwise, North-Holland, Amsterdam, 1977, 868-895.

Institut für Mathematische Logik und Grundlagenforschung,
Einsteinstrasse 62, W–4400 Münster, Germany

Provable computable selection functions on abstract structures

J. TUCKER & J. ZUCKER

Provable Computable Selection Functions on Abstract Structures

J.V. TUCKER*

Department of Mathematics and Computer Science,
University College of Swansea, Swansea SA2 8PP, Wales

J.I. ZUCKER**

Department of Computer Science and Systems,
McMaster University, Hamilton, Ontario L8S 4K1, Canada

ABSTRACT. We work in the context of abstract data types, modelled as classes of many-sorted algebras closed under isomorphism. We develop notions of computability over such classes, in particular notions of primitive recursiveness and μ-recursiveness, which generalize the corresponding classical notions over the natural numbers. We also develop classical and intuitionistic formal systems for theories about such data types, and prove (in the case of universal theories) that if an existential assertion is provable in either of these systems, then it has a primitive recursive selection function. It is a corollary that if a μ-recursive scheme is provably total, then it is extensionally equivalent to a primitive recursive scheme. The methods are proof-theoretical, involving cut elimination. These results generalize to an abstract setting previous results of C. Parsons and G. Mints over the natural numbers.

* Research supported by SERC Research Grant GR/F 59070.

**Research supported by SERC Research Grant GR/F 10606 under the Alvey Programme, by a grant from the Science & Engineering Research Board of McMaster University, by a grant from the Natural Sciences and Engineering Research Council of Canada, and by an academic travel grant from the British Council.

1 INTRODUCTION

We will examine the provability or verifiability in formal systems of program properties, such as termination or correctness, from the point of view of the general theory of computable functions over abstract data types. In this theory an abstract data type is modelled semantically by a class K of many-sorted algebras, closed under isomorphism, and many equivalent formalisms are used to define computable functions and relations on an algebra A, uniformly for all $A \in \mathsf{K}$. Some of these formalisms are generalizations to A and K of sequential deterministic models of computation on the natural numbers. Here we use a parallel deterministic functional model that generalizes the definition of the partial recursive functions by schemes as defined by Kleene [1952].

We will consider the following questions. Let $\mathcal{L}$ be a formal logical language and ***Proof***(T) be a proof system based on a theory T written in $\mathcal{L}$. Suppose T is an axiomatic specification for K.

> *For which computable functions over K is it possible to prove in* ***Proof***(T) *that they are total and, more generally, that they meet formal specifications written in $\mathcal{L}$?*
>
> *Is there an $\mathcal{L}$ and* ***Proof***(T) *on which it is possible to base a Generalized Church-Turing Thesis that characterises the computable functions on K that are formally verifiable?*

In order to approach these questions, we will define precisely a means of specifying functions in a language $\mathcal{L}$ and then establish the expressiveness of $\mathcal{L}$ with respect to algorithmic properties of interest. We will select an appropriate $\mathcal{L}$, give proof systems to prove termination and correctness of functions on K, and classify the verifiable functions in our system.

1.1 Summary of Results

Let us consider the issues and results in detail.

A partial function f on A is specified by a precondition S and postcondition R by requiring that for $a \in A$,

$$a \in S \text{ implies } f(a)\downarrow \text{ and } R(a, f(a)).$$

On expressing S and R in the language $\mathcal{L}$, this means that f is a *selection function*, *realizing function* or *witnessing function* for R in the formula

$$\forall x[S(x) \rightarrow \exists y R(x,y)].$$

There may be more than one selection function for a formula. Many functions of interest arise as selection functions (for equations, for example). If $\mathcal{L}$ is strong enough to express the graph of f, then f may be specified uniquely.

To compute a function f on A we augment A by adding to its carriers the natural numbers and finite sequences of elements of its carriers, together with appropriate operations, to make a new algebra A^*. The computable functions on A may be defined by recursive functions on A^* obtained from its basic operations by composition, simultaneous primitive recursion and least number search. Equivalently, they may be defined on A directly if *course of values (cov)* recursion replaces primitive recursion. This gives the class of μCR functions on A. The subclass defined without use of the least number operator is the class of CR functions on A.

Our classes $\mathbb{K}$ will contain (only) such structures, augmented by the natural numbers. See Tucker and Zucker [1988] for a detailed account of this computability theory.

Let ***Lang***** be the many-sorted first order language of A^*, and let $\mathbb{K}^*$ be the class of structures A^* for $A \in \mathbb{K}$. As a specification language for $\mathbb{K}^*$ we can take the subclass $\mathbf{\Sigma}_1^*$ of ***Lang*****, consisting of quantifier-free formulae prefixed by existential quantifiers and bounded universal number quantifiers. In this specification language we can express domains, ranges and graphs of computable functions, termination, and the class of effectively testable specifications. See Tucker and Zucker [1988, 1989, 1992*a*, 1992*b*, 1992*c*] for work relating to expressiveness and completeness of Floyd-Hoare logic, Horn clauses and logic programming, nondeterministic specification, and computability on the real and complex numbers,

To prove properties of specifications and programs for a class $\mathbb{K}$ we build intuitionistic and classical proof systems $\mathbf{\Sigma}_1^*$-$\boldsymbol{Ind_i}(T)$ and $\mathbf{\Sigma}_1^*$-$\boldsymbol{Ind_c}(T)$ for reasoning about $\mathbb{K}^*$ in ***Lang*****. The systems are based on an axiomatization T of $\mathbb{K}$ and includes the induction rule applied to $\mathbf{\Sigma}_1^*$ formulae.

THEOREM. *Let T be a universal theory true of $\mathbb{K}$. Suppose the specification is provable*

$$\mathbf{\Sigma}_1^*\text{-}\boldsymbol{Ind_\ell}(T) \vdash \forall x[S(x) \to \exists y R(x,y)]$$

where $\ell = i$ or c, R is $\mathbf{\Sigma}_1^*$ and S is quantifier-free. Then we can construct a CR scheme α that computes a selection function f for R on S, uniformly on all $A \in \mathbb{K}$. Conversely, every CR scheme gives the unique selection function for some such specification.

In other words, if a specification is provable in our systems for $\mathbb{K}^*$ then it is implementable by primitive recursion on $\mathbb{K}^*$; further the program can be synthesised from the proof.

The proof uses proof-theoretic techniques, notably the method of "cut reduction".

It is interesting to note that any first order theory can be translated into an equivalent universal theory by Skolemization.

Given the general idea of specification, and the special properties of the specification language and proof systems for computation, the result provides a simple reference point for establishing the scope and limits of verifiable computation. For example the result is relevant to the theoretical foundations of logic programming (see Lloyd [1987], Tucker and Zucker [1989, 1992*a*]) and program synthesis (see Constable *et al.* [1986] and Wainer [1990]).

Furthermore, since termination can be expressed in the specification language, the theorem may be used in the proof of the following:

COROLLARY. *Let α be a μCR scheme on $\mathbb{K}$. Then α is provably total in* Σ_1^*-$\boldsymbol{Ind}_\ell(T)$, *for $\ell = i$ or c, if, and only if, α is equivalent to a CR scheme β on $\mathbb{K}$.*

This result provides an example, in the context of verifiable specifications on abstract data types, of the general programme proposed by Kreisel [1971] of discovering "what more we know when we have proved a theorem than if we only know that it is true".

These theorems generalize to an abstract setting certain results known in the special case of the natural numbers, from work in proof theory in Parsons [1971, 1972] and Mints [1973]. Our method actually has much in common with that of Mints [1973]. The starting point for the present analysis was the proofs of the results (again over the natural numbers) given in Copestake and Wainer [1988]. We have also profited from unpublished work of A.J. Wilkie and H. Simmons on model theoretic proofs of the results in the natural number case. The analysis of the general problem of the limits of specifiability and verifiability of programs on abstract data types, and the concepts and methods necessary, are new.

The results presented here were announced in Tucker, Wainer and Zucker [1990]. We are deeply indebted to S.S. Wainer for many discussions on the proof theoretic and recursion theoretic issues presented here. We also thank W. Pohlers for valuable comments.

1.2 Structure of this Paper

In Section 2 we review the definitions of many-sorted algebras, especially *standard structures* and their extensions to *starred structures*. In Section 3 we define the different notions of computability considered in this paper — primitive and μ computability, intended to generalize the notions of primitive recursiveness and μ-recursiveness respectively. In Section 4 we introduce the proof system Σ_1^*-***Ind***, characterized by the restriction of the induction rule to Σ_1^* formulae. In Section 5 we set the groundwork for stating one of the main results by defining the *computation predicate* corresponding to a particular computation scheme, and (hence) the notion of *provable totality* of such a scheme in Σ_1^*-***Ind***. We can then state properly the corollary quoted above. In Section 6 we prove the main theorem, that a specification which is provable in Σ_1^*-***Ind*** is realizable by a primitive computable witnessing function. The method of proof involves cut reduction. Finally, in Section 7 we discuss the restriction of T to a *universal theory.* We note that any first order theory can be reduced to such a theory by Skolemization.

2 STANDARD STRUCTURES; STARRED STRUCTURES

In this section we review some concepts defined in Tucker and Zucker [1988, 1989, 1992*a*].

2.1 Standard Signatures and Structures; Classes of Structures

A *standard signature* Σ specifies (1) a finite set of *sorts*: *algebraic sorts* $1, \ldots, r$ (for some $r \geq 0$), and the *numerical sort* N and *boolean sort* B; and (2) finitely many *function symbols* F, each having a *type* $(i_1, \ldots, i_m; i)$, where $m \geq 0$ is the arity of F, $i_1, \ldots, i_m$ are the argument sorts and i is the value sort (including the case $m = 0$ for *constant symbols*). These include symbols for certain *standard operations* associated with the sorts N and B: (*a*) *arithmetical operations*, namely the constant '0', successor operation S and order relation '$<$' on the natural numbers; and (*b*) *boolean operations*, including a complete set of propositional connectives, the constants **true** and **false**, and an *equality* operator $\mathbf{eq}_i$ at some sorts i , including (at least) $i = \mathsf{N}$ and $i = \mathsf{B}$. We call those sorts i with the equality operator $\mathbf{eq}_i$, *equality sorts.* (We do not want to assume that all sorts have computable equality; for example, we may have a sort of reals.)

Relations can be represented by their (boolean-valued) characteristic functions.

We make one further assumption on Σ:

INSTANTIATION ASSUMPTION. *Each sort of Σ is* instantiated, *i.e. there is a closed term of each sort.*

We will see later where this assumption is used.

A Σ-structure A has, for each sort i of Σ, a domain A_i, and for each function symbol F of type $(i_1, \ldots, i_m; i)$, a function $F^A : A_{i_1} \times \cdots \times A_{i_m} \to A_i$. The structure A is *standard* if $A_{\mathsf{N}} = \mathsf{N}$, the domain of natural numbers, $A_{\mathsf{B}} = \mathsf{B} = \{\mathbf{tt}, \mathbf{ff}\}$, the domain of truth values, and the arithmetical and boolean function symbols have their *standard interpretations* on N and B, and the equality symbol is interpreted as identity on the relevant sort.

We only consider standard signatures and structures. Note, in this connection, that any many-sorted structure B can be *standardized* to such a structure A by the adjunction of the sets N and B, together with their standard operations, so that B is a reduct of A to the signature of B.

This notion of *reduct* will be used later, so we define it here.

DEFINITIONS. Let Σ and Σ' be signatures with $\Sigma \subset \Sigma'$.

(1) If A' is a Σ'-structure, then the *Σ-reduct of A'* is the structure

$$A' \mid_{\Sigma}$$

of signature Σ, consisting of the carriers of A' named by the sorts of Σ and equipped with the functions of A' named by the function symbols of Σ.

(2) If A' is a Σ'-structure and A a Σ-structure, then A' is a *Σ'-expansion* of A iff A is the Σ-reduct of A'.

2.2 Strictly Standard Signatures and Structures

We consider a notion stricter than standardness, namely *strict standardness*.

The signature Σ is *strictly standard* (with respect to the sorts N and B) if the *only operations* with sort N or B anywhere in their domain or range are the *standard operations* listed in §2.1. The structure A is *strictly standard* if its signature is.

Note that any standardized structure is automatically strictly standard.

Now fix a (not necessarily strictly) standard signature Σ. We will consider *classes* K of Σ-structures. We impose no restriction on K other than that it be *closed under isomorphism*. Such a class can be thought of as an *abstract data type*.

Fix such a class K, and consider a particular Σ-structure $A \in \mathsf{K}$. We will expand A in two stages.

2.3 The Unspecified Value $\mathbf{u}$; Structures A^{u} of Signature Σ^{u}

For each sort i let $\mathbf{u}_i$ be a new object, representing an "unspecified value", and let $A_i^{\mathsf{u}} = A_i \cup \{\mathbf{u}_i\}$. For each function symbol F of Σ of type $(i_1, \ldots, i_m; i)$, extend its interpretation F^A on A to a function

$$F^{A,\mathsf{u}} : A_{i_1}^{\mathsf{u}} \times \cdots \times A_{i_m}^{\mathsf{u}} \longrightarrow A_i^{\mathsf{u}}$$

by *strictness*— *i.e.*, the value is defined as $\mathbf{u}$ whenever any argument is $\mathbf{u}$. Then the structure A^{u} with signature Σ^{u}, contains:

(*i*) the original domains A_i of sort i, and functions F^A on them;

(*ii*) the new domains A_i^{u} of sort i^{u}, and functions $F^{A,\mathsf{u}}$ on them;

(*iii*) a constant unspec_i of type i^{u} to denote $\mathbf{u}_i$ as a distinguished element of A_i^{u};

(*iv*) a boolean-valued function Unspec_i of type $(i; \mathsf{B})$, the characteristic function of $\mathbf{u}_i$;

(*v*) an *embedding function* i_i of sort $(i; i^{\mathsf{u}})$ to denote the embedding of A_i into A_i^{u}, and an inverse function j_i of sort $(i^{\mathsf{u}}; i)$, which maps $\mathbf{u}_i$ to the denotation of some closed term in A_i (this being possible by the Instantiation Assumption) for each sort i; and finally

(*vi*) an *equality* operator on A_i^{u} for each equality sort i.

Also, K^{u} is the class of structures A^{u} for $A \in \mathsf{K}$.

REMARKS. (1) The structure A^{u} is a Σ^{u}-*expansion* of A.

(2) (*Two- and three-valued boolean operations.*) A^{u} is itself a standard structure. However it contains the domain $\mathsf{B}^{\mathsf{u}} = \{\mathbf{tt}, \mathbf{ff}, \mathbf{u}\}$ as well as B, with associated extensions of the original standard boolean operations, leading to a *weak 3-valued logic* (see Tucker and Zucker [1988], §1.1.6]). Further, there are *two equality operations* on A_i^{u} for each equality sort i: (*a*) the extension by strictness of eq_i^A to a 3-valued function

$$\mathsf{eq}_i^{A,\mathsf{u}} : A_i^{\mathsf{u}} \times A_i^{\mathsf{u}} \to \mathsf{B}^{\mathsf{u}}$$

which has the value $\mathbf{u}_{\mathsf{B}}$ if either argument is $\mathbf{u}_i$; (*b*) the "standard (2-valued) equality" on A_i^{u}

$$\mathsf{eq}_i^{A^{\mathsf{u}}} : A_i^{\mathsf{u}} \times A_i^{\mathsf{u}} \to \mathsf{B},$$

which we will usually denote by '=' in infix.

2.4 Structures A^* of Signature Σ^*

Define, for each sort i, the domain A_i^* to be the set of pairs $a^* = (\xi, l)$ where $\xi : \mathsf{N} \to A_i^{\mathsf{u}}$, $l \in \mathsf{N}$ and for all $n \geq l$, $\xi(n) = \mathbf{u}_i$. So l is a witness to the "finiteness" of ξ, or an "effective upper bound" for a^*. The elements of the domain A_i^* have "starred sort" i^*, and can be considered as finite sequences or *arrays*. The resulting structures A^* have signature Σ^*, which extends Σ^{u} by including, for each sort i, the new "starred sorts" i^*as well as i^{u}, and also the following new function symbols:

(i) the Lgth_i operator, of type $(i^*; \mathsf{N})$, where

$$\mathsf{Lgth}_i^A((\xi, l)) = l,$$

(ii) the application operator Ap_i of type $(i^*, N; i^{\mathsf{u}})$, where

$$\mathsf{Ap}_i^A((\xi, l), n) = \xi(n),$$

(iii) the null array Null_i of type i^*, where

$$\mathsf{Null}_i^A = (\lambda n \cdot \mathbf{u}_i, 0) \in A_i^*,$$

(iv) the Update_i operator of type $(i^*, \mathsf{N}, i^{\mathsf{u}}; i^*)$, where for $(\xi, l) \in A_i^*$, $n \in \mathsf{N}$ and $x \in A_i^{\mathsf{u}}$, $\mathsf{Update}_i^A((\xi, l), n, x)$ is the array $(\eta, l) \in A_i^*$ such that for all $k \in \mathsf{N}$,

$$\eta(k) = \begin{cases} \xi(k) & \text{if } k < l, k \neq n \\ x & \text{if } k < l, k = n \\ \mathbf{u}_i & \text{otherwise,} \end{cases}$$

(v) the $\mathsf{Newlength}_i$ operator of type $(i^*, \mathsf{N}; i^*)$, where $\mathsf{Newlength}_i^A((\xi, l), m)$ is the array (η, m) such that for all k,

$$\eta(k) = \begin{cases} \xi(k) & \text{if } k < m \\ \mathbf{u}_i & \text{if } k \geq m, \end{cases}$$

and (vi) the *equality* operator on i^*, for each *equality sort* i.

(The justification for this is that if a sort i has computable equality, then clearly so has the sort i^*, since it amounts to testing equality of finitely many pairs of objects of sort i, up to a computable length.)

For $a^* \in A_i^*$ and $n \in \mathsf{N}$, we write $a^*[n]$ for $\mathsf{j}_i^A(\mathsf{Ap}_i^A(a^*, n))$. (So $a^*[n]$ is the element of A_i "corresponding to" $\mathsf{Ap}(a^*, n) \in A_i^{\mathsf{u}}$.)

Also, K^* is the class of structures A^* for $A \in \mathsf{K}$.

REMARKS. (1) The structure A^* is a *Σ^*-expansion* of A and of A^{u}.

(2) Now we may also need to speak of finite sequences of starred sorts! However, we do not have to introduce a structure A^{**} of "doubly starred" domains (or two-dimensional arrays), since we can effectively code a finite sequence of starred objects of a given sort as a single starred object of the same sort, thanks to the explicit Lgth operation. More precisely, a sequence $x_0^*, \ldots, x_{k-1}^*$ of elements of A_h^* (for some sort h) can be coded as a *pair* $(y^*, n^*) \in A_h^* \times \mathsf{N}^*$, where $\mathsf{Lgth}(n^*) = k$, and for $0 \leq j < k$, $n^*[j] = \mathsf{Lgth}(x_j^*)$, and $\mathsf{Lgth}(y^*) = n^*[0] + \cdots + n^*[k]$, and for $1 \leq j \leq k$ and $0 \leq i < n^*[j]$, $y^*[n^*[0] + \cdots + n^*[j-1] + i] = x_j^*[i]$.

(3) As we will see, the reason for the use of starred sorts in the present work (as in Tucker and Zucker [1988, 1989]) is the lack of effective coding of finite sequences within abstract structures in general.

We note that starred sorts have significance in programming languages, since starred variables can be used to model arrays, and (hence) *finite but unbounded memory*.

3 COMPUTABILITY ON STANDARD STRUCTURES

In §3.1 three computability classes are introduced. In §3.2 three more classes are formed from these by adjoining the μ operator to each of the former three. These latter three classes were already considered in Tucker and Zucker [1988, 1989, 1992*a*] (with different terminology).

We use the following notation. If $\vec{k} = k_1, \ldots, k_n$ $(m \geq 0)$ is a list of sorts then $A[\vec{k}]$ denotes $A_{k_1} \times \cdots \times A_{k_n}$.

3.1 Primitive Computable Functions

We consider three classes of computable functions on A. Each class can be defined in two ways, by *schemes* and by loop programs.

3.1.1 PR computability. We define PR ("primitive recursive") schemes α (over Σ) which define functions α^A over A, or, more generally, *families of functions* $\{\alpha^A \mid A \in \mathsf{K}\}$ uniformly over K. These schemes generalize the schemes for primitive recursive functions over N in Kleene [1952]. They define, on each $A \in \mathsf{K}$, (total) functions as follows:

(*i*) *Initial functions and constants* corresponding to all the operations of Σ.

(*ii*) *Projection:*

$$f(\vec{x}) = x_i$$

of type $(\vec{k}; k_i)$, where $\vec{x}$ is a tuple of variables of sorts $\vec{k}$.

(iii) Composition:

$$f(\vec{x}) = h(g_1(\vec{x}),\dots,g_m(\vec{x}))$$

where $g_1,\dots,g_m$ and h are PR (of suitable type).

(iv) Definition by cases:

$$f(b,x,y) = \begin{cases} x & \text{if } b = \mathsf{tt} \\ y & \text{if } b = \mathsf{ff} \end{cases}$$

of type $(\mathsf{B},k,k;k)$, where x and y are variables of sort k.

(v) Simultaneous primitive recursion on N: This defines, on each $A \in \mathsf{K}$, for fixed $m > 0$ (the degree of simultaneity), $n \geq 0$ (the number of parameters), and sorts $\vec{k} = k_1,\dots,k_n$ and $\vec{l} = l_1,\dots,l_m$, an m-tuple of functions $\vec{f} = (f_1,\dots,f_m)$ with f_i of type $(\mathsf{N},\vec{k};l_i)$, such that for all $\vec{x} \in A[\vec{k}]$ and $i = 1,\dots,m$,

$$f_i(0,\vec{x}) = g_i(\vec{x})$$
$$f_i(z+1,\vec{x}) = h_i(z,\vec{x},f_1(z,\vec{x}),\dots,f_m(z,\vec{x}))$$

where for $i = 1,\dots,m$, g_i and h_i are PR (of suitable type).

The last scheme use the standardness of the structures, *i.e.* the domain N. (In fact, the schemes of definition-by-cases also use the boolean domain B.)

The class of functions defined by the PR schemes over A can be shown to *coincide* with the class of those computable over A by *simple* loop *programs* (in fact, uniformly over K).

It turns out, however, that a broader class of functions provides a better generalization of the notion of primitive recursiveness:

3.1.2 CR computability. To form CR ("cov recursive") schemes, we modify the PR schemes by replacing the scheme (v) for simultaneous primitive recursion by a scheme (v') for *simultaneous cov (= course-of-values) recursion.* This defines, on each $A \in \mathsf{K}$, for fixed $m > 0$ (the degree of simultaneity), $d > 0$ (the degree of the cov recursion), and $n \geq 0$ (the number of parameters), and sorts $\vec{k} = k_1,\dots,k_n$ and $\vec{l} = l_1,\dots,l_m$, an m-tuple of functions $\vec{f} = (f_1,\dots,f_m)$ with f_i of type $(\mathsf{N},\vec{k};l_i)$ such that for all $\vec{x} \in A[\vec{k}]$ and $i = 1,\dots,m$,

$$f_i(0,\vec{x}) = g_i(\vec{x})$$

and for $z > 0$,

$$\begin{aligned} f_i(z,\vec{x}) =& h_i(z,\vec{x},f_1(\hat{\delta}_1(z,\vec{x}),\vec{x}),\dots,f_m(\hat{\delta}_1(z,\vec{x}),\vec{x}),\dots \\ & \dots,f_1(\hat{\delta}_d(z,\vec{x}),\vec{x}),\dots,f_m(\hat{\delta}_d(z,\vec{x}),\vec{x})) \end{aligned}$$

where for $i = 1,\dots,m$, g_i and h_i are μPR (of suitable type), and for $i = 1,\dots,d$, $\hat{\delta}_i$ is defined by

$$\hat{\delta}_i(z,\vec{x}) = \min(\delta_i(z,\vec{x}), z \dot{-} 1),$$

for some CR δ_i of type $(\mathsf{N},\vec{k};\mathsf{N})$, so that for $z > 0$, $\hat{\delta}_i(z,\vec{x}) < z$.

(Over $\mathbb{N}$, all these schemes are equivalent to simple primitive recursion: see Kleene [1952, §46].)

The class of functions so defined can be shown to coincide with the class of those computable over A by **loop** *programs with array variables* (again, uniformly over $\mathbb{K}$). (The proof is a modification of the equivalence proof of μPR and '**while**' computability quoted below in §3.2.)

3.1.3 PR computability.* A function on A is PR* computable if it is defined by a PR scheme over Σ^*, interpreted on A^* (*i.e.*, using starred sorts in its definition).

This class of functions can shown to coincide with the class of those computable over A by **loop** *programs over* A^* (uniformly for $A \in \mathbb{K}$).

But further, it can be shown to coincide with the class (3.1.2) of CR functions; so "cov is equivalent to star". It is in proving this equivalence that the Instantiation Assumption is used. Details will be given in a forthcoming publication.

3.2 μ-Computable Functions

Each of the following classes of computable (partial) functions can be defined by schemes and by '**while**' programs.

3.2.1 μPR computability. The μPR *schemes* over Σ are formed by adding to the PR schemes of §3.1.1 the scheme:

(*vi*) *Least number* or *μ operator:*

$$f(\vec{x}) \simeq \mu z[g(\vec{x},z) = \mathtt{tt}]$$

of type $(\vec{k};\mathsf{N})$, where g is a μPR function of type $(\vec{k},\mathsf{N};\mathsf{B})$. Here $f(\vec{x}) \downarrow z$ if, and only if, $g(\vec{x},y) \downarrow \mathtt{ff}$ for each $y < z$ and $g(\vec{x},z) \downarrow \mathtt{tt}$.

Note that this scheme also uses the standardness of the structure. Also, μPR computable functions are, in general, *partial.*

These schemes generalize the schemes for *partial recursive functions* over $\mathbb{N}$ of Kleene [1952].

The class of functions defined by these schemes over A was shown in Tucker and Zucker [1988] to *coincide* with the class of those computable over A by *simple* 'while' *programs* (again, uniformly over $\mathbb{K}$).

The following simple lemma will be used in Section 7.

LEMMA. *If f is a μPR computable function on A of type $(\vec{k}; l)$ and $\vec{x} \in A[\vec{k}]$, then $f(\vec{x})$ lies in the Σ-substructure of A generated by $\vec{x}$.*

PROOF: By structural induction on the μPR scheme for f. In the case of simultaneous primitive recursion, use a secondary induction on the numerical argument of the function. □

Again, a broader class turns out to be more useful:

3.2.2 μCR computability. This is just CR computability with the μ operator.

Again, the class of μCR computable functions was shown to coincide with the class of those computable over A by 'while' *programs with array variables* (uniformly over $\mathbb{K}$).

3.2.3 μPR^* computability. This is just PR* computability with μ.

This class of functions coincides with the class of those computable over A by 'while' *programs over A^** (uniformly for $A \in \mathbb{K}$).

Further, it coincides with the class (3.2.2) of μCR functions; so once again, "cov is equivalent to star". (Again, the Instantiation Assumption is used to prove this equivalence).

All these equivalences can be summarized in a theorem:

THEOREM. *For a function f on A, the following are equivalent:*

(i) f is μCR computable
(ii) f is μPR^* computable
(iii) f is 'while' computable with arrays over A
(iv) f is 'while' computable over A^*.

There are a number of other models of computability, due to Friedman, Shepherdson and others, which also turn out to be equivalent to the above: see Tucker and Zucker [1988, §4.10]. All these equivalences have led to the postulation of a *Generalized Church-Turing Thesis for parallel deterministic computation on abstract structures* (Tucker and Zucker [1988, §4.11]).

An analogous *Church-Turing Thesis for nondeterministic specification* is presented in Tucker and Zucker [1989, 1992*a*, 1992*b*].

4 Σ_1^* FORMULAE; THE SYSTEM Σ_1^*-*Ind*

Let ***Lang*** = ***Lang***(Σ) be the first order language over the signature Σ, with equality at all sorts. Similarly, let ***Lang***** = ***Lang***(Σ^*) be the first order language with equality over Σ^*.

The exact formulation of the logical connectives is not too important. Let us assume we have true, $\wedge$, $\vee$, $\rightarrow$, $\neg$.

Let us call the sorts i *simple*, i^{u} *augmented* and i^* *starred.* There are variables of all these sorts.

The *atomic formulae* of ***Lang*** and ***Lang**** are equalities between terms of sort i (and also of sort i^{u} and i^* in the case of ***Lang****), for all sorts i of Σ (whether equality sorts or not).

We will define classical and intuitionistic sequent calculi in ***Lang****. Our formulation will closely follow that for Gentzen's systems *LK* and *LJ*. (See Gentzen [1969] or Takeuti [1987] for background information on these systems.) In preparation, we must define certain classes of formulae of ***Lang****. (Below, z denotes a variable of sort N.)

DEFINITIONS. (1) A *bounded quantifier* is a quantifier of the form '$\forall z < t$' or '$\exists z < t$', where t is a term of sort N. (The most elegant approach is to think of these as primitive constructs, with their own introduction rules: see below).

(2) A formula is *elementary* if it has only bounded quantifiers.

(3) A Σ_1^* *formula* is formed by prefixing an elementary formula with existential quantifiers only.

(4) An *extended* Σ_1^* *formula* is formed by prefixing an elementary formula with a string of existential quantifiers and bounded universal quantifiers (in any order).

The importance of elementary formulae is given by

LEMMA 1. *If P is an elementary formula all of whose variables are of equality sort, then the predicate defined by P is PR* computable.*

PROOF: By structural induction on P. Equations between variables of equality sort are PR* computable, as are boolean operations and bounded quantification. □

Now let T be any set of formulae in ***Lang***, satisfied by the class $\mathbb{K}$. We can think of T as an *axiomatization* for $\mathbb{K}$. (We could suppose further that T is a "complete standard axiomatization" for $\mathbb{K}$, *i.e.*, that $\mathbb{K}$ is the class of all standard Σ-structures satisfying T, although this is unnecessary for the subsequent development.)

A *sequent* can be defined as a figure of the form $\Gamma \longmapsto \Delta$, where Γ and Δ are finite sequences of formulae, with the intuitive meaning that the conjunction of the *antecedent* Γ implies the disjunction of the *succedent* Δ. We actually define two sequent calculi, $\mathbf{\Sigma_1^*}$-$\boldsymbol{Ind_\ell} = \mathbf{\Sigma_1^*}$-$\boldsymbol{Ind_\ell}(\Sigma, T)$, where the subscript ℓ can be either 'c' (for "classical") or '*i*' (for "intuitionistic"). In the intuitionistic version, the sequents have only one formula in the succedent. Further, both systems contain the the following rules:

(*i*) Rules for the *first order predicate calculus with equality* over the signature Σ^*, including *cut*. These rules can be taken as in Gentzen [1969], Section III, §1.2 or Takeuti [1987] §2. There are further rules for the bounded quantifiers:

$$\forall_b L : \frac{\Gamma \longmapsto \Delta, s < t \qquad P(s), \Pi \longmapsto \Lambda}{\forall z < tP(z), \Gamma, \Pi \longmapsto \Delta, \Lambda} \qquad\qquad \forall_b R : \frac{a < t, \Gamma \longmapsto \Delta, P(a)}{\Gamma \longmapsto \Delta, \forall z < tP(z)}$$

where s and t are terms of sort N, and a is a variable of sort N, the '*eigenvariable*' of the inference $\forall_b R$, which does not occur in the conclusion of that inference.

There are also two rules for the bounded existential quantifier, dual to the above, which are left as exercises to the reader. (Actually, the bounded existential quantifier is not really needed in the subsequent development.)

We should also draw attention to the formulation of the *initial sequents.* The *logical initial sequents* have the form

$$P \longmapsto P,$$

for any formula P. (All other initial sequents are called *non logical.*) There are also initial sequents for *equality*:

$$\longmapsto t = t, \qquad\qquad t_1 = t_2, P(t_1) \longmapsto P(t_2)$$

for *atomic* $P(t)$ and terms t, t_1 and t_2 of the same sort (for all sorts of Σ^*);

(*ii*) Axioms expressing the *standardness* of Σ, including properties of the standard boolean operations:

$$\longmapsto \mathsf{true} \neq \mathsf{false}, \qquad \longmapsto t = \mathsf{true} \vee t = \mathsf{false}$$

for any term t of sort B, and for conjunction and negation:

$$\begin{array}{rr} \longmapsto \mathsf{con}(\mathsf{true},\mathsf{true}) = \mathsf{true}, & \longmapsto \mathsf{con}(\mathsf{true},\mathsf{false}) = \mathsf{false}, \\ \longmapsto \mathsf{con}(\mathsf{false},\mathsf{true}) = \mathsf{false}, & \longmapsto \mathsf{con}(\mathsf{false},\mathsf{false}) = \mathsf{false}, \\ \longmapsto \mathsf{neg}(\mathsf{true}) = \mathsf{false}, & \longmapsto \mathsf{neg}(\mathsf{false}) = \mathsf{true}, \end{array}$$

and Peano's axioms for '0' and 'S', and the axioms for '<' (expressed by the predicate 'less_N'):

$$\begin{array}{rr} \longmapsto \mathsf{eq}_\mathsf{N}(0,0) = \mathsf{true}, & \longmapsto \mathsf{eq}_\mathsf{N}(\mathsf{S}t,0) = \mathsf{false}, \\ \longmapsto \mathsf{eq}_\mathsf{N}(0,\mathsf{S}t) = \mathsf{false}, & \longmapsto \mathsf{eq}_\mathsf{N}(\mathsf{S}t_1,\mathsf{S}t_2) = \mathsf{eq}_\mathsf{N}(t_1,t_2), \\ \longmapsto \mathsf{less}_\mathsf{N}(0,\mathsf{S}t) = \mathsf{true}, & \longmapsto \mathsf{less}_\mathsf{N}(0,0) = \mathsf{false}, \\ \longmapsto \mathsf{less}_\mathsf{N}(\mathsf{S}t,0) = \mathsf{false}, & \longmapsto \mathsf{less}_\mathsf{N}(\mathsf{S}t_1,\mathsf{S}t_2) = \mathsf{less}_\mathsf{N}(t_1,t_2) \end{array}$$

for all terms t, t_1 and t_2 of sort N, and properties of the *equality operators* at all *equality sorts* i:

$$\longmapsto \mathsf{eq}_i(t,t) = \mathsf{true}, \qquad \mathsf{eq}_i(t_1,t_2) = \mathsf{true} \longmapsto x_1 = x_2.$$

(*iii*) Axioms for the new operations of Σ^u:

$$\begin{array}{c} \longmapsto \mathsf{Unspec}_i(\mathsf{i}_i(x)) = \mathsf{false}, \\ \longmapsto \mathsf{Unspec}_i(\mathsf{unspec}_i) = \mathsf{true}, \qquad \mathsf{Unspec}_i(y) = \mathsf{true} \longmapsto y = \mathsf{unspec}_i, \\ \longmapsto \mathsf{j}_i(\mathsf{i}_i(x)) = x, \qquad \longmapsto \mathsf{j}_i(\mathsf{unspec}_i) = \mathsf{c}_i, \\ \mathsf{Unspec}_i(y) = \mathsf{false} \longmapsto \mathsf{i}_i(\mathsf{j}_i(y)) = y \end{array}$$

where c_i is the closed term of sort i guaranteed by the Instantiation Assumption;

$$\begin{array}{c} \longmapsto F^\mathsf{u}(\mathsf{i}_{k_1}(x_1),\ldots,\mathsf{i}_{k_n}(x_n)) = \mathsf{i}_l(F(x_1,\ldots,x_n)), \\ \longmapsto F^\mathsf{u}(x_1,\ldots,x_{i-1},\mathsf{unspec}_{k_i},x_{i+1},\ldots,x_n) = \mathsf{unspec}_l \end{array}$$

where F has type $(\vec{k}; l)$; and for the new operations of Σ^* (dropping sort subscripts now):

$$\begin{aligned}
&\longmapsto \mathsf{Lgth}(\mathsf{Null}) = 0,\\
\mathsf{less}_{\mathsf{N}}(z, \mathsf{Lgth}(a)) = \mathsf{false} &\longmapsto \mathsf{Ap}(a, z) = \mathsf{unspec},\\
&\longmapsto \mathsf{Lgth}(\mathsf{Update}(a, z, x)) = \mathsf{Lgth}(a),\\
\mathsf{eq}_{\mathsf{N}}(z, z_0) = \mathsf{false} &\longmapsto \mathsf{Ap}(\mathsf{Update}(a, z_0, x), z) = \mathsf{Ap}(a, z),\\
\mathsf{less}_{\mathsf{N}}(z, \mathsf{Lgth}(a)) = \mathsf{true} &\longmapsto \mathsf{Ap}(\mathsf{Update}(a, z, x), z) = x,\\
&\longmapsto \mathsf{Lgth}(\mathsf{Newlength}(a, z)) = z,\\
\mathsf{less}_{\mathsf{N}}(z, z_1) = \mathsf{true} &\longmapsto \mathsf{Ap}(\mathsf{Newlength}(a, z_1), z) = \mathsf{Ap}(a, z);
\end{aligned}$$

and finally axioms relating equality on i^* to equality on i, for all sorts i:

$$\mathsf{Lgth}(s_1) = \mathsf{Lgth}(s_2), \forall z < \mathsf{Lgth}(s_1)(\mathsf{Ap}(s_1, z) = \mathsf{Ap}(s_2, z)) \longmapsto s_1 = s_2.$$

(*iv*) The Σ_1^* *induction rule*:

$$\frac{\Gamma \longmapsto \Delta, P(0) \qquad P(a), \Pi \longmapsto \Lambda, P(\mathsf{S}a)}{\Gamma, \Pi \longmapsto \Delta, \Lambda, P(t)}$$

where $P(a)$ is a Σ_1^* formula, a is a variable of sort N, the *eigenvariable* of this inference, not occurring in the conclusion, and t is a term of sort N (and Δ and Λ are empty in the intuitionistic system). The occurrence of $P(t)$ shown is called the *principal formula* of the inference.

(*v*) The *axioms T for* $\mathbb{K}$, in sequent form.

REMARKS. (1) The system Σ_1^*-***Ind***$_i$ is, trivially, a *subsystem* of Σ_1^*-***Ind***$_c$.

(2) Note that the non-logical initial sequents (including the axioms of T) contain *elementary formulae* only. This is important for the proofs of both Theorems 3 and 4 in Section 6.

(3) In the intuitionistic system Σ_1^*-***Ind***$_i$, we can derive the *decidability of equality* at all simple *equality sorts*:

$$\longmapsto t_1 = t_2 \vee t_1 \neq t_2,$$

as well as the decidability of unspec_i at *all sorts* i^{u} (not just for equality sorts i):

$$\longmapsto t = \mathsf{unspec}_i \vee t \neq \mathsf{unspec}_i.$$

A useful lemma is one formalizing *concatenation of arrays* in Σ_1^*-***Ind***:

LEMMA 2 (CONCATENATION LEMMA). *The following sequent is derivable in* Σ_1^*-$\boldsymbol{Ind_i}$ *by* Σ_1^* *induction on* $\mathsf{Lgth}(y^*)$*:*

$$\begin{aligned} \longmapsto \forall x^* \forall y^* \exists z^* \big(&\mathsf{Lgth}(z^*) = \mathsf{Lgth}(x^*) + \mathsf{Lgth}(y^*) \wedge \\ &\forall z < \mathsf{Lgth}(x^*)(z^*[z] = x^*[z]) \wedge \\ &\forall z < \mathsf{Lgth}(y^*)(z^*[\mathsf{Lgth}(x^*) + z] = y^*[z])\big), \end{aligned}$$

PROOF: The derivation proceeds by Σ_1^* induction on $\mathsf{Lgth}(y^*)$. □

LEMMA 3 (FINITE CHOICE AXIOMS). *The following sequents are derivable in* Σ_1^*-$\boldsymbol{Ind_i}$*:*

$$\forall z < t \exists x P(z, x) \longmapsto \exists x^* \forall z < t P(z, x^*[z]) \tag{1}$$

where P is a Σ_1^* formula, t a term of sort N*, x is a variable of sort i (say) and x^* is a variable of the corresponding starred sort i^*; and*

$$\forall z < t \exists x^* P(z, x^*) \longmapsto \exists y^* \forall z < t P(z, y^*[z]) \tag{2}$$

where P is an extended Σ_1^* formula and t is of sort N *again, x^* is of sort i^*, and the variable y^*, of sort i^*, effectively codes a "doubly starred" object (as described in §2.3, Remark 2) which, when applied to the index z, yields a singly starred object (here also denoted $y^*[z]$ by abuse of notation).*

PROOF: First assume that P is *elementary*. For axiom (1), proceed as follows (arguing informally in Σ_1^*-$\boldsymbol{Ind_i}$). Assume $\forall z < t \exists x P(z, x)$. Then prove

$$z \leq t \;\rightarrow\; \exists x^* \big(\mathsf{Lgth}(x^*) = z \wedge \forall v < z\, P(v, x^*[v])\big)$$

(which is provably equivalent to a Σ_1^* formula), by Σ_1^* induction on z. Briefly, the idea is to extend the array x^* suitably by one item at each step.

Axiom (2) is proved similarly, except that at each step the array y^* is extended by a *segment*. The Concatenation Lemma can be used here.

Now let P be Σ_1^*. Use the above methods (in cases (1) and (2)) to "solve" simultaneously for x, as well as *all* existential quantifiers of P (starred and unstarred), as arrays, or functions of $z < t$. In this case, all these arrays are extended by one item simultaneously at each step. □

LEMMA 4. *In* Σ_1^*-$\boldsymbol{Ind_i}$*, every extended Σ_1^* formula is provably equivalent to some Σ_1^* formula.*

PROOF: The finite choice axioms are applied repeatedly (from the inside of the formula outwards), so as to shift all bounded universal quantifiers to the right. □

For a formula P of $\boldsymbol{Lang^*}$, we write $\boldsymbol{\Sigma_1^*}$-$\boldsymbol{Ind_\ell} \vdash P$ to mean that the sequent $\longmapsto P$ is provable in $\boldsymbol{\Sigma_1^*}$-$\boldsymbol{Ind_\ell}$ (for $\ell = c$ or i). We also write $\mathsf{K}^* \models P$ to mean that P is valid in K^*, *i.e.*, $A^* \models P$ for every $A \in \mathsf{K}$. The following *soundness* result then clearly holds:

LEMMA 4 (SOUNDNESS).

$$\boldsymbol{\Sigma_1^*}\text{-}\boldsymbol{Ind_c} \vdash P \quad \Longrightarrow \quad \mathsf{K}^* \models P.$$

5 COMPUTATION PREDICATES; PROVABLE TOTALITY OF SCHEMES

With each μPR* scheme α of type $(\vec{k};l)$ we can effectively associate a Σ_1^* formula $P_\alpha(\vec{x},y)$, the *computation predicate for* α, where $\vec{x}$ is a sequence of variables of sorts $\vec{k}$ and y has sort l, which represents the graph of the function defined by α. More precisely: for all $A \in \mathsf{K}$, and for all $\vec{a} \in A[\vec{k}]$ and $b \in A_l$,

$$A \models P_\alpha[\vec{a},b] \quad \Longleftrightarrow \quad \alpha^A(\vec{a}) \downarrow b.$$

This predicate formalizes the computational history given by the μPR* schemes. It is actually an existentially quantified form of a generalized version of Kleene's [1952] T predicate. (Another generalized version of the T predicate was defined in Tucker and Zucker [1988], as a formalization of '**while**' program computations over abstract structures.)

The construction of P_α proceeds by structural induction on the scheme α. (We will repeatedly use the equivalence of Σ_1^* and extended Σ_1^* formulae proved in Section 4, Lemma 4.) We proceed by cases, according to the construction of schemes α given in Section 3.

(*i*) *Initial functions and constants.* Suppose α is the scheme for the function symbol F of Σ^*, of type $(\vec{k};l)$. Then

$$P_\alpha(\vec{x},y) \quad \equiv \quad F(\vec{x}) = y.$$

(*ii*) *Projection.* If α is the scheme for projection of type $(\vec{k},k_i)$, then

$$P_\alpha(\vec{x},y) \quad \equiv \quad y = x_i.$$

(*iii*) *Composition.* Suppose α is the scheme for composition formed from the schemes $\beta, \gamma_1, \ldots, \gamma_m$. Then

$$P_\alpha(\vec{x}, y) \equiv \exists z_1, \ldots, z_m \left[P_{\gamma_1}(\vec{x}, z_1) \wedge \cdots \wedge P_{\gamma_1}(\vec{x}, z_m) \wedge P_\beta(\vec{z}, y)\right].$$

(*iv*) *Definition by cases.* Easy exercise.

(*v*) *Simultaneous primitive recursion.* Suppose (in the notation of §3.1.1) the functions f_i, given by schemes α_i, are formed by simultaneous primitive recursion from g_i and h_i, given by schemes β_i and γ_i respectively ($i = 1, \ldots, m$). Then for $i = 1, \ldots, m$,

$$\begin{aligned} P_{\alpha_i}(z, \vec{x}, y) \equiv \exists w_1^*, \ldots, w_m^* \Big[\bigwedge_{j=1}^{m} \big(&\mathsf{Lgth}(w_j^*) = z + 1 \ \wedge\ P_{\beta_j}(\vec{x}, w_j^*[0]) \\ &\wedge \forall v < z\, P_{\gamma_j}(v, \vec{x}, w_1^*[v], \ldots, w_m^*[v], w_j^*[v+1])\big) \\ &\wedge w_i^*[z] = y \Big]. \end{aligned}$$

Here the existentially quantified starred variables w_i^*, of sorts l_i^* ($i = 1, \ldots$ $\ldots, m$), code the initial segments of the functions f_i on the arguments $0, \ldots, z$.

We see here how starred existential quantifiers and bounded universal quantifiers enter into the definition of P_α.

(*vi*) μ *operator.* Suppose the function given by the scheme α is formed with the μ operator from the function given by the scheme β (see §3.2.1). Then

$$P_\alpha(\vec{x}, y) \equiv \forall z < y\, P_\beta(\vec{x}, z, \mathsf{false}) \wedge P_\beta(\vec{x}, y, \mathsf{true}).$$

Here we see another way in which bounded universal quantifiers can enter into the definition of P_α.

REMARK. Even if the scheme α is defined over Σ only (*i.e.*, the sorts involved in its definition are all simple), the definition of P_α generally involves existential quantification over *starred sorts*. This arises from the case (v) of simultaneous primitive recursion, as noted above.

DEFINITION. A scheme α is *provably total in* $\boldsymbol{\Sigma_1^*}$-***Ind***$_{\boldsymbol{t}}$ iff

$$\boldsymbol{\Sigma_1^*}\text{-}\boldsymbol{Ind_t} \vdash \forall \vec{x}\, \exists y P_\alpha(\vec{x}, y).$$

We can now state two of the main results of this paper. Remember that a PR* scheme is a special type of μPR* scheme, namely one in which the μ operator is not used.

THEOREM 1. *If α is a PR* scheme, then α is provably total in Σ_1^*-**Ind**$_i$ (and hence in Σ_1^*-**Ind**$_c$).*

PROOF: The required derivation is constructed by structural induction on α. There are five cases to consider, according to the five clauses in the definition of PR* schemes (§3.1.1). The first four cases are quite simple. We consider now case (v): simultaneous primitive recursion, and consider the computation predicates $P_{\alpha_i}(z, \vec{x}, y)$ $(i = 1, \ldots, m)$ defined above for this case. We must show how to prove, in Σ_1^*-**Ind**, $\exists y P_{\alpha_i}(z, \vec{x}, y)$ (a Σ_1^* formula) by induction on z.

Assume first that the ranges of the α_i are unstarred sorts. Then the induction step amounts to constructing appropriate one-step extensions to the initial segments (represented by) w_i^* $(i = 1, \ldots, m)$ of the functions defined by α_i, on the arguments $0, \ldots, z$. This is easily done with the help of the **Newlength** and **Update** operations.

Now assume that the ranges of the α_i may be starred sorts. In that case the variables w_i^* actually code two-dimensional arrays (as in §2.3, Remark 2), and the construction of their "one-step extensions" involves extending such arrays by *segments*. This can be done with the help of the Concatenation Lemma (Section 4, Lemma 2). The argument then proceeds as in the unstarred case. □

In order to formulate a converse result, we must now make an assumption on T.

ASSUMPTION (UNIVERSAL AXIOMATIZATION). *The axioms T for $\mathbb{K}$ are universal.*

This assumption is not unduly restrictive, as it includes, in particular, axiomatizations by *Horn formulae*, which are central to the theory of logic programming and abstract data types (see Meinke and Tucker [1990]). Note, incidentally, that Horn formulae lend themselves well to the sequent calculus formalism.

Now, as a sort of converse to Theorem 1, we have the following, to be proved in Section 6.

THEOREM 2. *Let α be a μPR* scheme. If α is provably total in Σ_1^*-**Ind**$_\ell$ ($\ell = c$ or i), then α is "extensionally PR* on $\mathbb{K}$", i.e., there is a PR* scheme β such that $\alpha^A = \beta^A$ for all $A \in \mathbb{K}$.*

6 COMPUTABLE SELECTION FUNCTIONS

This section is devoted to the proof of Theorem 2. This has two major steps. The first is a "cut reduction theorem".

DEFINITIONS. (1) A sequent is called Σ_1^* if all its formulae are Σ_1^*.

(2) A cut is called Σ_1^* if the cut formula is Σ_1^*.

(3) A derivation is *reduced* if all its cuts are Σ_1^*.

THEOREM 3 (CUT REDUCTION THEOREM). *Every derivation* D *in* Σ_1^*-$\boldsymbol{Ind}_\ell$ *($\ell = c$ or i) can be transformed into a reduced derivation* D' *of the same end-sequent. Moreover, if the end-sequent is* Σ_1^* *then every formula in* D' *is* Σ_1^*.

PROOF: By a technique similar to that in the proof of Gentzen's *Hauptsatz* (see Gentzen [1969, III, §3] or Takeuti [1987, Chapter 1, §5]). For convenience, for the duration of this proof (only) we work with a modified form of cut, the 'mix' inference:

$$\frac{\Gamma \longmapsto \Delta \qquad \Pi \longmapsto \Lambda}{\Gamma, \Pi^* \longmapsto \Delta^*, \Lambda}$$

where the sequences Δ and Π each contain at least one occurrence of the mix formula, say A, and Δ^* and Π^* denote these same sequences, with all such occurrences of A deleted.

Note that there is a simple effective way of transforming a cut into a mix (of the same formula), plus a sequence of thinnings and interchanges. Conversely, there is a simple effective way of transforming a mix into a sequence of interchanges and cuts (of the same formula).

The theorem follows easily from the following

LEMMA. *A derivation which contains only one non-Σ_1^* mix, occurring as the last inference, can be replaced by a reduced derivation (i.e., containing only Σ_1^* mixes) of the same sequent.*

The proof of the lemma is by a double induction on the *degree* and the *rank* of the derivation (defined in the above references). There are the following new cases to consider when the rank is 2, *i.e.*, when each occurrence of the mix formula is either the "principal formula" of an inference or in an initial sequent:

(1) The left mix formula is the principle formula of a Σ_1^* *induction inference*. But in that case the mix would be Σ_1^*, contrary to assumption.

(2) One of the mix formulae is in one of the *non-logical initial sequents*. But that would make it quantifier-free (see Remark 1 in §4). So again the mix would be Σ_1^*, contrary to assumption.

(3) Both mix formulae are principle formulae of inferences for *bounded quantifiers* (universal, let us say). The technique here combines those for the cases of the inferences for (unbounded) universal quantifiers and implication:

$$\cfrac{\cfrac{a < t, \Gamma_1 \longmapsto \Delta_1, P(a)}{\Gamma_1 \longmapsto \Delta_1, \forall z < tP(z)}\ \forall_b R \qquad \cfrac{\Gamma_2 \longmapsto \Delta_2, s < t \quad P(s), \Gamma_3 \longmapsto \Delta_3}{\forall z < tP(z), \Gamma_2, \Gamma_3 \longmapsto \Delta_2, \Delta_3}\ \forall_b L}{\Gamma_1, \Gamma_2, \Gamma_3 \longmapsto \Delta_1, \Delta_2, \Delta_3}\ \text{mix}$$

This is transformed to

$$\cfrac{\cfrac{\Gamma_2 \longmapsto \Delta_2, s < t \qquad \cfrac{s < t, \Gamma_1 \longmapsto \Delta_1, P(s) \qquad P(s), \Gamma_3 \longmapsto \Delta_3}{s < t, \Gamma_1, \Gamma_3^* \longmapsto \Delta_1^*, \Delta_3}\ \text{mix}}{\Gamma_2, \Gamma_1^*, \Gamma_3^* \longmapsto \Delta_2^*, \Delta_1^*, \Delta_3}\ \text{mix}}{\cfrac{\text{thinnings and interchanges}}{\Gamma_2, \Gamma_1, \Gamma_3 \longmapsto \Delta_2, \Delta_1, \Delta_3}}$$

(Above the upper sequent of the $\forall_b R$ inference, the eigenvariable a has been replaced by the term s. This is legitimate, provided the eigenvariables of the derivation have been suitably chosen.) The mix has been replaced by two mixes of lower degree, which can be eliminated in turn, by the main induction hypothesis (unless they are Σ_1^*, in which case they can be ignored).

For the second statement of the theorem, we can show that if the conclusion of a reduced derivation D is Σ_1^*, then all sequents of D are Σ_1^*, by a simple induction on the length of D. (Just consider all possibilities for the last inference rule in D. The two interesting cases, Σ_1^* induction and Σ_1^* mix, do not spoil the pattern of Σ_1^* sequents.) □

The second major step in the proof of Theorem 2 involves the construction of primitive recursive schemes to "witness" existential assertions provable in Σ_1^*-$\boldsymbol{Ind_t}$. This result (Theorem 4) can, in fact, be viewed as the central result of this paper.

THEOREM 4. *Suppose*

$$\Sigma_1^*\text{-}\boldsymbol{Ind}_\ell \vdash \exists y P(\vec{x}, y)$$

($\ell = c$ or i), where $P(\vec{x}, y)$ is a Σ_1^* formula, with free variables $\vec{x}$ of sorts $\vec{k}$ and y of sort l. Then there is a PR scheme β of type $(\vec{k}; l)$ such that for all $A \in \mathsf{K}$, and for all $\vec{a} \in A[\vec{k}]$,*

$$A \models P[\vec{a}, \beta^A(\vec{a})].$$

REMARK. The function β^A is called a *selection function, Skolem function, realizing function* or *witnessing function* for y in P.

PROOF: We consider the classical case, which trivially implies the intuitionistic case. We must actually prove a more general result, from which the theorem immediately follows:

For any Σ_1^* sequent $\Gamma \longmapsto \Delta$ provable in $\Sigma_1^*\text{-}\boldsymbol{Ind}_c$, there are PR* schemes for selection functions for all the existentially quantified variables in Δ, as functions of the free variables in $\Gamma \longmapsto \Delta$ *and also* of the existentially quantified variables in Γ. In symbols: Suppose $\Gamma = \langle \exists \vec{z}_j Q_j(\vec{x}, \vec{z}_j) \mid j = 1, \ldots, m\rangle$ and $\Delta = \langle \exists \vec{y}_i P_i(\vec{x}, \vec{y}_i) \mid i = 1, \ldots, n\rangle$, where Q_j and P_i are elementary, $\vec{x}$ contains all free variables in the sequent, and each $\vec{z}_j$ and $\vec{y}_i$ is a (possibly empty) list of (starred or unstarred) variables. Then we can construct vectors of PR* schemes $\vec{\beta}_1, \ldots, \vec{\beta}_n$ such that (using "vector notation" for function application) the sequent

$$\ldots, Q_j(\vec{x}, \vec{z}_j), \ldots \longmapsto \ldots, P_i(\vec{x}, \vec{\beta}_i(\vec{x}, \vec{z}_1, \ldots, \vec{x}, \vec{z}_m)), \ldots \tag{3}$$

is K-*valid*, which means that for all $A \in \mathsf{K}$ and vectors $\vec{a}, \vec{c}_1, \ldots, \vec{c}_m$ from A (of the correct sorts),

$$A \models \bigwedge_{i=1}^{m} Q_j[\vec{a}, \vec{c}_j] \rightarrow \bigvee_{i=1}^{n} P_i[\vec{a}, \vec{\beta}_i^A(\vec{a}, \vec{c})].$$

We will call (3) the *Skolem form* of the given sequent $\Gamma \longmapsto \Delta$. By Theorem 3, we may assume we have a *reduced* derivation of $\Gamma \longmapsto \Delta$, in which every sequent is Σ_1^*. The required PR* schemes are then constructed by induction on the length of such a derivation.

The *base case* involves initial sequents. Since all such sequents, including the axioms for T, contain only elementary formulae, the result holds trivially for them. (This issue is discussed further in Section 7.)

For the *induction step*, there are different cases according to the last inference of the derivation.

The cases of *thinning*, *interchange* and *contr:L* (contraction on the left) are trivial.

If it is a *propositional* or *bounded* $\forall$ inference, then the principle formula must be elementary (by the definition of Σ^* formulae), so such a case is also trivial — except that in the cases of $\wedge R$ (in the classical system) and $\vee L$ (in both systems) we must use definition by cases because of the implicit contraction of the (non-principle) formulae in the succedent (see the case *contr:R* below).

It cannot be a $\forall$ inference, since then the principle formula would not be Σ_1^*, contradicting the assumption that the derivation is reduced.

Suppose it is *contr:R*, say

$$\frac{\ldots, \exists\vec{z}_j Q_j(\vec{x},\vec{z}_j), \ldots \longmapsto \ldots, \exists\vec{y}_i P_i(\vec{x},\vec{y}_i), \ldots, \exists\vec{y}R(\vec{x},\vec{y}), \exists\vec{y}R(\vec{x},\vec{y})}{\ldots, \exists\vec{z}_j Q_j(\vec{x},\vec{z}_j), \ldots \longmapsto \ldots, \exists\vec{y}_i P_i(\vec{x},\vec{y}_i), \ldots, \exists\vec{y}R(\vec{x},\vec{y})}$$

with principle formula $\exists\vec{y}R$ (R elementary). By induction hypothesis there are PR* schemes $\vec{\beta}_i, \vec{\gamma}_1, \vec{\gamma}_2$ such that

$$\ldots, Q_j(\vec{x},\vec{z}_j), \ldots \longmapsto \ldots, P_i(\vec{x},\vec{\beta}_i(\vec{x},\vec{z})), \ldots, R(\vec{x},\vec{\gamma}_1(\vec{x},\vec{z})), R(\vec{x},\vec{\gamma}_2(\vec{x},\vec{z}))$$

is K-valid (where $\vec{z} \equiv \vec{z}_1, \ldots, \vec{z}_n$). Then $\vec{\beta}_i$ also provides selection functions for the formulae $\exists\vec{y}_i R(\vec{x},\vec{y}_i)$ in the conclusion. As for the principle formula $\exists\vec{y}S$, define the vector of PR* schemes

$$\vec{\gamma}(\vec{x},\vec{z}) = \begin{cases} \vec{\gamma}_1(\vec{x},\vec{z}) & \text{if } R(\vec{x},\vec{\gamma}_1(\vec{x},\vec{z})) \\ \vec{\gamma}_2(\vec{x},\vec{z}) & \text{otherwise} \end{cases}$$

using definition by cases (by Section 4, Lemma 1). Then $\vec{\gamma}$ provides selection functions for $\exists\vec{y}S$ in the conclusion.

Suppose the last inference is $\exists R$:

$$\frac{\ldots, \exists\vec{z}_j Q_j(\vec{x},\vec{z}_j), \ldots \longmapsto \ldots, \exists\vec{y}_i P_i(\vec{x},\vec{y}_i), \ldots, \exists\vec{y}R(\vec{x},t,\vec{y})}{\ldots, \exists\vec{z}_j Q_j(\vec{x},\vec{z}_j), \ldots \longmapsto \ldots, \exists\vec{y}_i P_i(\vec{x},\vec{y}_i), \ldots, \exists y\exists\vec{y}R(\vec{x},y,\vec{y}).}$$

Now the term t may contain extra free variables $\vec{v}$ not occurring elsewhere in the premiss (or the conclusion). So put $t \equiv t(\vec{v},\vec{x})$, where the free variables in the premiss are among $\vec{v},\vec{x}$. Then, by induction hypothesis, there are PR* schemes $\vec{\beta}'_i, \vec{\gamma}'$ such that the sequent

$$\ldots, Q_j(\vec{x}, \vec{z}_j), \ldots \longmapsto \ldots, P_i(\vec{x}, \vec{\beta}'_i(\vec{v}, \vec{x}, \vec{z})), \ldots, R(\vec{x}, t, \vec{\gamma}'(\vec{v}, \vec{x}, \vec{z}))$$

is K-valid. Now let $\vec{t}_0$ be a vector of *closed terms* of the same sorts as the vector $\vec{v}$. The existence of such closed terms is guaranteed by the Instantiation Assumption! Then (since the variables $\vec{v}$ are not free in the conclusion) PR* selection functions $\vec{\beta}_i$ for $\exists \vec{y}_i P_i$ in the conclusion are given by

$$\vec{\beta}_i(\vec{x}, \vec{z}) =_{df} \vec{\beta}'_i(\vec{t}_0, \vec{x}, \vec{z}),$$

and selection functions $\gamma, \vec{\gamma}$ for the principle formula $\exists y \exists \vec{y} R(\vec{x}, y, \vec{y})$ are given by

$$\gamma(\vec{x}, \vec{z}) =_{df} \vec{t}(\vec{t}_0, \vec{x})$$
$$\vec{\gamma}(\vec{x}, \vec{z}) =_{df} \vec{\gamma}'(\vec{t}_0, \vec{x}, \vec{z}).$$

(We are using here an obvious lemma, that the value of any term of the signature Σ^* is PR* in its free variables.)

If the last inference is $\exists L$, then exactly the same selection functions for the premiss work for the conclusion. The only difference is that one of the arguments of these functions is represented in the premiss by a free variable (the eigenvariable of the inference), and in the conclusion by an existentially quantified variable (in the antecedent).

Now suppose the last inference is *cut*, with premisses

$$\ldots, \exists \vec{z}_j Q_j(\vec{x}, \vec{z}_j), \ldots \longmapsto \ldots, \exists \vec{y}_i P_i(\vec{x}, \vec{y}_i), \ldots, \exists \vec{y} R(\vec{v}, \vec{x}, \vec{y}), \tag{4}$$
$$\exists \vec{y} R(\vec{v}, \vec{x}, \vec{y}), \ldots, \exists \vec{z}'_j Q'_j(\vec{x}, \vec{z}'_j), \ldots \longmapsto \ldots, \exists \vec{y}'_i P'_i(\vec{x}, \vec{y}'_i), \ldots \tag{5}$$

(where $\vec{x}$ contains the free variables in both premisses) and conclusion

$$\ldots, \exists \vec{z}_j Q_j(\vec{x}, \vec{z}_j), \ldots, \exists \vec{z}'_j Q'_j(\vec{x}, \vec{z}'_j), \ldots \longmapsto$$
$$\ldots, \exists \vec{y}_i P_i(\vec{x}, \vec{y}_i), \ldots, \exists \vec{y}'_i P'_i(\vec{x}, \vec{y}'_i), \ldots. \tag{6}$$

Note that the cut formula $\exists \vec{y} R(\vec{v}, \vec{x}, \vec{y})$ (where R is elementary) may have extra free variables $\vec{v}$ not occurring elsewhere in the two premisses (or the conclusion).

By induction hypothesis, there are PR* schemes $\vec{\beta}_i, \gamma, \vec{\beta}'_i$ such that the sequents

$$\ldots, Q_j(\vec{x}, \vec{z}_j), \ldots \longmapsto \ldots, P_i(\vec{x}, \vec{\beta}_i(\vec{v}, \vec{x}, \vec{z})), \ldots, R(\vec{v}, \vec{x}, \gamma(\vec{v}, \vec{x}, \vec{z})), \quad (4')$$

$$R(\vec{v}, \vec{x}, \vec{y}), \ldots, Q'_j(\vec{x}, \vec{z}'_j), \ldots \longmapsto \ldots, P'_i(\vec{x}, \vec{\beta}'_i(\vec{v}, \vec{x}, \vec{y}, \vec{z}')), \ldots \quad (5')$$

are valid. Let $\vec{t}_0$ be a vector of closed terms of the same sorts as $\vec{v}$ (guaranteed again by the Instantiation Assumption). Now *replace*, in sequents (4′) and (5′), $\vec{v}$ by $\vec{t}_0$, and $\vec{y}$ by $\gamma(\vec{t}_0, \vec{x}, \vec{z})$. The resulting two sequents are again valid, and can be used as premisses of a cut, with cut formula $R(\vec{t}_0, \gamma(\vec{t}_0, \vec{x}, \vec{z}))$. By comparing the (valid) conclusion of this cut with sequent (6), we can see that selection functions (in the arguments $\vec{x}, \vec{z}, \vec{z}'$) can be given as required for (6) as follows:

$$\vec{\beta}_i(\vec{t}_0, \vec{x}, \vec{z}) \quad \text{for} \quad \exists \vec{y}_i P_i,$$

$$\vec{\beta}'_i(\vec{t}_0, \vec{x}, \gamma(\vec{t}_0, \vec{x}, \vec{z}), \vec{z}') \quad \text{for} \quad \exists \vec{y}'_i P'_i.$$

Suppose, finally, that the last inference is an induction, with premisses

$$\ldots, \exists \vec{z}_j Q_j(\vec{x}, \vec{z}_j), \ldots \longmapsto \ldots, \exists \vec{y}_i P_i(\vec{x}, \vec{y}_i), \ldots, \exists \vec{y} R(0, \vec{x}, \vec{y}), \quad (7)$$

$$\exists \vec{y} R(a, \vec{x}, \vec{y}), \ldots, \exists \vec{z}'_j Q'_j(\vec{x}, \vec{z}'_j), \ldots \longmapsto \ldots, \exists \vec{y}'_i P'_i(\vec{x}, \vec{y}'_i), \ldots, \exists \vec{y} R(\mathsf{S}a, \vec{x}, \vec{y}) \quad (8)$$

and conclusion

$$\ldots, \exists \vec{z}_j Q_j(\vec{x}, \vec{z}_j), \ldots, \exists \vec{z}'_j Q'_j(\vec{x}, \vec{z}'_j), \ldots \longmapsto \ldots, \exists \vec{y}_i P_i(\vec{x}, \vec{y}_i), \ldots, \exists \vec{y}'_i P'_i(\vec{x}, \vec{y}'_i), \ldots, \exists \vec{y} R(t, \vec{x}, \vec{y}) \quad (9)$$

(where $\vec{x}$ contains the free variables in both premisses and in $t \equiv t(\vec{x})$).

By induction hypothesis (applied to (7) and (8)), there are PR* schemes $\vec{\beta}_i, \vec{\beta}'_i, \vec{\gamma}, \vec{\delta}$ such that the sequents

$$\ldots, Q_j(\vec{x}, \vec{z}_j), \ldots \longmapsto \ldots, P_i(\vec{x}, \vec{\beta}_i(\vec{x}, \vec{z})), \ldots, R(0, \vec{x}, \gamma(\vec{x}, \vec{z})), \quad (7')$$

$$R(a, \vec{x}, \vec{w}), \ldots, Q'_j(\vec{x}, \vec{z}'_j), \ldots \longmapsto \ldots, P'_i(\vec{x}, \vec{\beta}'_i(a, \vec{x}, \vec{z}', \vec{w})), \ldots R(\mathsf{S}a, \vec{x}, \vec{\delta}(a, \vec{x}, \vec{z}', \vec{w})) \quad (8')$$

are valid. Define a vector $\vec{\rho}$ of PR* schemes by simultaneous primitive recursion:

$$\vec{\rho}(0, \vec{x}, \vec{z}, \vec{z}\,') = \gamma(\vec{x}, \vec{z})$$
$$\vec{\rho}(n+1, \vec{x}, \vec{z}, \vec{z}\,') = \vec{\delta}(n, \vec{x}, \vec{z}\,', \vec{\rho}(n, \vec{x}, \vec{z}, \vec{z}\,')).$$

Now we can construct selection functions as required for (9) (in the arguments $\vec{x}, \vec{z}, \vec{z}\,'$) as follows:

$$\begin{aligned} \vec{\beta}_i(\vec{x}, \vec{z}) \quad & \text{for} \quad \exists \vec{y}_i P_i \quad \text{(as in the premiss (7))}, \\ \vec{\beta}'_i(t(\vec{x}), \vec{x}, \vec{z}\,', \vec{\rho}(t(\vec{x}), \vec{x}, \vec{z}, \vec{z}\,')) \quad & \text{for} \quad \exists \vec{y}'_i P'_i, \\ \vec{\rho}(t(\vec{x}), \vec{x}, \vec{z}, \vec{z}\,') \quad & \text{for} \quad \exists \vec{y} R(t(\vec{x}), \vec{x}, \vec{y}). \end{aligned}$$

These make the Skolem form of (9) valid, as can be proved by (metamathematical) induction on the value of the term $t(\vec{x})$ (for a given evaluation of $\vec{x}$), using the validity of (7′) and (8′). □

Theorem 2 now follows easily from Theorem 4, applied to the predicate P_α.

Notice also the following (obvious) converse to Theorem 4: every PR* scheme α gives the unique selection function for some Σ_1^* predicate, namely the predicate P_α itself!

7 UNIVERSAL AXIOMATIZATION OF THE THEORY T

The requirement of universal axiomatization of T is used in the proofs of Theorems 3 and 4. Actually, the proof of Theorem 3 only requires existential (Σ_1^*) axiomatization of T. However the proof of Theorem 4 requires quantifier-free (or universal) axiomatization of T. The reason for this can be seen by considering the inductive construction of PR* selection functions given by the proof. The base case involves initial sequents, including those expressing the axioms of T. If these sequents were not quantifier-free, it would, in general, be impossible, at this stage already, to construct such a PR* selection function!

Here are two examples to clarify this.

(1) Consider two axiomatizations of *group theory*:

(i) with (as usual) a function symbol f for the inverse of the group operation '$*$' and with the appropriate axiom in the quantifier-free form

$$x * f(x) = 1;$$

(*ii*) without such an symbol for the inverse, and with the corresponding axiom in the (existentially quantified!) form

$$\exists y(x * y = 1).$$

It should be clear that with the axiomatization (*ii*), there is (in general) no PR* selector for this axiom. Here is a specific counterexample. Let A be the additive group of integers (standardized as described in §2.1), with signature Σ containing (apart from the standard part) only 0 and +. Now by the Lemma in §3.2.1 (applied to Σ^*), for any μPR* operation $f : A \to A$, $f(1)$ must lie in the Σ^*-substructure of A generated by $\{1\}$, which (as is easy to see) must lie within $\{x \in A \mid x \geq 0\}$. Hence the unary minus operation cannot be μPR*, let alone PR*.

We note that axiomatizations of theories in model theory often use form (*ii*), *i.e.*, $\forall\exists$ formulae, in order to avoid the problems raised by partial selection functions; for example, in the axiomatization of fields in the signature of rings.

(2) Here is another simple example with T not universal. Let Σ contain (in addition to the standard parts N and B) a sort i, and a constant c of sort i (to fulfil the Instantiation Assumption), and let T contain (only) the axiom

$$\exists y^i(y^i \neq x^i).$$

This says that the domain A_i has at least two elements. Now a selection function for this axiom is just a function on A_i which moves every point. But in any model of T, the Σ^*-substructure of A^* generated by $\emptyset$ contains, at sort i, only the element c^A. Hence, by the Lemma in §3.2.1 again, for any μPR* (and hence PR*) function f of type $(i;i)$, $f(c^A) = c^A$. (In fact more is true: the only μPR* functions of type $(i;i)$ are the identity function on A_i and the constant function with value c^A.)

REMARK (SKOLEMIZATION OF ARBITRARY THEORIES). Given an arbitrary axiomatization T in ***Lang***(Σ), we can adjoin *Skolem functions* for T to the signature, and add the appropriate axioms for these, so as to reduce T to a universal theory $T^\forall$ (see Gallier [1986, Chapter 7]). We could then apply our results to this theory, and so, by Theorem 4, find selectors for $T^\forall$ which are PR* in the enlarged signature.

REFERENCES

C.S. Copestake, S.S. Wainer (1988), *A proof theoretic approach to the termination of computer programs*, Report 26.88, Centre for Theoretical Computer Science, University of Leeds.

R.L. Constable *et al.*(1986), *Implementing Mathematics with the Nuprl Development System*, Prentice-Hall.

J.H. Gallier (1986), *Logic for Computer Science*, Harper & Row.

G. Gentzen (1969), *Investigations into logical deduction*, The Collected Papers of Gerhard Gentzen, (ed. M.E. Szabo), North-Holland.

J.V. Guttag and J.J. Horning (1978), *The algebraic specification of abstract data types*, Acta Informatica **10**, 27-52.

S.C. Kleene (1952), *Introduction to Metamathematics*, North-Holland.

G. Kreisel (1971), *A survey of proof theory II*, Proc. Second Scandinavian Logic Symposium, (ed. J.E. Fenstad), North-Holland.

J.W. Lloyd (1987), *Foundations of Logic Programming* (Second edition), Springer-Verlag.

A.I. Mal'cev (1973), *Algebraic Systems*, Springer-Verlag.

K. Meinke and J.V. Tucker (1990), *Universal algebra*, Handbook of Logic in Computer Science (S. Abramsky, D. Gabbay and T. Maibaum, eds.), Oxford University Press (to appear).

G. Mints (1973), *Quantifier-free and one-quantifier systems*, J. Soviet Math. **1**, 71–84.

C. Parsons (1971), *On a number theoretic choice scheme II*, (Abstract), J. Symbolic Logic **36**, 587.

C. Parsons (1972), *On n-quantifier induction*, J. Symbolic Logic **37**, 466–482.

G. Takeuti (1987), *Proof Theory* (Second edition), North-Holland.

J.V. Tucker, S.S. Wainer and J.I. Zucker (1990), *Provable computable functions on abstract data types*, Proceedings of the 17th International Colloquium on Automata, Languages and Programming, Warwick University, England, July 1990, Lecture Notes in Computer Science 443, Springer-Verlag, pp. 745–760.

J.V. Tucker and J.I. Zucker (1988), *Program Correctness over Abstract Data Types, with Error-State Semantics*, CWI Monograph 6, North-Holland and the Centre for Mathematics and Computer Science (CWI), Amsterdam.

J.V. Tucker and J.I. Zucker (1989), *Horn programs and semicomputable relations on abstract structures*, Proc. 16th International Colloquium on Automata, Languages and Programming, Stresa, Italy, Lecture Notes in Computer Science 372, Springer-Verlag, pp. 745–760.

J.V. Tucker and J.I. Zucker (1992*a*), *Deterministic and nondeterministic computation, and Horn programs, on abstract data types*, J. Logic Programming (to appear).

J.V. Tucker and J.I. Zucker (1992*b*), *Projections of semicomputable relations on abstract data types*, International J. Foundations of Computer Science (to appear).

J.V. Tucker and J.I. Zucker (1992*c*), *Examples of semicomputable sets of real and complex numbers*, Constructivity in Computer Science: Proceedings of a Summer Symposium, San Antonio, Texas, June 1991 (M.J. O'Donnell and J.P. Myers, Jr., eds.) (to appear).

S.S. Wainer (1990), *Computability – logical and recursive complexity*, Proc. NATO International Summer School on Logic, Algebra and Computation, Marktoberdorf, July–Aug. 1989, Springer-Verlag.